British Railways

LOCOMOTIVES &

COACHING STOCK

1997

The Complete Guide to all
Locomotives & Coaching Stock
Vehicles Which Run On
Britain's Mainline Railways

Peter Fox

ISBN 1 872524 97 4

© 1997. Platform 5 Publishing Ltd., 3 Wyvern House, Sark Road, Sheffield, S2
4HG.

CONTENTS

CONTENTS

HIGH SPEED IN EUROPE

by David Haydock

High Speed in Europe is a comprehensive review of the progress made to date in implementing high speed rail travel. Each country is addressed in turn with new trains and new infrastructure examined in detail, including Eurostar, and the Channel Tunnel Rail Link. There are features on the new High Speed trains and routes in Germany, France, Spain, Italy and Sweden including TGV, ICE, X 2000, AVE etc. Also includes Appendices of European High Speed Line Statistics and High Speed Train Numbering. **A4 size. Thread Sewn. 80 pages including 38 in full colour. £9.95.** *See the back pages for ordering details.*

ORGANISATION OF BRITAIN'S RAILWAY SYSTEM

INFRASTRUCTURE

Britains state-owned railway infrastructure, i.e. the track, signalling, stations and overhead line equipment is now owned by a new company known as ''Railtrack''. This has recently been privatised. Many stations and maintenance depots are leased to train operating companies. The exception is the infrastructure on the Isle of Wight, which is leased to Island Line.

DOMESTIC PASSENGER TRAIN OPERATIONS

Passenger trains are operated by train operating companies (TOCs). All TOCs have now been franchised to private operators. A list of these is appended below:

TOC	Operator
Anglia Railways	GB Trains
Inter City East Coast	Sea Containers Ltd.
Inter City West Coast	Virgin Group
Cross-Country Trains	Virgin Group
Great Western Trains	Great Western Holdings
North West Regional Railways	Great Western Holdings
Midland Main Line	National Express
Gatwick Express	National Express
North London Railways	National Express
Central Trains	National Express
Scotrail	National Express
Merseyrail Electrics	MTL Holdings
Regional Railways North East	MTL Holdings
LTS Rail	Prism
South Wales & West Railway	Prism
Cardiff Railway Co.	Prism
West Anglia Great Northern	Prism
South West Trains	Stagecoach
Island Line	Stagecoach
Network South Central	Connex
South East Trains	Connex
Great Eastern	FirstBus
Thameslink	GOVIA
Chiltern railways	M40 Trains
Thames Trains	Victory Rail

InterCity East Coast has now been renamed Great North Eastern Railway (GNER). Cross Country trains is now known as Virgin CrossCountry. Network South Central and South East Trains are now known as Connex South Central and Connex South Eastern respectively.

NOTES ON TRAIN OPERATING COMPANIES

Connex

This is a French company owned by Société Générale des Entreprises Automobiles, a subsidiary of Compagnie Générale des Eaux.

FirstBus

This is a large bus company which was originally formed by the amalgamation of Badgerline and GRT bus group.

GB Trains

This is a company set up specifically to exploit the opportunities afforded by rail privatisation.

GOVIA

A joint venture between the Go-Ahead bus company and VIA, a French public transport operating company.

Great Western Holdings

This is a jointly owned by the former Great Western Trains management, 3i plc and FirstBus.

National Express

This is a transport operator which runs express coach services by sub-contracting them to various bus companies. It also owns east Midlands Airport.

M40 Trains

This is owned by the former management of Chiltern Railways.

MTL Holdings

This is the former municipal bus operator Merseyside PTE which operates buses in Merseyside and London.

Prism

This is a company whose shares are owned by individuals and financial institutions. Its chairman, Godfrey Burley, is joint managing director of EYMS, a bus company.

Sea Containers

This is a Bermuda-based shipping company which also owns the Venice-Simplon-Orient Express

Stagecoach

The largest private bus operator in the UK.

Victory Railway Holdings

This is a joint venture between the Go Ahead group and Thames Trains management..

Virgin Group

This is the well-known company headed by Richard Branson which has interests in travel, leisure and retailing.

CHANNEL TUNNEL PASSENGER TRAIN OPERATIONS

Eurostar trains are operated by Eurostar (UK) Ltd. jointly with French Railways (SNCF) and Belgian Railways (NMBS/SNCB). Eurostar (UK) will also operate the Night Service trains jointly with SNCF, Netherlands Railways (NS) and German Railways (DB).

FREIGHT TRAIN OPERATIONS

The three trainload freight companies LoadHaul, Mainline and TransRail which were set up on the government's orders in readiness for privatisation have been sold to the North & South Railway Company whose main shareholder is Wisconsin Central Transportation Corporation of the USA. Rail Express Systems, which operates mail and charter trains has also been sold to this company. The four concerns have been combined and now known as the English, Welsh and Scottish Railway Ltd. (EWS). EWS has also been named as preferred bidder for Railfreight Distribution (RfD) which operates general freight, particularly Channel Tunnel traffic.

The container train operation known as Freightliner has been sold to a management buyout known as Freightliner (1995) Ltd.

Certain other companies e.g. Direct Rail Services and National Power operate freight trains with their own locomotives.

OWNERSHIP OF LOCOMOTIVES AND ROLLING STOCK

The locomotives of EWS and those of Eurostar are owned by those companies. Most locomotives, hauled coaching stock and multiple unit vehicles used by the passenger train operating companies are owned by three leasing companies which were originally set up by British Railways as subsidiaries and then privatised. These are:

Eversholt Holdings (formerly Eversholt Leasing)
Angel Trains
Porterbrook Leasing Company Ltd.

Other vehicles are owned by various private companies such as The Carriage and Traction Co. Ltd., Carnforth Railway Restoration & Engineering Serv ices Ltd., Titanstar Ltd. and the Venice Simplon-Orient Express Ltd.

Further details of these companies will be found in the section on abbreviations and codes. Thus for each vehicle it is generally necessary to specify both the owner and the TOC which currently operates the vehicle.

A number of 'service' type vehicles are owned by Railtrack (e.g. Sandite vehicles) and others are owned by former BR Headquarters organisations which have now been privatised e.g. Railtest or by railway vehicle manufacturing and repair companies. Royal Train vehicles are owned by Railtrack.

For locomotiives, owning companies are detailed in the information section at the head of each class, whereas for coaching stock and multiple units a new format is used with separate columns for owner and operation (see the specific sections for details).

All locomotives are presumed to be owned by the operator specified by the pool code, except where indicated otherwise in the text.

1. LOCOMOTIVES

The following notes are applicable to locomotives:

DETAILS & DIMENSIONS

Principal details and dimensions are given for each class in metric units. Imperial equivalents are also given for power. Maximum speeds are still quoted in miles per hour since imperial units are still used in day to day railway operations in Britain.. Since the present maximum permissible speed of certain classes of locomotives is different from the design speed, these are now shown separately in class details. In some cases certain low speed limits are arbitrary and may occasionally be raised when necessary if a locomotive has to be pressed into passenger service.

LOCOMOTIVE DETAIL DIFFERENCES

Detail differences which affect the areas and types of train which locos work are shown. Where detail differences occur within a class or part class of locomotives., these are shown against the individual locomotive number. Except where shown, diesel locomotives have no train heating equipment. Electric or electro-diesel locomotives are assumed to have train heating unless shown otherwise. Standard abbreviations used are:

a	Train air brakes only.
c	Fitted with Scharfenberg couplers for Eurostar working.
e	Fitted with electric heating apparatus (ETH).
j	Fitted with RCH jumper cables for operating with PCVs (propelling control vehicles)
r	Fitted with radio electronic token block equipment.
s	Slow speed control fitted (and operable).
t	Fitted with automatic vehicle identification transponders.
v	Train vacuum brakes only.
x	Dual train brakes (air & vacuum).
y	ETH equipped but equipment isolated.
+	Extended range locos with Additional fuel tank capacity compared with others in class.

After the locomotive number are shown any notes regarding braking, heating etc., the livery code (in **bold** type), the pool code where applicable, the depot code and name if any. Locomotives which have been renumbered in recent years show the last number in parentheses after the current number. For previous numbers of other locos, please refer to the Platform 5 Book ''Diesel & Electric Loco. Register''

NAMES

All official names are shown as they appear on the locomotive i.e. all upper case or upper & lower case lettering. Where only a few locomotives in a class are named, these are shown in a separate table at the end of the class or sub-class.

DEPOT ALLOCATIONS & POOL CODES

The depot at which a locomotive is allocated is the one at which it receives its main examinations. This depot may be a long way away from where it normally performs its duties. The pool code is a better means of ascertaining where a locomotive may operate, but it should be borne in mind that often locomotives of the same company may be used in pools other than their official pool. In addition, English Welsh & Scottish Railway are moving towards a common user system. (S) denotes stored serviceable and (U) stored unserviceable. Locos may not be stored at their home depots. Thus the layout is as follows:

No.	Old No.	Notes	Liv.	Pool	Depot	Name
47777	(47636)		**RX**	PXLB	CD	Restored

GENERAL INFORMATION ON BRITISH RAILWAYS' LOCOMOTIVES

CLASSIFICATION & NUMBERING

Initially BR diesel locomotives were allocated numbers in the 1xxxx series, with electrics allotted numbers in the 2xxxx series. Around 1957 diesel locomotives were allocated new numbers with between one and four digits with 'D' prefixes. Diesel electric shunters in the 13xxx series had the '1' replaced by a 'D', but diesel mechanical shunters were completely renumbered. Electric locomotives retained their previous numbers but with an 'E' prefix.

When all standard gauge steam locomotives had been withdrawn, the prefix letter was removed. In 1972, the present TOPS numbering system was introduced whereby the loco number consisted of a two-digit class number followed by a serial number. In some cases the last two digits of the former number were generally retained (Classes 20, 37, 50), but in other classes this is not the case. In this book former TOPS numbers carried byrecently- converted locos. are shown in parentheses. Full renumbering information is to be found in the 'Diesel & Electric loco Register', the new third edition of which is now available.

Diesel locomotives are classified as "types" depending on their engine horsepower as follows:

Type	Engine hp.	Old Number Range	Current Classes
1	800-1000	D 8000-D 8999	20.
2	1001-1499	D 5000-D 6499/D 7500-D 7999	31.
3	1500-1999	D 6500-D 7499	33, 37.
4	2000-2999	D 1-D 1999	46, 47.
5	3000+	D 9000-D 9499	55, 56, 58, 59, 60.
Shunter	300-799	D 3000-D 4999	08, 09.

Class 14 (650 hp diesel hydraulics) were numbered in the D95xx series.

Electric and electro-diesel locomotives are classified according to their supply system. Locomotives operating on a d.c. system are allocated classes 71-80, whilst a.c. or dual voltage locomotives start at Class 81. Departmental locomotives which remain self propelled or which are likely to move around on a day to day basis are classified Class 97.

WHEEL ARRANGEMENT

For main line diesel and electric locomotives the system whereby the number of driven axles on a bogie or frame is denoted by a letter (A = 1, B = 2, C = 3 etc.) and the number of undriven axles is noted by a number is used. The letter 'o' after a letter indicates that each axle is individually powered and a + sign indicates that the bogies are intercoupled. For shunters the Whyte notation is used. In this notation, generally used in Britain for steam locomotives, the number of leading wheels are given, followed by the number of driving wheels and then the trailing wheels.

HAULING CAPABILITY OF DIESEL LOCOS

The hauling capability of a diesel locomotive depends basically upon three factors:

1. Its adhesive weight. The greater the weight on its driving wheels, the greater the adhesion and thus more tractive power can be applied before wheel slip occurs.

2. The characteristics of its transmission. In order to start a train the locomotive has to exert a pull at standstill. A direct drive diesel engine cannot do this, hence the need for transmission. This may be mechanical, hydraulic or electric. The current British standard for locomotives is electric transmission. Here the diesel engine drives a generator or alternator and the current produced is fed to the traction motors. The force produced by each driven wheel depends on the current in its traction motor. In other words the larger the current, the harder it pulls.

As the locomotive speed increases, the current in the traction motors falls hence the *Maximum Tractive Effort* is the maximum force at its wheels that the locomotive can exert at a standstill. The electrical equipment cannot take such high currents for long without overheating. Hence the *Continuous Tractive Effort* is quoted which represents the current which the equipment can take continuously.

3. The power of its engine. Not all of this power reaches the rail as electrical machines are approximately 90% efficient. As the electrical energy passes through two such machines (the generator/alternator and the traction motors), the *Power At Rail* is about 81% (90% of 90%) of the engine power, less a further amount used for auxiliary equipment such as radiator fans, traction motor cooling fans, air compressors, battery charging, cab heating, ETH, etc. The power of the locomotive is proportional to the tractive effort times the speed. Hence when on full power there is a speed corresponding to the continuous tractive effort.

HAULING CAPABILITY OF ELECTRIC LOCOS

Unlike a diesel locomotive, an electric locomotive does not develop its power on board and its performance is determined only by two factors, namely its weight and the characteristics of its electrical equipment. Whereas a diesel locomotive tends to be a constant power machine, the power of an electric locomotive varies considerably. Up to a certain speed it can produce virtually a constant tractive effort. Hence power rises with speed according to the formula given in section 3 above, until a maximum speed is reached at which tractive effort falls, such that the power also falls. Hence the power at the speed corresponding to the maximum tractive effort is lower than the maximum.

BRAKE FORCE

The brake force is a measure of the braking power of a locomotive. This is shown on the locomotive data panels so that railway staff can ensure that sufficient brake power is available on freight trains.

TRAIN HEATING AND POWER EQUIPMENT

The standard system in use in Britain for heating loco hauled trains is by means of electricity and is now known as ETS (Electric train supply). Locomotives which were equipped to provide steam heating have had this equipment removed or rendered inoperable (isolated). Electric heat is provided from the locomotive by means of a separate alternator on the loco, except in the case of Class 33 which have a d.c. generator. The *ETH Index* is a measure of the electrical power available for train heating. All electrically heated coaches have an ETH index and the total of these in a train must not exceed the ETH power of a locomotive.

ROUTE AVAILABILITY

This is a measure of a railway vehicle's axle load. The higher the axle load of a vehicle, the higher the RA number on a scale 1 to 10. Each route on BR has an RA number and in theory no vehicle with a higher RA number may travel on that route without special clearance. Exceptions are made, however.

MULTIPLE AND PUSH-PULL WORKING

Multiple working between diesel locomotives in Britain has usually been provided by means of an electro-pneumatic system, with special jumper cables connecting the locos. A coloured symbol is painted on the end of the locomotive to denote which system is in use. Class 47s nos. 47701-17 used a time-division multiplex (t.d.m.) system which utilised the existing RCH (an abbreviation for the former railway clearing house, a pre-nationalisation standards organisation) jumper cables for push-pull working. These had in the past only been used for train lighting control, and more recently for public address (pa) and driver-guard communication. A new standard t.d.m. system is now fitted to all a.c. electric locomotives and other vehicles, enabling them to work in both push-pull and multiple working modes. Certain RfD and Freightliner 1995 Ltd. Class 47 locomotives have been fitted with a 'green circle' multiple working system. Full details of the mechanism of this new multiple-working system are not to hand.

1.1. DIESEL LOCOMOTIVES

CLASS 08   BR SHUNTER   0-6-0

Built: 1953–62 by BR at Crewe, Darlington, Derby, Doncaster or Horwich Works.
Engine: English Electric 6KT of 298 kW (400 hp) at 680 rpm.
Main Generator: English Electric 801.
Traction Motors: Two English Electric 506.
Max. Tractive Effort: 156 kN (35000 lbf).
Cont. Tractive Effort: 49 kN (11100 lbf) at 8.8 m.p.h.
Power At Rail: 194 kW (260 hp).   **Length over Buffers:** 8.92 m.
Brake Force: 19 t.   **Wheel Diameter:** 1372 mm.
Design Speed: 20 m.p.h.   **Weight:** 50 t.
Max. Speed: 15 or 20* m.p.h.   **RA:** 5.

Non-standard liveries:

08077 is RFS grey with blue and yellow stripes.
08296, 08602, 08846 and 08943 are grey and carry numbers 001, D 3769, D 4144 and 002 respectively.
08414 is 'D' with RfD brandings and also carries its former number D 3529.
08460 is light grey with a dark grey roof, black cab doors and window surrounds and 'TLF South East' branding.
08500 is red lined out in black & white.
08519 is BR black.
08527 is light grey with a black roof, blue bodyside stripe and 'Ilford Level 5' branding.
08593 is Great Eastern blue lined out in red and also carries its former number D 3760.
08601 is London Midland & Scottish Railway black.
08629 is Royal purple.
08642 is London & South Western Railway black and also carries its former number D 3809.
08649 is grey with blue, white and red stripes and 'WTL' branding. Carries its original number D 3816.
08689 is 'D' with Railfreight general markings.
08699 is grey and carries no number.
08715 is in experimental dayglo orange livery.
08721 is blue with a red & yellow stripe ('Red Star' livery).
08730 is BR black.
08805 is LMS maroon and also carries its former number 3973.
08867 is BR black.
08879 is turquoise with full yellow ends, black cab doors, black numbers on a yellow background and RfD brandings.
08883 is Caledonian blue.
08907 is London & North Western Railway black.
08938 is grey and red.
08616 carries its former number D 3783. 08830 is on long-term lease to the East Somerset Railway.

n – Waterproofed for working at Oxley Carriage Depot.
z – Fitted with buckeye adaptor at nose end for HST depot shunting.
§ – Fitted with yellow flashing light and siren for working between Ipswich Yard and Cliff Quay.
Originally numbered in series D 3000 – 4192.

Ownership:

08296/527/73/602/82/92/9/823/46/943 are owned by ADtranz.
08484/568/629/730 are owned by Railcare Ltd.
08649/847 are owned by Wessex Traincare Ltd.
Great North Eastern Railway locos. Nos. 08331/892 are owned by RFS.

CLASS 08/0. Standard Design.

08077	x	**0**	DFLS	EH	08500	x	**0**	FDSD	DR
08296	x	**0**		ZC	08506	a			LGML	ML
08331	x	**GN**	HBSH	EC	08509	a	**F**	FDSD	DR
08388	a	**FP**	FDSX	IM (U)	08510	a		FDSD	DR
08389	a		DAWE	AN	08511	a		ENSN	DR
08393	a	**D**	DAWE	AN	08512	a	**F**	FDSD	DR
08397	a	**F**	LWSP	SP	08514	a		FDSD	DR
08401	a	**D**	FDSI	IM	08516	a	**D**	FDSK	TO
08402	a	**D**	PXLT	CD	08517	a		EWSX	SF (S)
08405	a	**D**	FDSI	IM	08519	a	**0**	LCWX	BS (U)
08410	a	**D**	HJXX	PM	08523	x	**ML**	EWOC	OC
08411	a		LGML	ML	08525	x	**F**	HISL	NL
08413	a	**D**	DAXT	TI	08526	x		EWOC	OC
08414	a* §| **0**	EWSX	SF	08527	x	**0**		ZI
08417	a		CDJD	DY	08528	x	**D**	ENSN	TO
08418	a	**F**	FDSD	DR	08529	x		ENSN	TO
08428	a		LCWX	BS (U)	08530	x	**D**	DFLS	SF
08441	a		ENSN	TO	08531	x	**D**	DFLS	SF
08442	a	**F**	FDSK	KY	08534	x	**D**	LGML	ML
08445	a		FDSX	IM (U)	08535	x	**D**	DASY	TI
08448	a		LCXX	BS (U)	08536	x		HISE	DY
08449	a		ENXX	TO (U)	08538	x	**D**	ENSN	TO
08451	x		HFSN	WN	08540	x	**D**	ENZX	TO (U)
08454	x		HFSN	WN	08541	x	**D**	EWSF	SF
08460	a	**0**	EWSX	SF	08542	x	**F**	EWSX	SF
08466	a	**F0**	FDSX	IM (U)	08543	x	**D**	LBBS	BS
08472	a		HBSH	BN	08561	a		LGML	ML
08480	az	**G**	EWOC	OC	08567	x		LBBS	BS
08481	x		LNCF	CF	08568	x			ZH
08482	a	**D**	DAWE	AN	08569	x		DAAN	AN
08483	a	**D**	HJXX	PM	08571	xz		HBSH	EC
08484	a	**D**		ZN	08573	x			ZI
08485	a		LWSP	SP	08575	x	**BS**	DFLS	TI
08489	a	**F**	LWSP	SP	08576	x		LNCF	CF
08492	a		ENSN	TO	08577	x		FMSY	TE
08493	a		LNCF	CF	08578	x	**R**	PXLS	HT
08495	x		ENSN	TO	08580	x		ENSN	TO
08499	a	**F**	FDSK	KY	08581	x	**BS**	FDSX	DR (S)

08582	a	D	FMSY	TE	08683	x		LBBS	BS
08585	x		DFLS	CD	08685	x		PXLS	WN
08586	a	F	LCXX	AY (U)	08689	a	0	EWSX	SF
08587	x		FDSD	DR	08690	a		HISE	DY
08588	xz	BS	HISL	NL	08691	x	G	DFLS	CD
08593	x	0	EWSF	SF	08692	x	0		ZC (U)
08594	x		PXLT	TO (U)	08693	x		LCWX	ML (U)
08597	x		ENZX	KY	08694	x		DASY	TI
08599	x		PXLS	CD	08695	x		PXLT	CD
08600	a	D	EWSX	SF	08696	a	D	HFSN	WN
08601	x	0	LBBS	BS	08697	x		HISE	DY
08602	x	0		ZD	08698	a		EWSU	SU
08605	x		FDSK	KY	08699	a			ZC
08607	x		ENXX	TO (U)	08700	a		EWSX	SF (S)
08610	x		LCXX	BS (U)	08701	x	RX	PXLS	CD
08611	x		HFSL	LO	08702	x		PXLS	WN
08616	x	G	HGSS	TS	08703	a		DAAN	AN
08617	x		HFSN	WN	08706	x		FDSK	KY
08619	x		LCXX	SP (S)	08709	x		EWOC	OC
08622	x		LCWX	ML (U)	08711	x	RX	EWSF	SF
08623	x		LBBS	BS	08713	a		FDSX	DR (U)
08624	x		DFLS	CD	08714	x	RX	PXLS	TO
08625	x		LBBS	BS	08715	v	0	EWSX	SF
08628	x		LBBS	BS	08718	x		LCWX	ML (U)
08629	x	0		ZN	08720	x	D	LGML	ML
08630	x		LGML	ML	08721	x	0	HFSL	LO
08632	x		FDSI	IM	08723	x		ENXX	TO (U)
08633	x	RX	PXLS	CD	08724	x		HBSH	BN
08635	x		PXLS	OC	08730	x	0		ZH
08641	xz	D	HJSL	LA	08731	x		LCWX	ML (U)
08642	x*	0	DFLS	EH	08734	x		LCWX	BS (U)
08643	x	D	HJXX	PM	08735	x		LGML	ML
08644	xz	I	HJSL	LA	08737	x	FE	DAWE	AN
08645	xz	D	HJSL	LA	08738	x	D	LGML	ML
08646	a	F	EWOC	OC	08739	x		DAAN	AN
08647	x	G	PXXA	CD	08740	x	F	EWSX	SF
08648	x*	D	HJSL	LA	08742	x	RX	PXLS	CD
08649	x	0		ZG	08745	xz	FE	DFLS	CD
08651	xz	D	EWOC	OC	08746	x	D	LBBS	BS
08653	x*	FE	DAXT	AN	08750	x		EWSF	SF
08655	x*	F	DAWE	AN	08751	x	FE	DASY	TI
08661	a	FE	DAYX	AN (U)	08752	x	C	EWSF	SF
08662	x		FDSK	KY	08754	x		HASS	IS
08663	a	D	HJSL	LA	08756	x	D	LNCF	CF
08664	x		EWOC	OC	08757	x	RX	PXLS	HT
08665	x		FDSI	IM	08758	x		EWSX	SF
08668	x		PXXA	CD	08762	x		HASS	IS
08670	a		EWSX	SF	08765	xn	D	LBBS	BS
08675	x	F	LGML	ML	08768	x		LGML	ML
08676	x		LWSP	SP	08770	a	D	LNCF	CF
08682	x			ZF	08773	x		ENXX	TO (U)

08775	x		EWSF	SF	08879	x	0	DATI	TI
08776	a	D	FDSK	KY	08881	x	D	LGML	ML
08780	x		HJSE	LE	08882	x		LGML	ML
08782	a		FDSK	KY	08883	x	0	LGML	ML
08783	a		FDSK	KY	08884	x		LWSP	SP
08784	x		DAXT	AN	08886	x	EW	ENSN	TO
08786	a	D	LNCF	CF	08887	x		HFSN	WN
08790	x		HFSL	LO	08888	xz	EW	FDSI	IM
08792	x		LNWK	CF	08890	x	D	PXLS	WN
08795	x	M	HJSE	LE	08891	x		DFLS	AN
08798	x		LNCF	CF	08892	x*	GN	HBSH	BN
08799	x		DAAN	AN	08893	x	D	LCXX	BS (U)
08801	x		LNCF	CF	08894	x		LWSP	SP
08802	x	RX	PXLS	CD	08896	x		PXLS	CD (S)
08804	x		PXLS	CD	08897	x	D	PXLS	CD
08805	x	0	HGSS	TS	08899	x		HISE	DY
08806	a	F	FMSY	TE	08900	x	D	LNWK	CF
08807	x	BS	LBBS	BS	08901	xn		LCXX	BS (U)
08810	a		HSSN	NC	08902	x		DAYX	AN (U)
08811	a*		EWSX	SF (S)	08904	x		EWOC	OC
08813	x	D	FMSY	TE	08905	x	FE	DASY	TI
08815	x		LCWX	SP (U)	08906	x		LGML	ML
08817	x	BS	LWSP	SP	08907	x	0	DAAN	AN
08818	x		PXXA	CD	08908	xz		HISL	NL
08819	x	D	LNCF	CF	08909	x		EWSF	SF
08822	x	M	HJSE	LE	08910	x		LGML	ML
08823	a			ZF	08911	x	D	LWSP	SP
08824	a	F	FDSI	IM	08912	x		LGML	ML
08825	a		DAAN	AN	08913	x	D	DAWE	AN
08826	a		LCWX	ML (U)	08914	x		LBBS	BS
08827	a		LGML	ML	08915	x	F	LWSP	SP
08828	a		EWSX	SF	08918	x		LWSP	SP
08830	x*		HLSV	CF	08919	x	RX	PXLS	CD
08834	x	FD	HBSH	BN	08920	x	F	LBBS	BS
08836	x	I	HJXX	OO	08921	x	EW	PXLS	CD
08837	x*	D	DAAN	AN	08922	x	D	LGML	ML
08842	x		DAXT	AN	08924	x	D	EWOC	OC
08844	x		DAWE	AN	08925	x		LWSP	SP
08846	a	0		ZC	08926	x		DAYX	AN (U)
08847	x*			ZG	08927	x		LBBS	BS
08853	xr		HBSH	EC	08928	x	FR	HSSN	NC
08854	x*		EWEH	EH	08931	x		FDSX	TE (U)
08856	x		DAAN	AN	08932	x		LNWK	CF
08865	x		PXLT	TO	08933	x*	EW	EWSX	SF
08866	x		EWSF	SF	08934	x		HFSN	WN
08867	x	0	LWSP	SP	08938	xr	0	LCWX	ML (U)
08869	x	G	HSSN	NC	08939	x		DAAN	AN
08872	x	D	DAAN	AN	08940	x		EWEH	EH
08873	x	RX	PXLS	CD	08941	x		LNCF	CF
08877	x	D	FDSD	DR	08942	x		LNWK	CF
08878	x		EWSX	SF (U)	08943	x	0		ZT

08944	x	D	EWOC	OC
08946	x	FE	DASY	TI
08947	x		EWOC	OC
08948	xc	E	GPSS	OC
08950	x	I	HISL	NL
08951	x	D	DAAN	AN
08952	x		LCWX	ML (U)

08953	x	D	LNCF	CF
08954	x	FT	LNWK	CF
08955	x		LNWK	CF
08956	x		CDJD	DY
08957	x		EWSX	SF
08958	x		EWSX	SF (U)

Names:

08578	Libert Dickinson
08647	Crimpsall
08649	G.H. Stratton
08661	Europa
08682	Lionheart
08701	The Sorter
08711	EAGLE C.U.R.C.

08714	Cambridge
08790	M.A. SMITH
08869	The Canary
08879	Sheffield Children's Hospital
08888	Postman's Pride
08919	Steep Holm
08950	Neville Hill 1st

Class 08/9. Fitted with cut-down cab and headlight for Cwmmawr branch.

08993	x	FT	LNWK	CF	ASHBURNHAM
08994	a	D	LNWK	CF	GWENDRAETH
08995	a	FT	LNWK	CF	KIDWELLY

CLASS 09   BR SHUNTER   0 – 6 – 0

Built: 1959 – 62 by BR at Darlington or Horwich Works.
Engine: English Electric 6KT of 298 kW (400 hp) at 680 rpm.
Main Generator: English Electric 801.
Traction Motors: English Electric 506.
Max. Tractive Effort: 111 kN (25000 lbf).
Cont. Tractive Effort: 39 kN (8800 lbf) at 11.6 m.p.h.
Power At Rail: 201 kW (269 hp).
Brake Force: 19 t.   **Length over Buffers:** 8.92 m.
Weight: 50 t.   **Wheel Diameter:** 1372 mm.
Max. Speed: 27 m.p.h.   **RA:** 5.
Train Brakes: Air & Vacuum.

Class 09/0 were originally numbered 3665 – 71, 3719 – 21, 4099 – 4114.

CLASS 09/0. Built as Class 09.

09001		LNCF	CF
09003		EWHG	SL
09004		HWSU	SU
09005	D	FMSY	TE
09006	ML	EWOC	OC
09007	ML	EWOC	OC
09008	D	LNCF	CF
09009	EW	EWHG	SL
09010	D	EWSF	SF
09011	D	DAWE	AN
09012	D	EWOC	OC

09013	D	LNCF	CF
09014	D	FDSK	KY
09015	D	LNCF	CF
09016	D	EWOC	OC
09018	ML	EWOC	OC
09019	ML	EWHG	SL
09020		EWSF	SF
09021	FE	DAWE	AN
09022		DAYX	AN (U)
09023		EWSU	SU
09024	ML	EWHG	SL

| 09025 | | HWSU | SU | 09026 | D | HWSU | SU |

Names:

| 09009 Three Bridges C.E.D. | 09026 William Pearson |
| 09012 Dick Hardy | |

CLASS 09/1. Converted from Class 08. 110 V electrical equipment.

09101	D	EWOC	OC	09105	D	LNCF	CF
09102	D	EWOC	OC	09106	D	FMSY	TE
09103	D	LGML	ML	09107	D	LNCF	CF
09104	D	LBBS	BS				

CLASS 09/2. Converted from Class 08. 90 V electrical equipment.

09201	D	ENSN	TO	09204	D	FMSY	TE
09202	D	LGML	ML	09205	D	LGML	ML
09203	D	LNCF	CF				

CLASS 20   ENGLISH ELECTRIC TYPE 1   Bo – Bo

Built: 1957 – 68 by English Electric Company at Vulcan Foundry, Newton le Willows or Robert Stephenson & Hawthorn, Darlington. 20001 – 128 were originally built with disc indicators whilst 20129 – 228 were built with four character headcode panels.
Engine: English Electric 8SVT Mk. II of 746 kW (1000 hp) at 850 rpm.
Main Generator: English Electric 819/3C.
Traction Motors: English Electric 526/5D (20001 – 48) or 526/8D (others).
Max. Tractive Effort: 187 kN (42000 lbf).
Cont. Tractive Effort: 111 kN (25000 lbf) at 11 m.p.h.

Power At Rail: 574 kW (770 hp).	**Length over Buffers:** 14.25 m.
Brake Force: 35 t.	**Wheel Diameter:** 1092 mm.
Design Speed: 75 m.p.h.	**Weight:** 73.5 t.
Max. Speed: 60 m.p.h.	**RA:** 5.

Train Brakes: Air & Vacuum.
Multiple Working: Blue Star Coupling Code (Class 20/3 have non-standard jumpers).

Originally numbered in series D 8007 – 8190, D 8315 – 8325.

CLASS 20/0. EWS or Racal-BRT owned Locomotives.

Note: The Racal-BRT locomotives in traffic are operated by EWS.

20007	st		TAKX	CE (U)	
20016	st		LCXX	BS (U)	
20032	s		TAKX	CE	
20057	st		LCXX	BS (U)	
20059	st	FR	LCXX	BS (U)	
20066			LCXX	BS (U)	
20072	st		TAKX	CE (U)	
20075	st	T	TAKB	BS	Sir William Cooke
20081	st		LCXX	BS (U)	
20087	st	BS	LCXX	BS (U)	
20092		CS	LCXX	BS (U)	

20104	st	FR		TAKX	CE (U)	
20117	st			TAKX	CE (U)	
20118		FR		LCWX	BS (U)	
20121	st			TAKX	CE (U)	
20128	st	T		TAKB	BS	Guglielmo Marconi
20131	st	T		TAKB	BS	Almon B. Strowger
20132	st	FR		LCWX	BS (U)	
20138		FR		LCWX	BS (U)	
20165		FR		LCWX	BS (U)	
20168	st			LCWX	BS (U)	
20169	st	CS		LCWX	BS (U)	
20187	st	T		TAKB	BS	Sir Charles Wheatstone
20190	st			TAKX	CE (U)	
20215	st	FR		TAKX	CE (U)	

CLASS 20/3. Privately-owned by Direct Rail Services.

Used on radioactive waste trains between Sellafield, Barrow Docks and Drigg and chemical trains to Northwich.
All have train air brakes only and twin fuel tanks.

Non-standard Livery: Dark blue with light blue roof and green lettering.

20301	(20047)	0	XHSD	SD	FURNESS RAILWAY 150
20302	(20084)	0	XHSD	SD	
20303	(20127)	0	XHSD	SD	
20304	(20120)	0	XHSD	SD	
20305	(20095)	0	XHSD	SD	

CLASS 20/9. Privately-owned by Hunslet – Barclay Ltd.

Used mainly on weedkilling trains.

Non-standard Livery: Hunslet – Barclay two-tone grey with red solebars and black lettering.

20901	(20101)	t	0	XYPD	ZK	NANCY
20902	(20060)		0	XYPD	ZK	LORNA
20903	(20083)		0	XYPD	ZK	ALISON
20904	(20041)		0	XYPD	ZK	JANIS
20905	(20225)	t	0	XYPD	ZK	IONA
20906	(20219)		0	XYPD	ZK	Kilmarnock 400

CLASS 31   BRUSH TYPE 2   A1A – A1A

Built: 1957 – 62 by Brush Traction at Loughborough.
31102/5 – 7/10/25/34/44/444/50/61 retain two headcode lights. Others have roof-mounted headcode boxes.
Engine: English Electric 12SVT of 1100 kW (1470 hp) at 850 rpm.
Main Generator: Brush TG160-48.
Traction Motors: Brush TM73-68.
Max. Tractive Effort: 160 kN (35900 lbf) (190 kN (42800 lbf)*).
Cont. Tractive Effort: 83 kN (18700 lbf) at 23.5 m.p.h. (99 kN (22250 lbf) at 19.7 m.p.h. *.)
Power At Rail: 872 kW (1170 hp).   **Length over Buffers:** 17.30 m.

Brake Force: 49 t.
Design Speed: 90 (80*) m.p.h.
Weight: 107 – 111 t.
RA: 5 or 6.
Max. Speed: 60 m.p.h. (90 m.p.h. 31/4).
Multiple Working: Blue Star Coupling Code.
Communication Equipment: Cab to shore radio-telephone.

Driving Wheel Diameter: 1092 mm.
Centre Wheel Diameter: 1003 mm.
Train Brakes: Air & Vacuum.
ETH Index (Class 31/4): 66.

Non-standard liveries:

31116 is red, yellow, red and grey with 'Infrastructure' branding.
31413 is BR blue with yellow cabsides, a light blue stripe along the bottom of
the body and a red band around the bottom of the cabs.

Originally numbered D 5520 – 5699, D 5800 – 5862 (not in order).

CLASS 31/1. Standard Design. RA5.

31102	C	LCXX	BS (U)	31186	C	ENXX	TO (U)
31105 *	FT	LCWX	BS	31187	C	ENXX	TO (U)
31106 *	C	LCWX	BS (U)	31188	C	LWNW	CD
31107	C	LCWX	BS (U)	31190	C	LCWX	SP (U)
31110	C	LWNW	CD	31191	C	ENXX	TO (U)
31112 *	CT	LCWX	BS	31199	FC	LCWX	SP (U)
31113	C	LWNW	CD	31200	FC	LCXX	SP (U)
31116	O	ENXX	TO (U)	31201	FC	LWNW	CD
31119	C	LCWX	SP (S)	31203	C	LWNW	CD
31125	C	LCXX	BS (U)	31205	FR	ENXX	TO (U)
31126	C	LCWX	SP (U)	31206	C	LCWX	BS (U)
31128	FO	LCXX	BS (U)	31207	C	LWNW	CD
31130	FC	LWNW	CD	31219	C	ENXX	TO (U)
31132	FO	LCWX	BS (U)	31224	C	LCWX	SP (S)
31134	C	LCWX	SP (U)	31229	C	LWNW	CD
31135	C	ENXX	TO (U)	31230 *	FO	ENXX	TO (U)
31142	C	LWNW	CD	31232	C	LCWX	BS (U)
31144	C	LCWX	SP (U)	31233	C	LWNW	CD
31145	C	LCXX	SP	31235	C	LCWX	SP (S)
31146 r	C	LWNW	CD	31237	C	LCWX	BS (U)
31147 r	C	LCWX	BS (U)	31238	C	LCWX	SP (U)
31149	FR	ENXX	TO (U)	31242	C	LCWX	SP (S)
31154	C	LWNW	CD	31247	FR	ENXX	TO (U)
31155	FA	LCXX	BS (U)	31248	FO	LCXX	BS (U)
31158	C	LCXX	BS (U)	31250	C	ENXX	TO (U)
31160	F	LCXX	SP (U)	31252	FO	ENXX	TO (U)
31163	C	LWNW	CD	31255	C	LWNW	CD
31164	FO	LCWX	BS (U)	31263	C	LCXX	SP (U)
31165	G	ENXX	TO (U)	31268	C	ENXX	TO (U)
31166 r	C	LWNW	CD	31270	FC	LCWX	SP (S)
31171	FO	LCXX	BS (U)	31271	FA	ENXX	TO (S)
31174	C	LCXX	BS (U)	31273	C	LWNW	CD
31178	C	LCWX	BS (U)	31275	FC	LWNW	CD
31181	C	ENXX	TO (U)	31276	FC	ENXX	TO (U)
31185	C	LWNW	CD (S)	31285	C	LCWX	SP (S)

31294	**FA**	ENXX	TO (U)	31308	**C**	ENXX	TO (S)
31301	**FR**	LCXX	SP (U)	31312	**FC**	LCXX	SP (U)
31302	**FP**	LCWX	SP (U)	31317	**FO**	LCWX	BS (U)
31304	**FC**	LCXX	SP (U)	31319	**FC**	LCWX	CD (U)
31306	**C**	LWNW	CD	31327	**FR**	LCWX	SP (S)

Names:

31102 Cricklewood
31105 Bescot TMD
31106 The Blackcountryman
31130 Calder Hall Power Station
31146 Brush Veteran
31147 Floreat Salopia
31233 Severn Valley Railway

CLASS 31/4. Equipped with Train Heating. RA6.
CLASS 31/5. Train Heating Equipment isolated. RA6.

31405	**M**	LWNW	CD	31537	**C**	LCWX	BS (U)
31407	**ML**	ENTN	TO	31538		LCWX	SP (S)
31408		LCXX	SP (S)	31439	**RR**	LWNW	CD
31410	**RR**	LWNW	CD	31541	**C**	ENXX	TO (U)
31411	**D**	LCXX	BS (U)	31444	**C**	LCXX	SP (U)
31512	**C**	LWNW	CD	31545		LWNW	CD
31413	**O**	LCXX	BS (U)	31546	**C**	LCWX	BS (U)
31514	**C**	LWNW	CD	31548	**C**	LCXX	BS (U)
31415		LCXX	BS (U)	31549	**C**	ENXX	TO (U)
31516	**C**	LCXX	BS (U)	31450		LWNW	CD
31417	**D**	LCXX	BS (U)	31551	**C**	ENXX	TO (U)
31519	**C**	LCXX	SP (U)	31552	**C**	ENXX	TO (S)
31420	**M**	LWNW	CD	31554	**C**	LWNW	CD
31421	**RR**	LWNW	CD	31455	**RR**	LCWX	SP (U)
31422	**M**	LCWX	BS (U)	31556	**C**	LCWX	SP (U)
31423	**M**	LCWX	BS (U)	31558	**C**	ENXX	TO (U)
31524	**C**	LCWX	BS (U)	31459		ENXX	TO (U)
31526	**C**	LCXX	BS (U)	31461	**D**	ENXX	TO (U)
31427		LCWX	SP (S)	31462	**D**	LWNW	CD
31530	**C**	LCWX	BS (U)	31563	**C**	ENXX	TO (U)
31531	**C**	ENXX	TO (U)	31465	**RR**	LWNW	CD
31432		LCWX	SP (U)	31466	**C**	ENTN	TO
31533	**C**	LCXX	BS (U)	31467		LWNW	CD
31434		LWNW	CD	31468	**C**	LCWX	BS (U)
31435	**C**	LCWX	BS (U)				

Names:

31405 Mappa Mundi
31423 Jerome K. Jerome
31439 North Yorkshire Moors Railway
31468 The Enginemen's Fund

CLASS 33   BRCW TYPE 3   Bo – Bo

Built: 1960 – 62 by the Birmingham Railway Carriage & Wagon Company, Smethwick.
Engine: Sulzer 8LDA28 of 1160 kW (1550 hp) at 750 rpm.
Main Generator: Crompton Parkinson CG391B1.
Traction Motors: Crompton Parkinson C171C2.
Max. Tractive Effort: 200 kN (45000 lbf).
Cont. Tractive Effort: 116 kN (26000 lbf) at 17.5 m.p.h.
Power At Rail: 906 kW (1215 hp).   **Length over Buffers:** 15.47 m.
Brake Force: 35 t.   **Wheel Diameter:** 1092 mm.
Design Speed: 85 m.p.h.   **Weight:** 77.5 t (78.5 t Class 33/1).
Max. Speed: 60 m.p.h.   **RA:** 6.
Train Heating: Electric (y isolated).   **ETH Index:** 48.
Train Brakes: Air & vacuum.
Multiple Working: Blue Star Coupling Code.
Communication Equipment: Cab to shore radio-telephone.

Originally numbered in series D 6500 – 97 but not in order.
33116 carries its original number D 6535.

Class 33/0. Standard Design.

33002	y	C	ENXX	SL (U)
33008	y	G	ENXX	SL (U)
33012	e		ENXX	SL (S)
33019	e	C	EWDB	SL	Griffon
33023	e		ENXX	SL (U)
33025	e	C	EWDB	SL	Sultan
33026	e	C	EWDB	SL	Seafire
33029	e		ENXX	SL (U)
33030	e	C	EWDB	SL
33046	y	C	EWDB	SL	Merlin
33048	es		ENXX	SL (S)
33051	e	C	EWDB	SL	Shakespeare Cliff
33052	e		ENXX	SL (S)
33053	e	FA	ENXX	SL (U)
33057	ys	C	ENXX	SL (U)
33063	ys	FM	ENXX	SL (S)
33065	e	C	ENXX	SL (S)

Class 33/1. Fitted with Buckeye Couplings & SR Multiple Working Equipment for use with SR EMUs, TC stock & class 73.

Also fitted with flashing light adaptor for use on Weymouth Quay line.

33103	e	C	ENXX	SL (S)
33109	e	D	ENXX	SL (U)
33116	e		EWDB	SL	Hertfordshire Rail Tours
33117	e		ENXX	SL (U)

Class 33/2. Built to Former Loading Gauge of Tonbridge – Battle Line.

33202	ys	C	EWDB	SL	The Burma Star

33204	es	**FM**	ENXX	SL (U)
33205	es	**FD**	ENZX	SL (U)
33207	ys	**FA**	ENXX	SL (U)
33208	es	**C**	EWDB	SL

CLASS 37   ENGLISH ELECTRIC TYPE 3   Co–Co

Built: 1960 – 5 by English Electric Company at Vulcan Foundry, Newton le Willows or Robert Stephenson & Hawthorn, Darlington. 37003 – 115/340/1/3/350/1/9 with the exception of 37019*/047/065*/072*/073/074/075*/100* (* one end only) retain box-type route indicators, the remainder having central headcode panels/marker lamps.
Engine: English Electric 12CSVT of 1300 kW (1750 hp) at 850 rpm.
Main Generator: English Electric 822/10G.
Traction Motors: English Electric 538/A.
Max. Tractive Effort: 245 kN (55500 lbf).
Cont. Tractive Effort: 156 kN (35000 lbf) at 13.6 m.p.h.
Power At Rail: 932 kW (1250 hp).   **Length over Buffers:** 18.75 m.
Brake Force: 50 t.   **Wheel Diameter:** 1092 mm.
Design Speed: 90 m.p.h.   **Weight:** 103 – 108 t.
Max. Speed: 80 m.p.h.   **RA:** 5 or 7.
Train Heating: Electric (Class 37/4 only). **ETH Index:** 30.
Train Brakes: Air & Vacuum.
Multiple Working: Blue Star Coupling Code.
Communication Equipment: Cab to shore radio-telephone.

Non-standard livery: 37116 is BR blue with Transrail markings.

a Vacuum brake isolated.

Originally numbered D 6600 – 8, D 6700 – 6999 (not in order).
37274 is the second loco to carry that number. It was renumbered to avoid confusion with Class 37/3 locos.
Class 37/3 locos.

Class 37/0. Unrefurbished Locos. Technical details as above. RA5.

37003	+	**C**	FDYX	IM (U)	
37010		**C**	ENTN	TO	
37012		**C**	ENTN	TO	
37013	+	**ML**	ENTN	TO	
37019	+	**FD**	FDYX	IM (U)	
37023		**ML**	EWDB	SF	Stratford TMD Quality Approved
37025		**BR**	LWCW	CD	Inverness TMD Quality Assured
37026	+	**FD**	LCWX	SP (S)	
37035		**C**	ENXX	SL (U)	
37037		**FM**	EWDB	SL	
37038		**C**	ENTN	TO	
37040		**EW**	EWRB	SL	
37042	+	**EW**	ENTN	TO	
37043		**CT**	LGBM	ML	
37045	+	**F**	FDYX	TE (U)	
37046		**C**	ENTN	TO	

37047	+	**ML**	EWDB	SF	
37048		**FM**	ENXX	TO (U)	
37051		**EW**	ENTN	TO	Merehead
37054		**C**	EWDB	SL	
37055	+	**ML**	ENTN	TO	RAIL Celebrity
37057	+	**EW**	ENTN	TO	Viking
37058	+	**C**	FDYX	IM (U)	
37059	+	**FD**	FDYX	IM (U)	
37063	+	**FD**	FDYX	TE (U)	
37065	+	**ML**	ENTN	TO	
37066	+	**C**	LCWX	SP (U)	
37068	+	**FD**	FDYX	IM (U)	
37069	+	**C**	LGBM	ML	
37071	+	**C**	LWCW	CD	
37072	+	**D**	ENTN	TO	
37073	+	**FT**	LWCW	CD	Fort William/An Gearasdan
37074	+	**ML**	EWDB	SL	
37075	+	**F**	FDYX	TE (U)	
37077		**ML**	EWDB	SL	
37078	+	**FS**	LCXX	ML (U)	
37079	+	**FD**	ENTN	TO	
37083	+	**C**	FDYX	IM (U)	
37087		**C**	LWCW	CD	
37088		**CT**	LCWX	ML (U)	Clydesdale
37092		**C**	ENXX	TO (U)	
37095	+	**C**	LWCW	CD	
37097		**C**	ENTN	TO	
37098	+	**C**	ENTN	TO	
37099		**C**	LCWX	BS (U)	Clydebridge
37100	+	**FT**	LGBM	ML	
37101	+	**FD**	FDYX	IM (U)	
37104		**C**	FDYX	IM (U)	
37106	+	**C**	EWDB	SF	
37107	+	**FD**	LCWX	SP (U)	
37108	+	**F**	LCWX	BS (U)	
37109		**EW**	EWDB	SL	
37110	+	**F**	`FDYX	IM (U)	
37111		**FT**	LCWX	BS (U)	
37114	+	**EW**	ENTN	TO	City of Worcester
37116	+	**O**	LWCW	CD	Sister Dora
37131	+	**F**	FDRI	IM	
37133		**C**	EWDB	SL	
37137		**FM**	ENTN	TO	
37139	+	**FC**	FDYX	IM (U)	
37140		**C**	EWDB	SF	
37141		**C**	LWCW	CD	
37142		**C**	LWCW	CD	
37144 r		**FA**	FDYX	IM (U)	
37146		**C**	LWCW	CD	
37152		**I**	LGBM	ML	
37153		**CT**	LGBM	ML	

37154	+	FT	LBSB	BS
37156	r	FT	LCWX	ML (S)
37158		C	LWCW	CD
37162	+	D	ENTN	TO
37165	+	C	LGBM	ML
37167	+	ML	EWDB	SL
37170	r	C	LGBM	ML
37174		U	EWRB	SL
37175		C	LGBM	ML
37178	+	F	LBSB	BS
37184		C	LCWX	BS
37185	+	C	ENTN	TO Lea & Perrins
37188		C	LCWX	BS (U)
37191		C	LWCW	CD
37194	+	FM	EWRB	SL British International Freight Association
37196		C	LBSB	BS
37197	+	CT	LNSK	CF
37198	+	ML	EWDB	SL
37201		CT	LCWX	BS (S) Saint Margaret
37203		ML	EWDB	SL
37207		C	LCWX	BS (U)
37209		BR	FDYX	IM (U)
37211		C	LWCW	CD
37212	+	FT	LWCW	CD
37213	+	FC	LCWX	CF (U)
37214	+	FT	LWCW	CD
37216	r+	ML	EWDB	SF Great Eastern
37217	+		FDYX	IM (U)
37218	+	F	FDYX	IM (U)
37219	r	ML	EWDB	SL
37220	+	EW	EWRB	SL
37221		FT	LGBM	ML
37222	+	FM	ENTN	TO
37223	+	FC	FDYX	IM (U)
37225	+	F	FDRI	IM
37227	+	FM	ENTN	TO
37229	+	FC	LNSK	CF
37230	+	CT	LNSK	CF
37232	r	CT	LCWX	ML (U)The Institution of Railway Signal Engineers
37235	+	F	FDYX	IM (U)
37238	+	F	ENTN	TO
37240	+	C	LWCW	CD
37241		F	ENXX	SF (U)
37242	+	ML	EWDB	SF
37244	+	F	ENTN	TO
37245		C	EWRB	SL
37248	+	ML	ENTN	TO Midland Railway Centre
37250	+	FT	LGBM	ML
37251	+	I	LCWX	ML (U)The Northern Lights
37254	+	C	LNSK	CF

37255	+	C	LBSB	BS	
37258	+	C	LBSB	BS	
37261	+	FD	LGBM	ML	Caithness
37262	+	D	LBSB	BS	Dounreay
37263		C	LNSK	CF	
37264		C	ENTN	TO	
37274	+	ML	EWDB	SL	
37275	+		LNSK	CF	Oor Wullie
37278	+	FC	ENXX	TO (U)	
37293	+	ML	EWRB	SL	
37294	+	C	LGBM	ML	
37298	+	F	FDYX	IM (U)	

Class 37/3. Unrefurbished locos fitted with regeared (CP7) bogies.
Details as Class 37/0 except:
Max. Tractive Effort: 250 kN (56180 lbf).
Cont. Tractive Effort: 184 kN (41250 lbf) at 11.4 m.p.h.

37330	+	BR	FDRI	IM	
37331		F	FDYX	IM (U)	
37332	+	FC	FDRI	IM	The Coal Merchants' Association of Scotland
37333	+	FD	FDYX	IM (U)	
37334	+	F	LBSB	BS	
37335	+	F	FDYX	IM (U)	
37340	+	FD	FDYX	IM (U)	
37341	+	F	FDYX	TE (U)	
37343		C	FDYX	IM (U)	
37344	+	FD	FDYX	IM (U)	
37350	+	FP	FDRI	IM	
37351	+	CT	LGBM	ML	
37358		F	FDRI	IM	
37359	+	FP	FDYX	TE (U)	
37370		EW	EWRB	SL	
37371	+	ML	EWDB	SL	
37372		ML	EWRB	SL	
37375	+	C	EWDB	SL	
37376	+	FC	ENTN	TO	
37377	+	C	EWDB	SL	
37379		ML	EWDB	SF	Ipswich WRD Quality Assured
37380		FM	EWRB	SL	
37381	+	FD	FDYX	IM (U)	
37382		FP	FDYX	IM (U)	

Class 37/4. Refurbished locos fitted with train heating. Main generator replaced by alternator. Regeared (CP7) bogies. Details as class 37/0 except:

Main Alternator: Brush BA1005A.
Max. Tractive Effort: 256 kN (57440 lbf).
Cont. Tractive Effort: 184 kN (41250 lbf) at 11.4 m.p.h.
Power At Rail: 935 kW (1254 hp).
All have twin fuel tanks.

37401	r	FT	LGHM	ML	Mary Queen of Scots
37402	r	F	LWMC	CD	Bont Y Bermo
37403	r	G	LGHM	ML	Ben Cruachan
37404	r	FT	LGHM	ML	Loch Long
37405	r	M	LWCW	CD	Strathclyde Region
37406	r	FT	LGHM	ML	The Saltaire Society
37407	r	FT	LWCW	CD	Blackpool Tower
37408		BR	LWMC	CD	Loch Rannoch
37409	r	FT	LGHM	ML	Loch Awe
37410	r	FT	LGHM	ML	Aluminium 100
37411		EW	LNCK	CF	
37412		FT	LNCK	CF	Driver John Elliot
37413	r	FT	LWCW	CD	Loch Eil Outward Bound
37414	r	RR	LWMC	CD	Cathays C&W Works 1846 – 1993
37415	r	EW	LWCW	CD	
37416	r	EW	LNCK	CF	
37417	r	F	LWMC	CD	Highland Region
37418	r	EW	LWMC	CD	
37419		EW	LWCW	CD	
37420	r	RR	LWMC	CD	The Scottish Hosteller
37421	r	RR	LWMC	CD	The Kingsman
37422	r	RR	LWMC	CD	Robert F. Fairlie Locomotive Engineer 1831 – 1885
37423	r	FT	LCWX	ML (U)	Sir Murray Morrison 1873 – 1948 Pioneer of British Aluminium Industry
37424	r	FT	LGHM	ML	
37425	r	RR	LWMC	CD	Sir Robert McAlpine/ Concrete Bob (opposite sides)
37426	r	M	LWCW	CD	
37427	r	EW	LNCK	CF	
37428	r	F	LGHM	ML	David Lloyd George
37429	r	RR	LWMC	CD	Eisteddfod Genedlaethol
37430	r	FT	LGHM	ML	Cwmbrân
37431	r	M	LCWX	ML (U)	

Class 37/5. Refurbished locos. Main generator replaced by alternator. Regeared (CP7) bogies. Details as class 37/4 except:

Max. Tractive Effort: 248 kN (55590 lbf).
All have twin fuel tanks.

37503		EW	FDCI	IM	
37505		FT	LWCW	CD	British Steel Workington
37509		FT	LWCW	CD	
37510		I	LGBM	ML	
37513		LH	FDCI	IM	
37515	s	FS	FDCI	IM	
37516	s	LH	FDCI	IM	
37517	ars	EW	FDCI	IM	
37518		EW	LWCW	CD	
37519		FS	FDCI	IM	
37520		FS	LWCW	CD	

37521   **EW** LNLK   CF

Class 37/6. Refurbished locos for use on Channel Tunnel Night services. All have train air brakes only, UIC brake and coaching stock jumpers, RCH jumpers, ETH through wires.

37601 (37501)	**E** GPSV	OC		37607 (37511)	**E** GPSV	OC
37602 (37502)	**E** GPSV	OC		37608 (37512)	**E** GPSV	OC
37603 (37504)	**E** GPSV	OC		37609 (37514)	**E** GPSV	OC
37604 (37506)	**E** GPSV	OC		37610 (37687)	**E** GPSV	OC
37605 (37507)	**E** GPSV	OC		37611 (37690)	**E** GPSV	OC
37606 (37508)	**E** GPSV	OC		37612 (37691)	**E** GPSV	OC

Class 37/5 continued.

37667	s	**F** EWDB	SF	
37668	s	**EW** LNLK	CF	
37669		**FT** LNLK	CF	
37670		**FT** LNLK	CF	St. Blazey T&RS Depot
37671		**FT** LNLK	CF	Tre Pol and Pen
37672	s	**FD** LNLK	CF	Freight Transport Association
37673		**FT** LNLK	CF	
37674		**FT** LNLK	CF	Saint Blaise Church 1445 – 1995
37675	s	**FT** LGBM	ML	
37676		**F** EWDB	SF	
37677		**F** FDCI	IM	
37678		**FA** EWDB	SF	
37679		**F** EWDB	SF	
37680		**FA** FDCI	IM	
37682	r	**EW** FDCI	IM	Hartlepool Pipe Mill
37683		**FT** LGBM	ML	
37684		**EW** FDCI	IM	Peak National Park
37685		**I** LGBM	ML	
37686		**FA** FDCI	IM	
37688		**EW** FDCI	IM	
37689	s	**F** FDCI	IM	
37692	s	**FC** LGBM	ML	The Lass O' Ballochmyle
37693	s	**FT** LGBM	ML	
37694	s	**FC** FDCI	IM	
37695	s	**EW** LWCW	CD	
37696	s	**FT** LNLK	CF	
37697	s	**EW** FDCI	IM	
37698	s	**LH** FDCI	IM	
37699		**FC** FDYX	IM (U)	

Class 37/7. Refurbished locos. Main generator replaced by alternator. Regeared (CP7) bogies. Ballast weights added. Details as class 37/4 except:

Main Alternator: GEC G564AZ (37796 – 803) Brush BA1005A (others).
Max. Tractive Effort: 276 kN (62000 lbf).
Weight: 120 t.   **RA:** 7.
All have twin fuel tanks.

37701   s   **FT** LNCK   CF

37702	s	**FT** LGBM	ML	Taff Merthyr
37703	s	**FM** EWDB	SL	
37704	s	**EW** LNCK	CF	
37705		**FM** EWDB	SL	
37706		**EW** FDCI	IM	
37707		**EW** FDCI	IM	
37708		**FP** FDCI	IM	
37709		**FM** EWDB	SL	
37710		**LH** FDCI	IM	
37711		**FS** FDCI	IM	
37712		**FP** LGBM	ML	Teesside Steelmaster
37713		**LH** FDCI	IM	
37714		**FS** LGBM	ML	
37715		**FM** ENTN	TO	British Petroleum
37716		**FS** FDCI	IM	British Steel Corby
37717		**EW** FDCI	IM	Maltby Lilly Hall Junior School Rotherham Railsafe Trophy Winners 1996
37718		**EW** FDCI	IM	
37719		**FP** FDCI	IM	
37796	s	**FC** LGBM	ML	
37797	s	**FC** LGBM	ML	
37798	s	**ML** ENTN	TO	
37799	s	**FT** LGBM	ML	Sir Dyfed/County of Dyfed
37800	s	**FM** EWDB	SL	
37801	s	**EW** LGBM	ML	
37802	s	**FT** LGBM	ML	
37803	s	**ML** EWDB	SL	
37883		**EW** FDCI	IM	
37884		**LH** FDCI	IM	Gartcosh
37885		**EW** FDCI	IM	
37886		**EW** FDCI	IM	
37887	s	**FT** LNCK	CF	Caerphilly Castle/Castell Caerffili
37888		**F** LNCK	CF	
37889		**FT** LNCK	CF	
37890	a	**FM** EWDB	SL	The Railway Observer
37891		**FM** EWDB	SL	
37892		**FM** EWDB	SL	Ripple Lane
37893		**EW** LGBM	ML	
37894	s	**FC** LNCK	CF	
37895	s	**EW** LNCK	CF	
37896	s	**FT** LNCK	CF	
37897	s	**FT** LNCK	CF	
37898	s	**FT** LNCK	CF	Cwmbargoed DP
37899	s	**FC** LNCK	CF	County of West Glamorgan/ Sir Gorllewin Morgannwg

Class 37/9. Refurbished Locos. Fitted with manufacturers prototype power units and ballast weights. Main generator replaced by alternator. Details as Class 37/0 except:

Engine: Mirrlees MB275T of 1340 kW (1800 hp) at 1000 rpm (37901 – 4), Ruston RK270T of 1340 kW (1800 hp) at 900 rpm (37905 – 6).

Main Alternator: Brush BA1005A (GEC G564, 37905/6).
Max. Tractive Effort: 279 kN (62680 lbf).
Cont. Tractive Effort: 184 kN (41250 lbf) at 11.4 m.p.h.
Weight: 120 t.   **RA:** 7.
All have twin fuel tanks.

37901	**FT**	LNCK	CF	Mirrlees Pioneer
37902	**FS**	LNCK	CF	
37903	**FS**	LNCK	CF	
37904	**FS**	LCWX	CF (U)	
37905 s	**FS**	LCWX	CF (U)	Vulcan Enterprise
37906 s	**FT**	LCWX	CF (U)	

CLASS 43   HST POWER CAR   Bo – Bo

Built: 1976 – 82 by BREL Crewe Works. Originally numbered as coaching stock but now classified as locomotives. Fitted with luggage compartment.
Engine: Paxman Valenta 12RP200L (Paxman VP185*) of 1680 kW (2250 hp) at 1500 rpm.
Main Alternator: Brush BA1001B.
Traction Motors: Brush TMH68 – 46 or GEC G417AZ (43124 – 151/180). Frame mounted.
Max. Tractive Effort: 80 kN (17980 lbf).
Cont. Tractive Effort: 46 kN (10340 lbf) at 64.5 m.p.h.
Power At Rail: 1320 kW (1770 hp).   **ETH:** Non standard 3-phase system.
Brake Force: 35 t.   **Length over Buffers:** 17.79 m.
Weight: 70 t.   **Wheel Diameter:** 1020 mm.
Max. Speed: 125 m.p.h.   **RA:** 5.
Train Brakes: Air.
Multiple Working: With one other similar vehicle.
Communication Equipment: All equipped with driver – guard telephone and cab to shore radio-telephone.

§ Modified to be able to remotely control a class 91 locomotive and to be remotely controlled by a class 91 locomotive. Fitted with buffers. Tdm and Class 91 control equipment now isolated.

Ownership:

Midland Mainline and Virgin CrossCountry locos are owned by Porterbrook Leasing Company. Great North Eastern Railway, Great Western Trains and West Coast locos are owned by Angel Train Contracts. The Above does not apply to Virgin CrossCountry locos 43006-8, 178, 84 which are owned by Angel Train Contracts and are due to be transferred to Great Western Trains shortly. 43104 and 43180 are spare power cars which are used to cover for failures and shortages.

43002	**I**	IWRP	PM
43003	**GW**	IWRP	PM
43004	**I**	IWRP	PM
43005	**I**	IWRP	PM
43006	**I**	ICCS	EC
43007	**I**	ICCS	EC
43008	**I**	ICCP	LA

43009		IWRP	PM	
43010	GW	IWRP	PM	
43011	I	IWRP	PM	Reader 125
43012	I	IWRP	PM	
43013 §	I	ICCS	EC	CROSSCOUNTRY VOYAGER
43014 §	I	ICCS	EC	
43015	GW	IWRP	PM	
43016	I	IWRP	PM	
43017	I	IWRP	LA	
43018	GW	IWRP	LA	
43019	I	IWRP	LA	City of Swansea/Dinas Abertawe
43020	I	IWRP	LA	John Grooms
43021	I	IWRP	LA	
43022	I	IWRP	LA	
43023	I	IWRP	LA	County of Cornwall
43024	I	IWRP	LA	
43025	I	IWRP	LA	Exeter
43026	I	IWRP	LA	City of Westminster
43027	I	IWRP	LA	Glorious Devon
43028	I	IWCP	LO	
43029	I	IWCP	LO	
43030	I	IWRP	PM	
43031	I	IWRP	PM	
43032	I	IWRP	PM	The Royal Regiment of Wales
43033	I	IWRP	PM	
43034	I	IWRP	PM	The Black Horse
43035	I	IWRP	PM	
43036	I	IWRP	PM	
43037	I	IWRP	PM	
43038	I	IECP	NL	National Railway Museum
				The First Ten Years 1975 – 1985
43039	I	IECP	NL	
43040	I	IWRP	PM	
43041	I	IWCP	LO	City of Discovery
43042	I	IWCP	LO	
43043	I	IMLP	NL	
43044	I	IMLP	NL	Borough of Kettering
43045	I	IMLP	NL	The Grammar School Doncaster AD 1350
43046	I	IMLP	NL	Royal Philharmonic
43047 *	I	IMLP	NL	Rotherham Enterprise
43048	I	IMLP	NL	
43049	I	IMLP	NL	Neville Hill
43050	I	IMLP	NL	
43051	I	IMLP	NL	The Duke and Duchess of York
43052	I	IMLP	NL	City of Peterborough
43053	I	IMLP	NL	Leeds United
43054	I	IMLP	NL	
43055	I	IMLP	NL	Sheffield Star
43056	I	IMLP	NL	University of Bradford
43057	I	IMLP	NL	Bounds Green
43058	MM	IMLP	NL	MIDLAND PRIDE

Number					Name
43059	*	MM	IMLP	NL	
43060		I	IMLP	NL	County of Leicestershire
43061		I	IMLP	NL	City of Lincoln
43062		I	ICCS	EC	
43063		VC	ICCS	EC	Maiden Voyager
43064		I	IMLP	NL	City of York
43065	§	I	ICCS	EC	City of Edinburgh
43066		I	IMLP	NL	Nottingham Playhouse
43067	§	I	ICCS	EC	
43068	§	VC	ICCS	EC	
43069		I	ICCS	EC	
43070		I	ICCS	EC	
43071		I	ICCS	EC	Forward Birmingham
43072		I	IMLP	NL	Derby Etches Park
43073		I	IMLP	NL	
43074	*	I	IMLP	NL	
43075	*	I	IMLP	NL	
43076		I	IMLP	NL	BBC East Midlands Today
43077		I	IMLP	NL	County of Nottingham
43078		I	ICCS	EC	Golowan Festival Penzance
43079		I	ICCS	EC	
43080	§	I	ICCS	EC	
43081		I	IMLP	NL	
43082		I	IMLP	NL	
43083		I	IMLP	NL	
43084	§	I	ICCS	EC	County of Derbyshire
43085		I	IMLP	NL	City of Bradford
43086		I	ICCS	EC	
43087		I	ICCP	LA	
43088		I	ICCP	LA	XIII Commonwealth Games Scotland 1986
43089		I	ICCP	LA	
43090		I	ICCP	LA	
43091		I	ICCP	LA	Edinburgh Military Tattoo
43092		I	ICCS	EC	
43093		VC	ICCS	EC	Lady in Red
43094		I	ICCS	EC	
43095		I	IECP	NL	
43096		I	IECP	NL	
43097		I	ICCS	EC	
43098		I	ICCS	EC	
43099		I	ICCS	EC	
43100		I	ICCS	EC	Craigentinny
43101		I	ICCP	LA	Edinburgh International Festival
43102		I	ICCP	LA	
43103		I	ICCP	LA	John Wesley
43104		I	IECP	EC	County of Cleveland
43105		GN	IECP	NL	
43106		GN	IECP	NL	
43107		I	IECP	NL	
43108		GN	IECP	NL	
43109		I	IECP	NL	Yorkshire Evening Press

43110	I	IECP	EC	Darlington
43111	GN	IECP	EC	
43112	I	IECP	EC	
43113	I	IECP	EC	City of Newcastle-upon-Tyne
43114	GN	IECP	EC	
43115	I	IECP	EC	Yorkshire Cricket Academy
43116	GN	IECP	EC	
43117	GN	IECP	EC	
43118	GN	IECP	EC	
43119	GN	IECP	EC	
43120	GN	IECP	EC	
43121	I	ICCP	LA	West Yorkshire Metropolitan County
43122	I	ICCP	LA	South Yorkshire Metropolitan County
43123 §	I	ICCS	EC	
43124	I	IWRP	PM	
43125	I	IWRP	PM	Merchant Venturer
43126	I	IWRP	PM	City of Bristol
43127	I	IWRP	PM	
43128	I	IWRP	PM	
43129	GW	IWRP	PM	
43130	I	IWRP	PM	Sulis Minerva
43131	I	IWRP	PM	Sir Felix Pole
43132	I	IWRP	PM	
43133	I	IWRP	PM	
43134	I	IWRP	PM	County of Somerset
43135	GW	IWRP	PM	
43136	I	IWRP	PM	
43137	I	IWRP	PM	
43138	I	IWRP	PM	
43139	GW	IWRP	PM	
43140	I	IWRP	PM	
43141	I	IWRP	PM	
43142	I	IWRP	PM	
43143	I	IWRP	PM	
43144	I	IWRP	PM	
43145	I	IWRP	PM	
43146	I	IWRP	PM	
43147	I	IWRP	PM	The Red Cross
43148	I	IWRP	PM	
43149	I	IWRP	PM	BBC Wales Today
43150	I	IWRP	PM	Bristol Evening Post
43151	I	IWRP	PM	
43152	I	IWRP	PM	
43153	I	ICCP	LA	University of Durham
43154	I	ICCP	LA	INTERCITY
43155	I	ICCP	LA	BBC Look North
43156	I	ICCP	LA	
43157	I	ICCP	LA	Yorkshire Evening Post
43158	I	ICCP	LA	Dartmoor The Pony Express
43159	I	ICCP	LA	
43160	I	ICCP	LA	Storm Force

43161	I	ICCP	LA	Reading Evening Post
43162	I	ICCP	LA	Borough of Stevenage
43163	I	IWRP	LA	
43164	I	IWCP	LO	
43165	I	IWCP	LO	
43166	I	IWCP	LO	
43167 *	I	IECP	NL	
43168 *	GW	IWRP	LA	
43169 *	I	IWRP	LA	The National Trust
43170 *	I	IWRP	LA	Edward Paxman
43171	I	IWRP	LA	
43172	I	IWRP	LA	
43173	I	IWRP	LA	Swansea University
43174	I	IWRP	LA	
43175	I	IWRP	LA	
43176	I	IWRP	LA	
43177	I	IWRP	LA	University of Exeter
43178	I	ICCP	LA	
43179	GW	IWRP	LA	Pride of Laira
43180	I	IMLP	NL	
43181	I	IWRP	LA	Devonport Royal Dockyard 1693 – 1993
43182	I	IWRP	LA	
43183	GW	IWRP	LA	
43184	I	ICCP	LA	
43185	GW	IWRP	LA	Great Western
43186	I	IWRP	LA	Sir Francis Drake
43187	GW	IWRP	LA	
43188	GW	IWRP	LA	City of Plymouth
43189	I	IWRP	LA	RAILWAY HERITAGE TRUST
43190	I	IWRP	LA	
43191	GW	IWRP	LA	Seahawk
43192	I	IWRP	LA	City of Truro
43193	I	ICCP	LA	Plymouth SPIRIT OF DISCOVERY
43194	I	ICCP	LA	
43195	I	ICCP	LA	British Red Cross 125th Birthday 1995
43196	I	ICCP	LA	The Newspaper Society Founded 1836
43197	I	ICCP	LA	Railway Magazine 1897 Centenary 1997
43198	I	ICCP	LA	

CLASS 46   BR TYPE 4   1Co – Co1

Built: 1962 by BR Derby Locomotive Works.
Engine: Sulzer 12LDA28B of 1860 kW (2500 hp) at 750 rpm.
Main Generator: Brush TG160-60.
Traction Motors: Brush TM73-68 Mk3 (axle hung).
Max. Tractive Effort: 245 kN (55000 lbf).
Cont. Tractive Effort: 141 kN (31600 lbf) at 22.3 m.p.h.
Power At Rail: 1460 kW (1960 hp).   **Length over Buffers:** 20.70 m.
Brake Force: 63 t.   **Wheel Diameter:** 914/1143 mm.
Design Speed: 90 m.p.h.   **Weight:** 141 t.
Max. Speed: 75 m.p.h.   **RA:** 7.

▲ Wessex Traincare liveried Class 08 No. 08649 'G.H. Stratton' is pictured at Eastleigh on 27th July 1996. This loco carries its former number D3816   *John A. Day*

▼ The first Class 09 to carry new Railfreight Distribution colours, No. 09021 is seen at Stratford Freight Terminal on 19th October 1996.
                                                                                            Darren Ford

Class 20s Nos 20128 'Guglielmo Marconi' and 20075 'Sir William Cooke' approach Norton Bridge with a Crewe–Bescot ballast working on 8th May 1996. Both locos carry Racal-BR Telecom livery.
Hugh Ballantyne

▲ The sole Mainline freight liveried Class 31, No. 31407 is seen at Great Yarmouth on 31st August 1996 after arriving with the 14.35 from Norwich. *Brian Denton*

▼ Regional Railways liveried Class 31s Nos. 31455 and 31 410 doublehead an Ince Moss to Warrington ballast at Winwick on 5th July 1996. *Paul Senior*

▲ Civil-link liveried Class 33 No. 33051 'Shakespeare Cliff' at Hoo Junction on 10th October 1995 after arriving with a train from East Peckham tip.   *Rodney Lissenden*

▼ A Fawley to Eastleigh trip working consisting of empty bogie tankers passes through Southampton on 8th February 1996 behind Mainline freight liveried Class 37 No. 37167.   *Nic Joynson*

▲ English, Welsh & Scottish Railway liveried Class 37 No. 37419 is pictured near Sellafield on 24th July 1996 with a nuclear flask train working. *Dave McAlone*

▼ New Railfreight Distribution liveried Class 47 No. 47310 'Henry Ford' passes Droitwich Spa with a Washwood Heath to MoD Long Marston train on 16th October 1996. *Bob Sweet*

An HST set in the new Great Western Trains livery catches the early morning sun as it passes through Dawlish with Class 43 power cars Nos. 43183 and 43185 'Great Western' in charge. The train is the 05.15 Penzance–London Paddington.

Colin J. Marsden

Class 47 No. 47345 passes the M27 motorway near Eastleigh with the daily 09.00 Southampton–Coatbridge service on 26th April 1996. This loco carries Freightliner livery.
Nic Joynson

Still carrying the obsolete Trainload Metals livery, Class 56 No. 56061 passes Clay Cross with a Tees yard to Etruria service on 31st May 1996.

Hugh Ballantyne

▲ Class 56 No. 56089 is pictured on the Felixstowe branch at Levington on 10th July 1996. The train is a special Crewe–Felixstowe Freightliner service. *John A. Day*

▼ Two-tone grey with Mainline branding is the livery carried by Class 58 No. 58035 in this view of the loco taken at Stratford. The date is 17th August 1996. *Kevin Conkey*

Foster Yeoman Class 59 No. 59005 'KENNETH J. PAINTER' approaches West Ealing from the east with an empty stone train on 28th July 1995.

Ian A. Lyall

Loadhaul liveried Class 60 No. 60007 passes Gateforth with a Leeds to Lindsey tank train on 20th May 1996.

Ian A. Lyall

The 11.12 Jarrow–Stanlow empty tank train is pictured passing Cowperthwaite, north of Oxenholme behind Transrail liveried Class 60 No. 60056 'William Beveridge'. The date is 17th July 1996.

Nic Joynson

▲ Freshly repainted in English, Welsh & Scottish Railway (EW&S) livery, Class 73 No. 73128 is pictured stabled at Eastleigh T&RSMD on 24th September 1996.   *Brian Denton*

▼ InterCity liveried Class 86 No. 86229 'Sir John Betjeman' passes Mealbank with the Glasgow Central–Brighton 'Sussex Scot' service on 26th May 1995.   *Dave McAlone*

A Euston bound train is seen passing the site of the Keswick branch at Penrith on 5th August 1995 behind Class 87 No. 87029 'Earl Marischal'.

Dave McAlone

▲ Rail express systems liveried Class 90 No. 90019 'Penny Black' passes Hambleton South Junction with the 14.50 Low Fell–London Kings Cross mail train on 12th July 1995.   *Hugh Ballantyne*

▼ Class 91 No. 91019 'Scottish Enterprise' is pictured at Esholt whilst working the 11.38 Bradford Forster Square–London Kings Cross service on 21st October 1996. Both the loco and the coaching stock are carrying the new Great North Eastern Railway livery   *Les Nixon*

Class 92s are now starting to enter traffic. Here, Class 92 No. 92010 'Molière' passes Otford Junction with the 09.37 Wembley–Dollands Moor service on 1st October 1996. The loco carries European Passenger Services livery.

Rodney Lissenden

Train Brakes: Air & vacuum.
Multiple Working: Not equipped.

Ownership: Owned by Carriage & Traction Company Ltd.

Carries original number D 172.

46035	**G**	MBDL	CQ	Ixion

CLASS 47   BRUSH TYPE 4   Co – Co

Built: 1963 – 67 by Brush Traction, Loughborough or BR Crewe Works.
Engine: Sulzer 12LDA28C of 1920 kW (2580 hp) at 750 rpm.
Main Generator: Brush TG160-60 Mk2, TG160-60 Mk4 or TM172-50 Mk1.
Traction Motors: Brush TM64-68 Mk1 or Mk1A (axle hung).
Max. Tractive Effort: 267 kN (60000 lbf).
Cont. Tractive Effort: 133 kN (30000 lbf) at 26 m.p.h.
Power At Rail: 1550 kW (2080 hp).   **Length over Buffers:** 19.38 m.
Brake Force: 61 t.   **Wheel Diameter:** 1143 mm.
Design Speed: 95 m.p.h.   **Weight:** 120.5 – 125 t.
Max. Speed: various.   **RA:** 6 or 7.
Train Brakes: Air & vacuum.
Multiple Working: Green Circle (m) or Blue Star (*) Coupling Code. Otherwise
not equipped.
ETH Index (47/4, 47/6 and 47/7): 66 (75 Class 47/6).
Communication Equipment: Cab to shore radio-telephone.

Non standard liveries:

47145 is dark blue with Railfreight Distribution markings.
47798/9 are Royal train purple.
47803 is grey, red and yellow.

Originally numbered D 1100 – 11, D 1500 – 1999 not in order.

Ownership:

Freightliner 1995 locos Nos. 47052/60/142/7/57/87/97/206/12/25/31 . 70/
9/83/9/96/301/5/17/22/37/9/45/7/9/54/8/71/6/7 plus Great Western Trains
and Virgin CrossCountry locos are owned by Porterbrook Leasing Company.

a Vacuum brake isolated.

Class 47/0. Built with train heating boiler. RA6. Max. Speed 75 m.p.h.

47004	**G**	ENRN	TO	Old Oak Common Traction & Rolling Stock Depot
47016	**FO**	ENRN	TO	ATLAS
47019	**FO**	DHLT	CD (U)	
47033 am +	**FE**	DAET	TI	The Royal Logistics Corps
47049 am +	**FE**	DAET	TI	GEFCO
47051 am +	**FE**	DAET	TI	
47052	**FF**	DFLR	CD	
47053 am +	**FE**	DAET	TI	Dollands Moor International
47060 a	**F**	DFLT	CD	
47079	**FE**	DFLT	CD	

47085 am+	**FE**	DAET	TI	REPTA 1893 – 1993
47095 am+	**FE**	DAET	TI	
47114 am+	**FD**	DFLM	CD	
47125 am+	**FE**	DAET	TI	
47142	**FR**	DHLT	CD	
47144 am+	**FD**	DAXT	TI	
47145 am	**0**	DAET	TI	
47146 am	**FE**	DAET	TI	Loughborough Grammar School
47147	**F**	DFLT	CD	
47150 am+	**FE**	DAET	TI	
47152 am+	**FF**	DFLM	CD	
47156 am+	**FD**	DHLT	CD (U)	
47157	**FF**	DHLT	CD	Johnson Stevens Agencies
47186 am+	**FE**	DAET	TI	Catcliffe Demon
47187	**F**	DHLT	CD	
47188 am+	**FE**	DAET	TI	
47193	**FP**	LCWX	BS (U)	
47194 am+	**FD**	DAET	TI	
47197	**F**	DFLT	CD	
47200 am+	**FE**	DAET	TI	Herbert Austin
47201 am+	**FE**	DAET	TI	
47204 am+	**F**	DFLM	CD	
47205 am+	**FF**	DFLM	CD	
47206	**FF**	DFLR	CD	The Morris Dancer
47207	**F**	DFLT	CD	
47209 am+	**FF**	DFLR	CD	
47210 am+	**FD**	DAET	TI	
47211 am+	**FD**	DAET	TI	
47212 +	**FF**	DFLR	CD	
47213 am+	**FD**	DAET	TI	Marchwood Military Port
47217 am+	**FE**	DAET	TI	
47218 am+	**FE**	DAET	TI	United Transport Europe
47219 am+	**FE**	DAET	TI	Arnold Kunzler
47221 +	**FP**	FDYX	IM (U)	
47222 am+	**FD**	DAYX	TI (U)	
47223 +	**F**	ENXX	SF (U)	
47224 +	**FP**	FDKI	IM	
47225	**FF**	DFLR	CD	
47226 am+	**FD**	DAET	TI	
47228 am+	**FE**	DAET	TI	axial
47229 am+	**FE**	DAET	TI	
47231	**F**	DFLT	CD	
47234 am+	**FE**	DFLM	CD	
47236 am+	**FE**	DAET	TI	ROVER GROUP QUALITY ASSURED
47237 am+	**FE**	DAET	TI	
47238	**FD**	LCXX	BS (U)	Bescot Yard
47241 am+	**FE**	DAET	TI	Halewood Silver Jubilee 1988
47245 am+	**FE**	DAET	TI	The Institute of Export
47256	**FD**	FDYX	IM (U)	
47258 am+	**FE**	DAET	TI	
47270	**FF**	DFLT	CD	Cory Brothers 1842 – 1992

47276 am +	**FD**	DAET	TI	
47277	**FD**	FDYX	IM (U)	
47278	**FP**	ENXX	SF (U)	
47279	**FF**	DHLT	CD	
47280 am +	**FD**	DAET	TI	Pedigree
47281 am +	**FD**	DAET	TI	
47283	**F**	DFLT	CD	
47284 am +	**FD**	DAET	TI	
47285 am +	**FE**	DAET	TI	
47286 am +	**FE**	DAET	TI	Port of Liverpool
47287 am +	**FE**	DAET	TI	
47289 a	**FF**	DFLT	CD	
47290 am +	**FE**	DFLR	CD	
47291 am +	**FD**	DAYX	TI (U)	
47292 am +	**FD**	DFLM	CD	
47293 am +	**FE**	DAET	TI	
47294 +	**FD**	FDYX	IM (U)	
47295 +	**FP**	LCWX	BS (U)	
47296	**FF**	DFLR	CD	
47297 am +	**FE**	DAET	TI	Cobra RAILFREIGHT
47298 am +	**FD**	DAET	TI	Pegasus
47299 am +	**FE**	DAET	TI	

Class 47/3. Built without Train Heat. (except 47300). RA6. Max. Speed 75 m.p.h. All equipped with slow speed control.

47300	**C**	LCWX	BS (U)	
47301	**FF**	DFLR	CD	Freightliner Birmingham
47302 a	**FR**	DFLT	CD	
47303 am +	**FE**	DFLM	CD	
47304 am +	**FD**	DAET	TI	
47305	**FF**	DFLR	CD	
47306 am +	**FE**	DAET	TI	The Sapper
47307 am +	**FE**	DAET	TI	
47308	**C**	LCWX	BS (U)	
47309 am +	**FD**	DAET	TI	The Halewood Transmission
47310 am +	**FE**	DAET	TI	Henry Ford
47312 am +	**FE**	DAET	TI	
47313 am +	**FD**	DAET	TI	
47314 am +	**FD**	DAET	TI	Transmark
47315	**C**	ENRN	TO	
47316 am +	**FE**	DAXT	TI	
47317	**F**	DFLT	CD	
47319 +	**FP**	FDYX	IM (U) Norsk Hydro	
47322	**FR**	DHLT	CD	
47323 am +	**FE**	DFLR	CD	
47326 am +	**FE**	DAET	TI	Saltley Depot Quality Approved
47328 am +	**FD**	DAET	TI	
47329	**C**	LCWX	BS (U)	
47330 am +	**FD**	DAET	TI	
47331	**C**	FDKI	IM	
47332	**C**	LCWX	BS (U)	

47333		C	LCWX	BS (U)
47334		C	LCWX	BS (U)
47335	am +	FD	DAET	TI
47337	am	FF	DFLR	CD
47338	am +	FE	DAET	TI
47339		FF	DFLR	CD
47340		C	DHLT	CD
47341		C	LCWX	BS (U)
47344	am +	FE	DAET	TI
47345		FF	DFLR	CD
47346		C	FDYX	IM (U)
47347	a	F	DHLT	CD (U)
47348	am	FE	DAET	TI St. Christopher's Railway Home
47349		F	DFLT	CD
47350		FO	DFLT	CD (U)
47351	am +	FE	DAET	TI
47352		C	FDYX	IM (U)
47353		C	LCWX	BS (U)
47354	a	FF	DFLR	CD
47355	am +	FD	DAET	TI
47356		FO	DHLT	CD (U)
47357		C	LCXX	BS (U)
47358		FF	DFLT	CD
47359		FD	FDYX	IM (U)
47360	am +	FE	DAET	TI
47361	am +	FF	DFLM	CD
47362	am +	FD	DAET	TI
47363	am +	F	DAET	TI
47365	am +	FE	DAET	TI ICI Diamond Jubilee
47366		C	ENXX	TO (U)
47367		FR	DHLT	CD
47368		F	ENXX	SF (U)
47369		FD	FDYX	IM (U)
47370		FF	DFLR	CD Andrew A Hodgkinson
47371		FF	DFLR	CD
47372		C	LCWX	BS (U)
47375	am +	FE	DAET	TI Tinsley Traction Depot
				Quality Approved
47376		FF	DFLR	CD Freightliner 1995
47377	a	F	DFLR	CD
47378	am +	FD	DAET	TI
47379	am +	F	DAET	TI

Class 47/4. Equipped with train heating. RA6. Max speed 95 m.p.h. (75 m.p.h.)

47462	R	ENXX	SF (U)
47467	BR	PXLC	CD
47471	IO	PXXA	CD (U)
47473	BR	DHLT	CD
47474	R	PXXA	CD (S) Sir Rowland Hill
47475	RX	LWRC	CD Restive
47476	R	FDKI	IM Night Mail

47478		LCWX	BS (U)	
47481	BR	PXXA	CD (U)	
47484	G	ENXX	SF (U) ISAMBARD KINGDOM BRUNEL
47489	R	LWRC	CD	
47492	RX	PXLC	CD	
47501	R	LWRC	CD	Craftsman
47513	BR	PXLD	CD	Severn
47519 +	G	LWRC	CD	
47520	I	LWRC	CD	
47522 §	R	FDKI	IM	Doncaster Enterprise
47523	M	LWRC	CD	
47524	RX	PXLD	CD (S)	
47525	FE	DAET	TI	
47526	BR	ENXX	SF (S)	
47528	M	LWRC	CD	The Queen's Own Mercian Yeomanry
47530	RX	PXLD	CD (S)	
47532	RX	PXLD	CD (S)	
47535	RX	LWRC	CD	
47536	RX	PXLD	CD (S)	
47539	RX	PXXA	CD	
47540	C	DAET	TI	The Institution of Civil Engineers
47543	R	FDKI	IM	
47547	N	PXXA	CD (U)	
47550	M	FDYX	IM (U)	University of Dundee
47555	FE	DAYX	TI	The Commonwealth Spirit
47565	RX	PXLC	CD	Responsive
47566	RX	PXLD	CD (U)	
47572	R	PXLC	CD	Ely Cathedral
47574	R	FDYX	IM (U)	Benjamin Gimbert G.C.
47575	R	PXLC	CD	City of Hereford
47576	RX	PXLD	CD (S)	
47584	RX	PXLC	CD	THE LOCOMOTIVE &
				CARRIAGE INSTITUTION
47596	RX	PXLC	CD	
47624	RX	PXLC	CD	Saint Andrew
47627	RX	PXLC	CD	
47628 j	RX	PXLC	CD	
47634	R	PXLC	CD	Holbeck
47635 j	R	PXLC	CD	
47640 j	R	PXLC	CD	University of Strathclyde

Class 47/6. Equipped with high phosphorous brake blocks. RA6. Max speed 75 m.p.h.

47676	I	FDYX	IM (U)
47677	I	FDYX	IM (U)

Class 47/7. Fitted with an older form of TDM. RA6. Max. Speed 95 m.p.h. All have twin fuel tanks.

47702	F	ENRN	TO	County of Suffolk
47704	RX	LWRC	CD	
47710	W	PWLO	CD	
47711	N	ENXX	TO (U)	County of Hertfordshire

47712	**W** PWLO	CD	DICK WHITTINGTON
47715	**N** PXLD	CD (S) Haymarket
47716	**RX** PXLD	CD (S)
47717	**R** PXXA	CD (U)

Class 47/7. Parcels dedicated locos. RA6. Max. Speed 95 m.p.h.
All have twin fuel tanks and are fitted with RCH jumper cables for operating
with propelling control vehicles (PCVs).

47721 (47557)		**RX** PXLB	CD	Saint Bede
47722 (47558)	a	**RX** PXLB	CD	The Queen Mother
47725 (47567)		**RX** PXLB	CD	The Railway Mission
47726 (47568)		**RX** PXLB	CD	Progress
47727 (47569)	a	**RX** PXLB	CD	Duke of Edinburgh's Award
47732 (47580)		**RX** PXLB	CD	Restormel
47733 (47582)	a	**RX** PXLB	CD	Eastern Star
47734 (47583)		**RX** PXLB	CD	Crewe Diesel Depot
				Quality Approved
47736 (47587)	a	**RX** PXLB	CD	Cambridge Traction
				& Rolling Stock Depot
47737 (47588)		**RX** PXLB	CD	Resurgent
47738 (47592)	a	**RX** PXLB	CD	Bristol Barton Hill
47739 (47594)	a	**RX** PXLB	CD	Resourceful
47741 (47597)		**RX** PXLB	CD	Resilient
47742 (47598)		**RX** PXLB	CD	The Enterprising Scot
47744 (47600)	a	**RX** PXLB	CD	Saint Edwin
47745 (47603)		**RX** PXLB	CD	Royal London Society
				for the Blind
47746 (47605)	a	**RX** PXLB	CD	The Bobby
47747 (47615)	a	**RX** PXLB	CD	Res Publica
47749 (47625)		**RX** PXLB	CD	Atlantic College
47750 (47626)	a	**RX** PXLB	CD	Royal Mail Cheltenham
47756 (47644)		**RX** PXLB	CD	Royal Mail Tyneside
47757 (47585)	a	**RX** PXLB	CD	Restitution
47758 (47517)		**RX** PXLB	CD	
47759 (47559)		**RX** PXLB	CD	
47760 (47562)		**RX** PXLB	CD	Restless
47761 (47564)		**RX** PXLB	CD	
47762 (47573)		**RX** PXLB	CD	
47763 (47581)		**RX** PXLB	CD	
47764 (47630)		**RX** PXLB	CD	Resounding
47765 (47631)		**RX** PXLB	CD	Ressaldar
47766 (47642)		**RX** PXLB	CD	Resolute
47767 (47641)		**RX** PXLB	CD	Saint Columba
47768 (47490)		**RX** PXLB	CD	Resonant
47769 (47491)		**RX** PXLB	CD	Resolve
47770 (47500)		**RX** PXLB	CD	Reserved
47771 (47503)		**RX** PXLB	CD	Heaton Traincare Depot
47772 (47537)		**RX** PXLB	CD	
47773 (47541)		**RX** PXLB	CD	Reservist
47774 (47551)		**RX** PXLB	CD	Poste Restante
47775 (47531)		**RX** PXLB	CD	Respite

47776	(47578)	**RX**	PXLB	CD	Respected
47777	(47636)	**RX**	PXLB	CD	Restored
47778	(47606)	**RX**	PXLB	CD	Irresistible
47779	(47612)	**RX**	PXLB	CD	
47780	(47618)	**RX**	PXLB	CD	
47781	(47653)	**RX**	PXLB	CD	Isle of Iona
47782	(47824)	**RX**	PXLB	CD	
47783	(47809)	**RX**	PXLB	CD	Saint Peter
47784	(47819)	**RX**	PXLB	CD	Condover Hall
47785	(47820)	**RX**	PXLB	CD	The Statesman
47786	(47821) a	**RX**	PXLB	CD	Roy Castle OBE
47787	(47823)	**RX**	PXLB	CD	Victim Support
47788	(47833) a	**RX**	PXLB	CD	Captain Peter Manisty RN
47789	(47616) a	**RX**	PXLB	CD	Lindisfarne
47790	(47673) a	**RX**	PXLB	CD	Saint David/Dewi Sant
47791	(47675) a	**RX**	PXLB	CD	VENICE SIMPLON ORIENT EXPRESS
47792	(47804)	**RX**	PXLB	CD	Saint Cuthbert
47793	(47579)	**RX**	PXLB	CD	Saint Augustine

Class 47/4 continued. RA6. Max. Speed 95 m.p.h.

47798	a	**0**	PXLP	CD	Prince William
47799	a	**0**	PXLP	CD	Prince Henry
47802	+	**I**	ENXX	SF (S)	
47803	+	**0**	ENXX	SF (S)	
47805	a+	**I**	ILRA	CD	
47806	a+	**I**	ILRA	CD	
47807	a+	**PL**	ILRB	CD	
47810	a+	**I**	ILRA	CD	PORTERBROOK
47811	a+	**I**	IWLX	LA	
47812	a+	**I**	ILRA	CD	
47813	a+	**I**	IWLX	LA	
47814	a+	**I**	ILRA	CD	
47815	a+	**I**	IWLA	LA	
47816	a+	**I**	IWLA	LA	Bristol Bath Road Quality Approved
47817	a+	**PL**	ILRB	CD	
47818	a+	**I**	ILRA	CD	
47822	a+	**I**	ILRA	CD	
47825	a+	**I**	ILRA	CD	Thomas Telford
47826	a+	**I**	ILRA	CD	
47827	a+	**I**	ILRA	CD	
47828	a+	**I**	ILRA	CD	
47829	a+	**I**	ILRA	CD	
47830	a+	**I**	SBXL	LA (U)	
47831	a+	**I**	ILRA	CD	Bolton Wanderer
47832	a+	**I**	IWLA	LA	
47839	a+	**I**	ILRA	CD	
47840	a+	**I**	ILRA	CD	NORTH STAR
47841	a+	**I**	ILRA	CD	The Institution of Mechanical Engineers
47843	a+	**I**	ILRA	CD	

47844 a+	I	ILRA	CD	Derby & Derbyshire Chamber of Commerce & Industry
47845 a+	I	IWLX	LA	County of Kent
47846 a+	U	IWLA	LA	THOR
47847 a+	I	ILRA	CD	
47848 a+	I	ILRA	CD	
47849 a+	I	ILRA	CD	
47851 a+	I	ILRA	CD	
47853 a+	I	ILRA	CD	
47854 a+	I	ILRA	CD	Women's Royal Voluntary Service
47971 *	BR	PXLK	CD	Robin Hood
47972	CS	LWRC	CD	The Royal Army Ordnance Corps
47976 *	C	PXLK	CD	Aviemore Centre

Class 47/3 continued. RA6. Max. Speed 75 m.p.h.

47981	C	FDKI	IM

CLASS 55   DELTIC   Co–Co

Built: 1961 by English Electric, Vulcan Foundry.
Engines: Two Napier Deltic T18-25 of 1230 kW (1650 h.p.) at 1500 rpm.
Main Generators: Two English Electric EE829.
Traction Motors: EE538 (axle hung).
Max. Tractive Effort: 222 kN (50000 lbf).
Cont. Tractive Effort: 136 kN (30500 lbf) at 32.5 m.p.h.
Power At Rail: 1969 kW (2640 hp). **Length over Buffers:** 17.65 m.
Brake Force: 51 t. **Wheel Diameter:** 1092 mm.
Design Speed: 100 m.p.h. **Weight:** 105 t.
Max. Speed: 90 m.p.h. **RA:** 5.
Train Brakes: Air & vacuum. **Multiple Working:** Not equipped.
ETH Index: 66.

Ownership:

Owned by 9000 locomotives Ltd.

Carries original number D 9000.

55022	G	MBDL	BN	ROYAL SCOTS GREY

CLASS 56   BRUSH TYPE 5   Co–Co

Built: 1976 – 84 by Electroputere at Craiova, Romania (as sub contractors for Brush) or BREL at Doncaster or Crewe Works.
Engine: Ruston Paxman 16RK3CT of 2460 kW (3250 hp) at 900 rpm.
Main Alternator: Brush BA1101A.
Traction Motors: Brush TM73-62.
Max. Tractive Effort: 275 kN (61800 lbf).
Cont. Tractive Effort: 240 kN (53950 lbf) at 16.8 m.p.h.
Power At Rail: 1790 kW (2400 hp). **Length over Buffers:** 19.36 m.
Brake Force: 60 t. **Wheel Diameter:** 1143 mm.
Design Speed: 80 m.p.h. **Weight:** 125 t.
Max. Speed: 80 m.p.h. **RA:** 7.

Train Brakes: Air.
Multiple Working: Red Diamond coupling code.
Communication Equipment: Cab to shore radio-telephone.
All equipped with slow speed control.

56001	FA	LCYX	CF (U)	
56003	LH	FDBI	IM	
56004		FDBI	IM	
56006	LH	FDBI	IM	Ferrybridge 'C' Power Station
56007	FT	FDBI	IM	
56008		FDYX	IM (U)	
56010	FT	LNBK	CF	
56011	F	FDYX	IM	
56012	FC	FDYX	IM (U)	
56014	FC	FDYX	IM (U)	
56018	FT	LNBK	CF	
56019	FR	LCWX	CF (U)	
56020		LCWX	CF (U)	
56021	LH	FDBI	IM	
56022	FT	FDBI	IM	
56025	FT	FDBI	IM	
56027	LH	FDBI	IM	
56029	F	FDBI	IM	
56031	C	FDBI	IM	
56032	FS	LNBK	CF	Sir De Morgannwg/ County of South Glamorgan
56033	FT	FDBI	IM	Shotton Paper Mill
56034	LH	FDBI	IM	Castell Ogwr/Ogmore Castle
56035	LH	FDBI	IM	
56036	CT	FDBI	IM	
56037	FT	FDBI	IM	Richard Trevithick
56038	FT	FDBI	IM	Western Mail
56039	LH	FDBI	IM	ABP Port of Hull
56040	FT	LNBK	CF	Oystermouth
56041	EW	FDBI	IM	
56043	FS	FDBI	IM	
56044	FT	LNBK	CF	Cardiff Canton Quality Assured
56045	LH	FDBI	IM	
56046	C	FDBI	IM	
56047	CT	FDBI	IM	
56048	C	FDBI	IM	
56049	CT	FDBI	IM	
56050	LH	FDBI	IM	British Steel Teeside
56051	EW	FDBI	IM	Isle of Grain
56052	FT	LNBK	CF	
56053	FT	LNBK	CF	Sir Morgannwg Ganol/ County of Mid Glamorgan
56054	FT	FDBI	IM	British Steel Llanwern
56055	LH	FDBI	IM	
56056	FT	LGAM	ML	
56057	EW	LGAM	ML	British Fuels

56058	EW	LGAM	ML	
56059	EW	FDBI	IM	
56060	FT	LCWX	CF(U)	The Cardiff Rod Mill
56061	FS	FDBI	IM	
56062	F	FDBI	IM	Mountsorrel
56063	F	FDBI	IM	Bardon Hill
56064	FT	LNBK	CF	
56065	FA	FDBI	IM	
56066	FT	FDBI	IM	
56067	EW	FDBI	IM	
56068	U	FDBI	IM	
56069	FS	FDBI	IM	Thornaby TMD
56070	FT	FDBI	IM	
56071	FT	FDBI	IM	
56072	FT	LGAM	ML	
56073	FT	LNBK	CF	Tremorfa Steelworks
56074	LH	FDBI	IM	Kellingley Colliery
56075	F	FDBI	IM	West Yorkshire Enterprise
56076	FS	LNBK	CF	
56077	LH	FDBI	IM	Thorpe Marsh Power Station
56078	F	FDBI	IM	
56079	FT	LGAM	ML	
56080	F	FDBI	IM	Selby Coalfield
56081	F	FDBI	IM	
56082	F	FDBI	IM	
56083	LH	FDBI	IM	
56084	LH	FDBI	IM	
56085	LH	FDBI	IM	
56086	FT	FDBI	IM	The Magistrates' Association
56087	FS	FDBI	IM	
56088	EW	FDBI	IM	
56089	EW	FDBI	IM	
56090	LH	FDBI	IM	
56091	F	FDBI	IM	Castle Donington Power Station
56092	FT	FDBI	IM	
56093	FT	FDBI	IM	The Institution of Mining Engineers
56094	FC	FDBI	IM	Eggborough Power Station
56095	F	FDBI	IM	Harworth Colliery
56096	EW	FDBI	IM	
56097	FS	FDBI	IM	
56098	F	FDBI	IM	
56099	FT	FDBI	IM	Fiddlers Ferry Power Station
56100	LH	FDBI	IM	
56101	FT	FDBI	IM	Mutual Improvement
56102	LH	FDBI	IM	Scunthorpe Steel Centenary
56103	FT	LNBK	CF	
56104	FC	LGAM	ML	
56105	EW	FDBI	IM	
56106	LH	FDBI	IM	
56107	LH	FDBI	IM	
56108	F	FDBI	IM	

56109	LH	FDBI	IM	
56110	LH	FDBI	IM	Croft
56111	LH	FDBI	IM	
56112	LH	FDBI	IM	Stainless Pioneer
56113	FT	LNBK	CF	
56114	EW	FDBI	IM	Maltby Colliery
56115	FT	LNBK	CF	
56116	LH	FDBI	IM	
56117	FC	FDBI	IM	Wilton-Coalpower
56118	LH	FDBI	IM	
56119	FT	LNBK	CF	
56120	EW	FDBI	IM	
56121	FC	LNBK	CF	
56123	FT	LGAM	ML	Drax Power Station
56124	FC	LGAM	ML	
56125	FT	FDBI	IM	
56126	FC	FDBI	IM	
56127	FT	FDBI	IM	
56128	FC	LGAM	ML	
56129	FT	LGAM	ML	
56130	LH	FDBI	IM	Wardley Opencast
56131	F	FDBI	IM	Ellington Colliery
56132	FT	FDBI	IM	
56133	FT	FDBI	IM	Crewe Locomotive Works
56134	FC	FDBI	IM	Blyth Power
56135	F	FDBI	IM	Port of Tyne Authority

CLASS 58   BREL TYPE 5   Co–Co

Built: 1983 – 87 by BREL at Doncaster Works.
Engine: Ruston Paxman RK3ACT of 2460 kW (3300 hp) at 1000 rpm.
Main Alternator: Brush BA1101B.
Traction Motors: Brush TM73-62.
Max. Tractive Effort: 275 kN (61800 lbf).
Cont. Tractive Effort: 240 kN (53950 lbf) at 17.4 m.p.h.
Power At Rail: 1780 kW (2387 hp). **Length over Buffers:** 19.13 m.
Brake Force: 62 t.   **Wheel Diameter:** 1120 mm.
Design Speed: 80 m.p.h.   **Weight:** 130 t.
Max. Speed: 80 m.p.h.   **RA:** 7.
Train Brakes: Air.
Multiple Working: Red Diamond coupling code.
Communication Equipment: Cab to shore radio-telephone.
All equipped with slow speed control.

58001	FM	ENBN	TO	
58002	ML	ENBN	TO	Daw Mill Colliery
58003	FM	ENBN	TO	Markham Colliery
58004	FM	ENBN	TO	
58005	ML	ENBN	TO	Ironbridge Power Station
58006	F	ENBN	TO	
58007	FM	ENBN	TO	Drakelow Power Station

58008	ML	ENBN	TO	
58009	FM	ENBN	TO	
58010	FM	ENBN	TO	
58011	FM	ENBN	TO	Worksop Depot
58012	FM	ENBN	TO	
58013	ML	ENBN	TO	
58014	ML	ENBN	TO	Didcot Power Station
58015	FM	ENBN	TO	
58016	EW	ENBN	TO	
58017	FM	ENBN	TO	Eastleigh Depot
58018	FM	ENBN	TO	High Marnham Power Station
58019	FM	ENBN	TO	Shirebrook Colliery
58020	FM	ENBN	TO	Doncaster Works
58021	ML	ENBN	TO	Hither Green Depot
58022	FM	ENBN	TO	
58023	ML	ENBN	TO	Peterborough Depot
58024	EW	ENBN	TO	
58025	FM	ENBN	TO	
58026	FM	ENBN	TO	
58027	FM	ENBN	TO	
58028	FM	ENBN	TO	
58029	FM	ENBN	TO	
58030	FM	ENBN	TO	
58031	FM	ENBN	TO	
58032	ML	ENBN	TO	Thoresby Colliery
58033	EW	ENBN	TO	
58034	FM	ENBN	TO	Bassetlaw
58035	FM	ENBN	TO	
58036	ML	ENBN	TO	
58037	EW	ENBN	TO	
58038	ML	ENBN	TO	
58039	FM	ENBN	TO	Rugeley Power Station
58040	FM	ENBN	TO	Cottam Power Station
58041	FM	ENBN	TO	Ratcliffe Power Station
58042	ML	ENBN	TO	Petrolea
58043	FM	ENBN	TO	
58044	FM	ENBN	TO	Oxcroft Opencast
58045	FM	ENBN	TO	
58046	ML	ENBN	TO	Asfordby Mine
58047	FM	ENBN	TO	Manton Colliery
58048	EW	ENBN	TO	
58049	EW	ENBN	TO	Littleton Colliery
58050	ML	ENBN	TO	Toton Traction Depot

CLASS 59   GENERAL MOTORS TYPE 5   Co – Co

Built: 1985 (59001 – 4), 1989 (59005) by General Motors, La Grange, Illinois, U.S.A. or 1990 (59101 – 4), 1994 (59201) and 1995 (59202 – 6) by General Motors, London, Ontario, Canada.
Engine: General Motors 645E3C two stroke of 2460 kW (3300 hp) at 900 rpm.
Main Alternator: General Motors AR11 MLD-D14A.

Traction Motors: General Motors D77B.
Max. Tractive Effort: 506 kN (113 550 lbf).
Cont. Tractive Effort: 291 kN (65 300 lbf) at 14.3 m.p.h.
Power At Rail: 1889 kW (2533 hp).   **Length over Buffers:** 21.35 m.
Brake Force: 69 t.   **Wheel Diameter:** 1067 mm.
Weight: 121 t.   **RA:** 7.
Design Speed: 60 m.p.h. (75 m.p.h Cl. 59/2).
Max. Speed: 60 m.p.h. (75 m.p.h. Cl. 59/2).

Class 59/0. Owned by Foster-Yeoman Ltd. Blue/silver/blue livery with white lettering and cast numberplates. 59003 is blue and red with DB logo.

59001	**0**	XYPO	MD	YEOMAN ENDEAVOUR
59002	**0**	XYPO	MD	ALAN J DAY
59003	**0**	XYPO	MD	YEOMAN HIGHLANDER
59004	**0**	XYPO	MD	PAUL A HAMMOND
59005	**0**	XYPO	MD	KENNETH J. PAINTER

Note: 59003 is to be tranferred to Germany, where it will be renumbered
259 003-2.

Class 59/1. Owned by ARC Limited. Yellow/grey with grey lettering and cast
numberplates.

59101	**0**	XYPA	WH	Village of Whatley
59102	**0**	XYPA	WH	Village of Chantry
59103	**0**	XYPA	WH	Village of Mells
59104	**0**	XYPA	WH	Village of Great Elm

Class 59/2. Owned by National Power. Grey, red, white and blue with white
and red lettering and cast numberplates.

59201	**0**	XYPN	FB	Vale of York
59202	**0**	XYPN	FB	Vale of White Horse
59203	**0**	XYPN	FB	Vale of Pickering
59204	**0**	XYPN	FB	Vale of Glamorgan
59205	**0**	XYPN	FB	Vale of Evesham
59206	**0**	XYPN	FB	

CLASS 60   BRUSH TYPE 5   Co – Co

Built: 1989 – 1993 by Brush Traction at Loughborough.
Engine: Mirrlees MB275T of 2310 kW (3100 hp) at 1000 rpm.
Main Alternator: Brush .
Traction Motors: Brush separately excited.
Max. Tractive Effort: 500 kN (106500 lbf).
Cont. Tractive Effort: 336 kN (71570 lbf) at 17.4 m.p.h.
Power At Rail: 1800 kW (2415 hp).   **Length over Buffers:** 21.34 m.
Brake Force: 74 t.   **Wheel Diameter:** 1118 mm.
Design Speed: 62 m.p.h.   **Weight:** 129 t (130 t +).
Max. Speed: 60 m.p.h.   **RA:** 7.
Multiple Working: Within class.
Communication Equipment: Cab to shore radio-telephone.
All equipped with slow speed control.

60001		FA	ENAN	SL	
60002	+	EW	FDAI	IM	
60003		FP	FDAI	IM	Christopher Wren
60004	+	EW	FDAI	IM	
60005		FT	ENAN	TO	Skiddaw
60006		FM	ENAN	TO	Great Gable
60007	+	LH	FDAI	IM	
60008		LH	FDAI	IM	GYPSUM QUEEN II
60009	+	FM	LNAK	CF	Carnedd Dafydd
60010		EW	ENAN	TO	
60011		ML	ENAN	TO	Cader Idris
60012	+	EW	ENAN	TO	
60013		FP	ENAN	TO	Robert Boyle
60014		EW	ENAN	TO	
60015	+	FT	LNAK	CF	Bow Fell
60016		FA	LNAK	CF	Langdale Pikes
60017	+	EW	LNAK	CF	Shotton Works Centenary Year 1996
60018		FM	ENAN	SL	Moel Siabod
60019		EW	ENAN	SL	
60020	+	EW	FDAI	IM	
60021	+	FS	FDAI	IM	Pen-y-Ghent
60022	+	U	ENAN	TO	
60023		FS	FDAI	IM	The Cheviot
60024		EW	FDAI	IM	
60025	+	LH	FDAI	IM	
60026	+	EW	FDAI	IM	
60027	+	EW	FDAI	IM	
60028	+	EW	FDAI	IM	
60029		FT	ENAN	TO	Ben Nevis
60030		FS	FDAI	IM	Cir Mhor
60031		FS	FDAI	IM	Ben Lui
60032		FT	ENAN	TO	William Booth
60033		FT	LNAK	CF	Anthony Ashley Cooper
60034		FT	LNAK	CF	Carnedd Llewelyn
60035		FT	LNAK	CF	Florence Nightingale
60036		FT	LNAK	CF	Sgurr Na Ciche
60037		FT	LNAK	CF	Helvellyn
60038	+	LH	FDAI	IM	
60039		FM	ENAN	SL	Glastonbury Tor
60040		EW	ENAN	SL	
60041	+	EW	LNAK	CF	
60042		FM	ENAN	SL	Dunkery Beacon
60043		FM	ENAN	SL	Yes Tor
60044		ML	ENAN	TO	Ailsa Craig
60045		FT	ENAN	TO	Josephine Butler
60046		FT	ENAN	TO	William Wilberforce
60047	+	EW	ENAN	TO	
60048		FM	ENAN	TO	Saddleback
60049		EW	FDAI	IM	
60050		EW	FDAI	IM	

60051		FP	FDAI	IM	Mary Somerville
60052		EW	FDAI	IM	
60053		FP	FDAI	IM	John Reith
60054	+	FP	FDAI	IM	Charles Babbage
60055		FT	ENAN	TO	Thomas Barnardo
60056		FT	ENAN	TO	William Beveridge
60057		FC	ENAN	TO	Adam Smith
60058		FT	ENAN	TO	John Howard
60059	+	LH	FDAI	IM	Swinden Dalesman
60060		FC	ENAN	TO	James Watt
60061		FT	ENAN	TO	Alexander Graham Bell
60062		FT	LNAK	CF	Samuel Johnson
60063		FT	LNAK	CF	James Murray
60064	+	FL	FDAI	IM	Back Tor
60065		FT	ENAN	TO	Kinder Low
60066		FT	ENAN	TO	John Logie Baird
60067		F	FDAI	IM	James Clerk-Maxwell
60068		F	FDAI	IM	Charles Darwin
60069		F	FDAI	IM	Humphry Davy
60070	+	FL	FDAI	IM	John Loudon McAdam
60071	+	FM	ENAN	TO	Dorothy Garrod
60072		FM	ENAN	TO	Cairn Toul
60073		FM	ENAN	TO	Cairn Gorm
60074		FM	ENAN	TO	Braeriach
60075		FM	ENAN	TO	Liathach
60076		FM	ENAN	TO	Suilven
60077	+	FM	ENAN	TO	Canisp
60078		ML	ENAN	TO	
60079		FM	ENAN	TO	Foinaven
60080	+	FT	LNAK	CF	Kinder Scout
60081		FT	LNAK	CF	Bleaklow Hill
60082		FA	LNAK	CF	Mam Tor
60083		FM	ENAN	TO	Shining Tor
60084		FT	LNAK	CF	Cross Fell
60085		FT	ENAN	TO	Axe Edge
60086		FM	ENAN	TO	Schiehallion
60087		FM	ENAN	TO	Slioch
60088		FM	ENAN	TO	Buachaille Etive Mor
60089		FT	LNAK	CF	Arcuil
60090	+	FC	FDAI	IM	Quinag
60091		FC	FDAI	IM	An Teallach
60092		FT	ENAN	TO	Reginald Munns
60093		FT	LNAK	CF	Jack Stirk
60094		FM	ENAN	TO	Tryfan
60095		FA	ENAN	TO	Crib Goch
60096		FT	LNAK	CF	Ben Macdui
60097		FT	ENAN	TO	Pillar
60098		EW	ENAN	TO	Charles Francis Brush
60099		FM	ENAN	SL	Ben More Assynt
60100		FM	ENAN	SL	Boar of Badenoch

1.2 ELECTRIC LOCOMOTIVES

CLASS 71   BR DESIGN   Bo-Bo

Built: 1958-60 by BR at Doncaster Works
Supply System: 660-850 V d.c. from third rail or overhead supply.
Traction Motors:
Max. Tractive Effort: 191 kN (43000 lbf).
Continuous Rating: 1715 kW (2300 hp).
Cont. Tractive Effort: 55 kN (12400 lbf) at 69.6 m.p.h.
Maximum Rail Power:
Brake Force: 68 t.   **Length over Buffers:**   m.
Design Speed: m.p.h.   **Weight:** 77 t.
Max. Speed: 90 m.p.h.   **RA:** 9.
Wheel Diameter: 1219 mm.   **ETH Index:**
Train Brakes: Air, Vacuum and electro-pneumatic.
Multiple Working: With Class 33/1, Class 73 and various 750 V d.c. EMUs.
Couplings: Drop-head buckeye.

Ownership:

Part of the National Collection.

Carries original number E 5001.

71001   **G**   MBEL   SE

CLASS 73/0   ELECTRO-DIESEL   Bo-Bo

Built: 1962 by BR at Eastleigh Works.
Supply System: 660-850 V d.c. from third rail.
Engine: English Electric 4SRKT of 447 kW (600 hp) at 850 rpm.
Main Generator: English Electric 824/3D.
Traction Motors: English Electric 542A.
Max. Tractive Effort: Electric 187 kN (42000 lbf). Diesel 152 kN (34100 lbf).
Continuous Rating: Electric 1060 kW (1420 hp) giving a tractive effort of 43 kN (9600 lbf) at 55.5 m.p.h.
Cont. Tractive Effort: Diesel 72 kN (16100 lbf) at 10 m.p.h.
Maximum Rail Power: Electric 1830 kW (2450 hp) at 37 m.p.h.
Brake Force: 31 t.   **Length over Buffers:** 16.36 m.
Design Speed: 80 m.p.h.   **Weight:** 76.5 t.
Max. Speed: 60 m.p.h.   **RA:** 6.
Wheel Diameter: 1016 mm.   **ETH Index:** Electric 66.
Train Brakes: Air, Vacuum and electro-pneumatic.
Multiple Working: Within sub-class, with Class 33/1, Class 71 and various 750 V d.c. EMUs.
Communication Equipment: All equipped with driver-guard telephone.
Couplings: Drop-head buckeye.

Non-standard Livery:

73005 is Network SouthEast blue.

Formerly numbered E 6002/5.

73002	**BR**	HEBD	BD (U)
73005	**O**	HEBD	BD

CLASS 73/1 & 73/2   ELECTRO-DIESEL   Bo-Bo

Built: 1965-67 by English Electric Co. at Vulcan Foundry, Newton le Willows.
Supply System: 660-850 V d.c. from third rail.
Engine: English Electric 4SRKT of 447 kW (600 hp) at 850 rpm.
Main Generator: English Electric 824/5D.
Traction Motors: English Electric 546/1B.
Max. Tractive Effort: Electric 179 kN (40000 lbf). Diesel 160 kN (36000 lbf).
Continuous Rating: Electric 1060 kW (1420 hp) giving a tractive effort of 35 kN (7800 lbf) at 68 m.p.h.
Cont. Tractive Effort: Diesel 60 kN (13600 lbf) at 11.5 m.p.h.
Maximum Rail Power: Electric 2350 kW (3150 hp) at 42 m.p.h.
Brake Force: 31 t.   **Length over Buffers:** 16.36 m.
Design Speed: 90 m.p.h.   **Weight:** 77 t.
Max. Speed: 60 (90*) m.p.h.   **RA:** 6.
Wheel Diameter: 1016 mm.   **ETH Index:** Electric 66.
Train Brakes: Air, Vacuum and electro-pneumatic.
Multiple Working: Within sub-class, with Class 33/1, Class 71 and various 750 V d.c. EMUs.
Communication Equipment: All equipped with driver-guard telephone.
Couplings: Drop-head buckeye.

Ownership:

All Gatwick Express locos are owned by Porterbrook Leasing Company.

a Vacuum brake isolated.

Formerly numbered E 6001-20/22-26/28-49 (not in order).

73101	**EW**	EWEB	EH	
73103	**IO**	EWEB	EH	
73104	**IO**	EWEB	EH	
73105	**C**	EWEB	EH	
73106	**D**	EWEB	EH	
73107	**C**	EWEB	EH	Redhill 1844-1994
73108	**C**	EWEB	EH	
73109 *	**SC**	HYSB	BM	Battle of Britain 50th Anniversary
73110	**C**	EWEB	EH	
73114	**ML**	EWEB	EH	Stewarts Lane Traction Maintenance Depot
73117	**IO**	EWEB	EH	University of Surrey
73118 c	**E**	GPSN	SL	
73119	**C**	EWEB	EH	Kentish Mercury
73126	**N**	ENXX	SL (U)	Kent & East Sussex Railway
73128	**EW**	EWRB	EH	
73129	**N**	EWEB	EH	City of Winchester
73130 c	**E**	GPSN	SL	
73131	**EW**	EWRB	EH	
73132	**IO**	EWRB	EH	

73133	**ML**	EWEB	EH	The Bluebell Railway
73134	**IO**	EWEB	EH	Woking Homes 1885-1985
73136	**ML**	EWEB	EH	Kent Youth Music
73138	**C**	EWEB	EH	
73139	**IO**	EWRB	EH	
73140	**IO**	EWRB	EH	
73141	**IO**	EWRB	EH	
73201 a*	**GX**	IVGA	SL	Broadlands
73202 a*	**GX**	IVGA	SL	Royal Observer Corps
73203 a*	**GX**	IVGA	SL	
73204 a*	**GX**	IVGA	SL	Stewarts Lane 1860-1985
73205 a*	**GX**	IVGA	SL	
73206 a*	**GX**	IVGA	SL	Gatwick Express
73207 a*	**GX**	IVGA	SL	County of East Sussex
73208 a*	**GX**	IVGA	SL	Croydon 1883-1983
73209 a*	**GX**	IVGA	SL	
73210 a*	**GX**	IVGA	SL	Selhurst
73211 a*	**GX**	IVGA	SL	
73212 a*	**GX**	IVGA	SL	Airtour Suisse
73213 a*	**GX**	IVGA	SL	University of Kent at Canterbury
73235 a*	**GX**	IVGA	SL	

CLASS 73/9   ELECTRO-DIESEL   Bo-Bo

For details see Class 73/0. Sandite fitted locos.

Formerly numbered E 6001/6.

| 73901 | **MD** | HEBD | BD |
| 73906 | **MD** | HEBD | BD |

NOTES FOR CLASSES 86-91.

The following common features apply to all locos of Classes 86-91.

Supply System: 25 kV a.c. from overhead equipment.
Communication Equipment: Driver-guard telephone and cab to shore radio-telephone.
Multiple Working: Time division multiplex system.

a vacuum brake isolated.

Class 86 were formerly numbered E 3101-3200 (not in order).

CLASS 86/1   BR DESIGN   Bo-Bo

Built: 1965-66 by English Electric Co. at Vulcan Foundry, Newton le Willows or BR at Doncaster Works. Rebuilt with Class 87 type bogies and motors. Tap changer control.
Traction Motors: GEC G412AZ frame mounted.
Max. Tractive Effort: 258 kN (58000 lbf).
Continuous Rating: 3730 kW (5000 hp) giving a tractive effort of 95 kN (21300 lbf) at 87 m.p.h.

Maximum Rail Power: 5860 kW (7860 hp) at 50.8 m.p.h.
Brake Force: 40 t.   **Length over Buffers:** 17.83 m.
Design Speed: 110 m.p.h.   **Weight:** 87 t.
Max. Speed: 110 m.p.h.   **RA:** 6.
ETH Index: 74.   **Wheel Diameter:** 1150 mm.
Train Brakes: Air & Vacuum.   **Electric Brake:** Rheostatic.

Ownership:

Owned by Eversholt Train Leasing Company.

86101		I	IWPA	WN	Sir William A Stanier FRS
86102 a		I	IWPA	WN	Robert A Riddles
86103		I	SAXL	WN	André Chapelon

CLASS 86/2   BR DESIGN   Bo-Bo

Built: 1965-66 by English Electric Co. at Vulcan Foundry, Newton le Willows or BR at Doncaster Works. Later rebuilt with resilient wheels and flexicoil suspension. Tap changer control.
Traction Motors: AEI 282BZ.
Max. Tractive Effort: 207 kN (46500 lbf).
Continuous Rating: 3010 kW (4040 hp) giving a tractive effort of 85 kN (19200 lbf) at 77.5 m.p.h.
Maximum Rail Power: 4550 kW (6100 hp) at 49.5 m.p.h.
Brake Force: 40 t.   **Length over Buffers:** 17.83 m.
Design Speed: 125 m.p.h.   **Weight:** 85 t-86 t.
Max. Speed: 100 (110*) m.p.h.   **RA:** 6.
ETH Index: 74.   **Wheel Diameter:** 1156 mm.
Train Brakes: Air & Vacuum.   **Electric Brake:** Rheostatic.

Ownership:

All Anglia Railways, Virgin CrossCountry and West Coast locos are owned by Eversholt Train Leasing Company.

86204		I	IANA	NC	City of Carlisle
86205 a		I	ICCA	LG	City of Lancaster
86206 a		I	ICCA	LG	City of Stoke on Trent
86207 a		I	IWPA	WN	City of Lichfield
86208 a		I	PXLE	CE	City of Chester
86209 a*		I	IWPA	WN	City of Coventry
86210	RX		PXLE	CE	C.I.T. 75th Anniversary
86212		I	ICCA	LG	Preston Guild 1328-1992
86213		I	SAXL	LG	Lancashire Witch
86214		I	ICCA	LG	Sans Pareil
86215 a		I	IANA	NC	Norwich Cathedral
86216 a		I	ICCA	LG	Meteor
86217 a		I	IANA	NC	City University
86218		I	IANA	NC	Harold MacMillan
86219 a		I	SAXL	WN (S)	Phoenix
86220 a		I	IANA	NC	The Round Tabler
86221 a		I	IANA	NC	B.B.C. Look East
86222		I	ICCA	LG	Clothes Show Live

86223	a	I	IANA	NC	Norwich Union
86224	a*	I	IWPA	WN	Caledonian
86225	a*	I	IWPA	WN	Hardwicke
86226		I	ICCA	LG	CHARLES RENNIE MACKINTOSH
86227	a	I	ICCA	LG	Sir Henry Johnson
86228		I	IANA	NC	Vulcan Heritage
86229		I	ICCA	LG	Sir John Betjeman
86230	a	I	IANA	NC	The Duke of Wellington
86231	a*	I	IWPA	WN	Starlight Express
86232	a	I	IANA	NC	Norfolk and Norwich Festival
86233		I	ICCA	LG	Laurence Olivier
86234		I	ICCA	LG	J B Priestley OM
86235	a	I	IANA	NC	Crown Point
86236	a	I	IWPA	WN	Josiah Wedgwood MASTER POTTER 1736-1795
86237	a	I	IANA	NC	University of East Anglia
86238	a	I	IANA	NC	European Community
86239	a	I	IWPA	WN	Bishop Eric Treacy
86241		RX	PXLE	CE	Glenfiddich
86242		I	IWPA	WN	James Kennedy GC
86243		RX	PXLE	CE	
86244		I	ICCA	LG	The Royal British Legion
86245		I	IWPA	WN	Dudley Castle
86246	a	I	IANA	NC	Royal Anglian Regiment
86247	a	I	ICCA	LG	Abraham Darby
86248		I	IWPA	WN	Sir Clwyd/County of Clwyd
86249	a	I	SAXL	WN (S)	County of Merseyside
86250	a	I	IANA	NC	The Glasgow Herald
86251		I	IWPA	WN	The Birmingham Post
86252		I	ICCA	LG	The Liverpool Daily Post
86253	a	I	IWPA	WN	The Manchester Guardian
86254		RX	PXLE	CE	
86255		I	ICCA	LG	Penrith Beacon
86256		I	IWPA	WN	Pebble Mill
86257	a	I	IANA	NC (U)	Snowdon
86258	a	I	IWPA	WN	Talyllyn-The First Preserved Railway
86259	a	I	ICCA	LG	Greater MANCHESTER THE LIFE & SOUL OF BRITAIN
86260	a	I	ICCA	LG	Driver Wallace Oakes G.C.
86261		RX	PXLE	CE	

CLASS 86/4 & 86/6   BR DESIGN   Bo-Bo

Built: 1965-66 by English Electric Co. at Vulcan Foundry, Newton le Willows or BR at Doncaster Works. Later rebuilt with resilient wheels and flexicoil suspension. Tap changer control.
Traction Motors: AEI 282AZ.
Max. Tractive Effort: 258 kN (58000 lbf).
Continuous Rating: 2680 kW (3600 hp) giving a tractive effort of 89 kN (20000 lbf) at 67 m.p.h.

Maximum Rail Power: 4400 kW (5900 hp) at 38 m.p.h.
Brake Force: 40 t.   **Length over Buffers:** 17.83 m.
Design Speed: 100 m.p.h.   **Weight:** 83 t-84 t.
Max. Speed: 100 (75*) m.p.h.   **RA:** 6.
ETH Index: 74.   **Wheel Diameter:** 1156 mm.
Train Brakes: Air & Vacuum.   **Electric Brake:** Rheostatic.

Class 86/6 have the ETH equipment isolated.

Ownership:

Freightliner 1995 locos Nos. 86612-39 are owned by Porterbrook Leasing Company.

86401	**RX**	PXLE	CE	
86602 a*	**F**	DFNC	CE	
86603 a*	**FD**	DFNC	CE	
86604 a*	**FF**	DFNC	CE	
86605 a*	**FD**	DFNC	CE	
86606 a*	**FF**	DFNC	CE	
86607 a*	**FD**	DFNC	CE	The Institution of Electrical Engineers
86608 a*	**FE**	DFNC	CE	St. John Ambulance
86609 a*	**FD**	DFNC	CE	
86610 a*	**FD**	DFNC	CE	
86611 a*	**FD**	DFNC	CE	Airey Neave
86612 a*	**FF**	DFNC	CE	Elizabeth Garrett Anderson
86613 a*	**F**	DFNC	CE	County of Lancashire
86614 a*	**FD**	DFNC	CE	Frank Hornby
86615 a*	**F**	DFNC	CE	Rotary International
86416	**RX**	PXLE	CE	
86417	**RX**	PXLE	CE	
86618 a*	**FF**	DFNC	CE	
86419	**RX**	PXLE	CE	
86620 a*	**F**	DFNC	CE	
86621 a*	**FD**	DFNC	CE	London School of Economics
86622 a*	**FE**	DFNC	CE	
86623 a*	**FF**	DFNC	CE	
86424	**RX**	PXLE	CE	
86425	**RX**	PXLE	CE	Saint Mungo
86426	**RX**	PXLE	CE	
86627 a*	**F**	DFNC	CE	The Industrial Society
86628 a*	**FF**	DFNC	CE	Aldaniti
86430	**RX**	PXLE	CE	Saint Edmund
86631 a*	**FD**	DFNC	CE	
86632 a*	**F**	DFNC	CE	Brookside
86633 a*	**F**	DFNC	CE	Wulfruna
86634 a*	**F**	DFNC	CE	University of London
86635 a*	**FD**	DFNC	CE	
86636 a*	**F**	DFNC	CE	
86637 a*	**FF**	DFNC	CE	
86638 a*	**FF**	DFNC	CE	
86639 a*	**FD**	DFNC	CE	

CLASS 87   BR DESIGN   Bo-Bo

Built: 1973-75 by BREL at Crewe Works.
Traction Motors: GEC G412AZ frame mounted (87/0), G412BZ (87/1).
Max. Tractive Effort: 258 kN (58000 lbf).
Continuous Rating: 3730 kW (5000 hp) giving a tractive effort of 95 kN (21300 lbf) at 87 m.p.h. (Class 87/0), 3620 kW (4850 hp) giving a tractive effort of 96 kN (21600 lbf) at 84 m.p.h. (Class 87/1).
Maximum Rail Power: 5860 kW (7860 hp) at 50.8 m.p.h.

Brake Force: 40 t.	**Length over Buffers:** 17.83 m.
Design Speed: 110 m.p.h.	**Weight:** 83.5 t.
Max. Speed: 110 (75*) m.p.h.	**RA:** 6.
ETH Index: 95 (75§).	**Wheel Diameter:** 1150 mm.
Train Brakes: Air.	**Electric Brake:** Rheostatic.

Ownership:

All West Coast locos are owned by Porterbrook Leasing Company.

Class 87/0. Standard Design. Tap Changer Control.

87001	I	IWCA	WN	Royal Scot
87002	I	IWCA	WN	Royal Sovereign
87003	I	IWCA	WN	Patriot
87004	I	IWCA	WN	Britannia
87005	I	IWCA	WN	City of London
87006	I	IWCA	WN	City of Glasgow
87007	I	IWCA	WN	City of Manchester
87008	I	IWCA	WN	City of Liverpool
87009 §	I	IWCA	WN	City of Birmingham
87010	I	IWCA	WN	King Arthur
87011	I	IWCA	WN	The Black Prince
87012	I	IWCA	WN	The Royal Bank of Scotland
87013	I	IWCA	WN	John O' Gaunt
87014	I	IWCA	WN	Knight of the Thistle
87015	I	IWCA	WN	Howard of Effingham
87016	I	IWCA	WN	Willesden Intercity Depot
87017	I	IWCA	WN	Iron Duke
87018	I	IWCA	WN	Lord Nelson
87019	I	IWCA	WN	Sir Winston Churchill
87020	I	IWCA	WN	North Briton
87021	I	IWCA	WN	Robert the Bruce
87022	I	IWCA	WN	Cock o' the North
87023	I	IWCA	WN	Velocity
87024	I	IWCA	WN	Lord of the Isles
87025	I	IWCA	WN	County of Cheshire
87026	I	IWCA	WN	Sir Richard Arkwright
87027	I	IWCA	WN	Wolf of Badenoch
87028	I	IWCA	WN	Lord President
87029 §	I	IWCA	WN	Earl Marischal
87030	I	IWCA	WN	Black Douglas
87031	I	IWCA	WN	Hal o' the Wynd

87032	I	IWCA	WN	Kenilworth
87033	I	IWCA	WN	Thane of Fife
87034	I	IWCA	WN	William Shakespeare
87035	I	IWCA	WN	Robert Burns

Class 87/1. Thyristor Control.

| 87101 | * | | DAMC | CE | STEPHENSON |

CLASS 89   BRUSH DESIGN   Co-Co

Built: 1987 by BREL at Crewe Works.
Traction Motors: Brush design frame mounted.
Max. Tractive Effort: 205 kN (46000 lbf).
Continuous Rating: 2390 kW (3200 hp) giving a tractive effort of 105 kN (23600 lbf) at 92 m.p.h.
Maximum Rail Power:
Brake Force: 40 t.
Design Speed: 125 m.p.h.
Max. Speed: 125 m.p.h.
ETH Index: 95.
Train Brakes: Air.
Couplings: Drop-head buckeye.

Length over Buffers: 18.80 m.
Weight: 104 t.
RA: 6.
Wheel Diameter: 1150 mm.
Electric Brake: Rheostatic.

Ownership:

Owned by Sea Containers Ltd.

| 89001 | **GN** | IECA | BN |

CLASS 90   GEC DESIGN   Bo-Bo

Built: 1987-90 by BREL at Crewe Works. Thyristor control.
Traction Motors: GEC G412CY separately excited frame mounted.
Max. Tractive Effort: 258 kN (58000 lbf).
Continuous Rating: 3730 kW (5000 hp) giving a tractive effort of 95 kN (21300 lbf) at 87 m.p.h.
Maximum Rail Power: 5860 kW (7860 hp) at 68.3 m.p.h.
Brake Force: 40 t.
Design Speed: 110 m.p.h.
Max. Speed: 110 (75*) m.p.h.
ETH Index: 95.
Train Brakes: Air.
Couplings: Drop-head buckeye (removed on Class 90/1).

Length over Buffers: 18.80 m.
Weight: 84.5 t.
RA: 7.
Wheel Diameter: 1156 mm.
Electric Brake: Rheostatic.

Non-standard Liveries:

90128 is in SNCB/NMBS (Belgian Railways) electric loco livery.
90129 is in DB (German Federal Railways) 'neurot' livery.
90130 is in SNCF (French Railways) 'Sybic' livery.
90136 is in livery **FE**, but with full yellow ends and roof and red 'Railfreight Distribution' lettering.

Ownership:

All West Coast and Freightliner 1995 locos are owned by Porterbrook

Leasing Company.

Class 90/0. As built.

90001	I	IWCA	WN	BBC Midlands Today
90002	I	IWCA	WN	The Girls' Brigade
90003	I	IWCA	WN	THE HERALD
90004	I	IWCA	WN	The D' Oyly Carte Opera Company
90005	I	IWCA	WN	Financial Times
90006	I	IWCA	WN	High Sheriff
90007	I	IWCA	WN	Lord Stamp
90008	I	IWCA	WN	The Birmingham Royal Ballet
90009	I	IWCA	WN	The Economist
90010	I	IWCA	WN	275 Railway Squadron (Volunteers)
90011	I	IWCA	WN	The Chartered Institute of Transport
90012	I	IWCA	WN	British Transport Police
90013	I	IWCA	WN	The Law Society
90014	I	IWCA	WN	'The Liverpool Phil'
90015	I	IWCA	WN	BBC North West
90016	RX	PXLE	CE	
90017	RX	PXLE	CE	Rail express systems Quality Assured
90018	RX	PXLE	CE	
90019	RX	PXLE	CE	Penny Black
90020	RX	PXLE	CE	Colonel Bill Cockburn CBE TD
90021	FE	DAMC	CE	
90022	FE	DAMC	CE	Freightconnection
90023	FE	DAMC	CE	
90024	FE	DAMC	CE	

Class 90/1. ETH equipment isolated.

90125	*	FE	DAMC	CE	
90126	*	FE	DAMC	CE	Crewe International Electric Maintenance Depot
90127	*	FD	DAMC	CE	Allerton T&RS Depot Quality Approved
90128	*	0	DAMC	CE	Vrachtverbinding
90129	*	0	DAMC	CE	Frachtverbindungen
90130	*	0	DAMC	CE	Fretconnection
90131	*	FE	DAMC	CE	
90132	*	FE	DAMC	CE	Cerestar
90133	*	FE	DAMC	CE	
90134	*	FE	DAMC	CE	
90135	*	FE	DAMC	CE	Crewe Basford Hall
90136	*	0	DAMC	CE	
90137	*	F	DAMC	CE	
90138	*	FE	DAMC	CE	
90139	*	FD	DAMC	CE	
90140	*	FD	DAMC	CE	
90141	*	F	DFLC	CE	
90142	*	F	DFLC	CE	
90143	*	FF	DFLC	CE	Freightliner Coatbridge
90144	*	F	DFLC	CE	
90145	*	FD	DFLC	CE	

90146	*	FF	DFLC	CE
90147	*	FF	DFLC	CE
90148	*	FF	DFLC	CE
90149	*	F	DFLC	CE
90150	*	FF	DFLC	CE

CLASS 91   GEC DESIGN   Bo-Bo

Built: 1988-91 by BREL at Crewe Works. Thyristor control.
Traction Motors: GEC G426AZ.
Continuous Rating: 4540 kW (6090 hp).
Maximum Rail Power: 4700 kW (6300 hp).

Brake Force: 45 t.	Length over Buffers: 19.40 m.
Design Speed: 140 m.p.h.	Weight: 84 t.
Max. Speed: 140 m.p.h.	RA: 7.
ETH Index: 95.	Wheel Diameter: 1000 mm.
Train Brakes: Air.	Electric Brake: Rheostatic.

Couplings: Drop-head buckeye.

Ownership:

Owned by Eversholt Train Leasing Company.

91001	GN	IECA	BN	
91002	I	IECA	BN	Durham Cathedral
91003	GN	IECA	BN	
91004	GN	IECA	BN	
91005	I	IECA	BN	Royal Air Force Regiment
91006	GN	IECA	BN	
91007	GN	IECA	BN	
91008	I	IECA	BN	Thomas Cook
91009	I	IECA	BN	Saint Nicholas
91010	GN	IECA	BN	
91011	I	IECA	BN	Terence Cuneo
91012	I	IECA	BN	
91013	I	IECA	BN	Michael Faraday
91014	I	IECA	BN	Northern Electric
91015	I	IECA	BN	
91016	I	IECA	BN	
91017	GN	IECA	BN	
91018	I	IECA	BN	Robert Louis Stevenson
91019	GN	IECA	BN	
91020	GN	IECA	BN	
91021	I	IECA	BN	Royal Armouries
91022	I	IECA	BN	Robert Adley
91023	I	IECA	BN	
91024	I	IECA	BN	Reverend W Awdry
91025	GN	IECA	BN	
91026	I	IECA	BN	Voice of the North
91027	I	IECA	BN	Great North Run
91028	I	IECA	BN	Guide Dog
91029	I	IECA	BN	Queen Elizabeth II

91030	I	IECA	BN	Palace of Holyroodhouse
91031	**GN**	IECA	BN	

CLASS 92   BRUSH DESIGN   Co-Co

Built: 1993-5 by Brush Traction at Loughborough. Thyristor control.
Supply System: 25 kV a.c. from overhead equipment and 750 V d.c. third rail.
Electrical equipment: ABB Transportation, Zürich, Switzerland.
Traction Motors: Brush design.
Max. Tractive Effort: 400 kN (90 000 lbf).
Continuous Rating at Motor Shaft: 5040 kW (6760 hp).
Maximum Rail Power (25 kV a.c.): 5000 kW (6700 hp).
Maximum Rail Power (750 V d.c.): 4000 kW (5360 hp).
Brake Force: t.   **Length over Buffers:** 21.34 m.
Design Speed: 140 km/h (87.5 m.p.h.).   **Weight:** 126 t.
Max. Speed: 140 km/h (87.5 m.p.h.).   **RA:** 8.
ETH Index: 108. **Wheel Diameter:** 1160 mm.
Train Brakes: Air.
Electric Brake: Rheostatic & regenerative.
Multiple Working: Time division multiplex system.
Communication Equipment: Driver-guard telephone and cab to shore radio-telephone.
Cab Signalling: Fitted with TVM430 cab signalling for Channel Tunnel.

Ownership:

92006/10/4/8/23/8/33/8/43 are owned by SNCF.
92020/1/32/40/4-6 are owned by Eurostar (UK) Ltd.

92001	E	DAEC	CE	Victor Hugo
92002	E	DADC	CE	H G Wells
92003	E	DAEC	CE	Beethoven
92004	E	DADC	CE	Jane Austen
92005	E	DAVC	CE	Mozart
92006	E	DAVC	CE	Louis Armand
92007	E	DAVC	CE	Schubert
92008	E	DAVC	CE	Jules Verne
92009	E	DAVC	CE	Elgar
92010	E	DADC	CE	Molière
92011	E	DADC	CE	Handel
92012	E	DADC	CE	Thomas Hardy
92013	E	DAEC	CE	Puccini
92014	E	DAVC	CE	Emile Zola
92015	E	DADC	CE	D H Lawrence
92016	E	DAEC	CE	Brahms
92017	E	DAEC	CE	Shakespeare
92018	E	DAVC	CE	Stendhal
92019	E	DAEC	CE	Wagner
92020	E	DADC	CE	Milton
92021	E	DAVC	CE	Purcell
92022	E	DAVC	CE	Charles Dickens
92023	E	DAVC	CE	Ravel

92024	E	DAEC	CE	J S Bach
92025	E	DAEC	CE	Oscar Wilde
92026	E	DAVC	CE	Britten
92027	E	DAVC	CE	George Eliot
92028	E	DADC	CE	Saint Saëns
92029	E	DAVC	CE	Dante
92030	E	DADC	CE	Ashford
92031	E	DAEC	CE	
92032	E	DAEC	CE	César Franck
92033	E	DAEC	CE	Berlioz
92034	E	DAVC	CE	Kipling
92035	E	DAVC	CE	Mendelssohn
92036	E	DAVC	CE	Bertolt Brecht
92037	E	DADC	CE	Sullivan
92038	E	DADC	CE	Voltaire
92039	E	DADC	CE	Johann Strauss
92040	E	DAVC	CE	Goethe
92041	E	DAVC	CE	Vaughan Williams
92042	E	DAVC	CE	Honegger
92043	E	DAVC	CE	Debussy
92044	E	DAVC	CE	Couperin
92045	E	DAVC	CE	Chaucer
92046	E	DAVC	CE	Sweelinck

1.3 SERVICE LOCOMOTIVES

CLASS 97/6   RUSTON SHUNTER   0-6-0

Built: 1959 by Ruston & Hornsby at Lincoln.
Engine: Ruston 6VPH of 123 kW (165 hp).
Main Generator: British Thomson Houston RTB6034.
Traction Motor: One British Thomson Houston RTA5041.
Max. Tractive Effort: 75 kN (17000 lbf).
Brake Force: 16 t.   **Length over Buffers:** 7.62 m.
Weight: 31 t.   **Wheel Diameter:** 978 mm.
Max. Speed: 20 mph.   **RA:** 1.

Non-Standard Livery: Civil Engineer's Yellow.

| 97651 | (PWM 651) | v | 0 | RNRG | RG (U) |
| 97654 | (PWM 654) | v | 0 | RNRG | RG |

CLASS 97/8   EE SHUNTER   0-6-0

For details see Class 09. Severn Tunnel emergency train locomotive.

Non-Standard Livery: BR blue with grey cab.

| 97806 | (09017) | x | 0 | LNCF | CF | Normally kept at Sudbrook. |

1.4 LOCOMOTIVES AWAITING DISPOSAL

03079		Sandown	31428	Bescot Yard
03179	N	Ryde T&RSMD	31442	Crewe Carriage Shed
08222		Bounds Green T&RSMD	31460	Bescot Yard
08390		ADtranz Crewe Works	31547 C	Toton Yard
08419		ADtranz Crewe Works	31553 C	Toton Yard
08473		Leicester LIP	31569 C	Toton Yard
08515		Gateshead WRD	31970 O	ADtranz Crewe Works
08562		Stratford TMD	33021 FM	Eastleigh T&RSMD
08565		Motherwell TMD	33035 N	Eastleigh T&RSMD
08609		Willesden TMD	33038	Stratford TMD
08618		Gateshead WRD	33047 C	Eastleigh Yard
08634		Stratford TMD	33050 FA	Stewarts Lane T&RSMD
08666		Allerton TMD	33064 FA	Old Oak Common TMD
08673	IO	Allerton TMD	33101 D	Eastleigh T&RSMD
08677		Willesden TMD	33108 C	Eastleigh T&RSMD
08707		ADtranz Crewe Works	33113	Stewarts Lane T&RSMD
08733		Motherwell TMD	33118 C	Eastleigh T&RSMD
08755		Millerhill FP	33201 C	Stewarts Lane T&RSMD
08760		Wessex Traincare	33206 FD	Eastleigh T&RSMD
08793	O	Aberdeen Guild St Yard	37031 FD	Cardiff Canton T&RSMD
08829		Toton TMD	37080 FP	Cardiff Canton T&RSMD
08849		ADtranz Crewe Works	37252 FD	Doncaster TMD
08855		Aberdeen Guild St Yard	37280 FP	Old Oak Common TMD
08880		Allerton TMD	37373 FR	Old Oak Common TMD
08895		Margam WRD	45015	Toton TMD
08898		Bescot TMD	47096	Tinsley TMD
20073		Bescot Yard	47102	Tinsley TMD
20119		Toton TMD	47108	Old Oak Common TMD
20154		Toton TMD	47112 FO	Old Oak Common TMD
20177		Toton TMD	47121	Old Oak Common TMD
25083		Crewe Carriage Shed	47190 FP	Tinsley TMD
31168		Bescot Yard	47214 FD	Tinsley TMD
31180	FR	Toton Yard	47249 FR	Tinsley TMD
31184	FO	Toton Yard	47318 FO	Bescot Yard
31196	C	Stratford TMD	47321 F	Tinsley TMD
31209	FA	Toton Yard	47325 FO	Tinsley TMD
31217	FC	Toton Yard	47421	ADtranz Crewe Works
31282	FR	Bescot Yard	47423	Old Oak Common TMD
31283	O	Stratford TMD	47425	Old Oak Common TMD
31286		Bescot Yard	47426 BR	Old Oak Common TMD
31289		Bescot Yard	47430 FA	Old Oak Common TMD
31290	C	Toton Yard	47431 BR	Old Oak Common TMD
31296	FA	Crewe Carriage Shed	47438 BR	Old Oak Common TMD
31299	FO	Stratford TMD	47439 BR	ADtranz Crewe Works
31320		Stratford TMD	47440 BR	Old Oak Common TMD
31402		Bescot Yard	47441 BR	Old Oak Common TMD
31403		Toton Yard	47442 BR	ADtranz Crewe Works

47446	**BR**	Old Oak Common TMD		47850	**I**	ADtranz Crewe Works
47452	**BR**	Old Oak Common TMD		47973	**M**	ADtranz Crewe Works
47453	**BR**	Old Oak Common TMD		56013	**FC**	Toton TMD
47457	**BR**	Old Oak Common TMD		56016	**FC**	Cardiff Canton T&RSMD
47465	**BR**	Old Oak Common TMD		56023	**FC**	Toton TMD
47466	**BR**	ADtranz Crewe Works		56028	**FC**	Margam WRD
47472		Old Oak Common TMD		56030	**FC**	Margam WRD
47485	**BR**	ADtranz Crewe Works		56122	**FC**	Toton TMD
47515	**M**	Crewe Coal Siding		73003	**G**	Old Oak Common TMD
47538	**BR**	ADtranz Crewe Works		73111	**IO**	Stewarts Lane T&RSMD
47707	**RX**	Crewe Basford Hall Yard		86239	**RX**	Crewe Int. TMD (E)
47714	**RX**	Crewe Basford Hall Yard		97653	**O**	Reading T&RSMD

Non-Standard Liveries:

08793 is in London & North Eastern Railway Apple Green.
31283 is BR blue with large numbers.
31970 is BR Research light grey, dark grey, white and red.
97653 is Departmental yellow.

2. LOCOMOTIVE-HAULED PASSENGER STOCK

Coaches are listed in batches, according to their class, with lot number information for the various batches being shown above the listings. Where a coach has been renumbered, the former number is shown in parentheses. If the coach has been renumbered more than once, both the original number and last number are shown in parentheses. Where the old number of a coach due to be converted or renumbered is known and the conversion or renumbering has not yet taken place, the coach is listed both under its old number with its depot allocation, and under its new number without an allocation. 'Preserved' coaches are now listed in the main section, as their is now no official distinction between those and other coaches registered to operate on Railtrack metals, all coaches in use now being privately-owned.

NUMBERING SYSTEMS

Six different numbering systems were in use on BR. These were the BR series, the four pre-nationalisation companies' series' and the Pullman Car Company's series. BR number series coaches and former Pullman Car Company series ones are listed separately and there is also a list of pre-nationalistaion coaches registered to run on Railtrack metals . Please note that the Mark 2 Manchester Pullman vehicles were ordered after the Pullman Car Company had been nationalised and are therefore numbered in the BR series.

DETAILED INFORMATION AND CODES

After the heading, the following details are shown:

- Diagram code. This consists of the first three characters of the TOPS code followed by two numbers which relate to the particular design of vehicle.
- 'Mark' of coach (see below).
- Number of first class seats , standard class seats and lavatory compartments shown as F/S nT respectively.
- Bogie type (see below).
- Brake type. (see below).
- Additional features.
- ETH Index.

TOPS CODES

TOPS (Total operations processing system) codes are allocated to all coaching stock. For passenger stock the code consists of:

(1) Two letters denoting the layout of the vehicle as follows:

AA	Gangwayed Corridor
AB	Gangwayed Corridor Brake
AC	Gangwayed Open (2 + 2 seating)
AD	Gangwayed Open (2 + 1 seating)
AE	Gangwayed Open Brake
AF	Gangwayed Driving Open Brake
AG	Micro-Buffet

AH	Brake Micro-Buffet
AI	As 'AC' but fitted with drop-head buckeye and no gangway at one end.
AJ	Restaurant Buffet with Kitchen
AK	Kitchen Car
AL	As 'AC' but with disabled person's toilet (Mark 4 only)
AN	Miniature Buffet
AP	Pullman First with Kitchen
AQ	Pullman Parlour First
AR	Pullman Brake First
AS	Sleeping Car
AT	Royal Train Coach
AU	Sleeping Car with Pantry
AX	Generator Van
AY	Eurostar Barrier Vehicle
AZ	Special saloon
GF	DMU/EMU/Mark 4 Barrier Vehicle
GX	Generator Van
NM	Sandite Coach

(2) A digit for the class of passenger accommodation:

1	First	4	Unclassified
2	Standard (formerly second)	5	None
3	Composite		

(3) A suffix relating to the build of coach.

1 Mark 1	A Mark 2A	C Mark 2C	E Mark 2E	G Mark 3 or	H Mark 3B
Z Mark 2	B Mark 2B	D Mark 2D	F Mark 2F	Mark 3A	J Mark 4

OPERATOR CODES

The normal operator codes are given in brackets after the TOPS codes. These are as follows:

B	Brake	C	Composite
F	First	O	Open
S	standard (formerly second)	K	Side corridor with lavatory

Various other letters are in use and the meaning of these can be ascertained by referring to the titles at the head of each class.

BOGIE TYPES

BR Mk 1 (BR1). Standard double bolster leaf spring bogie. 90 m.p.h. Weight: 6.1 t.
BR Mk 2 (BR2). Single bolster leaf-spring bogie used on certain types of non-passenger stock and suburban stock (all now withdrawn). Weight: 5.3 t.
COMMONWEALTH (C). Heavy, cast steel coil spring bogie. 100 m.p.h. Weight: 6.75 t.
B4. Coil spring fabricated bogie for 100 m.p.h. Weight: 5.2 t.Note: B4 bogies are allowed to run at 110 m.p.h. provided that they hav aspecial maintenance regime. This applies to certain BGs (NHA).
B5. Heavy duty version of B4. 100 m.p.h. Weight: 5.3 t.
B5 (SR). A bogie used on ex Southern Region EMUs, similar in design to the B5 above. 100 m.p.h.
BT10. A fabricated bogie designed for 125 m.p.h. Air suspension.
T4. A 125 m.p.h. bogie from BREL (now ADtranz).

BT41. Fitted to Mark 4 vehicles. Manufactured by the Swiss firm of SIG. At present limited to 125 m.p.h. but designed for 140 m.p.h.

BRAKE TYPE CODES.

a	Air braked.	x	Dual braked (air and vacuum).
v	Vacuum braked.		

HEATING

All heating on British main-line trains is now electric. Certain coaches for use on charter trains may, hoewever have steam heating facilities also.

PUBLIC ADDRESS

It is assumed that all coaches are now fitted with public address, although certain stored coaches may not have the feature. In addition, it is assumed that all vehicles with a guard's compartment have public address transmission facilities, as have catering vehicles.

ADDITIONAL FEATURE CODES.

d	Secondary door locking provided.
f	Facelifted or fluorescent lighting provided.
k	Composition brake blocks (instead of cast iron).
n	Day/night lighting.
p	Fitted with public telephone.
pg	Public address transmission and driver-guard communication.
q	Fitted with catering staff to shore telephone.
w	Fitted with wheelchair space.
z	Fitted with wheelchair space and disabled persons' toilet.

NOTES ON ETH INDICES.

The sum of ETH indices in a train must not be more than that of the locomotive. The normal voltage on BR is 1000. Suffix 'X' denotes 600 amp wiring instead of 400 amp. Trains whose ETH index comes to more than 66 must be formed completely with 600 amp wired stock.

LAYOUT

The layout in this section consists of number, roiginal and last numbers in parentheses if applicable, notes (if any), livery, owner code, operation code and depot. All coaches are in InterCity livery unless otherwise stated.

Thus an example of the layout is as follows:

No.	Notes	Liv.	Owner	Op.	Depot
1696	a	G	M	SS	BN

Note: For off-loan vehicles, the last storage location is given where known.

THE DEVELOPMENT OF BR STANDARD COACHES

The standard BR coach built from 1951 to 1963 is the mark 1. This has a separate underframe and body. The underframe is normally 64'6'' long, but certain vehicles were built on short (57') frames. Tungsten lighting is standard and until 1961, BR mark 1 bogies were generally provided. In 1959 TSOs to lot No. 30525 appeared with fluorescent lighting and melamine interior panels and from 1961 onwards Commonwealth bogies were fitted in an attempt to improve the quality of ride which became very poor when the tyre profiles on the wheels of the Mark 1 bogies became worn. The further batches of TSOs and BSOs retained the features of lot 30525, but the BSKs, SKs, BCKs and CKs, whilst utilising melamine panelling in standard class, still retained tungsten lighting. Wooden interior finish was retained in first class compartments. The FOs had fluorescent lighting with wooden panelling except for lot No. 30648 which had tungsten lighting. In later years many mark 1s had their mark 1 bogies replaced by B4s.

In 1964, a new train was introduced. Known as ''XP64'', it featured new seat designs, pressure ventilation, aluminium compartment doors and corridor partitions, foot pedal operated toilets, and B4 bogies. The vehicles were on standard mark 1 underframes. Folding doors were fitted but these proved troublesome and were later replaced with hinged doors. All XP64 coaches have now been withdrawn, but some have been preserved.

The prototype mark 2 vehicle (W 13252) was produced in 1963. This was an FK of semi-integral construction and was pressure ventilated. Tungsten lighting was provided and B4 bogies. This vehicle has been preserved by the National Railway Museum. The production build was similar, but wider windows were used. The standard class open vehicles used the new seat design similar to that in the XP64 and fluorescent lighting was provided. Interior finish reverted to wood. MK 2s were built from 1964-66.

The mark 2As, built 1967-68, incorporated the rest of the novel features first used in the XP64 set, i.e. foot pedal operated toilets (except BSOs), new first seat design, aluminium compartment doors and partitions together with fluorescent lighting in first class compartments. Folding gangway doors (lime green coloured) were used instead of the traditional variety. The following list summarises the changes made in the later Mk 2 variants:

Mk 2B: Wide wrap round doors, no centre doors, slightly longer body. In standard class, one toilet at each end instead of two at one end as previously . Red gangway doors.

Mk 2C: Lowered ceiling with twin strips of fluorescent lighting, ducting for air conditioning, but no air conditioning.

Mk 2D: Air conditioning. No opening lights in windows.

Mk 2E: Smaller toilets with luggage racks opposite. Fawn gangway doors.

Mk 2F: Plastic interior panels. Inter-City 70 seats. Modified air conditioning system.

The Mark 3 coach has BT10 bogies, is 75' long and is of fully integral construction with Inter-City 70 seats. Gangway doors are yellow (red in RFB). Loco-hauled coaches are classified Mark 3A, Mark 3 being reserved for HST trailers. A new batch of FOs and BFOs classified Mark 3B was built in 1985 with APT style seating and revised lighting. The last vehicles in the Mark 3 series were the driving brake vehicles (officially called driving van trailers) which have been built for West Coast Main Line services.

The Mark 4 coach built by Metro-Cammell for the East Coast Main Line electrification scheme features a body profile suitable for tilting trains, although tilt is not fitted, and is not intended to be. They are suitable for 140 m.p.h. running, although are restricted to 125 m.p.h. pending the installation of a more advanced signalling system on the East Coast Main Line.

2.1. BR NUMBER SERIES STOCK

AJ11 (RF)   RESTAURANT FIRST

Dia. AJ106. Mark 1. Gas cooking. 24/-. B5 bogies. ETH 2. This coach spent most of its life as a Royal train vehicle and was numbered 2907 for a time.

Lot No. 30633 Ashford/Swindon 1961. a. 41 t.

325   **WV** M SS   BN

AP1Z (PK)   PULLMAN FIRST WITH KITCHEN

Dia. AP101. Mark 2. Pressure Ventilated. Electric cooking. 18/- 2T. B5 bogies. a. ETH 6.

Lot No. 30755 Derby 1966. 40 t.

Non-Standard Livery: Maroon & beige.

504	**0**	C SS	CS	THE WHITE ROSE
506	**0**	C SS	CS	THE RED ROSE

AQ1Z (PC)   PULLMAN PARLOUR FIRST

Dia. AQ101. Mark 2. Pressure Ventilated. 36/- 2T. B4 bogies. a. ETH 5.

Lot No. 30754 Derby 1966. 35 t.

Non-Standard Livery: Maroon & beige.

546	**0**	C SS	CS	CITY OF MANCHESTER
548	**0**	C SS	CS	ELIZABETHAN
549	**0**	C SS	CS	PRINCE RUPERT
550	**0**	C	CS	GOLDEN ARROW
551	**0**	C SS	CS	CALEDONIAN
552	**0**	C SS	CS	SOUTHERN BELLE
553	**0**	C SS	CS	KING ARTHUR

AR1Z (PB)   PULLMAN BRAKE FIRST

Dia. AR101. Mark 2. Pressure Ventilated. 30/- 2T. B4 bogies. a. ETH 4.

Lot No. 30753 Derby 1966. 35 t.

Non-Standard Livery: Maroon & beige.

586	**0**	C SS	CS	TALISMAN

AJ1F (RFB)   BUFFET OPEN FIRST

Dia. AJ104. Mark 2F. Air conditioned. Electric cooking. Converted 1988-9/91 at BREL, Derby from Mark 2F FOs. 1200/1/3/6/11/14-17/20/21/50/2/5/6/9 have Stones equipment, others have Temperature Ltd. -/26 1T. B4 bogies. a.

payphone. Catering staff-shore telephone. Secondary door locks. ETH 6X.

1200/3/6/11/14/16/20/52/5/6. Lot No. 30845 Derby 1973. 33 t.
1201/4/5/7/8/10/12/13/15/17-9/21/50/1/4/9. Lot No. 30859 Derby 1973-4.
33 t.
1202/9/53/8. Lot No. 30873 Derby 1974-5. 33 t.

1200	(3287, 6459)		E	XC	DY
1201	(3361, 6445)		E	XC	DY
1202	(3436, 6456)		E	XC	DY
1203	(3291)		E	XC	DY
1204	(3401)		E	XC	MA
1205	(3329, 6438)		E	XC	DY
1206	(3319)		E	XC	MA
1207	(3328, 6422)		E	XC	MA
1208	(3393)		E	XC	MA
1209	(3437, 6457)	w	E	XC	DY
1210	(3405, 6462)		E	XC	DY
1211	(3305)		E	XC	MA
1212	(3427, 6453)		E	XC	DY
1213	(3419)		E	XC	DY
1214	(3317, 6433)		E	XC	MA
1215	(3377)		E	XC	MA
1216	(3302)	w	E	XC	DY
1217	(3357, 6444)		E		ZH
1218	(3332)	w	E	XC	DY
1219	(3418)		E	XC	MA
1220	(3315, 6432)		E	XC	MA
1221	(3371)		E	XC	MA
1250	(3372)		E	XC	MA
1251	(3383)		E	XC	MA
1252	(3280)		E	XC	DY
1253	(3432)		E	XC	ZP
1254	(3391)		E	XC	DY
1255	(3284)		E	XC	MA
1256	(3296)		E	XC	MA
1258	(3322)		E	XC	DY
1259	(3439)	w	E	XC	MA
1260	(3378)		E	XC	MA

AK51 (RKB)   KITCHEN BUFFET

Dia. AK502. Mark 1. Gas Cooking. No seats. B5 bogies. a. ETH 1.

Lot No. 30624 Cravens 1960-1. 41 t.

1566	**G**	V SS	SL		

AJ41 (RBR)   RESTAURANT BUFFET

Dia. AJ403. Mark 1. Gas cooking. Built with 23 loose chairs (dia. AJ402). All
remaining vehicles refurbished with 23 (21 w) fixed polypropylene chairs and
fluorescent lighting. ETH 2 (2X*).

r Further refurbished with 21 chairs, payphone, wheelchair space and carpets (Dia. AJ417).

1644-1699. Lot No. 30628 Pressed Steel 1960-61. Commonwealth bogies. 39 t.
1730. Lot No. 30512 BRCW 1960-61. B5 bogies. 37 t.

1691 is leased to the Venice Simplon Orient Express.

1644	a		W		OM	1675	x*		X	Ferme Park
1645	a		M SS		HT	1678	x*	**M**	M SS	BN
1649	aw		E		Kineton	1679	a		M SS	BN
1650	aw		W		OM	1680	x*w	**WV**	M SS	BN
1652	aw		W		OM	1683	ar		E AR	NC
1653	aw		M SS		BN	1684	x*	**BG**	W	Carlisle Yard
1655	a		W		Carlisle Yard	1686	ar		E	Long Marston
1658	a		M SS		BN	1688	aw	**BG**	W	OM
1659	a		X		Ferme Park	1689	ar		E	Long Marston
1663	x*		W		Ferme Park	1691	ar	**G**	E SS	SL
1666	x*		W		OM	1692	ar	**CH**	R	CQ
1667	x		M SS		BN	1693	x*		X	Ferme Park
1670	x*w	**BG**	W		OM	1696	a	**G**	M SS	BN
1671	x*		M SS		BN	1697	ar		E	CP
1672	x*		W		BN	1698	a	**WV**	M SS	BN
1673	aw		E		Kineton	1699	ar		E AR	NC
1674	a		M SS		HT	1730	x	**M**	S SS	BO

AN21 (RMB)   MINIATURE BUFFET CAR

Dia. AN203. Mark 1. Gas cooking. -/44 2T. These vehicles are basically an open standard with two full window spaces removed to accommodate a buffet counter, and four seats removed to allow for a stock cupboard. All remaining vehicles now have fluorescent lighting. All vehicles have Commonwealth bogies except 1850 (B5). ETH 3 (3X*).

1813-1832. Lot No. 30520 Wolverton 1960. 38 t.
1842-1850. Lot No. 30507 Wolverton 1960. 37 t (1850 is 36 t).
1853-1863. Lot No. 30670 Wolverton 1961-2. 38 t.
1871-1882. Lot No. 30702 Wolverton 1962. 38 t.

1842/50/71 have been been refurbished and are fitted with a microwave oven and payphone. Dia. AN208.

1813	x	**CC**	M SS		BN	1859	x	**M**	S SS	BO
1816	x*	**B**	X		BQ	1860	x	**M**	C SS	CS
1832	x		M SS		HT	1861	x	**M**	M SS	BN
1842	x		E AR		NC	1863	x	**CH**	R SS	CO
1850	a		E AR		NC	1871	x		E AR	NC
1853	x		M SS		BN	1882	a	**M**	C SS	CS

AJ41 (RBR)   RESTAURANT BUFFET

Dia. AJ414. Mark 1. Gas cooking. These vehicles were built as unclassified restaurant (RU). All remaining vehicles were rebuilt with buffet counter and 23 fixed polypropylene chairs (RBS). They were then further refurbished by fitting fluorescent lighting and reclassified RBR. 1966-84 have 21 chairs. ETH 2 (2X*).

1953. Lot No. 30575 Ashford/Swindon 1960. B4/B5 bogies. 36.5 t.
1966-1984. Lot No. 30632 Ashford/Swindon 1960-61. Commonwealth bogies. 39 t.

1953	**O**	D SS	CS	1972	**BG** E	Kineton
1966		E	Kineton	1984	**BG** E	Kineton
1971		E	Kineton			

AS41   FIRST CLASS SLEEPING CAR

Dia. AS101. Mark 1. Pressure Ventilated. 11 single-berth compartments plus an attendant's compartment with gas cooking. a. ETH 3 (3X*).

2013. Lot No. 30159 Wolverton 1958. B5 bogies. 39 t.
2127. Lot No. 30687 Wolverton 1961. Commonwealth bogies. 41 t.

2013 was numbered 2908 for a time when in use with the Royal Train.

| 2013 | **M** N | SO | 2127 | * | **M** G SS | EN |

AU51   CHARTER TRAIN STAFF COACHES

Dia. AU501. Mark 1. Converted from BCKs. ETH 2.

Lot No. 30732 Derby 1964. Commonwealth bogies. a. 37 t.

| 2833 | (21270) | M SS | BN | 2834 | (21267) | **WV** M SS | BN |

AT5G   ROYAL SALOONS

HM The Queen's Saloon.

Dia. AT525. Mark 3. Converted from a FO built 1972. Consists of a lounge, bedroom and bathroom for HM The Queen, and a combined bedroom and bathroom for the Queen's dresser. One entrance vestibule has double doors. Air conditioned. a. BT10 bogies. ETH 9X.

Lot No. 30886 Wolverton 1977. 36 t.

| 2903 | (11001) | **RT** Q RT | ZN |

HRH The Duke of Edinburgh's Saloon.

Dia. AT526. Mark 3. Converted from a TSO built 1972. Consists of a combined lounge/dining room, a bedroom and a shower room for the Duke, a kitchen and a valet's bedroom and bathroom. Air conditioned. a. BT10 bogies. ETH 15X.

Lot No. 30887 Wolverton 1977. 36 t.

| 2904 | (12001) | **RT** Q RT | ZN |

AT5B   ROYAL STAFF COUCHETTES

Dia. AT527. Mark 2B. Converted from a BFK built 1969. Consists of luggage accommodation, guard's compartment, 350 kW diesel generator and Staff sleeping accommodation. Pressure ventilated. a. B5 bogies. ETH 5X.

Lot No. 30888 Wolverton 1977. 46 t.

2905 (14105) RT Q RT ZN

Dia. AT528. Mark 2B. Converted from a BFK built 1969. Pressure ventilated. a. B5 bogies. ETH 4X.

Lot No. 30889 Wolverton 1977. 35.5 t.

2906 (14112) RT Q RT ZN

AT5G   ROYAL STAFF SLEEPING CARS

Dia. AT531. Mark 3A Details as for 10646-732 except that controlled emission toilets are not fitted. ETH11X.

Lot No. 31002 Derby/Wolverton 1985. 42.5 t (44 t*).

2914   RT Q RT ZN
2915 *   RT Q RT ZN

AT5G   ROYAL KITCHEN/DINING CARS

Dia. AT537 (AT539*). Mark 3. Converted from HST TRUKs built 1976/7. a. BT10 bogies. ETH 13X.

Lot No. 31059 (31084*) Wolverton 1988 (1990*). 43 t.

2916 (40512)   RT Q RT ZN
2917 (40514) *   RT Q RT ZN

AT5G   ROYAL HOUSEHOLD CARS

Dia. AT538 (AT540*). Mark 3. Converted from HST TRUKs built 1976/7. a. BT10 bogies. ETH 10X.

Lot Nos. 31083 (31085*) Wolverton 1989. 41.05 t.

2918 (40515)   RT Q RT ZN
2919 (40518) *   RT Q RT ZN

AT5B   ROYAL STAFF COUCHETTES

Dia. AT536 (AT541*). Mark 2B. Converted from BFKs built 1969. B5 bogies. ETH2X (ETH 7X*).

Lot No. 31044 Wolverton 1986. With generator (similar to 2905). 48 t.

2920 .(14109, 17109)   RT Q RT ZN

Lot No. 31086 Wolverton 1990. 41.5 t.

2921 (14107, 17107) *   RT Q RT ZN

AT5G   HRH THE PRINCE OF WALES'S SLEEPING CAR

Dia. AT534. Mark 3B. a. BT10 bogies.

Lot No. 31035 Derby/Wolverton 1987.

| 2922 | | **RT** Q RT   ZN |

AT5G   HRH THE PRINCE OF WALES'S SALOON

Dia. AT535. Mark 3B. a. BT10 bogies.

Lot No. 31036 Derby/Wolverton 1987.

| 2923 | | **RT** Q RT   ZN |

AD11 (FO)   OPEN FIRST

Dia. AD103. Mark 1. 42/- 2T. ETH 3. Many now fitted with table lights.

Non-Standard liveries: 3125 is in green & cream. 3150 is in unlined **WV** livery.

3063-3069. Lot No. 30169 Doncaster 1955. B4 bogies. 33 t.
3096-3100. Lot No. 30576 BRCW 1959. B4 bogies. 33 t.

3063	a	**BG** V		SL		3096	x	**M** S SS		BO
3064	a	**BG** V		SL		3097	a	**WV** M SS		BN
3066	a	**G**	V SS	SL		3098	a	**CH** R		CQ
3068	a	**G**	V SS	SL		3100	x	**CC** M SS		BN
3069	a	**G**	V SS	SL						

Later design with fluorescent lighting, aluminium window frames and Commonwealth bogies.

3105-3128. Lot No. 30697 Swindon 1962-3. 36 t.
3130-3150. Lot No. 30717 Swindon 1963. 36 t.

3128/35/6/41/3/4/6/7/8 were renumbered 1058/9/60/3/5/6/8/9/70 when reclassified RUO, then 3600/1/5/8/9/2/6/4/10 when declassified, but have now regained their original numbers.

3105	x	**M** C SS	CS		3124	a		X	Ferme Park
3107	x	**M** SS	BN		3125	a	**0** D SS		CQ
3110	x	**CC** M SS	BN		3127	a		M SS	BN
3111	x	X	Ferme Park		3128	x	**M** C SS		CS
3112	x	**CH** R	CQ		3130	v	**M** C		CS
3113	x	**M** C SS	CS		3131	x	**M** M SS		BN
3114	a	M SS	BN		3132	x	**M** M SS		BN
3115	x	M SS	BN		3133	x	**M** M SS		BN
3117	x	**M** C SS	CS		3134	x		X	Ferme Park
3118	x	X	WN		3135	a		E	BN
3119	x	M SS	BN		3136	a		M SS	HT
3120	a	**WV** M SS	BN		3140	x		X	Ferme Park
3121	a	**WV** M SS	BN		3141	a		M SS	BN
3122	a	**BG** D	CQ		3143	a		N SS	Ferme Park
3123	a	M SS	BN		3144	a	**CC** M SS		BN

3146	a	**WV** M SS	BN	3149	a		M SS	HT
3147	a	**WV** M SS	BN	3150	a	**0**	M SS	BN
3148	a	M SS	BN					

Name: 3125 is named 'LOCH SHIEL'.

AD1D (FO)   OPEN FIRST

Dia. AD105. Mark 2D. Air conditioned. 3172-88 have Stones equipment. 3192/3202 have Temperature Ltd and require at least 800 V train heating supply. 42/- 2T. B4 bogies. a. ETH 5.

Lot No. 30821 Derby 1971-2. 32.5 t.

3172	X	DY	3186	X	DY
3174	X	Ferme Park	3187	W	Carlisle Yard
3178	X	DY	3188	D	DY
3181	D	CQ	3192	W	DY
3182	X	DY	3202	W	Carlisle Yard

AD1E (FO)   OPEN FIRST

Dia. AD106. Mark 2E. Air conditioned. Stones equipment. Require at least 800 V train heating supply. 42/- 2T (41/- 2T w). B4 bogies. a. ETH 5.

* Seats removed to accommodate catering module. 40F 1T.
§ Fitted with power supply for Mk. 1 RBR.

Lot No. 30843 Derby 1972-3. 32.5 t.

3221	w	E	Long Marston	3246	w	X	Ferme Park
3223		X	OM	3247		X	Hornsey Up CS
3225		W	Kineton	3248		X	DY
3226		W	Kineton	3249	*	E	Hornsey Up CS
3227		X	Ferme Park	3251	*	X	Ferme Park
3228	d §	E	Long Marston	3252	w	E	Long Marston
3229	d	E	Long Marston	3256	w	E	Long Marston
3230		X	DY	3257	w	X	Ferme Park
3231		X	Ferme Park	3258	n	W	Kineton
3232	dw	E	Long Marston	3259	d *	E	Hornsey Up CS
3233	**BG**	W	BK	3261	dw	E	Longtown
3234	w	X	Ferme Park	3267		R	CQ
3235	§	E	Long Marston	3268		X	Kineton
3237		X	BN	3269	d	E	Long Marston
3239		X	Ferme Park	3270		X	Ferme Park
3240	**CH**	R	CQ	3272		X	Hornsey Up CS
3241	d	E	Long Marston	3273		R	Crewe Coal Sdgs
3242	w §	E	Long Marston	3275		X	Hornsey Up CS
3244	dw	E	Long Marston				

AD1F (FO)   OPEN FIRST

Dia. AD107. Mark 2F. Air conditioned. 3277-3318/58-81 have Stones equipment. others have Temperature Ltd. 42/- 2T. All now refurbished with power-operated vestibule doors, new panels and new seat trim. B4 bogies. a. Secondary door locks. ETH 5X.

3277-3318. Lot No. 30845 Derby 1973. 33 t.
3325-3428. Lot No. 30859 Derby 1973-4. 33 t.
3429-3438. Lot No. 30873 Derby 1974-5. 33 t.

§ Fitted with power supply for Mk. 1 RBR.

3277		E	AR	NC	3362		E	WC	OY
3278		E	WC	OY	3363		E	WC	OY
3279		E	AR	NC	3364		E	WC	OY
3285		E	WC	OY	3366		E	WC	OY
3290		E	AR	NC	3368		E	AR	NC
3292		E	AR	NC	3369		E	WC	OY
3293		E	WC	OY	3373		E	AR	NC
3295		E	AR	NC	3374		E	WC	OY
3299		E	WC	OY	3375		E	AR	NC
3300		E	WC	OY	3379	§	E	AR	NC
3303		E	AR	NC	3381		E	AR	NC
3304		E	WC	OY	3384		E	WC	OY
3309		E	AR	NC	3385		E	WC	OY
3312		E	WC	OY	3386		E	WC	OY
3313		E	WC	OY	3387		E	WC	OY
3314		E	WC	OY	3388		E	AR	NC
3318		E	AR	NC	3389		E	WC	OY
3325		E	WC	OY	3390		E	WC	OY
3326		E	WC	OY	3392		E	WC	OY
3330		E	WC	OY	3395		E	WC	OY
3331		E	AR	NC	3397		E	WC	OY
3333		E	WC	OY	3399	§	E	AR	NC
3334		E	AR	NC	3400		E	AR	NC
3336	§	E	AR	NC	3402		E	WC	OY
3337		E	WC	OY	3403		E	WC	OY
3338	§	E	AR	NC	3408		E	WC	OY
3340		E	WC	OY	3411		E	WC	OY
3344		E	WC	OY	3414		E	AR	NC
3345		E	WC	OY	3416		E	AR	NC
3348		E	WC	OY	3417		E	AR	NC
3350		E.	WC	OY	3424		E	AR	NC
3351		E	AR	NC	3425		E	WC	OY
3352		E	WC	OY	3426		E	WC	OY
3353		E	WC	OY	3428		E	WC	OY
3354		E	WC	OY	3429		E	WC	OY
3356		E	WC	OY	3431		E	WC	OY
3358		E	AR	NC	3433		E	WC	OY
3359		E	WC	OY	3434		E	WC	OY
3360		E	WC	OY	3438		E	WC	OY

AG1E (FOt)   OPEN FIRST (PANTRY)

Dia. AG101. Mark 2E. Air conditioned. Converted from FO. Fitted with pantry, microwave oven and payphone for use on sleeping car services. 36/- 1T. B4 bogies. a. Secondary door locks. ETH 5X.

Lot No. 30843 Derby 1972-3. 32.5 t.

3520	(3253)	E GW LA	3523	(3238)	E SR IS
3521	(3271)	E GW LA	3524	(3254)	E SR IS
3522	(3236)	E GW LA	3525	(3255)	E CP

AC21 (TSO)   OPEN STANDARD

Dia. AC204. Mark 1. This vehicle has 2 + 2 seating and is classified TSO ('Tourist second open'-a former LNER designation). It has narrower seats than later vehicles. -/64 2T. x. ETH 4.

Lot No. 30079 York 1953. Commonwealth bogies. 36 t.

3766   M C SS   CS

AC21 (TSO)   OPEN STANDARD

Dia. AC201. Mark 1. These vehicles are a development of Dia. AC204 with fluorescent lighting and modified design of seat headrest. -/64 2T. ETH 4.

4831-4836. Lot No. 30506 Wolverton 1959. Commonwealth (BR1*) bogies. k. 33 t.
4842-4891. Lot No. 30525 Wolverton 1959-60. B4 bogies. 33 t. (4891 is 36 t.)

4831	xk	M	S SS	BO	4860	x	M	C	CS
4832	x	M	S SS	BO	4866	x	RR	E NW	LL
4836	xk	M	S SS	BO	4869	x		X	Ferme Park
4842	x		X	Ferme Park	4873	x	RR	E NW	LL
4849	x	RR	E NW	LL	4875	x	RR	E NW	LL
4854	x	RR	E NW	LL	4876	x	RR	E NW	LL
4856	x	M	S SS	BO	4880	x	RR	E NW	LL
4858	x		W	Carlisle Yard	4891	v C	N	X	Crewe Brook Sdgs

Lot No. 30646 Wolverton 1961. Built with Commonwealth bogies, but BR1 bogies substituted by the SR on 4902/5/9/10/12/15/16. All now re-rebogied. 34 t B4, 36 t C.

4902	x B4	CH	R SS	CO	4912	x C	M	C SS	CS
4905	v C	M	M SS	BN	4915	x B4	W	M SS	BN
4909	x B4		X	Ferme Park	4916	x B4		X	Ferme Park
4910	v C	M	M SS	BN	4917	x C	RR	E NW	LL

These two lots have Commonwealth bogies and aluminium window frames. 37 t.

4923/89 have BR2 bogies substituted and weigh 35.5 t.

4923-5044. Lot No. 30690 Wolverton 1961-2.
5067. Lot No. 30724 York 1963. Converted to 'LMS Club Car'.

4923	v	N	X	Crewe Brook Sdgs	4993	a		M SS	HT
4925	a		M SS	BN	4994	v	M	M SS	BN
4927	af		R	CP	4996	x	CC	M SS	BN
4930	af		R	CP	4997	v	BG	C	CS
4931	v	M	C SS	CS	4998	a		M SS	BN
4932	v	N	C	CS	4999	a		M SS	BN
4936	v	M	C	CS	5002	a	W	M SS	HT
4938	a	W	M SS	BN	5005	a	W	M SS	BN
4939	a		M SS	BN	5007	a		M SS	BN
4940	v	M	M SS	BN	5008	x	CC	M SS	BN
4946	x	CC	M SS	BN	5009	a		R	CQ
4949	a		M SS	BN	5010	a		R	CP
4951	v	M	M SS	BN	5023	a		M SS	BN
4954	v	M	C SS	CS	5025	x	CH	R SS	CO
4956	a		M SS	BN	5027	a		M SS	BN
4958	v	M	C SS	CS	5028	x	M	S	BO
4959	a		M SS	BN	5029	x	CH	R SS	CO
4960	v	M	M SS	BN	5030	x	CH	R SS	CO
4961	a		R	CP	5032	x	M	C	CS
4963	x	CH	R SS	CO	5033	x	M	C SS	CS
4966	a		R	CP	5035	x	M	C	CS
4973	v	M	M SS	BN	5037	a		M SS	BN
4977	a		M SS	BN	5038	x		W	OM
4979	a		X	CP	5040	x		R	CP
4980	v	M	X	Crewe Brook Sdgs	5041	a		X	Wolsingham
4984	v	M	M SS	BN	5042	x		X	Ferme Park
4986	a		M SS	BN	5044	x	M	C SS	CS
4989	v	N	X	CP	5067	a	M	D SS	CQ
4991	a	W	M SS	HT					

AC2Z (TSO)   OPEN STANDARD

Dia. AC205. Mark 2. Pressure ventilated. -/64 2T. B4 bogies. v. ETH 4.

Lot No. 30751 Derby 1965-7. 32 t.

5132	H	E	Longtown	5179	4	RR	E	Longtown
5135	RR	E	Longtown	5180		RR	E	Longtown
5148	RR	E	Longtown	5183		RR	E	Longtown
5154	H	E	Longtown	5186		RR	E	Longtown
5156	RR	E	Longtown	5191		H	E	Longtown
5157	RR	E	Longtown	5193		RR	E	Longtown
5158	RR	E	Longtown	5194		RR	E	Longtown
5159	RR	E	Longtown	5198		RR	E	Longtown
5161	RR	E	Longtown	5207		RR	E	Longtown
5163	RR	E	Longtown	5209		RR	E	Longtown
5166	H	E	Longtown	5212		H	E	Longtown
5167	RR	E	Longtown	5213		RR	E	Longtown
5173	RR	E	Longtown	5221		RR	E	Longtown
5174	RR	E	Longtown	5225		RR	E	Longtown
5175	N	X	CP	5226		RR	E	Longtown
5177	RR	E	Longtown					

Named vehicles:

5132	CLAN MUNRO	5166	CLAN MACKENZIE	5193	CLAN MACLEOD
5154	CLAN FRASER	5191	CLAN DONALD	5212	CAPERKAILZIE

AD2Z (SO)   OPEN STANDARD

Dia. AD203. Mark 2. Pressure ventilated. -/48 2T. B4 bogies. a. ETH 4.

Lot No. 30752 Derby 1966. 32 t.

| 5254 | BG E | DY | |

AC2A (TSO)   OPEN STANDARD

Dia. AC206. Mark 2A. Pressure ventilated. -/64 2T (-/62 2T w). B4 bogies. a.
ETH 4.

5265-5345. Lot No. 30776 Derby 1967-8. 32 t.
5350-5433. Lot No. 30787 Derby 1968. 32 t.

5265	RR E		Long Marston		5341	RR E			Long Marston
5266	RR E		Long Marston		5345	RR E	NW	LL	
5267	RR E		Long Marston		5350	NR E			Long Marston
5271	RR E		Long Marston		5353	RR E			Long Marston
5272	RR E		Long Marston		5354	RR E			Long Marston
5275	RR E		CP		5364	RR E			Long Marston
5276	RR E	NW	LL		5365	RR E			CP
5277	BG E		Long Marston		5366	RR E			Long Marston
5278	RR E	NW	LL		5373	RR E			CP
5279	BG E		Long Marston		5376	NR E			Long Marston
5282	RR E		Long Marston		5378	NR E			Long Marston
5290	NR E		Long Marston		5379	RR E			Long Marston
5291	RR E		ZF		5381	w	RR E	NW	LL
5292	RR E		Long Marston		5384		■ E		Long Marston
5293	NR E		Long Marston		5386	w	RR E	NW	LL
5299	M C SS		CS		5389	w	RR E	NW	LL
5300	BG E		Long Marston		5392	BG E			Long Marston
5304	RR E		Long Marston		5393	RR E			Long Marston
5307	RR E		CP		5396	RR E			Long Marston
5309	RR E	NW	LL		5401	RR E			Long Marston
5314	BG E		Long Marston		5410	■ E			Long Marston
5316	RR E		Long Marston		5412	w	RR E	NW	LL
5322	RR E	NW	LL		5419	w	RR E	NW	LL
5323	RR E		Long Marston		5420	w	RR E	NW	LL
5331	RR E	NW	LL		5432		RR E		LL
5335	RR E	NW	LL		5433	w	RR E	NW	LL
5337	BG E		Long Marston						

AC2B (TSO)   OPEN STANDARD

Dia. AC207. Mark 2B. Pressure ventilated. -/62 2T. B4 bogies. a. ETH 4.

Non-Standard livery: 5453 and 5478 are royal blue with white lining.

Lot No. 30791 Derby 1969. 32 t.

5439	**N**	E		Long Marston	5464	**N**	X	CP
5443	**N**	E		Long Marston	5468	**N**	E		Longtown
5446	**N**	E		Long Marston	5471	**N**	E		Long Marston
5447	**N**	E		Long Marston	5472	**N**	E		Long Marston
5449	**N**	X		Crewe Brook Sdgs	5475	**N**	E		Long Marston
5450	**N**	E		Long Marston	5476	**BG**	J		NL
5453	**O**	C	WW	BK	5478	**O**	C	WW	BK
5454	**N**	E		Long Marston	5480	**N**	E		Long Marston
5456	**N**	E		Longtown	5487	**M**	C	WW	BK
5462	**N**	X		Crewe Brook Sdgs	5491	**O**	C	WW	BK
5463	**M**	C	WW	BK	5494	**N**	X		CP

AC2C (TSO)   OPEN STANDARD

Dia. AC208. Mark 2C. Pressure ventilated. -/62 2T. B4 bogies. a. ETH 4.

Lot No. 30795 Derby 1969-70. 32 t.

5505	**RR**	C		CS	5574	**BG**	J		NL
5520	**RR**	J		Norwich Goods	5585	**BG**	J		NL
5533	**BG**	J		NL	5595	**BG**	J		NL
5554	**RR**	E		Long Marston	5600	**M**	C	SS	CS
5569	**M**	C	WW	BK	5614	**RR**	E		Long Marston

AC2D (TSO)   OPEN STANDARD

Dia. AC209. Mark 2D. Air conditioned. Stones (5653 has Temperature Ltd.) equipment. -/62 2T. B4 bogies. a. ETH 5.

Non-Standard Livery: Waterman VIP without lining.

Lot No. 30822 Derby 1971. 33 t.

5616			X	Ferme Park	5633			W		OM
5617			W	OM	5634			E		Long Marston
5618			E	Long Marston	5636	d		E		Long Marston
5620			E	Longtown	5638			E		Longtown
5623			E	Longtown	5640			E		Longtown
5624			E	Long Marston	5642			C		CS
5625			E	Long Marston	5645			C		CS
5626	d		E	Long Marston	5646	d		E		Long Marston
5628			E	Long Marston	5647		**O**	X	CA	BK
5629			E	Longtown	5648			W		Long Marston
5630		**O**	X	CA	BK	5650			E		Longtown
5631	d		E	Long Marston	5651			E		Long Marston
5632	d		E	Long Marston	5652	d		E		Long Marston

5653	d	E		Longtown	5703	d	E	Long Marston
5654	d	E		Long Marston	5704	**M** C SS		CS
5657		E		Long Marston	5705		E	Long Marston
5658		E		Longtown	5709	**BG** C		CS
5659		E		PC	5710	d	E	Long Marston
5660		E		Long Marston	5711		E	Longtown
5661		E		Kineton	5712		C	CS
5662		E		Long Marston	5714	**M** C SS		CS
5663		E		Kineton	5715		E	Longtown
5665		E		Long Marston	5716		E	Kineton
5669	d	E		Longtown	5718		E	Kineton
5671	d	E		Longtown	5719		E	Long Marston
5673	d	E		PC	5722		W	Carlisle Yard
5674		E		Kineton	5723		E	Longtown
5675		W		OM	5724		E	Longtown
5676	d	E		Long Marston	5726		E	Long Marston
5679	d	E		Long Marston	5727	**M** C SS		CS
5682	d	E		Long Marston	5728		E	Long Marston
5685		E		Long Marston	5729		X	OM
5686		E		Long Marston	5730		E	Long Marston
5687		E		Kineton	5731		E	Kineton
5690		E		Longtown	5732	**0** X CA		BK
5692		E		Long Marston	5735		E	Long Marston
5693		E		Long Marston	5737	d	E	Long Marston
5694		E		Kineton	5738		E	Kineton
5695		E		Long Marston	5739	**0** X CA		BK
5699		E		Long Marston	5740	d	E	Long Marston
5700	d	E		Long Marston	5743		E	Longtown
5701		E		Kineton				

AC2E (TSO)   OPEN STANDARD

Dia. AC210. Mark 2E. Air conditioned. Stones equipment. -/64 2T (-/62 2T w).
B4 bogies. Require at least 800 V train heat supply. a. ETH 5.

5744-5803. Lot No. 30837 Derby 1972. 33.5 t.
5810-5907. Lot No. 30844 Derby 1972-3. 33.5 t.

§ Fitted with centre luggage rack seating -/60 2T (-/58 2T w).

5744	d	E	XC	MA	5762		X		DY
5745	d§	E	XC	DY	5764	d	E		Longtown
5746	d	E	XC	MA	5766	d	E		Longtown
5747		X		DY	5768		E		ZG
5748	dw	E	XC	MA	5769	d	E	XC	MA
5750	d§	E	XC	DY	5772	dw	E	XC	DY
5751	dw	E	WC	OY	5773	d§	E	XC	DY
5752	dw	E	XC	DY	5775	d§	E	XC	DY
5754	dw	E	XC	MA	5776	d	E	XC	MA
5756		**M**	C	SS	CS	5777		X		CP
5759		X		DY	5778	dw	E	XC	MA
5760	d	E	XC	DY	5779	d	E	XC	MA

5780	dw		E	XC	MA	5847	dw		E	XC	MA
5781	dw		E	XC	MA	5851	d		E	WC	OY
5784	d		E	XC	MA	5852		W	M	SS	HT
5787	d§		E	XC	DY	5853	d		E		Longtown
5788	dw		E	XC	MA	5854	d		E	XC	MA
5789	dw		E	XC	MA	5859	d		E	XC	MA
5791	dw		E	XC	MA	5861			X		DY
5792	d		E	XC	MA	5863			M	SS	HT
5793			E	XC	DY	5866	d		E	XC	MA
5794	dw		E	XC	MA	5868	d		E	XC	MA
5796	dw		E	XC	MA	5869	d		E	XC	DY
5797	d		E	XC	MA	5871	d		E	XC	DY
5799	d		E	WC	OY	5873			C	SS	CS
5800		W	M	SS	HT	5874	dw		E	XC	DY
5801	d		E	XC	MA	5875	d		E		Longtown
5803			X	SS	CS	5876	d		E	XC	MA
5810	d§		E	XC	DY	5878			X	SS	CS
5811			C	SS	CS	5879		W			OM
5812	dw		E	XC	MA	5881	dw§		E	XC	DY
5814	d		E	XC	MA	5885			E		Crewe Coal Sdgs
5815	d§		E	XC	DY	5886	d§		E	XC	DY
5816	d		E	XC	MA	5887	dw		E	XC	MA
5821	d		E	XC	MA	5888	dw		E	XC	MA
5822	d		E	XC	MA	5889	d		E	XC	MA
5824	dw		E	XC	MA	5890	d		E	WC	OY
5826	d		E	XC	DY	5891			X		DY
5827	dw		E	XC	MA	5892	d		E	XC	DY
5828	dw		E	XC	MA	5893	d		E	XC	MA
5829			X		DY	5897	d		E	XC	MA
5831			M	SS	HT	5899	d		E	XC	MA
5832			L		ZC	5900	d§		E	XC	DY
5833	d		E	XC	MA	5901	d§		E	XC	DY
5835			C	SS	CS	5902			E	XC	MA
5836			X		DY	5903			E	XC	MA
5837			C	SS	CS	5904			E		PC
5840	d		E	WC	OY	5905	d		E	XC	MA
5842	w		X	SS	CS	5906	d		E	XC	MA
5843	dw		E	XC	DY	5907			E		Longtown
5845	dw		E	XC	MA						

AC2F (TSO)   OPEN STANDARD

Dia. AC211. Mark 2F. Air conditioned. Temperature Ltd. equipment. -/64 2T.
(-/62 2T w) Inter-City 70 seats. All now refurbished with power-operated
vestibule doors, new panels and new seat trim. B4 bogies. a. Secondary door
locks. ETH 5X.

* Early Mark 2 style seats.

5908-5958. Lot No. 30846 Derby 1973. 33 t.
5959-6170. Lot No. 30860 Derby 1973-4. 33 t.
6171-6184. Lot No. 30874 Derby 1974-5. 33 t.

5908		E	WC	OY	5962		E	XC	DY
5910	w	E	WC	OY	5963		E	WC	OY
5911		E	XC	MA	5964		E	AR	NC
5912		E	XC	DY	5965	w	E	XC	DY
5913		E	XC	DY	5966		E	AR	NC
5914		E	WC	OY	5967	w	E	XC	MA
5915		E	WC	OY	5968		E	AR	NC
5916	w	E	XC	DY	5969	w	E	WC	OY
5917		E	XC	DY	5971		E	XC	MA
5918	w	E	XC	DY	5973		E	AR	NC
5919		E	XC	DY	5975	*	E	XC	DY
5920		E	WC	OY	5976	w	E	XC	MA
5921		E	AR	NC	5977		E	WC	OY
5922		E	AR	NC	5978	*	E	WC	OY
5924		E	AR	NC	5980		E	WC	OY
5925	w	E	XC	MA	5981		E	XC	MA
5926		E	AR	NC	5983		E	XC	DY
5927		E	AR	NC	5984	*	E	WC	OY
5928		E	AR	NC	5985		E	AR	NC
5929		E	AR	NC	5986		E	WC	OY
5930	w	E	XC	MA	5987	*	E	WC	OY
5931	w	E	WC	OY	5988	w	E	WC	OY
5932		E	WC	OY	5989	w	E	XC	MA
5933		E	WC	OY	5991		E	XC	MA
5934		E	WC	OY	5993	*w	E	AR	NC
5935		E	AR	NC	5994	*	E	XC	MA
5936		E	AR	NC	5995		E	XC	DY
5937		E	WC	OY	5996		E	XC	DY
5939		E	WC	OY	5997		E	WC	OY
5940	w	E	WC	OY	5998		E	AR	NC
5941		E	WC	OY	5999		E	XC	MA
5943	w	E	WC	OY	6000		E	XC	DY
5944	w	E	AR	NC	6001	w	E	WC	OY
5945	w	E	WC	OY	6002		E	WC	OY
5946		E	WC	OY	6005	*	E	XC	MA
5947		E	XC	MA	6006		E	AR	NC
5948	w	E	WC	OY	6008		E	XC	MA
5949	w	E	WC	OY	6009		E	WC	OY
5950		E	AR	NC	6010	n	E	XC	MA
5951		E	XC	MA	6011		E	XC	DY
5952		E	WC	OY	6012	*	E	WC	OY
5953		E	WC	OY	6013	*	E	XC	DY
5954		E	AR	NC	6014		E	XC	DY
5955		E	WC	OY	6015	w	E	XC	DY
5956		E	AR	NC	6016		E	WC	OY
5957		E	WC	OY	6018	*	E	XC	DY
5958		E	XC	MA	6021		E	WC	OY
5959	n	E	AR	NC	6022	w	E	XC	DY
5960		E	XC	DY	6024		E	XC	MA
5961		E	XC	DY	6025	*w	E	XC	MA

6026	*	E	XC	DY	6119	w	E	XC	DY
6027	w	E	WC	OY	6120	w	E	XC	MA
6028		E	AR	NC	6121		E	WC	OY
6029		E	WC	OY	6122		E	XC	DY
6030	w	E	XC	MA	6123		E	AR	NC
6031		E	WC	OY	6124		E	XC	DY
6034		E	AR	NC	6134		E	WC	OY
6035	w	E	XC	DY	6135		E	XC	DY
6036	*	E	AR	NC	6136		E	WC	OY
6037		E	AR	NC	6137		E	XC	MA
6038		E	XC	DY	6138		E	WC	OY
6041		E	XC	DY	6139	*n	E	AR	NC
6042		E	AR	NC	6141	w	E	WC	OY
6043		E	WC	OY	6142	*	E	WC	OY
6045	w	E	WC	OY	6143	*	E	WC	OY
6046		E	XC	DY	6144	*	E	WC	OY
6047	*n	E	WC	OY	6145	*	E	XC	DY
6049		E	WC	OY	6146	*	E	AR	NC
6050		E	XC	DY	6147	*	E	WC	OY
6051	*	E	WC	OY	6148		E	XC	DY
6052	w	E	XC	MA	6149	*w	E	WC	OY
6053	*	E	AR	NC	6150	*	E	XC	DY
6054		E	WC	OY	6151	*	E	WC	OY
6055		E	WC	OY	6152	*	E	AR	NC
6056		E	WC	OY	6153	*	E	WC	OY
6057		E	WC	OY	6154	*	E	XC	DY
6059		E	XC	MA	6155	*	E	AR	NC
6060	*	E	WC	OY	6157	*	E	XC	MA
6061	*	E	XC	MA	6158	*	E	WC	OY
6062	*	E	WC	OY	6159	*n	E	XC	DY
6063	w	E	WC	OY	6160	*	E	AR	NC
6064		E	XC	MA	6161	*	E	WC	OY
6065		E	WC	OY	6162		E	XC	MA
6066		E	XC	DY	6163		E	WC	OY
6067		E	XC	MA	6164		E	WC	OY
6073		E	XC	DY	6165		E	WC	OY
6100	*	E	WC	OY	6166		E	AR	NC
6101		E	WC	OY	6167		E	AR	NC
6102		E	WC	OY	6168		E	XC	DY
6103		E	AR	NC	6170		E	XC	MA
6104		E	WC	OY	6171		E	WC	OY
6105		E	XC	DY	6172		E	XC	MA
6106		E	WC	OY	6173	w	E	XC	DY
6107		E	WC	OY	6174		E	AR	NC
6110	w	E	AR	NC	6175		E	WC	OY
6111		E	WC	OY	6176	w	E	XC	DY
6112		E	XC	MA	6177		E	XC	DY
6113		E	WC	OY	6178	w	E	XC	MA
6115		E	XC	DY	6179		E	WC	OY
6116		E	WC	OY	6180	w	E	WC	OY
6117	w	E	XC	DY	6181	wn	E	WC	OY
					6182		E	XC	DY

| 6183 | E XC MA | 6184 * | E XC MA |

AC2D (TSO)   OPEN STANDARD

Dia. AC217. Mark 2D. Air conditioned. Stones. -/58 2T. (-/58 1T*). B4 bogies.
a. ETH 5X. Rebuilt from FO with new style 2 + 2 seats.

Lot No. 30821 Derby 1971-2. 33.5 t.

6200	(3198)	d	E GW	LA
6201	(3210)	d*	E	Longtown
6202	(3191)	d*	E	Kineton
6203	(3180)	d	E	Kineton
6204	(3216)		X CA	BK
6205	(3193)		E	Long Marston
6206	(3183)	d	E GW	LA
6207	(3204)	d	E	Kineton
6208	(3205)	d	E	Kineton
6209	(3177)		X CA	BK
6210	(3196)	d*	E	Longtown
6211	(3215)	d	E	Longtown
6212	(3176)	d	E	Kineton
6213	(3208)	d	E GW	LA
6214	(3211)	d	E	Long Marston
6215	(3170)	d	E	Long Marston
6216	(3179)		E	Long Marston
6217	(3184)	d	E	Kineton
6218	(3209)	d	E	Longtown
6219	(3213)	d	E	Kineton
6220	(3175)	d	E	Longtown
6221	(3173)	d	E	Kineton
6222	(3171)	d	E	Kineton
6224	(3195)	d*	E	Long Marston
6226	(3203)	d	E GW	LA
6227	(3197)		E	Long Marston
6228	(3201)	d*	E	Long Marston
6229	(3212)		E	Long Marston
6230	(3185)		E	Long Marston
6232	(3199)	d*	E	Kineton
6233	(3206)		E	Long Marston
6234	(3207)	d	E	Kineton

GX51   GENERATOR VAN

Dia. GX501. Renumbered 1989 from BR departmental series. Converted from
NDA in 1973 to three-phase supply generator van for use with HST trailers. Used
at times of low availability of HST power cars. a. B4 bogies.

Lot No. 30400 Pressed Steel 1958.   t.

| 6310 | (81448, ADB 975325) | **PL** P | CQ |

AX51   GENERATOR VAN

Dia. AX501. Converted from NDA in 1992 to generator vans for use with pairs of Class 37s on Anglo-Scottish sleeping car services. Now normally used on tours hauled by steam locomotives. a. B4 bogies. ETH75.

Non-Standard Livery: 6311 is purple.

6313 is leased to the Venice Simplon Orient Express.

6311. Lot No. 30162 Pressed Steel 1958. 37.25 t.
6312. Lot No. 30224 Cravens 1956. 37.25 t.
6313. Lot No. 30484 Pressed Steel 1958. 37.25 t.

6311	(80903, 92911)	**0**	M	SS	BN
6312	(81023, 92925)		N		SK
6313	(81553, 92167)	**PC**	P	SS	SL

AZ5Z   SPECIAL SALOON

Dia. AZ501. Renumbered 1989 from LMR departmental series. Formerly the LMR General Manager's saloon. Rebuilt from LMS period 1 BFK M 5033 M to dia. 1654 and mounted on the underframe of BR suburban BS M 43232. B5 bogies. This vehicle has a maximum speed of 100 mph, but is restricted to 60 mph when carrying passengers with screw coupling operative.

LMS Lot No. 326 Derby 1927. x. t.

6320	(5033, 95707)	**M**	X	HT

GS5 (HSBV)   HST BARRIER VEHICLE

Various diagrams. Renumbered from departmental stock, or converted from various types. a. B4 bogies (Commonwealth bogies *).

6330. Lot No. 30786 Derby 1968. 32 t.
6334. Lot No. 30400 Pressed Steel 1957-8. 31.5 t.
6335. Lot No. 30775 Derby 1967-8. 32 t.
6336/8/44. Lot No. 30715 Gloucester 1962. 31 t.
6340. Lot No. 30669 Swindon 1962. 36 t.
6343. Lot No. 30795 Derby 1969/70. 32 t.
6346. Lot No. 30777 Derby 1967. 31.5 t.
6347. Lot No. 30787 Derby 1968. 31.5 t.
6348. Lot No. 30163 Pressed Steel 1957. 31.5 t.

6330	(14084, 97562)		A	AT	LA
6334	(81478, 92128)	**PL**	P	PL	NL
6335	(14065, 97565)		P		LA
6336	(81591, 92185)		A	AT	LA
6338	(8158, 92180)		A	AT	LA
6340	(21251, 97567)		A	AT	LA
6343	(5522)		P	PL	NL
6344	(81263, 92080)		A	AT	EC
6346	(9422)		A	AT	EC

| 6347 | (5395) | | A | AT | LA |
| 6348 | (81233, 92963) | | A | AT | LA |

GF5 (MFBV)   MARK 4 BARRIER VEHICLE

Various diagrams. Renumbered from departmental stock, or converted from FK, BSO or BG. a. B4 bogies.

6351. Lot No. 30091 Doncaster 1954. 33 t.
6352/3. Lot No. 30774 Derby 1968. 33 t.
6354-6. Lot No. 30820 Derby 1970. 32 t.
6357. Lot No. 30798 Derby 1970. 32 t.
6358-9. Lot No. 30788 Derby 1968. 31.5 t.
6390. Lot No. 30136 Metro-Cammell 1955. 31.5 t.

6351	(3050, 97543)		E	GN	EC
6352	(13465, 19465)	BG	E	GN	BN
6353	(13478, 19478)	BG	E	GN	EC
6354	(9459)		E	GN	BN
6355	(9477)	BG	E	GN	BN
6356	(9455)	BG	E	GN	BN
6357	(9443)	BG	E	GN	BN
6358	(9432)	BG	E	GN	BN
6359	(9429)	BG	E	GN	BN
6390	(80723, 92900)		E	GN	BN

GF5 (BV)   DMU/EMU* BARRIER VEHICLE

Various diagrams. Converted from BFK, BSO or BG. a. B4 (BR1*) bogies.

6360. Lot No. 30777 Derby 1967. 31.5 t.
6361-2. Lot No. 30820 Derby 1970. 32 t.
6363. Lot No. 30796 Derby 1970. 32 t.
6364. Lot No. 30039 Derby 1954. 32 t.
6365. Lot No. 30323 Pressed Steel 1957. 32 t.

6360	(9420)		RR	P	PL	NL
6361	(9460)		RR	P	PL	NL
6362	(9467)		RR	A	AT	LL
6363	(14117, 17117)		RR	A	AT	LL
6364	(80565)	*	RR	P	PL	TS
6365	(81296, 84296)	*	RR	P	PL	TS

AX5G   EURONIGHT GENERATOR VAN

Dia. AX502. Generator vans for European Night Services trains. Operate sandwiched between two Class 37 locomotives. Converted from Mark 3A sleeping cars. Gangways removed. Two Cummins diesel generator groups providing a 1500 V train supply. Hydraulic parking brake. 61-way ENS interface jumpers. a. BT10 bogies.

| 6371 | (10545) | E | U | ES | PM |
| 6372 | (10564) | E | U | ES | PM |

6373	(10568)	**E**	U ES	PM
6374	(10585)	**E**	U ES	PM
6375	(10587)	**E**	U ES	PM

AY5 (BV)   EUROSTAR BARRIER VEHICLE

Dia. AY501. Converted from GUVs. Bodies removed to allow for nose of Eurostar set. a. B4 bogies.

6380-6382/9. Lot No. 30417 Pressed Steel 1958-9. 40 t.
6383. Lot No. 30565 Pressed Steel 1959. 40 t.
6384/6/7. Lot No. 30616 Pressed Steel 1959-60. 40 t.
6385. Lot No. 30343 York 1957. 40 t.
6388. Lot No. 30403 York/Glasgow 1958-60. 40 t.

6380	(86386, 93386)	**B**	U ES	PI
6381	(86187, 93187)	**B**	U ES	PI
6382	(86295, 93295)	**B**	U ES	PI
6383	(86664, 93664)	**B**	U ES	PI
6384	(86955, 93955)	**B**	U ES	PI
6385	(86515, 93515)	**B**	U ES	PI
6386	(86859, 93859)	**B**	U ES	PI
6387	(86973, 93973)	**B**	U ES	PI
6388	(86562, 93562)	**B**	U ES	PI
6389	(86135, 93135)	**B**	U ES	PI

GS5 (HSBV)   HST BARRIER VEHICLE

Dia. Converted from BG. a. B4 bogies.

6392. Lot No. 30715 Gloucester 1962. 29.5 t.
6393/6/7. Lot No. 30716 Gloucester 1962. 29.5 t.
6394. Lot No. 30162 Pressed Steel 1956-7. 30.5 t.
6395. Lot No. 30484 Pressed Steel 1958. 30.5 t.
6398/9. Lot No. 30400 Pressed Steel 1957-8. 30.5 t.

6392	(81588, 92183)	**PL**	P PL	NL
6393	(81609, 92196)	**PL**	P PL	NL
6394	(80878, 92906)	**PL**	P PL	NL
6395	(81506, 92148)	**PL**	P PL	NL
6396	(81606, 92195)	**PL**	P PL	NL
6397	(81600, 92190)	**PL**	P PL	NL
6398	(81471, 92126)	**PL**	P PL	NL
6399	(81367, 92994)	**PL**	P PL	NL

AD2C (FO)   OPEN SECOND

Dia. AD205. Mark 2C. Pressure ventilated. Declassified open firsts. -/42 2T. B4 bogies. a. ETH 4.

Lot No. 30810 Derby 1970. 33 t.

| 6400 | (3167) | **BG** | J | Melmerby | 6415 | (3155) | **BG** | J | Melmerby |
| 6414 | (3161) | **BG** | J | Melmerby | | | | | |

AG2C (TSOT)   OPEN STANDARD (TROLLEY)

Dia. AG201. Mark 2C. Converted from TSO by removal of one seating bay and
replacing this by a counter with a space for a trolley. Adjacent toilet removed
and converted to steward's washing area/store. Pressure ventilated. -/54 1T. B4
bogies. a. ETH 4.

Lot No. 30795 Derby 1969-70. 32.5 t.

6510	(5518)	**BG**	J	Norwich Goods	6523	(5569)	**BG**	C	CS
6513	(5538)	**N**	E	OM	6528	(5592)	**M**	C	SS CS
6517	(5499)	**N**	E	OM					

AG2D (TSOT)   OPEN STANDARD (TROLLEY)

Dia. AG202. Mark 2D. Converted from TSO by removal of one seating bay and
replacing this by a counter with a space for a trolley. Adjacent toilet removed
and converted to steward's washing area/store. Air conditioned. Stones
equipment. -/54 1T. B4 bogies. a. ETH 5.

Lot No. 30822 Derby 1971. 33 t.

6609	(5698)		E	Kineton	6619	(5655)	E	Kineton

AN2D (RMBT)   MINIATURE BUFFET CAR

Dia. AN207. Mark 2D. Converted from TSOT by the removal of another seating
bay and fitting a proper buffet counter with boiler and microwave oven. Air
conditioned. Stones equipment. -/46 1T. B4 bogies. a. payphone. Catering staff-
shore telephone. Secondary door locks. ETH 5.

Lot No. 30822 Derby 1971. 33 t.

6652	(5622, 6602)	E	Long Marston
6660	(5627, 6610)	E	CP
6661	(5736, 6611)	E	CP
6662	(5641, 6612)	E	Long Marston
6665	(5721, 6615)	E	Long Marston

AN1F (RLO)   SLEEPER RECEPTION CAR

Dia. AN101 (AN102*). Mark 2F. Converted from FO, these vehicles consist of
pantry, microwave cooking facilities, seating area for passengers, telephone
booth and staff toilet. 6703-8 also have a bar. Converted at RTC, Derby (6700),
Ilford (6701-5) and Derby (6706-8). Air conditioned. 26/- 1T. B4 bogies. a.
payphone. Catering staff-shore telephone. Secondary door locks. ETH 5X.

6700-2/4/8. Lot No. 30859 Derby 1973-4. 33.5 t.
6703/5-7. Lot No. 30845 Derby 1973. 33.5 t.

6700	(3347)		E	SR	IS
6701	(3346)	*	E	SR	IS
6702	(3421)	*	E	SR	IS
6703	(3308)		E	SR	IS

6704	(3341)	E	SR	IS
6705	(3310, 6430)	E	SR	IS
6706	(3283, 6421)	E	SR	IS
6707	(3276, 6418)	E	SR	IS
6708	(3370)	E	SR	IS

AC2F (TSO)   OPEN STANDARD

Dia. AC224. Mark 2F. Renumbered 1985-6 from FO. Converted 1990 to TSO with mainly unidirectional seating and power-operated sliding doors. Air conditioned. B4 bogies. -/74 2T + one tip-up seat. 6800-14 were converted by BREL Derby and have Temperature Ltd. air conditioning. 6815-29 were converted by RFS Industries Doncaster and have Stones air conditioning. a. Secondary door locks. ETH 5X.

6800-07. 6810-12. 6813-14. 6819/22/28. Lot No. 30859 Derby 1973-4. 33 t.
6808-6809. Lot No. 30873 Derby 1974-5. 33.5 t.
6815-18. 6820-21. 6823-27. 6829. Lot No. 30845 Derby 1973. 33 t.

6800	(3323, 6435)	E	AR	NC
6801	(3349, 6442)	E	AR	NC
6802	(3339, 6439)	E	AR	NC
6803	(3355, 6443)	E	AR	NC
6804	(3396, 6449)	E	AR	NC
6805	(3324, 6436)	E	AR	NC
6806	(3342, 6440)	E	AR	NC
6807	(3423, 6452)	E	AR	NC
6808	(3430, 6454)	E	AR	NC
6809	(3435, 6455)	E	AR	NC
6810	(3404, 6451)	E	AR	NC
6811	(3327, 6437)	E	AR	NC
6812	(3394, 6448)	E	AR	NC
6813	(3410, 6463)	E	AR	NC
6814	(3422, 6465)	E	AR	NC
6815	(3282, 6420)	E	AR	NC
6816	(3316, 6461)	E	AR	NC
6817	(3311, 6431)	E	AR	NC
6818	(3298, 6427)	E	AR	NC
6819	(3365, 6446)	E	AR	NC
6820	(3320, 6434)	E	AR	NC
6821	(3281, 6458)	E	AR	NC
6822	(3376, 6447)	E	AR	NC
6823	(3289, 6424)	E	AR	NC
6824	(3307, 6429)	E	AR	NC
6825	(3301, 6460)	E	AR	NC
6826	(3294, 6425)	E	AR	NC
6827	(3306, 6428)	E	AR	NC
6828	(3380, 6464)	E	AR	NC
6829	(3288, 6423)	E	AR	NC

NM51   MERSEYRAIL SANDITE COACH

Dia. NM504. Mark 1. Former Class 501 750 V d.c. third rail EMU driving trailers converted for use as Sandite / de-icing coaches. Mark 1 Bogies.

Lot No. 30328 Ashford/Eastleigh 1958.   . t.

6910	(75178, 97734)	**MD** Q DI	BD
6911	(75180, 97734)	**MD** Q DI	BD

AH2Z (BSOT) OPEN BRAKE STANDARD (MICRO-BUFFET)

Dia. AH203. Mark 2. Converted from BSO by removal of one seating bay and replacing this by a counter with a space for a trolley. Adjacent toilet removed and converted to a steward's washing area/store. -/23 OL. v. ETH 4.

Lot No. 30757 Derby 1966. 31 t.

9100	(9405)	**RR** E	Longtown
9101	(9398)	**RR** E	Longtown
9105	(9404)	**RR** E	Longtown

AE21 (BSO)   OPEN BRAKE STANDARD

Dia. AE201. Mark 1. -/39 1T. Mark 1 bogies. xk. ETH 3.

Lot No. 30170 Doncaster 1955. 34 t.

9227   **M** S SS   BO

AE2Z (BSO)   OPEN BRAKE STANDARD

Dia. AE203. Mark 2. These vehicles use the same body shell as the mark 2 BFK and have first class seat spacing and wider tables. Pressure ventilated. -/31 1T. B4 bogies. v. ETH 4.

9385	**H** E	Longtown	BALMACARA
9388	**H** E	Longtown	BRAHAN SEER
9414	**H** E	Longtown	BAILECHAUL

AE2A (BSO)   OPEN BRAKE STANDARD

Dia. AE204. Mark 2A. These vehicles use the same body shell as the mark 2A BFK and have first class seat spacing and wider tables. Pressure ventilated. -/31 1T. B4 bogies. a. ETH 4.

9417-9424. Lot No. 30777 Derby 1967. 31.5 t.
9428-9438. Lot No. 30788 Derby 1968. 31.5 t.

9417	**RR** E	Long Marston	9424	**RR** E	CP
9418	**RR** E	Long Marston	9428	**RR** E	CP
9419	**RR** E	Long Marston	9431	**RR** E	Long Marston
9421	**RR** E	Long Marston	9434	**RR** E	LL

| 9435 | **RR** E | Long Marston | 9438 | **RR** E | CP |

AE2C (BSO)   OPEN BRAKE STANDARD

Dia. AE205. Mark 2C. Pressure ventilated. -/31 1T. B4 bogies. a. ETH 4.

9440-48. Lot No. 30798 Derby 1970. 32 t.
9458. Lot No. 30820 Derby 1970. 32 t.

Non-Standard Livery: 9440 is in Royal blue with white lining.

| 9440 | **0** C WW BK | | 9448 | **M** C WW BK | |
| 9444 | **BG** J | Norwich Goods | 9458 | **RR** E | LL |

AE2D (BSO)   OPEN BRAKE STANDARD

Dia. AE206. Mark 2D. Air conditioned (Stones). -/31 1T. B4 bogies. a. pg. ETH 5.

Lot No. 30824 Derby 1971. 33 t.

9479	d	E XC	MA	9486		E	Long Marston
9480	d	E XC	MA	9488	d	E	Long Marston
9481	d	E GW	LA	9489	d	E XC	MA
9482		E	NL	9490	d	E	Longtown
9483		E	Long Marston	9492	d	E GW	LA
9484	d	E	Longtown	9493	d	E XC	DY
9485		E	Longtown	9494		E	Long Marston

AE2E (BSO)   OPEN BRAKE STANDARD

Dia. AE207. Mark 2E. Air conditioned (Stones). -/32 1T. B4 bogies. a. pg. ETH 5.

Lot No. 30838 Derby 1972. 33 t.

9496	d	E XC	MA	9503	d	E XC	DY
9497	d	E XC	MA	9504	d	E XC	MA
9498	d	E XC	DY	9505	d	E XC	MA
9499		E	ZH	9506	d	E XC	MA
9500	d	E XC	MA	9507	d	E XC	MA
9501	d	E GW	LA	9508	d	E XC	DY
9502	d	E XC	DY	9509	d	E XC	MA

AE2F (BSO)   OPEN BRAKE STANDARD

Dia. AE208. Mark 2F. Air conditioned (Temperature Ltd.). All now refurbished with power-operated vestibule doors, new panels and seat trim. -/32 1T. B4 bogies. Secondary door locks. a. pg. ETH 5X.

Lot No. 30861 Derby 1974. 34 t.

9513		E XC	DY	9521		E XC	DY
9516	n	E XC	MA	9522		E XC	MA
9520	n	E XC	MA	9523		E XC	MA

9524	n	E	XC	DY	9531		E	XC	MA
9525		E	XC	DY	9537	n	E	XC	DY
9526	n	E	XC	DY	9538		E	XC	DY
9527	d	E	XC	DY	9539		E	XC	DY
9529		E	XC	MA					

AF2F (DBSO)   DRIVING OPEN BRAKE STANDARD

Dia. AF201. Mark 2F. Air conditioned (Temperature Ltd.). Push & pull (t.d.m. system). Converted from BSO, these vehicles originally had half cabs at the brake end. They have since been refurbished and have had their cabs widened and the outer gangways removed. Fitted with cowcatchers. Cab to shore communication. BR Cellnet phone and data transmitter. Secondary door locks. -/32 1T. B4 bogies. a. pg. ETH 5X.

9701-9710. Lot No. 30861 Derby 1974. Converted 1979. Disc brakes. 34 t.
9711-9713. Lot No. 30861 Derby 1974. Converted Glasgow 1985. 34 t.
9714. Lot No. 30861 Derby 1974. Converted Glasgow 1986. Disc brakes. 34 t.

9701	(9528)	E	AR	NC	9709	(9515)	E	AR	NC
9702	(9510)	E	AR	NC	9710	(9518)	E	AR	NC
9703	(9517)	E	AR	NC	9711	(9532)	E	AR	NC
9704	(9512)	E	AR	NC	9712	(9534)	E	AR	NC
9705	(9519)	E	AR	NC	9713	(9535)	E	AR	NC
9707	(9511)	E	AR	NC	9714	(9536)	E	AR	NC
9708	(9530)	E	AR	NC					

AJ1G (RFM) RESTAURANT BUFFET FIRST (MODULAR)

Dia. AJ103 (10200/1 are Dia. AJ101). Mark 3A. Air conditioned. Converted from HST TRFKs, RFBs and FOs. 22/- (24/-*). BT10 bogies. a. q. Fitted with payphone. Secondary door locks. ETH 14X.

10200-10211. Lot No. 30884 Derby 1977.
10212-10229. Lot\No. 30878 Derby 1975-6. 39.80 t.
10230-10260. Lot No. 30890 Derby 1979. 39.80 t.

10200	(40519) *	P		ZD	10216	(11041)	P	AR	NC
10201	(40520) *	P	WC	OY	10217	(11051)	P	WC	OY
10202	(40504)	P	WC	OY	10218	(11053)	P	WC	MA
10203	(40506)	P	AR	NC	10219	(11047)	P	WC	OY
10204	(40502)	P	WC	MA	10220	(11056)	P	WC	OY
10205	(40503)	P	WC	OY	10221	(11012)	P	WC	PC
10206	(40507)	P	WC	PC	10222	(11063)	P	WC	MA
10207	(40516)	P	WC	MA	10223	(11043)	P	AR	NC
10208	(40517)	P	WC	PC	10224	(11062)	P	WC	MA
10209	(40508)	P	WC	PC	10225	(11014)	P	WC	OY
10210	(40509)	P	WC	MA	10226	(11015)	P	WC	PC
10211	(40510)	P	WC	PC	10227	(11057)	P	WC	MA
10212	(11049)	P	WC	PC	10228	(11035)	P	AR	NC
10213	(11050)	P	WC	MA	10229	(11059)	P	WC	OY
10214	(11034)	P	AR	NC	10230	(10021)	P	WC	PC
10215	(11032)	P	WC	PC	10231	(10016)	P	WC	PC

10232 (10027)	P	WC	OY	10248 (10005)	P	WC	PC
10233 (10013)	P	WC	MA	10249 (10012)	P	WC	PC
10234 (10004)	P	WC	PC	10250 (10020)	P	WC	OY
10235 (10015)	P	WC	OY	10251 (10024)	P	WC	OY
10236 (10018)	P	WC	PC	10252 (10008)	P	WC	MA
10237 (10022)	P	WC	PC	10253 (10026)	P	WC	MA
10238 (10017)	P	WC	OY	10254 (10006)	P	WC	PC
10240 (10003)	P	WC	OY	10255 (10010)	P	WC	OY
10241 (10009)	P	AR	NC	10256 (10028)	P	WC	PC
10242 (10002)	P	WC	PC	10257 (10007)	P	WC	MA
10245 (10019)	P	WC	MA	10258 (10023)	P	WC	MA
10246 (10014)	P	WC	OY	10259 (10025)	P	WC	OY
10247 (10011)	P	AR	NC	10260 (10001)	P	WC	MA

AJ1J (RFM) RESTAURANT BUFFET FIRST (MODULAR)

Dia. AJ105. Mark 4. Air conditioned. 20/- 1T. SIG bogies (BT41). a. ETH   X.

Lot No. 31045 Metro-Cammell 1989 onwards. 45.5 t.

10300	**GN**	E	GN	BN	10317		E	GN	BN
10301		E	GN	BN	10318	**GN**	E	GN	BN
10302		E	GN	BN	10319	**GN**	E	GN	BN
10303		E	GN	BN	10320	**GN**	E	GN	BN
10304	**GN**	E	GN	BN	10321		E	GN	BN
10305		E	GN	BN	10322		E	GN	BN
10306		E	GN	BN	10323		E	GN	BN
10307		E	GN	BN	10324		E	GN	BN
10308		E	GN	BN	10325		E	GN	BN
10309		E	GN	BN	10326		E	GN	BN
10310		E	GN	BN	10327	**GN**	E	GN	BN
10311		E	GN	BN	10328		E	GN	BN
10312		E	GN	BN	10329		E	GN	BN
10313		E	GN	BN	10330		E	GN	BN
10314		E	GN	BN	10331		E	GN	BN
10315		E	GN	BN	10332		E	GN	BN
10316		E	GN	BN	10333		E	GN	BN

AU4G (SLEP)   SLEEPING CAR WITH PANTRY

Dia. AU401. Mark 3A. Air conditioned. 12 compartments with a fixed lower berth and a hinged upper berth, plus an attendants compartment with 2T (controlled emission). BT10 bogies. a. ETH 7X.

10569 is leased to the Venice Simplon Orient Express.

Lot No. 30960 Derby 1981-3.

10500		N	Ferme Park	10506	d	P	SR	IS
10501	d	P	SR	IS	10507	d	P	SR	IS
10502	d	P	SR	IS	10508	d	P	SR	IS
10503		N	Ferme Park	10510	d	P	SR	IS
10504	d	P	SR	IS	10512	d	P		ZG

10513 d		N	SR	Ferme Park	10567		P		ZG
10514		M	SS	BN	10569 d	PC	P	SS	SL
10515 d		P	SR	IS	10570		P		Kineton
10516 d		P	SR	IS	10571		X		Ferme Park
10519 d		P	SR	IS	10572 d		N		ZD
10520 d		P	SR	IS	10573 d		P		ZD
10522 d		P	SR	IS	10574		M	SS	BN
10523 d		P	SR	IS	10575		N		Ferme Park
10526 d		P	SR	IS	10577	BG	P		ZD
10527 d		P	SR	IS	10578		P		Kineton
10529 d		P	SR	IS	10579	BG	P		Kineton
10530 d		P		ZD	10580 d		P	SR	IS
10531 d		P	SR	IS	10582 d		P		ZD
10532 d		P	GW	LA	10583 d		P	GW	LA
10533		P		ZD	10584 d		P	GW	LA
10534 d		P	GW	LA	10586 d		P		Kineton
10535 d		P		ZD	10588 d		P	GW	LA
10536 d		P		Kineton	10589 d		P	GW	LA
10537 d		P		ZD	10590 d		P	GW	LA
10538 d		P		Kineton	10591		P		Kineton
10539 d		P		Kineton	10592		P		Kineton
10540 d		P		ZD	10593 d		P		Kineton
10541 d		G	SS	EN	10594 d		P	GW	LA
10542 d		P	SR	IS	10595	BG	P		Kineton
10543 d		P	SR	IS	10596 d		P		Kineton
10544 d		P	SR	IS	10597 d		P	SR	IS
10546		P		ZD	10598 d		P	SR	IS
10547 d		P	SR	IS	10599		P		Kineton
10548 d		P	SR	IS	10600 d		P	SR	IS
10549 d		P		ZD	10601		P		ZD
10550 d		P		ZD	10602		P		ZD
10551 d		P	SR	IS	10603		P		Kineton
10552 d		P		WB	10604		P		ZD
10553 d		P	SR	IS	10605 d		P	SR	IS
10554 d		P		ZD	10606		P		Kineton
10555 d		P		Kineton	10607 d		P	SR	IS
10556 d		G	SS	EN	10608		P		ZN
10557 d		P		ZD	10609	BG	P		ZG
10558 d		P		ZH	10610 d		P	SR	IS
10559 d		P		Kineton	10612 d		P	GW	LA
10560 d		P		ZD	10613 d		P	SR	IS
10561 d		P	SR	IS	10614 d		P	SR	IS
10562 d		P	SR	IS	10615		P		WB
10563 d		P	GW	LA	10616 d		P	GW	LA
10565 d		P	SR	IS	10617 d		P	SR	IS
10566 d		P		ZD					

AS4G (SLE)   SLEEPING CAR

Dia. AS403. Mark 3A. Air conditioned. 13 compartments with a fixed lower berth and a hinged upper berth. 2T (controlled emission). BT10 bogies. a. ETH 6X.

Lot No. 30961 Derby 1980-4.

No.	d	BG	Code	Sub	Location	No.	d	BG	Code	Sub	Location
10646	d		N	SS	Ferme Park	10693	d		P	SR	IS
10647	d		P		Kineton	10696	d		P		Kineton
10648	d		P	SR	IS	10697	d		P		Kineton
10649	d		P		Kineton	10699	d		P	SR	IS
10650	d		P	SR	IS	10700		BG	P		Kineton
10651	d		P		ZD	10701	d		P		Kineton
10653	d		P		ZD	10702			N	SS	Ferme Park
10654	d		P		ZD	10703	d		P	SR	IS
10655			N	SS	Ferme Park	10704	d		T	TT	ZA
10656			P		Kineton	10706	d		P	SR	IS
10657			N	SS	Ferme Park	10707			P		ZG
10658	d		P		Kineton	10708	d		P		ZD
10660	d		P		ZD	10709	d		P		ZD
10662			P		ZD	10710	d		P		Kineton
10663	d		P	SR	IS	10711	d		P		ZD
10665		BG	P		ZG	10712	d		P		ZD
10666	d		P	SR	IS	10713	d		P		ZD
10668	d		P		ZA	10714	d		P	SR	IS
10670			P		Kineton	10715	d		P		ZD
10672	d		P		ZG	10716	d		P		ZD
10674	d		P		ZG	10717	d		P		ZA
10675	d		P	SR	IS	10718	d		P	SR	IS
10678		BG	P		Kineton	10719	d		P	SR	IS
10679		BG	P		Kineton	10720			P		Kineton
10680	d		P	SR	IS	10722	d		P	SR	IS
10682	d		P		ZD	10723	d		P	SR	IS
10683	d		P	SR	IS	10724			N		Ferme Park
10684		BG	P		Kineton	10725			N		Ferme Park
10685	d		P		ZH	10726			N		Ferme Park
10686	d		P		ZD	10727			N		Ferme Park
10687	d		P		ZD	10728			P		ZN
10688	d		P	SR	IS	10729			N		Ferme Park
10689	d		P	SR	IS	10730	d		P		ZD
10690	d		P	SR	IS	10731	d		P		Kineton
10691	d		P		ZD	10732	d		P		Kineton
10692	d		P		ZD						

AD1G (FO)   OPEN FIRST

Dia. AD108. Mark 3A. Air conditioned. All now facelifted with new upholstery, carpets etc. 11005-7 have regained their original numbers, having being converted back from open composites 11905-7. 48/- 2T. BT10 bogies. Secondary door locks. a. ETH 6X.

Lot No. 30878 Derby 1975-6. 34.30 t.

11005	P WC PC		11031	P WC PC
11006	P WC PC		11033	P WC PC
11007	P WC PC		11036	P WC PC
11011 z	P WC PC		11037	P WC PC
11013	P WC PC		11038	P WC PC
11016	P WC PC		11039	P WC PC
11017	P WC PC		11040	P WC PC
11018	P WC PC		11042	P WC PC
11019	P WC PC		11044	P WC PC
11020	P WC PC		11045	P WC PC
11021	P WC PC		11046	P WC PC
11023	P WC PC		11048	P WC PC
11024	P WC PC		11052	P WC PC
11026	P WC PC		11054	P WC PC
11027	P WC PC		11055	P WC PC
11028	P WC PC		11058	P WC PC
11029	P WC PC		11060	P WC PC
11030	P WC PC			

AD1H (FO)   OPEN FIRST

Dia. AD109. Mark 3B. Air conditioned. Inter-City 80 seats. 48/- 2T. BT10 bogies. a. Secondary door locks. ETH 6X.

Lot No. 30982 Derby 1985. 36.46 t.

11064	P WC MA		11083 p	P WC MA
11065	P WC MA		11084 p	P WC MA
11066	P WC MA		11085 p	P WC MA
11067	P WC MA		11086 p	P WC MA
11068	P WC MA		11087 p	P WC MA
11069	P WC MA		11088 p	P WC MA
11070	P WC MA		11089 p	P WC MA
11071	P WC MA		11090 p	P WC MA
11072	P WC MA		11091 p	P WC MA
11073	P WC MA		11092 p	P WC MA
11074	P WC PC		11093 p	P WC MA
11075	P WC MA		11094 p	P WC MA
11076	P WC MA		11095 p	P WC MA
11077	P WC MA		11096 p	P WC MA
11078	P WC MA		11097 p	P WC MA
11079	P WC MA		11098 p	P WC MA
11080	P WC MA		11099 p	P WC MA
11081	P WC MA		11100 p	P WC MA
11082	P WC MA		11101 p	P WC MA

AD1J (FO)   OPEN FIRST

Dia. AD111. Mark 4. Air conditioned. Known as 'Pullman open' by GNER. 46/ 1T. SIG bogies (BT41). a. ETH 6.

11264-71 were cancelled.

Lot No. 31046 Metro-Cammell 1989-92. 39.70 t.

11200			E	GN	BN	11235	p	GN E	GN	BN
11201	p		E	GN	BN	11236		GN E	GN	BN
11202			E	GN	BN	11237	p	E	GN	BN
11203	p		E	GN	BN	11238		E	GN	BN
11204	p		E	GN	BN	11239	p	E	GN	BN
11205		GN	E	GN	BN	11240		E	GN	BN
11206			E	GN	BN	11241		E	GN	BN
11207	p		E	GN	BN	11242	p	E	GN	BN
11208			E	GN	BN	11243	p	E	GN	BN
11209			E	GN	BN	11244		GN E	GN	BN
11210			E	GN	BN	11245		GN E	GN	BN
11211	p		E	GN	BN	11246	p	E	GN	BN
11212			E	GN	BN	11247	p	E	GN	BN
11213	p		E	GN	BN	11248		GN E	GN	BN
11214	p		E	GN	BN	11249	p	GN E	GN	BN
11215			E	GN	BN	11250		E	GN	BN
11216			E	GN	BN	11251	p	E	GN	BN
11217	p		E	GN	BN	11252		E	GN	BN
11218			E	GN	BN	11253	p	E	GN	BN
11219	p		E	GN	BN	11254		E	GN	BN
11220			E	GN	BN	11255	p	E	GN	BN
11221	p		E	GN	BN	11256		E	GN	BN
11222	p		E	GN	BN	11257	p	E	GN	BN
11223			E	GN	BN	11258		E	GN	BN
11224			E	GN	BN	11259	p	E	GN	BN
11225	p		E	GN	BN	11260		E	GN	BN
11226			E	GN	BN	11261	p	E	GN	BN
11227	p		E	GN	BN	11262		E	GN	BN
11228	p	GN	E	GN	BN	11263	p	E	GN	BN
11229	p	GN	E	GN	BN	11272		E	GN	BN
11230			E	GN	BN	11273		E	GN	BN
11231	p		E	GN	BN	11274		E	GN	BN
11232		GN	E	GN	BN	11275		E	GN	BN
11233	p	GN	E	GN	BN	11276		E	GN	BN
11234		GN	E	GN	BN					

AC2G (TSO)   OPEN STANDARD

Dia. AC213 (AC220 z). Mark 3A. Air conditioned. All now refurbished with modified seat backs and new layout. 12169-72 have been converted from open composites 11908-10/22, formerly FOs 11008-10/22. -/76 2T (-/74 2T z). BT10 (BREL T4*, BT15 b) bogies. a. Secondary door locks. ETH 6X.

Lot No. 30877 Derby 1975-7. 34.30 t.

12004		P	WC	PC	12008		P	WC	PC
12005		P	WC	PC	12009		P	WC	MA
12007		P	WC	PC	12010	b	P	WC	PC

Pullman Stock. Umber & cream liveried Kitchen First No. 284 'VERA' is pictured at Southall, West London on 13th June 1996. The coach has had its Gresley bogies replaced with B5 (SR) bogies.
Kevin Conkey

▲ Parlour First No. 553 'KING ARTHUR' is pictured at Blackpool North carriage sidings on 20th July 1995. The vehicle is in a maroon and beige livery which is used on the former "Statesman" Pullman set. *Colin J. Marsden*

▼ **Mark 1 Stock.** Waterman Railways VIP liveried Resturant First No. 325 at Cheltenham Spa on 14th March 1996. The train was running in connection with the races taking place at that time. This vehicle was previously used as the Royal Train staff dining car. *Denise Johnson*

▲ Intercity liveried Restaurant Buffet No. 1699 passes Stratford in the formation of the 12.30 London Liverpool Street–Norwich on 13th June 1996. *Kevin Conkey*

▼ Green and cream Open First No. 3125 'LOCH SHIEL'. *Colin J. Marsden*

▲ Open Standard No. 5029 at Crewe in the formation of the 17.18 to Holyhead on 17th August 1996. The chocolate and cream liveried vehicle was on loan to North West Regional Railways at that time.
Martyn Hilbert

▼ Railfilms owned Open Standard No. 5067 pictured carrying LMS maroon livery on 17th August 1996. *Hugh Ballantyne*

▲ **Mark 2A Stock.** Corridor Brake First No. 35515 at Crewe on 7th September 1996. The Regional Railways liveried coach was in the formation of the 12.18 North West Regional Railways service to Holyhead. *Peter Fox*

▼ **Mark 2B Stock.** West Coast Railway Company Open Standard No. 5491 in royal blue livery at Westbury on 8th July 1996.

Colin J. Marsden

▲ **Mark 2E Stock.** Intercity liveried Open Standard No. 5903 at Penrith in the formation of the 16.08 Glasgow Central–Reading CrossCountry Trains service. The date is 26th June 1996.

Kevin Conkey

▼ **Mark 2F Stock.** Buffet Open First No. 1221 ascends Acton Bank as the rear vehicle in the formation of the 07.17 Manchester Piccadilly–Brighton CrossCountry Trains service on 20th November 1995.

Kevin Conkey

Driving Brake Standard Open No. 9703 leads the 11.30 London Liverpool Street-Norwich Anglia Railways service at Ipswich on 13th August 1996.
Colin J. Marsden

Mark 3 Stock. The new Great Western Trains livery of ivory and green is pictured here on HST Open First No. 41056 at Bristol Temple Meads on 30th September 1996.

Colin J. Marsden

Mark 3A Stock. Royal train staff sleeping car No. 2914 is pictured passing through Malvern Wells on 3rd May 1996. A dark purple livery is carried by all royal train coaches. *Stephen Widdowson*

Eurostar (GB) night stock generator coach No. 6372 is pictured between a pair of Class 37/6 locomotives at Old Oak Common on 5th October 1996. The coach carries a livery of two-tone grey with a dark blue roof, as applied to all Eurostar (GB) locomotives.
Kevin Conkey

▲ Venice Simplon Orient Express sleeping car No. 10569 'LEVIA-THAN' is seen at Stewarts Lane carriage sidings on 5th June 1996. Umber and cream Pullman livery is carried. *Brian Denton*

▼ Open Standard No. 12045 in the formation of the 11.20 Preston–London Euston West Coast service at Preston on 4th May 1996.
Martyn Hilbert

Mark 4 Stock. The new GNER livery of dark blue with an orange bodyside stripe is seen here on Open Standard No. 12313 at Copley Hill on 21st October 1996.

Les Nixon

NPCCS Mark 3B Driving Van Trailer 82138 leads the 15.40 Glasgow Central–London Euston Intercity West Coast service as it departs from Penrith on 23rd June 1996.
Kevin Conkey

The 18.00 Great North Eastern Railway service to London Kings Cross leaves Glasgow Central on 29th August 1996 with Mark 4 Driving Van Trailer No. 82219 at the front of the formation. *Colin J. Marsden*

▲ Royal Mail liveried Post Office Stowage Van No. 80416 at Didcot Railway Centre on 23rd September 1995. *Colin J. Marsden*

▼ Rail Express Systems liveried Super BG No. 94191 is pictured with another similar coach soon after conversion. The date is 9th August 1995. *Colin J. Marsden*

▲ Trials were conducted with the new Propelling Control Vehicles on the West Somerset Railway prior to their entry into traffic. PCV No. 94315 and Class 47 No. 47733 'Eastern Star' are pictured here at Blue Anchor on 15th August 1996. *Colin J. Marsden*

▼ Several GUVs have been converted to Super GUVs but without a central roller shutter door or the full Rail Express Systems livery. One of the vehicles, No. 95749 is seen here at Railcare's Glasgow Works after conversion on 29th August 1996. *Colin J. Marsden*

12011		P	WC	PC	12064	P WC PC
12012		P	WC	MA	12065	P WC PC
12013		P	WC	PC	12066	P WC PC
12014		P	WC	PC	12067	P WC PC
12015		P	WC	PC	12068	P WC MA
12016		P	WC	PC	12069	P WC PC
12017		P	WC	PC	12070	P WC MA
12019		P	WC	PC	12071	P WC MA
12020		P	WC	MA	12072	P WC MA
12021		P	WC	MA	12073	P WC PC
12022		P	WC	PC	12075	P WC MA
12023		P	WC	PC	12076	P WC MA
12024		P	WC	PC	12077	P WC MA
12025		P	WC	PC	12078	P WC PC
12026		P	WC	PC	12079	P WC PC
12027		P	WC	PC	12080	P WC MA
12028		P	WC	PC	12081	P WC MA
12029		P	WC	PC	12082	P WC PC
12030		P	WC	PC	12083	P WC MA
12031		P	WC	PC	12084	P WC MA
12032		P	WC	PC	12085 w	P WC PC
12033 z		P	WC	PC	12086 w	P WC MA
12034		P	WC	MA	12087 w	P WC MA
12035		P	WC	MA	12088 z	P WC PC
12036		P	WC	MA	12089	P WC MA
12037		P	WC	MA	12090	P WC MA
12038		P	WC	MA	12091	P WC MA
12040		P	WC	PC	12092	P WC PC
12041		P	WC	PC	12093	P WC MA
12042 w		P	WC	MA	12094	P WC PC
12043		P	WC	PC	12095	P WC PC
12044		P	WC	PC	12096	P WC PC
12045		P	WC	PC	12097	P WC PC
12046		P	WC	PC	12098	P WC MA
12047 z		P	WC	PC	12099	P WC MA
12048		P	WC	PC	12100 z	P WC PC
12049		P	WC	PC	12101 w	P WC MA
12050 w		P	WC	PC	12102	P WC MA
12051		P	WC	PC	12103 z	P WC PC
12052		P	WC	PC	12104	P WC PC
12053		P	WC	PC	12105	P WC MA
12054 z		P	WC	PC	12106	P WC MA
12055		P	WC	MA	12107	P WC MA
12056		P	WC	MA	12108 w	P WC MA
12057		P	WC	PC	12109 w	P WC MA
12058		P	WC	PC	12110	P WC MA
12059 w		P	WC	MA	12111	P WC PC
12060		P	WC	MA	12112 z	P WC PC
12061 w		P	WC	MA	12113	P WC MA
12062		P	WC	MA	12114	P WC PC
12063		P	WC	PC	12115	P WC PC

12116		P	WC	PC	12144	w	P	WC	MA
12117		P	WC	PC	12145		P	WC	PC
12118		P	WC	MA	12146			WC	MA
12119		P	WC	PC	12147		P	WC	PC
12120		P	WC	MA	12148		P	WC	PC
12121		P	WC	MA	12149		P	WC	PC
12122	z	P	WC	PC	12150		P	WC	PC
12123		P	WC	PC	12151		P	WC	PC
12124		P	WC	MA	12152		P	WC	MA
12125		P	WC	MA	12153		P	WC	MA
12126		P	WC	PC	12154		P	WC	MA
12127		P	WC	MA	12155	w	P	WC	MA
12128	w	P	WC	MA	12156		P	WC	PC
12129		P	WC	MA	12157		P	WC	MA
12130		P	WC	PC	12158		P	WC	MA
12131		P	WC	MA	12159		P	WC	MA
12132		P	WC	MA	12160	w	P	WC	MA
12133		P	WC	PC	12161	z	P	WC	PC
12134		P	WC	MA	12163		P	WC	PC
12135		P	WC	PC	12164		P	WC	MA
12136		P	WC	MA	12165		P	WC	PC
12137		P	WC	PC	12166		P	WC	PC
12138		P	WC	MA	12167		P	WC	MA
12139		P	WC	MA	12168	w	P	WC	MA
12140	*z	P	WC	PC	12169	z	P	WC	PC
12141		P	WC	MA	12170	z	P	WC	PC
12142	z	P	WC	PC	12171	z	P	WC	PC
12143		P	WC	MA	12172	z	P	WC	PC

AI2J (TSOE)   OPEN STANDARD (END)

Dia. AI201. Mark 4. Air conditioned. -/74 2T. SIG bogies (BT41). a. ETH 6.

12232 was converted from the original 12405.

Lot No. 31047 Metro-Cammell 1989-91. 39.5 t.

12200		E	GN	BN	12215			E	GN	BN
12201		E	GN	BN	12216			E	GN	BN
12202		E	GN	BN	12217	GN		E	GN	BN
12203		E	GN	BN	12218	GN		E	GN	BN
12204		E	GN	BN	12219			E	GN	BN
12205		E	GN	BN	12220			E	GN	BN
12206		E	GN	BN	12222	GN		E	GN	BN
12207		E	GN	BN	12223			E	GN	BN
12208		E	GN	BN	12224			E	GN	BN
12209		E	GN	BN	12225	GN		E	GN	BN
12210		E	GN	BN	12226			E	GN	BN
12211		E	GN	BN	12227			E	GN	BN
12212		E	GN	BN	12228			E	GN	BN
12213		E	GN	BN	12229			E	GN	BN
12214	GN	E	GN	BN	12230			E	GN	BN

| 12231 | | E | GN | BN | | 12232 | | E | GN | BN |

AL2J (TSOD) OPEN STANDARD (DISABLED ACCESS)

Dia. AL201. Mark 4. Air conditioned. -/72 + wheelchair space 1T (suitable for a disabled person). SIG bogies (BT41). a. p. ETH 6.

Lot No. 31048 Metro-Cammell 1989-91. 39.4 t.

12300		E	GN	BN		12316	GN	E	GN	BN
12301		E	GN	BN		12317	GN	E	GN	BN
12302		E	GN	BN		12318		E	GN	BN
12303		E	GN	BN		12319		E	GN	BN
12304		E	GN	BN		12320		E	GN	BN
12305		E	GN	BN		12321	GN	E	GN	BN
12306		E	GN	BN		12322		E	GN	BN
12307		E	GN	BN		12323		E	GN	BN
12308		E	GN	BN		12324		E	GN	BN
12309		E	GN	BN		12325		E	GN	BN
12310		E	GN	BN		12326		E	GN	BN
12311		E	GN	BN		12327		E	GN	BN
12312		E	GN	BN		12328		E	GN	BN
12313	GN	E	GN	BN		12329		E	GN	BN
12314	GN	E	GN	BN		12330		E	GN	BN
12315		E	GN	BN						

AC2J (TSO) OPEN STANDARD

Dia. AC214. Mark 4. Air conditioned. -/74 2T. SIG bogies (BT41). a. ETH 6X.

12405 is the second coach to carry that number. It was built from the bodyshell originally intended for 12221. The original 12405 is now 12232. 12490-12512 were cancelled.

Lot No. 31049 Metro-Cammell 1989 onwards. 39.9 t.

12400		E	GN	BN		12416		E	GN	BN
12401		E	GN	BN		12417		E	GN	BN
12402		E	GN	BN		12418		E	GN	BN
12403		E	GN	BN		12419		E	GN	BN
12404		E	GN	BN		12420		E	GN	BN
12405	GN	E	GN	BN		12421		E	GN	BN
12406	GN	E	GN	BN		12422		E	GN	BN
12407		E	GN	BN		12423		E	GN	BN
12408		E	GN	BN		12424		E	GN	BN
12409		E	GN	BN		12425		E	GN	BN
12410		E	GN	BN		12426		E	GN	BN
12411		E	GN	BN		12427		E	GN	BN
12412		E	GN	BN		12428		E	GN	BN
12413		E	GN	BN		12429		E	GN	BN
12414		E	GN	BN		12430		E	GN	BN
12415		E	GN	BN		12431		E	GN	BN

12432		E	GN	BN		12474		E	GN	BN
12433		E	GN	BN		12475		E	GN	BN
12434		E	GN	BN		12476		E	GN	BN
12435		E	GN	BN		12477		E	GN	BN
12436		E	GN	BN		12478		E	GN	BN
12437		E	GN	BN		12479		E	GN	BN
12438	GN	E	GN	BN		12480		E	GN	BN
12439		E	GN	BN		12481		E	GN	BN
12440		E	GN	BN		12482		E	GN	BN
12441		E	GN	BN		12483		E	GN	BN
12442		E	GN	BN		12484		E	GN	BN
12443		E	GN	BN		12485		E	GN	BN
12444		E	GN	BN		12486		E	GN	BN
12445	GN	E	GN	BN		12487		E	GN	BN
12446	GN	E	GN	BN		12488		E	GN	BN
12447	GN	E	GN	BN		12489		E	GN	BN
12448		E	GN	BN		12513		E	GN	BN
12449		E	GN	BN		12514	GN	E	GN	BN
12450		E	GN	BN		12515		E	GN	BN
12451		E	GN	BN		12516		E	GN	BN
12452		E	GN	BN		12517		E	GN	BN
12453		E	GN	BN		12518		E	GN	BN
12454		E	GN	BN		12519		E	GN	BN
12455		E	GN	BN		12520		E	GN	BN
12456		E	GN	BN		12521		E	GN	BN
12457		E	GN	BN		12522		E	GN	BN
12458		E	GN	BN		12523		E	GN	BN
12459		E	GN	BN		12524		E	GN	BN
12460	GN	E	GN	BN		12525		E	GN	BN
12461	GN	E	GN	BN		12526		E	GN	BN
12462	GN	E	GN	BN		12527		E	GN	BN
12463	GN	E	GN	BN		12528		E	GN	BN
12464		E	GN	BN		12529		E	GN	BN
12465		E	GN	BN		12530		E	GN	BN
12466		E	GN	BN		12531	GN	E	GN	BN
12467		E	GN	BN		12532		E	GN	BN
12468		E	GN	BN		12533		E	GN	BN
12469		E	GN	BN		12534	GN	E	GN	BN
12470	GN	E	GN	BN		12535		E	GN	BN
12471	GN	E	GN	BN		12536	GN	E	GN	BN
12472		E	GN	BN		12537		E	GN	BN
12473		E	GN	BN		12538	GN	E	GN	BN

AA11 (FK)   CORRIDOR FIRST

Dia. AA101. Mark 1. 42/- 2T. ETH 3.

13225-13230. Lot No. 30381 Ashford/Swindon 1959. B4 bogies. 33 t.
13306-13344. Lot No. 30667 Swindon 1962. Commonwealth bogies. 36 t.

f Fitted with fluorescent lighting.

13225	xk	RR	E		CQ
13227	xk	CH	R	SS	CO
13228	xk	M	S	SS	BO
13229	xk	M	S	SS	BO
13230	xk	M	S	SS	BO
13306	v	BG	W		Carlisle Yard
13317	x	M	C		CS

13318	a	M	SS		HT
13320	v	M	C		CS
13321	x	M	C	SS	CS
13323	x	M	C		CS
13331	vf	N	X		CP
13341	af	M	SS		HT
13344	vf	BG	X		Carlisle Yard

AA1A (FK)   CORRIDOR FIRST

Dia. AA106. Mark 2A. Pressure ventilated. 42/- 2T. a. B4 bogies. ETH 4.

13462. Lot No. 30774 Derby 1968. 33 t.
13467. Lot No. 30785 Derby 1968. 33 t.

13462 was renumbered 19462 for a time when declassified.

13462	a	N	X		CP

13467	a	N	X		CP

AA1B (FK)   CORRIDOR FIRST

Dia. AA107. Mark 2B. Pressure ventilated. 42/- 2T. B4 bogies. a. ETH 4.
Lot No. 30789 Derby 1969. 33 t.

13479 was renumbered 19479 for a time when declassified.

13479	N	X		CP

13482	N	X		CP

AA1D (FK)   CORRIDOR FIRST

Dia. AA109. Mark 2D. Air conditioned (Stones). 42/- 2T. B4 bogies. a. ETH 5.
13585-13607 require at least 800 V train heat supply.

Lot No. 30825 Derby 1971-2. 34.5 t.

13575	N	E	OM
13581		E	WB
13582		W	Kineton
13582		W	Kineton

13583	E	WB
13585	X	Kineton
13604	X	BN
13607	X	Hornsey Up CS

AA31 (CK)   CORRIDOR COMPOSITE

Dia. AA301. Mark 1. 24/18 1T. ETH 2.

Lot No. 30665 Derby 1961. Commonwealth bogies and metal window frames.
37 t. Numbered 7167/87/91 for a time.

16167	v	N	V		SL
16187	x	CH	R	SS	CO

16191	x	CH	R	SS	CO

AB11 (BFK)   CORRIDOR BRAKE FIRST

Dia. AB101. Mark 1. 24/- 1T. Commonwealth bogies. ETH 2.
17007. Lot No. 30382 Ashford/Swindon 1959. 35 t.

17013-17015. Lot No. 30668 Swindon 1961. 36 t.
17021-17023. Lot No. 30718 Swindon 1963. Metal window frames. 36 t.

Originally numbered 14007/13/15/21/23.

17007	x	**PC**	O LS	SO	17021	k	**M** O	OM
17013	v	**M**	N	SO	17023	x	M SS	BN
17015	x	**W**	M SS	BN				

Name: 17007 is named 'MERCATOR'.

AB1Z (BFK)   CORRIDOR BRAKE FIRST

Dia. AB102. Mark 2. Pressure ventilated. 24/- 1T. B4 bogies. d. ETH 4.

Lot No. 30756 Derby 1966. 31.5 t.

Originally numbered 14039/41/54.

17039	**RX**	E EW	CD	17054	**BG**	E	Crewe Brook Sdgs
17041	**M**	O LS	DI				

AB1A (BFK)   CORRIDOR BRAKE FIRST

Dia. AB103. Mark 2A. Pressure ventilated. 24/- 1T. B4 bogies. ETH 4.

17056-17077. Lot No. 30775 Derby 1967-8. 32 t.
17086-17102. Lot No. 30786 Derby 1968. 32 t.

Non-Standard Livery: Statesman Pullman maroon & beige. Branded 'ATTEND-ANTS CAR'.

Originally numbered 14056-102. 17089/90 were renumbered 35502/3 for a time when declassified.

17096 is leased to the Venice Simplon Orient Express.

17056	a	**N**	X	CP	17086	a	**N** E	Long Marston
17058	a	**N**	E	Long Marston	17090	v	**RR** E	Longtown
17064	v	**RR**	E	Longtown	17091	v	**RR** E	Longtown
17073	a	**N**	E	Long Marston	17096	a	**G** E SS	SL
17076	a	**N**	E	Eastleigh Dn Sdgs	17099	v	**RR** E	Longtown
17077	a	**N**	E	Long Marston	17102	a	**O** C SS	CS

AB1D (BFK)   CORRIDOR BRAKE FIRST

Dia. AB106. Mark 2D. Air conditioned (Stones equipment). 24/- 1T. B4 Bogies. 17163-17172 require at least 800 V train heat supply. a. ETH 5.

Non-Standard Livery: Waterman VIP without lining.

Originally numbered 14141-72.

Lot No. 30823 Derby 1971-2. 33.5 t.

17141	**O**	X CA	BK	17151		X	HT
17144		X	DY	17153	**W**	X SS	CS
17146		X	DY	17155		E	Kineton
17148		E	Kineton	17156		X	DY

17159		X	Hornsey Up CS	17167		X	HT
17161		W	OM	17168	M	C SS	CS
17163		E	Kineton	17169		X SS	CS
17164	0	X CA	BK	17170		X	DY
17165		X	Ferme Park	17171		W	Carlisle Yard
17166		E	Longtown	17172		X	Ferme Park

AE1G (BFO)   OPEN BRAKE FIRST

Dia. AE101. Mark 3B. Air conditioned. Fitted with hydraulic handbrake. 36/- 1T.
BT10 bogies. a. pg. Secondary door locks. ETH 5X.

Lot No. 30990 Derby 1986. 35.81 t.

17173	P WC MA	17175	P WC MA
17174	P WC MA		

AB31 (BCK)   CORRIDOR BRAKE COMPOSITE

Dia. AB301 (AB302*). Mark 1. There are two variants depending upon whether
the standard class compartments have armrests. Each vehicle has two first class
and three standard class compartments. 12/18 2T (12/24 2T*). ETH 2.

21096. Lot No. 30185. Metro-Cammell 1956. BR1 bogies. Steam heat only.
32.5 t.
21224. Lot No. 30245. Metro-Cammell 1958. B4 bogies. 33 t.
21236-21246. Lot No. 30669 Swindon 1961-2. Commonwealth bogies. 36 t.
21256. Lot No. 30731 Derby 1963. Commonwealth bogies. 37 t.
21265-21272. Lot No. 30732 Derby 1964. Commonwealth bogies. 37 t.

21096	x	M	O LS	WQ	21256	x	M	C SS	CS
21224		BG	D	Heysham	21265	a*	BG	W	Carlisle Yard
21236	v	M	R LS	ZG	21266	a*		N	Ferme Park
21241	x		M SS	HT	21268	a*		N	Ferme Park
21245	x	CC	M SS	BN	21269	a*	WV	M SS	BN
21246	a		M SS	BN	21272	x*	M	X	BN

AA21 (SK)   CORRIDOR STANDARD

Dia. AA201 (AA202*). Mark 1. Each vehicle has eight compartments. All
remaining vehicles have metal window frames and melamine interior panelling.
Commonwealth bogies. -/48 1T (-/64 1T*). ETH 4.

Non-Standard Livery: Pilkington's K (green with white red chevron and light blue
block).

25729-25893. Lot No. 30685 Derby 1961-2. 36 t.
25955. Lot No. 30686 Derby 1962. 36 t.
26013. Lot No. 30719 Derby 1962. 37 t.

f Facelifted with fluorescent lighting.

These coaches were renumbered 18729-19013 for a time.

| 25729 | x*f | M | C SS | CS | 25756 | x | 0 | C SS | CS |

25767	x	0	C SS	CS		25862	x	M	C SS	CS
25806	x	M	C SS	CS		25893	x	0	C SS	CS
25808	x	M	C SS	CS		25955	x*f	M	C SS	CS
25837	x	0	C SS	CS		26013	x	0	C SS	CS

AB21 (BSK)   CORRIDOR BRAKE STANDARD

Dia. AB201. Mark 1. Each vehicle has four compartments. -/24 1T (-/32 1T*).

Non-Standard Liveries: 30290 is black. 35407 is in London & North Western Railway livery.

34525-34556. Lot No. 30095 Wolverton 1955. BR1 bogies. 34 t. (34525 C 36 t.).
34952-34991. Lot No. 30229 Metro-Cammell 1956-7. BR1 bogies. 34 t. (34991 C 36 t.).
35073. Lot No. 30233 Gloucester 1956-7. BR1 bogies. 35 t.
35185-35207. Lot No. 30427 Wolverton 1959. B4 bogies. 33 t.
35290. Lot No. 30573 Gloucester 1960. B4 bogies. 33 t.

34525	ag	M	G SS	EN		35073	v	M	C		CS
34556	v	BG	V	SL		35185	x	0	V		SL
34952	v*	BG	V	SL		35207	x*	G	V LS		SL
34991	a*	PC	V SS	SL		35290	v	0	X		CQ

These lots have metal window frames and melamine interior panelling Commonwealth bogies. ETH 2.

35317-35337. Lot No. 30699 Wolverton 1962-3. Commonwealth bogies. 37 t.
35449. Lot No. 30728 Wolverton 1963. Commonwealth bogies. 37 t.
35407, 35452-35479. Lot No. 30721 Wolverton 1963. 37 t.

f Facelifted with fluorescent lighting.
g Converted to ETH generator vehicle.
§ Converted to charter train support coach.

35317	v	M	M SS	BN		35461	x	CH	R SS	CO
35322	x*f	M	O LS	DI		35463	v	M	C LS	CS
35333	x	CH	O LS	DI		35465	x §	WV	L LS	CQ
35407	xg	0	Y SS	CJ		35467	v	M	R LS	KR
35449	v	CH	O LS	SO		35468	v	M	O LS	YM
35452	x	RR	E NW	LL		35469	xg	WV	M SS	BN
35453	x	CH	R SS	CO		35476	v	CC	O LS	SK
35457	v	M	O LS	BQ		35479	v	M	M SS	BN
35459	x	M	C SS	CS						

AB2A/AB2C (BSK)   CORRIDOR BRAKE STANDARD

Dia. AB204. Mark 2A (2C*). Pressure ventilated. Renumbered from BFK. -/24 1T. B4 bogies. ETH 4.

35500/15-18. Lot No. 30786 Derby 1968. 32 t.
35505-9/11. Lot No. 30796. Derby 1969-70. 32.5 t.
35510/12-14. Lot No. 30775 Derby 1967-68. 32 t.

§ Cage removed from brake compartment.

```
35505 (14118, 17118) a*  RR E         LL
35507 (14123, 17123) a*  RR E         Long Marston
35508 (14128, 17128) a*  RR X         CP
35509 (14138, 17138) a*  RR E         Long Marston
35510 (14075, 17075) a   RR E         Long Marston
35511 (14130, 17130) a*  RR E         Kineton
35512 (14057, 17057) a§  RR E  NW  LL
35513 (14063, 17063) a§  RR E  NW  LL
35514 (14069, 17069) a§  RR E  NW  LL
35515 (14079, 17079) a§  RR E  NW  LL
35516 (14080, 17080) a§  RR E  NW  LL
35517 (14088, 17088) a§  RR E  NW  LL
35518 (14097, 17097) a§  RR E  NW  LL
```

2.2. PRE-NATIONALISATION STOCK

The following are pre-nationalisation preserved vehicles are at present passed for running on the Railtrack system. Vehicles are painted in their appropriate pre-nationalisation livery except for 902260 which is **M**. Original number is shown and other numbers may have been carried.

159	London & North Western Railway dining saloon	Y	SS	CJ
484	West Coast Joint Stock dining saloon	Y	SS	CJ
807	Great Northern Railway family saloon	Y	SS	CJ
9004	Great Western Railway first saloon	D	SS	CS
902260	LNER General Manager's Saloon	V	SS	EN

The following vehicle which had a BR freight stock number is also passed. It is in **PC** livery and carries the branding "BAGGAGE CAR No. 8".

889202	Ferry van	V	SS	SL

2.3. HIGH SPEED TRAIN TRAILER CARS

HSTs run in formations of 7 or 8 trailer cars with a driving motor brake (power car) at each end. All vehicles are classified mark 3. All trailer cars have BT10 bogies with disc brakes. Heating is by a three-phase supply and vehicles have air conditioning. Max. Speed is 125 mph.

GN4G (TRB)   TRAILER BUFFET FIRST

Dia. GN401. Converted from TRSB by fitting first class seats. Renumbered from 404xx series by subtracting 200. Secondary door locks. pq. 23/ – (22 ÷ w).

40204 – 40228. Lot No. 30883 Derby 1976 – 7. 36.12 t.
40231 – 40233. Lot No. 30899 Derby 1978 – 9. 36.12 t.

40204	A	XC	LA	40212 w	P	XC	LA
40205	A	GW	PM	40213	A	GW	PM
40206	A	GW	PM	40221	A	GW	PM
40207	A	GW	PM	40228	A	GW	PM
40208	A	XC	LA	40231	A	GW	LA
40209	A	GW	PM	40232	P	XC	LA
40210	A	GW	PM	40233 w	P	XC	LA
40211	P	XC	LA			

GK2G (TRSB)   TRAILER BUFFET STANDARD

Dia. GK202. Renumbered from 400xx series by adding 400. Secondary door locks. pq. – 35 (– 33 + tip-up seat w).

40401 – 40427. Lot No. 30883 Derby 1976 – 7. 36.12 t.
40429 – 40437. Lot No. 30899 Derby 1978 – 9. 36.12 t.

40401 w	P	XC	EC	40423	P	XC	EC
40402 w	P	XC	EC	40424 w	P	XC	LA
40403 w	P	XC	LA	40425 w	P	XC	EC
40414 w	P	XC	LA	40426 w	P	XC	EC
40415 w	P	XC	LA	40427	P	XC	EC
40416 w	P	XC	EC	40429 w	P	XC	EC
40417 w	P	XC	LA	40430 w	P	XC	EC
40418 w	P	XC	LA	40434 w	P	XC	LA
40419	P	XC	EC	40435	P	XC	EC
40420 w	P	XC	EC	40436 w	P	XC	LA
40422 w	P	XC	EC	40437 w	P	XC	EC

GL1G (TRFK)   TRAILER KITCHEN FIRST

Dia. GL101. Reclassified from TRUK. pq. 24/ – .

Lot No. 30884 Derby 1976 – 7. 37 t.

40501 d	P	ZD	40511	A	Kineton
40505	A	Kineton	40513 d	P	ZD

GK1G (TRFM)   TRAILER MODULAR BUFFET FIRST

Dia. GK102. Converted to modular catering from 40719. Secondary door locks. pq. 17/–.

Lot No. 30921 Derby 1978 – 9. 38.16 t.

| 40619 | | P | | DY | | |

GK1G (TRFB)   TRAILER BUFFET FIRST

Dia. GK101. These vehicles have larger kitchens than the 402xx and 404xx series vehicles, and are used in trains where full meal service is required. They were renumbered from the 403xx series (in which the seats were unclassified) by adding 400 to previous number. Secondary door locks. pq. 17/–.

40700 – 40721. Lot No. 30921 Derby 1978 – 9. 38.16 t.
40722 – 40735. Lot No. 30940 Derby 1979 – 80. 38.16 t.
40736 – 40753. Lot No. 30948 Derby 1980 – 1. 38.16 t.
40754 – 40757. Lot No. 30966 Derby 1982. 38.16 t.

* Prototype refurbished vehicle for Porterbrook Leasing Company.

40700		P	ML	NL		40730		P	ML	NL
40701		P	ML	NL		40731		A	GW	LA
40702		P	ML	NL		40732		A	WC	MA
40703		A	GW	LA		40733	GW	A	GW	LA
40704		A	GN	EC		40734		A	GW	LA
40705		A	GN	EC		40735		A	GN	EC
40706		A	GN	EC		40736		A	GW	LA
40707		A	GW	LA		40737		A	GN	EC
40708		P	ML	NL		40738		A	GW	LA
40709	GW	A	GW	LA		40739		A	GW	PM
40710		A	GW	LA		40740		A	GN	EC
40711		A	GN	EC		40741		P	ML	NL
40712		A	GW	LA		40742		A	WC	MA
40713	GW	A	GW	LA		40743		A	GW	LA
40714		A	GW	PM		40744		A	GW	PM
40715		A	GW	PM		40745		A	GW	PM
40716		A	GW	PM		40746	MM	P	ML	NL
40717		A	GW	PM		40747		A	GW	PM
40718		A	GW	LA		40748		A	GN	EC
40720		A	GN	EC		40749		P	ML	NL
40721		A	GW	LA		40750	GN	A	GN	EC
40722		A	GW	LA		40751		P	ML	NL
40723		A	WC	MA		40752		A	GW	PM
40724		A	GW	PM		40753		P	ML	NL
40725		A	GW	LA		40754	*	P	ML	NL
40726		A	GW	LA		40755		A	GW	LA
40727		A	GW	LA		40756		P	ML	NL
40728		P	ML	NL		40757		A	GW	LA
40729		P	ML	NL						

GH1G (TF)   TRAILER FIRST

Dia. GH102. Secondary door locks. 48/– 2T (47 ÷ 2T w).

41003 – 41056. Lot No. 30881 Derby 1976 – 7. 33.66 t.
41057 – 41120. Lot No. 30896 Derby 1977 – 8. 33.66 t.
41121 – 41148. Lot No. 30938 Derby 1979 – 80. 33.66 t.
41149 – 41166. Lot No. 30947 Derby 1980. 33.66 t.
41167 – 41169. Lot No. 30963 Derby 1982. 33.66 t.
41170. Lot No. 30967 Derby 1982. Ex prototype vehicle. 33.66 t.
41178. Lot No. 30882 Derby 1976 – 7. 33.60 t.

Note: 41170 was converted from 41001. 41178 is a prototype refurbished vehicle and has been converted from 42011 which was damaged by fire.

41003	p	I	A	GW	PM	41039		I	A	GN	EC
41004		I	A	GW	PM	41040	w	I	A	GN	EC
41005	p	I	A	GW	PM	41041	p	I	P	ML	NL
41006		I	A	GW	PM	41042		I	A	GW	PM
41007	p	I	A	GW	PM	41043	w	I	A	GN	EC
41008		I	A	GW	PM	41044	w	I	A	GN	EC
41009	pw	I	A	XC	LA	41045	w	I	P	XC	LA
41010		I	A		Kineton	41046		I	P	ML	NL
41011	p	I	A	GW	PM	41049		I	A	GW	PM
41012		I	A	GW	PM	41050		I	A	GW	PM
41013	p	I	A	GW	PM	41051		I	A	GW	LA
41014		I	A	GW	PM	41052		I	A	GW	LA
41015	p	I	A	GW	PM	41055		GW	A	GW	LA
41016		I	A	GW	PM	41056		GW	A	GW	LA
41017	pw	I	A	XC	LA	41057		I	P	ML	NL
41018		I	A	GW	PM	41058	w	I	P	ML	NL
41019	p	I	A	GW	PM	41059	w	I	P	XC	EC
41020		I	A	GW	PM	41060		I	A	GW	LA
41021	p	I	A	GW	PM	41061		I	P	ML	NL
41022		I	A	GW	PM	41062		I	P	ML	NL
41023	p	I	A	GW	LA	41063		I	P	ML	NL
41024		I	A	GW	LA	41064	w	I	P	ML	NL
41025	p	I	A	WC	MA	41065		I	A	GW	LA
41026		I	A	WC	MA	41066	p	I	A	WC	MA
41027	p	I	A	GW	LA	41067		I	P	ML	NL
41028		I	A	GW	LA	41068	w	I	P	ML	NL
41029	p	I	A	GW	LA	41069		I	P	ML	NL
41030		I	A	GW	LA	41070	w	I	P	ML	NL
41031	p	I	A	GW	LA	41071		I	P	ML	NL
41032		I	A	GW	LA	41072	w	I	P	ML	NL
41033	p	I	A	GW	LA	41075		I	P	ML	NL
41034		I	A	GW	LA	41076	w	I	P	ML	NL
41035	p	I	A	WC	MA	41077		I	P	ML	NL
41036		I	A	WC	MA	41078	w	I	P	ML	NL
41037	p	I	A	GW	LA	41079		I	P	ML	NL
41038		I	A	GW	LA	41080	w	I	P	ML	NL

41081	w	I		P	XC	EC	41127	p	I	A	GW	PM
41082	w	I		P	ML	NL	41128		I	A	GW	PM
41083	w	I		P	ML	NL	41129	p	I	A	GW	PM
41084		I		P	ML	NL	41130		I	A	GW	PM
41085		I		P	XC	EC	41131	p	I	A	GW	LA
41086		I		P	XC	EC	41132		I	A	GW	LA
41087		I		A	GN	EC	41133	p	I	A	GW	LA
41088	w	I		A	GN	EC	41134		I	A	GW	LA
41089		I		A	GW	LA	41135	p	I	A	GW	LA
41090	w	I		A	GN	EC	41136		I	A	GW	PM
41091		I		A	GN	EC	41137	p	I	A	GW	PM
41092	w	I		A	GN	EC	41138		I	A	GW	PM
41093		I		A	GW	LA	41139	p	I	A	GW	LA
41094		I		A	GW	LA	41140		I	A	GW	LA
41095		I		P	XC	EC	41141	p	I	A	GW	LA
41096	w	I		P	XC	EC	41142		I	A	GW	LA
41097		GN		A	GN	EC	41143	p	GW	A	GW	LA
41098		GN		A	GN	EC	41144		GW	A	GW	LA
41099		I		A	GN	EC	41145	p	I	A	GW	PM
41100		I		A	GN	EC	41146		I	A	GW	PM
41101		I		A	GW	LA	41147	w	I	P	XC	EC
41102		I		A	GW	LA	41148	w	I	P	XC	EC
41103		GW		A	GW	LA	41149	w	I	P	XC	EC
41104		GW		A	GW	LA	41150		I	A	GN	EC
41105		I		A	GW	PM	41151		I	A	GN	EC
41106		I		A	GW	PM	41152	w	I	A	GN	EC
41107	w	I		P	XC	EC	41153		I	P	ML	NL
41108	w	I		P	XC	LA	41154	w	I	P	ML	NL
41109	w	I		P	XC	LA	41155		MM	P	ML	NL
41110		I		A	GW	PM	41156	w	MM	P	ML	NL
41111	w	I		P	ML	NL	41157		I	A	GW	LA
41112		I		P	ML	NL	41158		I	A	GW	LA
41113		I		P	ML	NL	41159	w	I	P	XC	LA
41114	w	I		P	XC	EC	41160	w	I	P	XC	LA
41115		I		P	ML	NL	41161	w	I	P	XC	EC
41116		I		A	GW	LA	41162	w	I	P	XC	EC
41117		MM		P	ML	NL	41163	w	I	P	XC	LA
41118	w	I		A	GN	EC	41164	p	I	A	WC	MA
41119		I		P	XC	EC	41165	w	I	P	XC	LA
41120		I		A	GN	EC	41166	w	I	P	XC	LA
41121	p	I		A	GW	LA	41167	w	I	P	XC	LA
41122		I		A	GW	LA	41168	w	I	P	XC	LA
41123	p	I		A	GW	PM	41169	w	I	P	XC	LA
41124		I		A	GW	PM	41170		I	A	GN	EC
41125		I		A	GW	PM	41178		I	A		Kineton
41126	p	I		A	GW	PM						

GH2G (TS)   TRAILER STANDARD

Dia. GH203. Secondary door locks. –/76 2T (– 74 2T + centre luggage racks §).

42003 – 42090. Lot No. 30882 Derby 1976 – 7. 33.60 t.
42091 – 42250. Lot No. 30897 Derby 1977 – 9. 33.60 t.
42251 – 42305. Lot No. 30939 Derby 1979 – 80. 33.60 t.
42306 – 42322. Lot No. 30969 Derby 1982. 33.60 t.
42323 – 42341. Lot No. 30983 Derby 1984 – 5. 33.60 t.
42342. Lot No. 30949 Derby 1982. 33.47 t. Converted from TGS.
42343/5. Lot No. 30970 Derby 1982. 33.47 t. Converted from TGS.
42344. Lot No. 30964 Derby 1982. 33.47 t. Converted from TGS.
42346/7/50/1. Lot No. 30881 Derby 1976 – 7. 33.66 t. Converted from TF.
42348/9. Lot No. 30896 Derby 1977 – 8. 33.66 t. Converted from TF.
42353/5 – 7. Lot No. 30967 Derby 1982. Ex prototype vehicles. 33.66 t.
42352/4. Lot No. 30897 Derby 1977. Were TF from 1983 to 1992. 33.66 t.

Note: 42158 was also numbered 41177 for a time.

42003	I	A	GW	PM		42041	I	A	GW	LA
42004	I	A	XC	LA		42042	I	A	GW	LA
42005	I	A	GW	PM		42043	I	A	GW	LA
42006	I	A	GW	PM		42044	I	A	GW	LA
42007	I	A	GW	PM		42045	I	A	GW	LA
42008	I	A	XC	LA		42046	I	A	GW	LA
42009	I	A	GW	PM		42047	I	A	GW	LA
42010	I	A	GW	PM		42048	I	A	GW	LA
42011	I	A	GW	PM		42049	I	A	GW	LA
42012	I	A	XC	LA		42050	I	A	GW	LA
42013	I	A	XC	LA		42051	I	A	WC	MA
42014	I	A	XC	LA		42052	I	A	WC	MA
42015	I	A	GW	PM		42053	I	A	WC	MA
42016	I	A	GW	PM		42054	I	A	GW	LA
42017	I	A	GW	PM		42055	I	A	GW	LA
42018	I	A	GW	PM		42056	I	A	GW	LA
42019	I	A	GW	PM		42057	I	A	GN	EC
42020	I	A	GW	PM		42058	I	A	GN	EC
42021	I	A	GW	PM		42059	I	A	GN	EC
42022	I	A	GW	PM		42060	I	A	GW	PM
42023	I	A	GW	PM		42061	I	A	GW	PM
42024	I	A	XC	LA		42062	I	A	GW	LA
42025	I	A	XC	LA		42063	I	A	GN	EC
42026	I	A	XC	LA		42064	I	A	GN	EC
42027	I	A	GW	PM		42065	I	A	GN	EC
42028	I	A	GW	PM		42066	I	A	GW	LA
42029	I	A	GW	PM		42067	I	A	GW	LA
42030	I	A	GW	PM		42068	I	A	GW	LA
42031	I	A	GW	PM		42069	I	A	GW	PM
42032	I	A	GW	PM		42070	I	A	GW	PM
42033	I	A	GW	LA		42071	I	A	GW	PM
42034	I	A	GW	LA		42072	I	A	GW	PM
42035	I	A	GW	LA		42073	I	A	GW	PM
42036	I	A	WC	MA		42074	I	A	GW	PM
42037	I	A	WC	MA		42075	I	A	GW	LA
42038	I	A	WC	MA		42076	I	A	GW	LA
42039	I	A	GW	LA		42077	I	A	GW	LA
42040	I	A	GW	LA						

42078	I	A	GW	LA	42130	I	P	XC	EC
42079	I	A	GW	PM	42131	I	P	ML	NL
42080	I	A	GW	PM	42132	I	P	ML	NL
42081	GW	A	GW	LA	42133	I	P	ML	NL
42082	GW	A	GW	LA	42134	I	A	WC	MA
42083	GW	A	GW	LA	42135	I	P	ML	NL
42084	I	P	XC	EC	42136	I	P	ML	NL
42085	I	P	XC	EC	42137	I	P	ML	NL
42086	I	P	XC	EC	42138	I	A	GW	PM
42087	I	P	XC	EC	42139	I	P	ML	NL
42088	I	P	XC	EC	42140	I	P	ML	NL
42089	I	A	GW	PM	42141	I	P	ML	NL
42090	I	P	XC	EC	42143	I	A	GW	PM
42091	I	P	XC	EC	42144	I	A	GW	PM
42092	I	P	XC	LA	42145	I	A	GW	PM
42093	I	P	XC	LA	42146	I	A	GN	EC
42094	I	P	XC	LA	42147	I	P	ML	NL
42095	I	P	XC	LA	42148	I	P	ML	NL
42096	I	A	GW	LA	42149	I	P	ML	NL
42097	I	A	WC	MA	42150	I	A	GN	EC
42098	I	A	GW	LA	42151	I	P	ML	NL
42099	I	A	GW	LA	42152	I	P	ML	NL
42100	I	P	ML	NL	42153	I	P	ML	NL
42101	I	P	ML.	NL	42154	I	A	GN	EC
42102	I	P	ML	NL	42155	I	P	ML	NL
42103	I	P	XC	EC	42156	I	P	ML	NL
42104	I	A	GN	EC	42157	I	P	ML	NL
42105	I	P	XC	LA	42158	GN	A	GN	EC
42106	I	A	GN	EC	42159	I	P	ML	NL
42107	I	A	GW	LA	42160	I	P	ML	NL
42108	I	P	XC	LA	42161	I	P	ML	NL
42109	I	P	XC	LA	42162	I	P	XC	EC
42110	I	P	XC	LA	42163	I	P	ML	NL
42111	I	P	ML	NL	42164	I	P	ML	NL
42112	I	P	ML	NL	42165	I	P	ML	NL
42113	I	P	ML	NL	42166	I	P	XC	EC
42115	I	P	XC	EC	42167	I	P	XC	EC
42116	I	P	XC	EC	42168	I	P	XC	EC
42117	I	P	XC	EC	42169	I	P	XC	EC
42118	I	A	GW	PM	42170	I	P	XC	EC
42119	I	P	ML	NL	42171	I	A	GN	EC
42120	I	P	ML	NL	42172	I	A	GN	EC
42121	I	P	ML	NL	42173	I	P	XC	EC
42122	I	A	WC	MA	42174	I	P	XC	EC
42123	I	P	ML	NL	42175	I	P	XC	LA
42124	I	P	ML	NL	42176	I	P	XC	LA
42125	I	P	ML	NL	42177	I	P	XC	LA
42126	GW	A	GW	LA	42178	I	P	XC	EC
42127	I	P	XC	EC	42179	I	A	GN	EC
42128	I	P	XC	EC	42180	I	A	GN	EC
42129	I	A	GW	LA	42181	I	A	GN	EC

42182	I	A	GN	EC		42233	I	P	XC	EC
42183	I	A	GW	LA		42234	I	P	XC	EC
42184	I	A	GW	LA		42235	I	A	GN	EC
42185	I	A	GW	LA		42236	I	A	GW	PM
42186	I	A	GN	EC		42237	I	P	XC	EC
42187	I	P	XC	EC		42238	I	P	XC	EC
42188	I	P	XC	EC		42239	I	P	XC	EC
42189	I	P	XC	EC		42240	I	A	GN	EC
42190	I	A	GN	EC		42241	I	A	GN	EC
42191	GN	A	GN	EC		42242	I	A	GN	EC
42192	GN	A	GN	EC		42243	I	A	GN	EC
42193	GN	A	GN	EC		42244	I	A	GN	EC
42194	I	P	ML	NL		42245	I	A	GW	LA
42195	I	P	XC	EC		42246	I	P	XC	EC
42196	I	A	GW	PM		42247	I	P	XC	EC
42197	I	A	GW	PM		42248	I	P	XC	EC
42198	I	A	GN	EC		42249	I	P	XC	EC
42199	I	A	GN	EC		42250	I	A	GW	LA
42200	I	A	GW	LA		42251	I	A	GW	LA
42201	I	A	GW	LA		42252	I	A	GW	LA
42202	I	A	GW	LA		42253	I	A	GW	LA
42203	I	A	GW	LA		42254	I	P	XC	EC
42204	I	A	GW	LA		42255	I	A	GW	PM
42205	I	P	ML	NL		42256	I	A	GW	PM
42206	GW	A	GW	LA		42257	I	A	GW	PM
42207	GW	A	GW	LA		42258	I	P	XC	EC
42208	GW	A	GW	LA		42259	I	A	GW	PM
42209	GW	A	GW	LA		42260	I	A	GW	PM
42210	I	P	ML	NL		42261	I	A	GW	PM
42211	I	A	GW	PM		42262	I	P	XC	EC
42212	I	A	GW	PM		42263	I	A	GW	PM
42213	I	A	GW	PM		42264	I	A	GW	LA
42214	I	A	GW	PM		42265	I	A	GW	LA
42215	I	A	GN	EC		42266	I	P	XC	EC
42216	I	A	GW	LA		42267	I	A	GW	PM
42217	I	P	XC	EC		42268	I	A	GW	PM
42218	I	P	XC	EC		42269	I	A	GW	PM
42219	I	A	GN	EC		42270	I	P	XC	EC
42220 §	MM	P	ML	NL		42271	I	A	GW	LA
42221	I	A	GW	LA		42272	I	A	GW	LA
42222	I	P	XC	LA		42273	I	A	GW	LA
42223	I	P	XC	LA		42274	I	P	XC	EC
42224	I	P	XC	LA		42275	I	A	GW	LA
42225 §	MM	P	ML	NL		42276	I	A	GW	LA
42226	I	A	GN	EC		42277	I	A	GW	LA
42227	I	P	ML	NL		42278	I	P	XC	EC
42228	I	P	ML	NL		42279	I	A	GW	LA
42229	I	P	ML	NL		42280	I	A	GW	LA
42230 §	MM	P	ML	NL		42281	I	A	GW	LA
42231	I	P	XC	EC		42282	I	P	XC	EC
42232	I	P	XC	EC		42283	I	A	GW	PM

42284	I		A	GW	PM	42313	I	P	XC	LA
42285	I		A	GW	PM	42314	I	P	XC	LA
42286	I		P	XC	LA	42315	I	P	XC	LA
42287	I		A	GW	LA	42316	I	P	XC	LA
42288	I		A	GW	LA	42317	I	P	XC	LA
42289	I		A	GW	LA	42318	I	P	XC	LA
42290	I		P	XC	LA	42319	I	P	XC	LA
42291	I		A	GW	LA	42320	I	P	XC	LA
42292	I		A	GW	LA	42321	I	P	XC	LA
42293	I		A	GW	LA	42322	I	P	XC	LA
42294	I		P	XC	LA	42323	I	A	GN	EC
42295	GW	A	GW	LA	42324	I	P	ML	NL
42296	GW	A	GW	LA	42325	I	A	GW	PM
42297	GW	A	GW	LA	42326	I	P	XC	EC
42298	I		P	XC	LA	42327	I	P	ML	NL
42299	I		A	GW	PM	42328	I	P	ML	NL
42300	I		A	GW	PM	42329	I	P	ML	NL
42301	I		A	GW	PM	42330	I	P	XC	EC
42302	I		P	XC	LA	42331	I	P	ML	NL
42303	I		P	XC	LA	42332	I	A	GW	PM
42304	I		P	XC	LA	42333	I	A	GW	PM
42305	I		P	XC	LA	42334	I	P	XC	LA
42306	I		P	XC	LA	42335	I	P	ML	NL
42307	I		P	XC	LA	42336	I	P	XC	EC
42308	I		P	XC	LA	42337	I	P	ML	NL
42309	I		P	XC	LA	42338	I	P	XC	EC
42310	I		P	XC	LA	42339	I	P	ML	NL
42311	I		P	XC	LA	42340	I	A	GN	EC
42312	I		P	XC	LA	42341	I	P	ML	NL

42342	(44082)	I	A	WC	MA
42343	(44095)	I	A	GW	LA
42344	(44092)	I	A	GW	PM
42345	(44096)	I	A	GW	LA
42346	(41053)	I	A	GW	PM
42347	(41054)	I	A	GW	LA
42348	(41073)	I	A	GW	LA
42349	(41074)	I	A	GW	PM
42350	(41047)	GW	A	GW	LA
42351	(41048)	I	A	GW	PM
42352	(42142, 41176)	I	P	ML	NL
42353	(42001, 41171)	I	P	XC	EC
42354	(42114, 41175)	I	A	GN	EC
42355	(42000, 41172)	I	A	WC	MA
42356	(42002, 41173)	I	A	GW	LA
42357	(41002, 41174)	I	A	WC	MA

GJ2G (TGS)   TRAILER GUARD'S STANDARD

Dia. GJ205. Secondary door locks. pg. −/63 1T + tip-up seat and wheelchair space. Wheelchair space now being removed seating − 65 1T.

44000. Lot No. 30953 Derby 1980. 33.47 t.
44001 – 44090. Lot No. 30949 Derby 1980 – 2. 33.47 t.
44091 – 44094. Lot No. 30964 Derby 1982. 33.47 t.
44097 – 44101. Lot No. 30970 Derby 1982. 33.47 t.

§ Fitted with centre luggage racks seating – 63 1T.

44000	I		P	XC	EC			
44001	I		A	GW	LA			
44002	I		A	GW	PM			
44003	I		A	GW	PM			
44004	I		A	XC	LA			
44005	I		A	GW	PM			
44006	I		A	GW	PM			
44007	I		A	GW	PM			
44008	I		A	XC	LA			
44009	I		A	GW	PM			
44010	I		A	GW	PM			
44011	I		A	GW	LA			
44012	I		A	WC	MA			
44013	I		A	GW	LA			
44014	I		A	GW	LA			
44015	I		A	GW	LA			
44016	I		A	GW	LA			
44017	I		A	WC	MA			
44018	I		A	GW	LA			
44019	I		A	GN	EC			
44020	I		A	GW	PM			
44021	I		P	XC	EC			
44022	I		A	GW	LA			
44023	I		A	GW	PM			
44024	I		A	GW	PM			
44025	I		A	GW	LA			
44026	I		A	GW	PM			
44027	I		P	ML	NL			
44028	I		A	GW	LA			
44029	I		A	GW	PM			
44030	I		A	GW	PM			
44031	I		A	WC	MA			
44032	I		A	GW	PM			
44033	I		A	GW	LA			
44034	I		A	GW	LA			
44035	I		A	GW	LA			
44036	I		A	GW	PM			
44037	I		A	GW	LA			
44038	I		A	GW	LA			
44039	GW		A	GW	LA			
44040	I		A	GW	PM			
44041	I		P	ML	NL			
44042	I		P	XC	EC			
44043	GW		A	GW	LA			
44044	I		P	ML	NL			
44045	I		A	GN	EC
44046	I		P	ML	NL
44047	I		P	ML	NL
44048	I		P	ML	NL
44049	I		A	GW	PM
44050	I		P	ML	NL
44051	I		P	ML	NL
44052	I		P	ML	NL
44053	I		P	ML	NL
44054	I		P	ML	NL
44055	I		P	XC	EC
44056	I		A	GN	EC
44057	I		P	XC	LA
44058	I		A	GN	EC
44059	I		A	GW	LA
44060	I		P	XC	EC
44061	GN		A	GN	EC
44062	I		P	XC	EC
44063	I		A	GN	EC
44064	I		A	GW	LA
44065	I		P	XC	LA
44066	GW		A	GW	LA
44067	I		A	GW	PM
44068	I		P	XC	LA
44069	I		P	XC	EC
44070	I		P	ML	NL
44071	I		P	ML	NL
44072	I		P	XC	EC
44073	I		P	ML	NL
44074	I		P	XC	EC
44075	I		P	XC	EC
44076	I		P	XC	LA
44077	I		A	GN	EC
44078	I		P	XC	EC
44079	I		P	XC	EC
44080	I		A	GN	EC
44081	I		P	XC	LA
44083	I		P	ML	NL
44085	§	MM	P	ML	NL
44086	I		A	GW	LA
44087	I		P	XC	LA
44088	I		P	XC	LA
44089	I		P	XC	LA
44090	I		P	XC	LA
44091	I		P	XC	LA

44093	I	A	GW	LA		44099	I	A		Kineton
44094	I	A	GN	EC		44100	I	P	XC	EC
44097	I	P	XC	EC		44101	I	P	XC	LA
44098	I	A	GN	EC						

GH2G (TCSD)   TRAILER CONDUCTOR STANDARD

Dia. GH201. Converted from 44084. Guard's compartment converted to walk-through conductor's compartment with a disabled persons toilet also provided. The car is marshalled adjacent to the buffet. Secondary door locks.

45084. Lot No. 30949 Derby 1982. 33.47 t.

| 45084 | I | A | | Kineton | |

2.4. PULLMAN CAR COMPANY STOCK

VARIOUS PULLMAN CARS

Various Pullman cars built to early designs.

* Former 'Brighton Belle' EMU vehicle now used as hauled stock.

213	MINERVA	PPF		**PC**	V	SS	SL	26/-	1927	Midland
239	AGATHA	PPF		**PC**	V		SL	24/-	1928	Metro
243	LUCILLE	PPF		**PC**	V		SL	24/-	1928	Metro
245	IBIS	PKF		**PC**	V	SS	SL	20/-	1925	BRCW
254	ZENA	PPF		**PC**	V		SL	24/-	1928	Metro
255	IONE	PKF		**PC**	V	SS	SL	20/-	1928	Metro
261	CAR No. 83	PPS		**PC**	V		SL	-/42	1931	BRCW
280	AUDREY	PKF	*	**PC**	V	SS	SL	20/-	1932	Metro
281	GWEN	PKF	*	**PC**	V		SL	20/-	1932	Metro
284	VERA	PKF	*	**PC**	V	SS	SL	20/-	1932	Metro
286	CAR No. 86	PPS	*	**PC**	V		SL	-/56	1931	Metro
301	PERSEUS	PPF		**PC**	V	SS	SL	32/-	1951	BRCW
302	PHOENIX	PPF		**PC**	V	SS	SL	26/-	1952	Pullman Car Co.
307	CARINA	PKF		**PC**	V		SL	22/-	1951	BRCW
308	CYGNUS	PPF		**PC**	V	SS	SL	32/-	1951	BRCW

PULLMAN KITCHEN FIRST

Built by Metro-Cammell 1960/1 for East Coast Main-line services. x. Commonwealth bogies. 20/- 2T. 40 t. Used in the ''Royal Scotsman'' charter train set.

Some of these vehicles have been modified. Names not carried.

313	FINCH	**M**		G	SS	EN		319	SNIPE	M	G	SS	EN
317	RAVEN	**M**		G	SS	EN							

PULLMAN PARLOUR FIRST

Built by Metro-Cammell 1960/1 for East Coast Main-line services. x. Commonwealth bogies. 29/- 2T. 38.5 t. Used in the ?Royal Scotsman'' charter train set.

Some of these vehicles have been modified. Names not carried.

324	AMBER	**M**		G	SS	EN		331	TOPAZ	M	G	SS	EN
329	PEARL	**M**		G	SS	EN							

PULLMAN KITCHEN SECOND

Built by Metro-Cammell 1960/1 for East Coast Main-line services. x. Commonwealth bogies. -/30 1T. 40 t.

335   CAR No. 335   **PC**   N   On loan to Swanage Railwa

PULLMAN PARLOUR SECOND

Built by Metro-Cammell 1960/1 for East Coast Main-line services. x.
Commonwealth bogies. -/42 2T. 38.5 t.

347	CAR No. 347	**PC**	N	Crewe Carriage Shed
348	CAR No. 348	**PC**	N	On loan to Swanage Railway
349	CAR No. 349	**PC**	N	On loan to Kent & East Sussex Railway
350	CAR No. 350	**PC**	N	Crewe Carriage Shed
351	CAR No. 347	**PC**	N	Crewe Carriage Shed
352	CAR No. 348	**PC**	N	Crewe Carriage Shed
353	CAR No. 349	**PC**	N	On loan to Swanage Railway

THE HADRIAN BAR

Built by Metro-Cammell 1961 for East Coast Main-line services. x.
Commonwealth bogies. 24/- + bar seating 1T. 38.5 t.

354 THE HADRIAN BAR **PC**   N   Crewe Carriage Shed

2.5. COACHING STOCK AWAITING DISPOSAL

This list contains the last known locations of coaching stock awaiting disposal.
The definition of which vehicles are awaiting disposal is somewhat vague, but
generally speaking these are vehicles of types not now in normal service or
vehicles which have been damaged by fire, vandalism or collision.

6332	ZK
6339	EC
6345	EC
6900	Cambridge Station Yard
6901	Cambridge Station Yard
7183	CP
7213	OM
9533	MA
13237	Hull Paragon Station
18416	Crewe Brook Sidings
18750	Crewe Brook Sidings
19500	CP
24893	Mossend Yard

2.6. ADDITIONAL INFORMATION

The following table is presented to help readers identify vehicles which may still have their former private owner numbers painted on them. The private owner number is shown in column 1 and the number by which the vehicle is now identified is show in column 2.

99000	4946	99322	5600	99545	80207	99782	17007
99001	4996	99323	5704	99554	92904	99821	9227
99002	5008	99324	5714	99566	3066	99822	1859
99035	35322	99325	5727	99568	3068	99823	4832
99052	484	99326	4954	99670	546	99824	4831
99053	9004	99327	5044	99671	546	99826	13229
99080	21096	99328	5033	99672	548	99827	3096
99121	3105	99329	4931	99670	549	99828	13230
99125	3113	99356	21245	99674	551	99829	4856
99127	3117	99371	3128	99675	552	99831	4836
99131	902260	99530	301	99676	553	99880	159
99132	1861	99531	302	99677	586	99881	807
99141	17041	99532	308	99678	504	99886	35407
99241	35449	99534	245	99679	506	99887	2127
99304	21256	99535	213	99680	17102	99953	35468
99311	1882	99536	254	99710	25767	99961	324
99312	35463	99537	280	99712	25893	99962	329
99314	25729	99538	34991	99713	26013	99963	331
99315	25955	99539	255	99716	25808	99964	313
99316	13321	99540	3069	99717	25837	99965	319
99317	3766	99541	243	99718	25862	99966	34525
99318	4912	99542	889202	99721	25806	99967	317
99319	14168	99543	284	99722	25756	99993	5067
99321	5299	99544	35207	99723	35459	99995	35457

The following table lists support coaches and the locomotives which they normally support at present.

17007	35028	35322	70000	35463	48151	35468	NRM locos
17041	71000	35333	6024	35465	D 172	80217	60532
21096	4498	35449	34027	35467	KR locos	80220	31625
21236	30828	35457	44767				

2.7. NIGHTSTAR STOCK

These coaches are designed for use on new 'Nightstar' services between Britain and Continental Europe via the Channel Tunnel. The new generation of overnight trains offer high quality accommodation to both business and leisure customers.

This innovative venture is being developed by European Night Services Limited (ENS), a joint company of Eurostar (GB) Ltd., SNCF, DB and NS. It was originally intended that the trains would operate on the following routes, but it is understood that the project is being reassessed and that one or more or even all of these might be changed:

London Waterloo – Amsterdam CS.
London Waterloo – Dortmund Hbf./Frankfurt Hbf.
Glasgow/Manchester – Paris Nord.
Plymouth/Swansea – Paris Nord.

Both sleeping cars and reclining seat coaches will be used. Each train will be formed of two half-sets, London services having two reclining seat coaches, a service vehicle and five sleeping cars in each half-set to form a sixteen coach train, whilst services from the Provinces to Paris will be fourteen coaches long with each portion consisting of three sleeping cars, a service vehicle and three reclining seat coaches. The regional half-sets are numbered 1 – 9, whilst the London half-sets are numbered 10 – 18.

In the following lists, the UIC number for each vehicle is followed by the set number to which it belongs.

RECLINING SEAT CARS   SO End

Each car has 50 seats which are fully reclining, with generous leg space. A table is provided at each seat, and footrests will offer extra comfort. The seats are mounted on plinths, which enhance the customer's sense of personal space. Main luggage is stored beneath the seat, while hand baggage is stored in overhead lockers. Individually controlled reading lights are provided, with different levels of ambient lighting for sleeping and non-sleeping hours. Each car has three toilet compartments with washing facilities. These include facilities such as shaver sockets and hot-air hand dryers.

61 19 20-90 001-0 *1*	61 19 20-90 010-1 *10*
61 19 20-90 002-8 *2*	61 19 20-90 011-9 *11*
61 19 20-90 003-6 *3*	61 19 20-90 012-7 *12*
61 19 20-90 004-4 *4*	61 19 20-90 013-5 *13*
61 19 20-90 005-1 *5*	61 19 20-90 014-3 *14*
61 19 20-90 006-9 *6*	61 19 20-90 015-0 *15*
61 19 20-90 007-7 *7*	61 19 20-90 016-8 *16*
61 19 20-90 008-5 *8*	61 19 20-90 017-6 *17*
61 19 20-90 009-3 *9*	61 19 20-90 018-4 *18*

RECLINING SEAT CAR   SO

Details as above, but no coupling for locomotive.

61 19 20-90 019-2	*1*	61 19 20-90 034-1	*8*
61 19 20-90 020-0	*1*	61 19 20-90 035-8	*9*
61 19 20-90 021-8	*2*	61 19 20-90 036-6	*9*
61 19 20-90 022-6	*2*	61 19 20-90 037-4	*10*
61 19 20-90 023-4	*3*	61 19 20-90 038-2	*11*
61 19 20-90 024-2	*3*	61 19 20-90 039-0	*12*
61 19 20-90 025-9	*4*	61 19 20-90 040-8	*13*
61 19 20-90 026-7	*4*	61 19 20-90 041-6	*14*
61 19 20-90 027-5	*5*	61 19 20-90 042-4	*15*
61 19 20-90 028-3	*5*	61 19 20-90 043-2	*16*
61 19 20-90 029-1	*6*	61 19 20-90 044-0	*17*
61 19 20-90 030-9	*6*	61 19 20-90 045-7	*18*
61 19 20-90 031-7	*7*	61 19 20-90 046-5	*S*
61 19 20-90 032-5	*7*	61 19 20-90 047-3	*S*
61 19 20-90 033-3	*8*		

SLEEPING CARS   SLF End

ENS sleeping cars will set high standards, with service quality and facilities like those found in a good hotel. Main users are expected to be business travellers and comfort-seeking leisure travellers Each sleeping car will have 10 cabins. Six of these will have a compact en-suite shower room, with a washbasin, toilet and hairdryers. The remaining four cabins will include en-suite toilet and washing facilities, but without the shower.

All cabins will be convertible so that when the bunks are folded away by the attendant after passengers have got up, two comfortable armchairs with fold-out tables are revealed. The bunks themselves are generously sized one above the other and will already be made up with duvets, sheets and pillows When passengers arrive. Each cabin will have a fitted wardrobe and cupboard, together with facilities for making hot drinks. Cabin telephones are provided for room service.

61 19 70-90 001-9	*1*	61 19 70-90 010-0	*10*
61 19 70-90 002-7	*2*	61 19 70-90 011-8	*11*
61 19 70-90 003-5	*3*	61 19 70-90 012-6	*12*
61 19 70-90 004-3	*4*	61 19 70-90 013-4	*13*
61 19 70-90'005-0	*5*	61 19 70-90 014-2	*14*
61 19 70-90 006-8	*6*	61 19 70-90 015-9	*15*
61 19 70-90 007-6	*7*	61 19 70-90 016-7	*16*
61 19 70-90 008-4	*8*	61 19 70-90 017-5	*17*
61 19 70-90 009-2	*9*	61 19 70-90 018-3	*18*

SLEEPING CARS   SLF

Details as above, but no coupling for locomotive.

61 19 70-90 019-1	*1*	61 19 70-90 046-4	*12*
61 19 70-90 020-9	*1*	61 19 70-90 047-2	*12*
61 19 70-90 021-7	*2*	61 19 70-90 048-0	*12*
61 19 70-90 022-5	*2*	61 19 70-90 049-8	*13*
61 19 70-90 023-3	*3*	61 19 70-90 050-6	*13*
61 19 70-90 024-1	*3*	61 19 70-90 051-4	*13*
61 19 70-90 025-8	*4*	61 19 70-90 052-2	*13*
61 19 70-90 026-6	*4*	61 19 70-90 053-0	*14*
61 19 70-90 027-4	*5*	61 19 70-90 054-8	*14*
61 19 70-90 028-2	*5*	61 19 70-90 055-5	*14*
61 19 70-90 029-0	*6*	61 19 70-90 056-3	*14*
61 19 70-90 030-8	*6*	61 19 70-90 057-1	*15*
61 19 70-90 031-6	*7*	61 19 70-90 058-9	*15*
61 19 70-90 032-4	*7*	61 19 70-90 059-7	*15*
61 19 70-90 033-2	*8*	61 19 70-90 060-5	*15*
61 19 70-90 034-0	*8*	61 19 70-90 061-3	*16*
61 19 70-90 035-7	*9*	61 19 70-90 062-1	*16*
61 19 70-90 036-5	*9*	61 19 70-90 063-9	*16*
61 19 70-90 037-3	*10*	61 19 70-90 064-7	*16*
61 19 70-90 038-1	*10*	61 19 70-90 065-4	*17*
61 19 70-90 039-9	*10*	61 19 70-90 066-2	*17*
61 19 70-90 040-7	*10*	61 19 70-90 067-0	*17*
61 19 70-90 041-5	*11*	61 19 70-90 068-8	*17*
61 19 70-90 042-3	*11*	61 19 70-90 069-6	*18*
61 19 70-90 043-1	*11*	61 19 70-90 070-4	*18*
61 19 70-90 044-9	*11*	61 19 70-90 071-2	*18*
61 19 70-90 045-6	*12*	61 19 70-90 072-0	*18*

SERVICE VEHICLE/LOUNGE CAR   SV

Lounge cars are positioned in each half of the train, between the sleeping cars and the seated accommodation. These vehicles consist of of a sleeping cabin for a disabled passenger and companion with en-suite washroom, a parcels room, offices for train manager and control authority, a lounge with bar for sleeping car passengers and public telephone and a bar for seated passengers.

The vehicle also acts as a base for the sleeping car attendants and for the trolley service which will be provided for the seated passengers in the evening. There is also a seated passengers' counter so that snacks and drinks can be obtained during sleeping hours.

61 19 89-90 001-8	*1*	61 19 89-90 011-7	*11*
61 19 89-90 002-6	*2*	61 19 89-90 012-5	*12*
61 19 89-90 003-4	*3*	61 19 89-90 013-3	*13*
61 19 89-90 004-2	*4*	61 19 89-90 014-1	*14*
61 19 89-90 005-9	*5*	61 19 89-90 015-8	*15*
61 19 89-90 006-7	*6*	61 19 89-90 016-6	*16*
61 19 89-90 007-5	*7*	61 19 89-90 017-4	*17*
61 19 89-90 008-3	*8*	61 19 89-90 018-2	*18*
61 19 89-90 009-1	*9*	61 19 89-90 019-0	*S*
61 19 89-90 010-9	*10*	61 19 89-90 020-8	*S*

3. DIESEL MULTIPLE UNITS

Diesel Multiple Unit operation on Britain's main line railways increased enormously since the end of the steam era but there have been many changes in recent years. Electrification has meant the replacement of DMUs with EMUs on many routes, whilst on other services, DMUs have replaced loco-hauled trains. Very few first generation DMUs remain and most DMU services are now operated by "Pacer", "Sprinter" or other modern air-braked Express units. A few DEMUs will be found operating on the former Southern Region, but some of these now have ex-EMU centre cars. One vehicle (71634) started life as loco-hauled coach No. 4059, was converted to an EMU trailer and is now part of DEMU 205 205!

NUMBERING

Diesel mechanical and diesel hydraulic multiple unit vehicles are numbered in the series 51000-59999. All vehicles numbered in the 53000-53999 series were originally numbered in the series 50000-50999, and were renumbered by having 3000 added to their original numbers. All vehicles in the series 54000-54504 were originally numbered in the series 56000-56504, and were renumbered by having 2000 subtracted from their original numbers.

Diesel electric multiple unit vehicles are numbered in the series 60000-60918. A number of vehicles which were numbered in the series 60001-60100 were renumbered in 1989 to avoid conflicting with Class 60 locomotives.

DESIGN CONSIDERATIONS

Unless stated otherwise, all diesel multiple unit vehicles are of BR design, or designed by contractors for BR and have buckeye couplings and tread brakes. Seating is 3 + 2 in standard class open vehicles, 2 + 2 in first class open vehicles, 12 to a non-corridor standard class compartment, 8 to a corridor standard class compartment and 6 to a corridor first class compartment. In express stock, open standards have 2 + 2 seating and open firsts have 2 + 1 seating.

VEHICLE CODES

The codes used by the BR Operating Department to describe the various different types of DMU vehicles and quoted in the class headings are as follows:

Diesel Mechanical & Diesel Hydraulic Units.

DMBC   Driving Motor Brake Composite.
DMBS   Driving Motor Brake Standard.
DMC   Driving Motor Composite.
DMS   Driving Motor Standard.
DMPMV   Driving Motor Parcels & Miscellaneous Van
DTPMV   Driving Trailer Parcels & Miscellaneous Van
DTS   Driving Trailer Standard.
MS   Motor Standard.
TS   Trailer Standard.

It should be noted that as all vehicles are of an open configuration the letter 'O' is omitted for all vehicles. An 'L' suffix denotes that the vehicle is fitted with a lavatory compartment. The letters (A) and (B) may be added to the above codes to differentiate between two cars of the same operating type which have differences between them. Note that a consistent system is used, rather than the official operator codes which are sometimes inconsistent.

A composite is a vehicle containing both First and Standard class accommodation, and vehicles are described as such even though most first class accommodation has now been declassified on most vehicles. This is done so as to differentiate between the different styles of seat provided in standard and erstwhile first class areas of a vehicle. At the time of writing no heritage units retained first class accommodation in use as such.

A brake vehicle is a vehicle containing seperate specific accommodation for the guard (as opposed to the use of spare driving cabs on second generation units).

Diesel Electric Units.

DMBSO Driving Motor Brake Standard (Open).
DTCsoL Driving Trailer Composite with Lavatory (Semi-Open).
DTSOL   Driving Trailer Standard with Lavatory (Open).
DTSO   Driving Trailer Standard (Open).
TSO   Trailer Standard (Open).
TSOL   Trailer Standard with Lavatory (Open).

The notes as above apply regarding composite and brake vehicles. A semi-open composite vehicle has first class accommodation in compartments with a side corridor and standard class accommodation provided in an open saloon.

WEIGHTS & DIMENSIONS

Approximate weights in working order are given in tonnes for all vehicle types in the class headings and sub headings as appropriate.

The dimensions of each type of vehicle are given in metric units, with length followed by width. All lengths quoted are over buffers (1st generation vehicles) or couplings (2nd generation vehicles). All widths quoted are maxima.

DIAGRAMS AND DESIGN CODES

For each type of vehicle, the official design code consists of a seven character code of two letters, four numbers and another letter, e.g. DP2010A. The first five characters of this are the diagram code and are given in the class heading or sub heading. These are explained as follows:

1st Letter

This is always 'D' for a diesel multiple unit vehicle.

2nd Letter

as follows for various vehicle types (DMMU or DHMU unless otherwise stated):

B	Driving motor passenger vehicles with a brake compartment (DEMU).
E	Driving trailer passenger vehicles (DEMU).
H	Trailer passenger vehicles without a brake compartment (DEMU).
P	Driving motor passenger vehicles without a brake compartment.
Q	Driving motor passenger vehicles with a brake compartment.
R	Non-Driving motor passenger vehicles.
S	Driving trailer passenger vehicles.
T	Trailer passenger vehicles without a brake compartment.
X	Parcels and Mails vehicles and single unit railcars.

1st Figure

This denotes the class of accommodation as follows:

2	Standard class accommodation (incl. declassified seats).
3	Composite accommodation.
5	No passenger accommodation.

2nd & 3rd Figures

These distinguish between the different designs of vehicle, each different design being allocated a unique two digit number.

Special Note

Where vehicles have been declassified the correct design code for a declassified vehicle is given, even though this may be at variance with official records which do not show the reality of the current position. A declassified composite is still referred to as a composite if it still retains the first class style seats in the erstwhile first class section of the vehicle. Its declassification is denoted by the fact that the first figure of the design code is a '2'.

THE FOLLOWING DETAILS APPLY TO BOTH DMUS AND EMUS:

ACCOMMODATION

This information is given in class headings and sub headings in the form F/S nT, where F & S denote the number of first class nd standard class seats followed by n which denotes the number of toilets. (e.g. 12/54 1T denotes 12 first class seats, 54 standard class seats and one toliet). In declassified vehicles, the capacity is still shown in terms of first and standard class seats to differentiate between the two physically different seat types available, although all seats are officially standard class in such instances.

BUILD DETAILS

LOT NUMBERS

Each batch of vehicles is allocated a Lot (or batch) number when ordered and these are quoted in class headings and sub headings.

BUILDERS

These are shown in class headings . A list of builders is given in section 7.6.

LAYOUT

The layout in this section is as follows:

(1) Unit number.
(2) Notes (if any).
(3) Livery code.
(4) Owner code.
(5) Operation code.
(6) Depot code.
(7) Individual car numbers.
(8) Name (if any).

Thus an example of the layout is as follows:

No.	Liv.	Owner	Op.	Depot	Car 1	Car 2	Name
150257	**RR**	P	AR	NC	52257	57257	Queen Boadicea

Note: For off-loan vehicles, the last storage location is given where known.

3.1. 'HERITAGE' DIESEL MULTIPLE UNITS

Very few first generation diesel multiple units remain. These are now referred to as 'heritage' units. Standard features are as follows:

Brakes:

All units are vacuum braked.

Lighting:

All cars are now fitted with fluorescent lighting.

Couplings:

Screw couplings are used on all vehicles. All remaining first generation vehicles may be coupled together to work in multiple up to a maximum of 6 motor cars or 12 cars in total in a formation. First generation vehicles may not be coupled in multiple with second generation vehicles.

CLASS 101   METRO-CAMMELL

Engines: Two Leyland of 112 kW (150 hp) per power car.
Transmission: Mechanical. Cardan shaft and freewheel to a four-speed epicyclic gearbox with a further cardan shaft to the final drive, each engine driving the inner axle of one bogie.
Gangways: Midland scissors type. Within unit only.
Doors: Slam.
Bogies: DD15 (motor) and DT11 (trailer).
Dimensions: 18.49 x 2.82 m.
Seats: 3 + 2 facing (2 + 2 in first class).

51175 – 51253. DMBS. Dia. DQ202. Lot No. 30467 1958 – 59. –/52. 32.5 t.
51426 – 51463. DMBS. Dia. DQ202. Lot No. 30500 1959. –/52. (–/49 with additional luggage rack for Gatwick sets – Dia. DQ232) 32.5 t.
53164. DMBS. Dia. DQ202. Lot No. 30254 1956. –/52. 32.5 t.
53198 – 53204. DMBS. Dia. DQ202. Lot No. 30259 1957. –/52. 32.5 t.
53211 – 53228. DMBS. Dia. DQ202. Lot No. 30261 1957. –/52. 32.5 t.
53253 – 53256. DMBS. Dia. DQ202. Lot No. 30266 1957. –/52. 32.5 t.
53311 – 53314. DMBS. Dia. DQ202. Lot No. 30275 1958. –/52. (–/49 with additional luggage rack for Gatwick sets – Dia. DQ232) 32.5 t.
51496 – 51533. DMCL or DMSL. Dia. DP317 or DP210. Lot No. 30501 1959. 12/46 1T with additional luggage racks. 32.5t.
51800. DMBS. Dia. DQ202. Lot No. 30587 1956. –/52. 32.5 t.
51803. DMSL. Dia. DP210. Lot No. 30588 1959. –/72 1T. 32.5 t.
53160 – 53163. DMSL. Dia. DP214. Lot No. 30253 1956. –/72 1T. 32.5 t.
53170 – 53171. DMSL. Dia. DP214. Lot No. 30255 1957. –/72 1T. 32.5 t.
53177. DMSL. Dia. DP214. Lot No. 30256 1957. –/72 1T. 32.5 t.
53266 – 53269. DMSL. Dia. DP210. Lot No. 30267 1957. –/72 1T. 32.5 t.
53322 – 53327. DMCL. Dia. DP317. Lot No. 30276 1958. 12/46 1T with additional luggage racks. 32.5 t.
53746. DMSL. Dia. DP210. Lot No. 30271 1957. –/72 1T. 32.5 t.
54055 – 54061. DTSL. Dia. DS206. Lot No. 30260 1957. –/72 1T. 25.5 t.

54062 – 54091. DTSL. Dia. DS206. Lot No. 30262 1957. –/72 1T. 25.5 t.
54343 – 54408. DTSL. Dia. DS206. Lot No. 30468 1958. –/72 1T. 25.5 t.
59303. TSL. Dia. DT202. Lot No. 30273 1957. –/71 1T. 25.5 t.
59539. TSL. Dia. DT228. Lot No. 30502 1959. –/72 1T. 25.5 t.

Refurbished 2-car Sets. DMBS – DTSL.

101 651	**RR**	A	NW	LO	53201	54379
101 652	**RR**	A	NW	LO	53198	54346
101 653	**RR**	A	NW	LO	51426	54358
101 654	**RR**	A	NW	LO	51800	54408
101 655	**RR**	A	NW	LO	51428	54062
101 656	**RR**	A	NW	LO	51230	54056
101 657	**RR**	A	NW	LO	53211	54085
101 658	**RR**	A	NW	LO	51175	54091
101 659	**RR**	A	NW	LO	51213	54352
101 660	**RR**	A	NW	LO	51189	54343
101 661	**RR**	A	NW	LO	51463	54365
101 662	**RR**	A	NW	LO	53228	54055
101 663	**RR**	A	NW	LO	51201	54347
101 664	**RR**	A	NW	LO	51442	54061
101 665	**RR**	A	NW	LO	51429	54393

Refurbished Twin Power Car and 3-Car Sets. DMBS – DMSL or DMBS – TSL – DMSL.

Non-Standard livery: Caledonian Blue.

101 676	**RR**	A	NW	LO	51205		51803
101 677	**RR**	A	NW	LO	51179		51496
101 678	**RR**	A	NW	LO	51210		53746
101 679	**RR**	A	NW	LO	51224		51533
101 680	**RR**	A	NW	LO	53204		53163
101 681	**RR**	A	NW	LO	51228		51506
101 682	**RR**	A	NW	LO	53256		51505
101 683	**RR**	A	NW	LO	51177	59303	53269
101 684	**S**	A	SR	CK	51187		51509
101 685	**G**	A	NW	LO	53164	59539	53160
101 686	**S**	A	SR	CK	51231		51500
101 687	**S**	A	SR	CK	51247		51512
101 688	**S**	A	SR	CK	51431		51501
101 689	**S**	A	SR	CK	51185		51511
101 690	**S**	A	SR	CK	51435		53177
101 691	**S**	A	SR	CK	51253		53171
101 692	**0**	A	SR	CK	53253		53170
101 693	**S**	A	SR	CK	51192		53266
101 694	**S**	A	SR	CK	51188		53268
101 695	**S**	A	SR	CK	51226		51499

Note: The trailer cars of 101 683 and 101 685 are sometimes removed and stored at Chester CSD.

Unrefurbished Twin Power Car Sets. DMBS – DMCL. These sets have seats removed and additional luggage racks. These modifications were carried out when they were used on Reading – Gatwick Airport services.

Note: Some units show 'L' instead of the official class prefix.

101 835	**RR**	A	NW	LO	51432	51498
101 840	**N**	A	NW	LO	53311	53322
101 842	**N**	A	WW	PZ	53314	53327

CLASS 117   PRESSED STEEL SUBURBAN

DMBS – TSL – DMS or DMBS – DMS (DMBS – DMBS*).
Engines: Two Leyland 680/1 of 112 kW (150 hp) per power car.
Transmission: Mechanical. Cardan shaft and freewheel to a four-speed epicyclic gearbox with a further cardan shaft to the final drive, each engine driving the inner axle of one bogie.
Gangways: GWR suspension type. Within unit only.
Bogies: DD10 (motor) and DT9 (trailer).
Dimensions: 20.45 x 2.82 m.
Seats: 3 + 2 facing.

Non-standard Livery: 51368 of 117 305 is in GWR chocolate & cream whilst 51361 is in '**N**' livery (and is not refurbished).

DMBS. Dia. DQ220. Lot No. 30546 1959 – 60. – /65. 36.5 t.
TSL. Dia. DT230. Lot No. 30547 1959 – 60. – 78 2T. 30.5 t.
DMS. Dia. DP221. Lot No. 30548 1959 – 60. – /89. 36.5 t.

Note: Some units show 'L' instead of the official class prefix.

117 301	f	**RR**	A	SR	HA	51353	59505	51395
117 305	f*	**0**	A	WW	PZ	51368		51361
117 306	f	**RR**	A	SR	HA	51369	59521	51411
117 308	f	**RR**	A	SR	HA	51371	59509	51413
117 310	f	**RR**	A	SR	HA	51373	59486	51381
117 311	f	**RR**	A	SR	HA	51334	59500	51376
117 313	f	**RR**	A	SR	HA	51339	59492	51382
117 314	f	**RR**	A	SR	HA	51352	59489	51394
117 700		**N**	A	NL	BY	51332		51374
117 701		**N**	A	NL	BY	51350		51392
117 702		**N**	A	NL	BY	51356		51398
117 703		**N**	A		BY	51359		51401
117 704		**N**	A	NL	BY	51341		51383
117 705		**N**	A	NL	BY	51358		51400
117 706		**N**	A	NL	BY	51366		51408
117 707		**N**	A	NL	BY	51335		51377
117 708		**N**	A	WW	PZ	51336		51378
117 709		**N**	A	WW	PZ	51344		51386
117 720		**N**	A	NL	BY	51354		51396
117 721		**N**	A	NL	BY	51363		51405
117 724		**N**	A	NL	BY	51333		51375

Name: 51332 of 117 700 is named 'Marston Vale'.

CLASS 121   PRESSED STEEL SUBURBAN

DMBS.
Engines: Two Leyland 1595 of 112 kW (150 hp) per power car.
Transmission: Mechanical. Cardan shaft and freewheel to a four-speed epicyclic gearbox with a further cardan shaft to the final drive, each engine driving the inner axle of one bogie.
Gangways: Non gangwayed single cars with cabs at each end.
Bogies: DD10 (motor) and DT9 (trailer).
Dimensions: 20.45 x 2.82 m.
Seats: 3 + 2 facing.

DMBS. Dia. DX201. Lot No. 30518 1960. −/65. 38.0 t.

Notes: Some of the sets show 'L' instead of the official class prefix.

121 123	G	A	BY	55023
121 127	N	A NL	BY	55027
121 129	N	A NL	BY	55029
121 131	N	A NL	BY	55031

CLASS 122   GLOUCESTER SUBURBAN

DMBS.
Engines: Two AEC 220 of 112 kW (150 hp) per power car.
Transmission: Mechanical. Cardan shaft and freewheel to a four-speed epicyclic gearbox with a further cardan shaft to the final drive, each engine driving the inner axle of one bogie.
Gangways: Non gangwayed single car with cabs at each end.
Bogies: DD10 (motor) and DT9 (trailer).
Dimensions: 20.45 x 2.82 m.
Seats: 3 + 2 facing.

DMBS. Dia. DX202. Lot No. 30419 1958. −/65. 36.5 t.

Note: This unit is used as a crew-training vehicle and does not carry its unit number.

122 012	LH	W CT	TE	55012

3.2. SECOND GENERATION DMUS

Unit Types

There are five basic types of second generation vehicle as referred to in the class headings as follows:

● **Pacers** (Railbuses). Folding power operated exterior doors. Bus-type 3 + 2 (2 + 2 on class 141) largely unidirectional seating. Limited luggage space. Four wheel chassis. 75 mph.

● **Sprinter.** Sliding power operated exterior double doors to large entrance vestibules. High backed 3 + 2 seating. Limited luggage space. 75 mph.

● **Super Sprinter.** Sliding/sliding plug power-operated exterior doors. High backed 2 + 2 largely unidirectional seating with some tables. 75 mph.

● **Express.** Sliding plug power-operated exterior doors. Air conditioned. High backed 2 + 2 half-facing and half-unidirectional seating with some tables. 90 mph.

● **Network Turbo.** Sliding power operated exterior double doors to large entrance vestibules. 3 + 2 seating. Limited luggage space. 90 mph.

Public Address System: All vehicles are equipped with public address, with transmission equipment on driving vehicles.

Gangways: Unless stated otherwise, all vehicles have flexible diaphragm gangways.

Couplings: Unless otherwise stated all vehicles are fitted with BSI automatic couplings at their outer ends. Railbus types are fitted with bar couplings at their inner ends, but all other types have BSI couplings at their inner ends unless otherwise stated.

Brakes: All vehicles are fitted with electro-pneumatic and air brakes.

CLASS 141   LEYLAND BUS/BREL RAILBUS

DMS – DMSL. Built from Leyland National bus parts on four-wheeled underframes.

Engines: One Leyland TL11 152 kW (205 hp) (* Cummins LT10-R) per car.
Transmission: Hydraulic. Voith T211r with Gmeinder final drive.
Gangways: Within unit only.
Doors: Folding.
Dimensions: 15.45 x 2.50 m.
Accommodation: 2 + 2 bus style.
Maximum Speed: 75 mph.

DMS. Dia. DP228 Lot No. 30977 Derby 1984. Modified by Barclay 1988 – 89.
–/50. 26.0 t.
DMSL. Dia. DP229 Lot No. 30978 Derby 1984. Modified by Barclay 1988 – 89.
–/44. 1T. 26.5 t.

141 101		Y	P	NE	NL	55521 55541
141 102		Y	P	NE	NL	55502 55522
141 103		Y	P		ZB	55503 55523
141 104		Y	P		ZB	55505 55525
141 105		Y	P		ZB	55505 55525
141 106		Y	P		ZB	55506 55526
141 107		Y	P		ZB	55507 55527
141 108		Y	P		ZB	55508 55528
141 109		Y	P	NE	NL	55509 55529
141 110		Y	P		ZB	55510 55530
141 111		Y	P	NE	NL	55511 55531
141 112		Y	P		ZB	55512 55532
141 113	*	Y	P	NE	NL	55513 55533
141 114		Y	P	NE	NL	55514 55534
141 115		Y	P	NE	NL	55515 55535
141 116		Y	P		ZB	55516 55536
141 117		Y	P	NE	NL	55517 55537
141 118		Y	P		ZB	55518 55538
141 119		Y	P	NE	NL	55519 55539
141 120		Y	P		ZB	55520 55540

CLASS 142   LEYLAND BUS/BREL RAILBUS

DMS – DMSL. Development of Class 141 with wider body and improved appearance.

Engines: One Cummins LTA10-R of 170 kW (225 h.p.) per car.
Transmission: Hydraulic. Voith T211r with Gmeinder final drive.
Gangways: Within unit only.
Doors: Folding.
Dimensions: 15.55 x 2.80 m.
Accommodation: 2 + 3 bus style.
Maximum Speed: 75 mph.
Non-Standard Livery: Chocolate & Cream.

55542 – 55591. DMS. Dia. DP234 Lot No. 31003 Derby 1985 – 6. – /62.
24.5 t.
55592 – 55641. DMSL. Dia. DP235 Lot No. 31004 Derby 1985 – 6. – /59 1T.
25.0 t.
55701 – 55746. DMS. Dia. DP234 Lot No. 31013 Derby 1986 – 7. – /62.
24.5 t.
55747 – 55792. DMSL. Dia. DP235 Lot No. 31014 Derby 1986 – 7. – /59 1T.
25.0 t.

142 001	GM	A	NW	NH	55542	55592
142 002	GM	A	NW	NH	55543	55593
142 003	GM	A	NW	NH	55544	55594
142 004	GM	A	NW	NH	55545	55595
142 005	GM	A	NW	NH	55546	55596
142 006	GM	A	NW	NH	55547	55597
142 007	GM	A	NW	NH	55548	55598
142 008	GM	A	NW	NH	55549	55599
142 009	GM	A	NW	NH	55550	55600
142 010	GM	A	NW	NH	55551	55601
142 011	GM	A	NW	NH	55552	55602
142 012	GM	A	NW	NH	55553	55603
142 013	GM	A	NW	NH	55554	55604
142 014	GM	A	NW	NH	55555	55605
142 015	RR	A	NE	HT	55556	55606
142 016	RR	A	NE	HT	55557	55607
142 017	T	A	NE	HT	55558	55608
142 018	T	A	NE	HT	55559	55609
142 019	T	A	NE	HT	55560	55610
142 020	T	A	NE	HT	55561	55611
142 021	T	A	NE	HT	55562	55612
142 022	T	A	NE	HT	55563	55613
142 023	RR	A	NW	NH	55564	55614
142 024	0	A	NE	HT	55565	55615
142 025	0	A	NE	HT	55566	55616
142 026	0	A	NE	HT	55567	55617
142 027	0	A	NW	NH	55568	55618
142 028	GM	A	NW	NH	55569	55619
142 029	GM	A	NW	NH	55570	55620
142 030	GM	A	NW	NH	55571	55621
142 031	GM	A	NW	NH	55572	55622
142 032	GM	A	NW	NH	55573	55623
142 033	RR	A	NW	NH	55574	55624
142 034	GM	A	NW	NH	55575	55625
142 035	GM	A	NW	NH	55576	55626
142 036	RR	A	NW	NH	55577	55627
142 037	GM	A	NW	NH	55578	55628
142 038	GM	A	NW	NH	55579	55629
142 039	GM	A	NW	NH	55580	55630
142 040	GM	A	NW	NH	55581	55631
142 041	GM	A	NW	NH	55582	55632
142 042	GM	A	NW	NH	55583	55633

142 043	**GM**	A	NW	NH	55584 55634
142 044	**GM**	A	NW	NH	55585 55635
142 045	**GM**	A	NW	NH	55586 55636
142 046	**GM**	A	NW	NH	55587 55637
142 047	**RR**	A	NW	NH	55588 55638
142 048	**RR**	A	NW	NH	55589 55639
142 049	**PR**	A	NW	NH	55590 55640
142 050	**PR**	A	NE	HT	55591 55641
142 051	**MT**	A	NW	NH	55701 55747
142 052	**MT**	A	NW	NH	55702 55748
142 053	**MT**	A	NW	NH	55703 55749
142 054	**MT**	A	NW	NH	55704 55750
142 055	**MT**	A	NW	NH	55705 55751
142 056	**MT**	A	NW	NH	55706 55752
142 057	**MT**	A	NW	NH	55707 55753
142 058	**MT**	A	NW	NH	55708 55754
142 060	**PR**	A	NW	NH	55710 55756
142 061	**PR**	A	NW	NH	55711 55757
142 062	**PR**	A	NW	NH	55712 55758
142 063	**PR**	A	NW	NH	55713 55759
142 064	**PR**	A	NW	NH	55714 55760
142 065	**PR**	A	NE	HT	55715 55761
142 066	**PR**	A	NE	HT	55716 55762
142 067	**GM**	A	NW	NH	55717 55763
142 068	**GM**	A	NW	NH	55718 55764
142 069	**GM**	A	NW	NH	55719 55765
142 070	**PR**	A	NW	NH	55720 55766
142 071	**PR**	A	NE	HT	55721 55767
142 072	**RR**	A	NE	NL	55722 55768
142 073	**RR**	A	NE	NL	55723 55769
142 074	**RR**	A	NE	NL	55724 55770
142 075	**RR**	A	NE	NL	55725 55771
142 076	**RR**	A	NE	NL	55726 55772
142 077	**RR**	A	NE	NL	55727 55773
142 078	**RR**	A	NE	NL	55728 55774
142 079	**RR**	A	NE	NL	55729 55775
142 080	**RR**	A	NE	NL	55730 55776
142 081	**RR**	A	NE	NL	55731 55777
142 082	**RR**	A	NE	NL	55732 55778
142 083	**RR**	A	NE	NL	55733 55779
142 084	**RR**	A	NE	NL	55734 55780
142 085	**RR**	A	NE	NL	55735 55781
142 086	**RR**	A	NE	NL	55736 55782
142 087	**RR**	A	NE	NL	55737 55783
142 088	**PR**	A	NE	NL	55738 55784
142 089	**PR**	A	NE	NL	55739 55785
142 090	**PR**	A	NE	NL	55740 55786
142 091	**RR**	A	NE	NL	55741 55787
142 092	**RR**	A	NE	NL	55742 55788
142 093	**RR**	A	NE	NL	55743 55789
142 094	**RR**	A	NE	NL	55744 55790

| 142 095 | **RR** | A | NE | NL | 55745 55791 |
| 142 096 | **RR** | A | NE | NL | 55746 55792 |

CLASS 143   ALEXANDER/BARCLAY RAILBUS

DMS – DMSL. Similar design to Class 142, but bodies built by W. Alexander with Barclay underframes.

Engines: One Cummins LTA10-R of 170 kW (225 h.p.) per car.
Transmission: Hydraulic. Voith T211r with Gmeinder final drive.
Gangways: Within unit only.
Doors: Folding.
Dimensions: 15.55 x 2.70 m.
Accommodation: 2 + 3 bus style.
Maximum Speed: 75 mph.

DMS. Dia. DP236 Lot No. 31005 Andrew Barclay 1985 – 6. – /62. 24.5 t.
DMSL. Dia. DP237 Lot No. 31006 Andrew Barclay 1985-6. -60 1T. 25.0 t.

Note: 143 601104 are owned by Mid-Glamorgan County Council. 143 609 is owned by West Glamorgan County Council and 143 617-9 are owned by West Glamorgan County Council. They are all managed by Porterbrook Leasing Company.

g Fitted with global positioning system.

143 601		**RR**	P	WW	CF	55642 55667	
143 602	g	**RR**	P	CA	CF	55651 55668	
143 603	g	**RR**	P	CA	CF	55658 55669	
143 604	g	**RR**	P	CA	CF	55645 55670	
143 605	g	**RR**	P	CA	CF	55646 55671	
143 606	g	**RR**	P	CA	CF	55647 55672	
143 607	g	**RR**	P	CA	CF	55648 55673	
143 608	g	**RR**	P	CA	CF	55649 55674	
143 609	g	**RR**	P	CA	CF	55650 55675	
143 610		**RR**	P	WW	CF	55643 55676	
143 611	g	**RR**	P	CA	CF	55652 55677	
143 612		**RR**	P	WW	CF	55653 55678	
143 613	g	**RR**	P	CA	CF	55654 55679	
143 614		**RR**	P	WW	CF	55655 55680	
143 615	g	**RR**	P	CA	CF	55656 55681	
143 616	g	**RR**	P	CA	CF	55657 55682	
143 617		**RR**	P	WW	CF	55644 55683	Bewick's Swan
143 618		**RR**	P	WW	CF	55659 55684	Mute Swan
143 619		**RR**	P	WW	CF	55660 55685	Whooper Swan
143 620		**RR**	P	WW	CF	55661 55686	
143 621		**RR**	P	WW	CF	55662 55687	
143 622		**RR**	P	WW	CF	55663 55688	
143 623		**RR**	P	WW	CF	55664 55689	
143 624		**RR**	P	WW	CF	55665 55690	
143 625		**RR**	P	WW	CF	55666 55691	

CLASS 144   ALEXANDER/BREL RAILBUS

DMS – DMSL or DMS – MS – DMSL. Similar design to Class 143, but underframes built by BREL as subcontractor to W. Alexander.

Engines: One Cummins LTA10-R of 170 kW (225 h.p.) per car.
Transmission: Hydraulic. Voith T211r with Gmeinder final drive.
Gangways: Within unit only.
Doors: Folding.
Dimensions: 15.25 x 2.70 m.
Accommodation: 2 + 3 bus style.
Maximum Speed: 75 mph.

DMS. Dia. DP240 Lot No. 31015 Derby 1986 – 7. –/62 and wheelchair space.
24.2 t.
MS. Dia. DR205 Lot No. Derby 31037 1987. –/73. 22.6 t.
DMSL. Dia. DP241 Lot No. Derby 31016 1986 – 7. –/60 1T. 25.0 t.

Note: The centre cars of the three-car units are owned by West Yorkshire PTE,
although managed by Porterbrook Leasing Company.

144 001	Y	P	NE	NL	55801	55824
144 002	Y	P	NE	NL	55802	55825
144 003	Y	P	NE	NL	55803	55826
144 004	Y	P	NE	NL	55804	55827
144 005	Y	P	NE	NL	55805	55828
144 006	Y	P	NE	NL	55806	55829
144 007	Y	P	NE	NL	55807	55830
144 008	Y	P	NE	NL	55808	55831
144 009	Y	P	NE	NL	55809	55832
144 010	Y	P	NE	NL	55810	55833
144 011	RR	P	NE	NL	55811	55834
144 012	RR	P	NE	NL	55812	55835
144 013	RR	P	NE	NL	55813	55836
144 014	Y	P	NE	NL	55814 55850	55837
144 015	Y	P	NE	NL	55815 55851	55838
144 016	Y	P	NE	NL	55816 55852	55839
144 017	Y	P	NE	NL	55817 55853	55840
144 018	Y	P	NE	NL	55818 55854	55841
144 019	Y	P	NE	NL	55819 55855	55842
144 020	Y	P	NE	NL	55820 55856	55843
144 021	Y	P	NE	NL	55821 55857	55844
144 022	Y	P	NE	NL	55822 55858	55845
144 023	Y	P	NE	NL	55823 55859	55846

CLASS 150/0   BREL PROTOTYPE SPRINTER

DMSL – MS – DMS. Prototype Sprinter.

Engines: One Cummins NT855R5 of 210 kW (285 hp) per car.
Transmission: Hydraulic. Voith T211r with Gmeinder final drive.
Bogies: One BX8P and one BX8T.

Couplings: BSI at outer end of driving vehicles, bar non-driving ends.
Gangways: Within unit only.
Doors: Sliding.
Accommodation: 2 + 3 (mainly unidirectional).
Dimensions: 20.06 x 2.82 m (outer cars), 20.18 x 2.82 m (inner car).
Maximum Speed: 75 mph.

DMSL. Dia. DP230. Lot No. 30984 York 1984. –/72 1T. 35.8 t.
MS. Dia. DR202. Lot No. 30986 York 1984. –/92. 34.4 t.
DMS. Dia. DP231. Lot No. 30985 York 1984. –/76. 35.6 t.

Note: 150 002 was converted to 154 002 at RTC Derby in 1986, but was later converted back to a Class 150.

150 001	**CE**	A	CT	TS	55200 55400 55300	
150 002	**CE**	A	CT	TS	55201 55401 55301	

CLASS 150/1   **BREL SPRINTER**

DMSL – DMS or DMSL – DMSL (Class 150/2) – DMS or DMSL – DMS (Class 150/2) – DMS.

Engines: One Cummins NT855R5 of 210 kW (285 hp) per car.
Transmission: Hydraulic. Voith T211r with Gmeinder final drive.
Bogies: One BP38 and one BT38.
Gangways: Within unit only.
Doors: Sliding.
Accommodation: 2 + 3 facing. (★ Reseated with part unidirectional seating and part facing).
Dimensions: 20.06 x 2.82 m.
Maximum Speed: 75 mph.

DMSL. Dia. DP238. Lot No. 31011 York 1985 – 6. –/68 1T (–/64 1T*, –/72 1T★). 36.5 t.
DMS. Dia. DP239. Lot No. 31012 York 1985 – 6. –/70 (–/76★, –/66§). 38.45 t.

Note: The centre cars of three-car units are Class 150/2 vehicles. For details see next Class.

150 010	r★ **CE**	A	CT	TS	52110	57226	57110
150 011	r★ **CE**	A	CT	TS	52111	57206	57111
150 012	r★ **CE**	A	CT	TS	52112	52204	57112
150 013	r★ **CE**	A	CT	TS	52113	52226	57113
150 014	r★ **CE**	A	CT	TS	52114	57204	57114
150 015	r★ **CE**	A	CT	TS	52115	52206	57115
150 016	r★ **CE**	A	CT	TS	52116	57212	57116
150 017	r★ **CE**	A	CT	TS	52117	57209	57117
150 101	r★ **CE**	A	CT	TS	52101		57101
150 102	r★ **CE**	A	CT	TS	52102		57102
150 103	r★ **CE**	A	CT	TS	52103		57103
150 104	r★ **CE**	A	CT	TS	52104		57104
150 105	r★ **CE**	A	CT	TS	52105		57105

150 106	r★ **CE**	A	CT	TS	52106	57106
150 107	r★ **CE**	A	CT	TS	52107	57107
150 108	r★ **CE**	A	CT	TS	52108	57108
150 109	r★ **CE**	A	CT	TS	52109	57109
150 118	r★ **CE**	A	CT	TS	52118	57118
150 120	r★ **CE**	A	CT	TS	52120	57120
150 121	r★ **CE**	A	CT	TS	52121	57121
150 122	r★ **CE**	A	CT	TS	52122	57122
150 123	r★ **CE**	A	CT	TS	52123	57123
150 124	r★ **CE**	A	CT	TS	52124	57124
150 125	r★ **CE**	A	CT	TS	52125	57125
150 126	r★ **CE**	A	CT	TS	52126	57126
150 127	r★ **CE**	A	CT	TS	52127	57127
150 128	r★ **CE**	A	CT	TS	52128	57128
150 129	r★ **CE**	A	CT	TS	52129	57129
150 130	r★ **CE**	A	CT	TS	52130	57130
150 131	r★ **CE**	A	CT	TS	52131	57131
150 132	r★ **CE**	A	CT	TS	52132	57132
150 133	r* **GM**	A	NW	NH	52133	57133
150 134	r* **GM**	A	NW	NH	52134	57134
150 135	r* **GM**	A	NW	NH	52135	57135
150 136	r* **GM**	A	NW	NH	52136	57136
150 137	r§ **GM**	A	NW	NH	52137	57137
150 138	r* **GM**	A	NW	NH	52138	57138
150 139	r* **GM**	A	NW	NH	52139	57139
150 140	r* **GM**	A	NW	NH	52140	57140
150 141	r* **GM**	A	NW	NH	52141	57141
150 142	r§ **GM**	A	NW	NH	52142	57142
150 143	r* **P**	A	NW	NH	52143	57143
150 144	r§ **P**	A	NW	NH	52144	57144
150 145	r§ **P**	A	NW	NH	52145	57145
150 146	r§ **RR**	A	NW	NH	52146	57146
150 147	r§ **P**	A	NW	NH	52147	57147
150 148	r§ **P**	A	NW	NH	52148	57148
150 149	r§ **P**	A	NW	NH	52149	57149
150 150	r§ **P**	A	NW	NH	52150	57150

CLASS 150/2 — BREL SPRINTER

DMSL – DMS.

Engines: One Cummins NT855R5 of 210 kW (285 hp) per car.
Transmission: Hydraulic. Voith T211r with Gmeinder final drive.
Bogies: One BP38 and one BT38.
Gangways: Throughout.
Doors: Sliding.
Accommodation: 2 + 3 mainly unidirectional.
Dimensions: 20.06 x 2.82 m.
Maximum Speed: 75 mph.

DMSL. Dia. DP242. Lot No. 31017 York 1986 – 87. –/73 1T (– 70 1T*).
35.8 t.

DMS. Dia. DP243. Lot No. 31018 York 1986 – 7. –/76 (–/73§) and luggage space. 34.90 t.

g Fitted with global positioning system.

150 201	*	**MT**	A	NW	NH	52201 57201	
150 202		**CE**	A	CT	TS	52202 57202	
150 203	*	**MT**	A	NW	NH	52203 57203	
150 205	*	**MT**	A	NW	NH	52205 57205	
150 207	§	**MT**	A	NW	NH	52207 57207	
150 208		**RR**	P	SR	HA	52208 57208	
150 210		**CE**	A	CT	TS	52210 57210	
150 211	§	**MT**	A	NW	NH	52211 57211	
150 213		**RR**	P	AR	NC	52213 57213	Lord Nelson
150 214		**CE**	A	CT	TS	52214 57214	
150 215		**GM**	A	NW	NH	52215 57215	
150 216		**CE**	A	CT	TS	52216 57216	
150 217		**RR**	P	AR	NC	52217 57217	Oliver Cromwell
150 218	* §	**GM**	A	NW	NH	52218 57218	
150 219		**RR**	P	WW	CF	52219 57219	
150 220		**CE**	A	CT	TS	52220 57220	
150 221		**RR**	P	WW	CF	52221 57221	
150 222	§	**GM**	A	NW	NH	52222 57222	
150 223	*	**GM**	A	NW	NH	52223 57223	
150 224	*	**GM**	A	NW	NH	52224 57224	
150 225	§	**GM**	A	NW	NH	52225 57225	
150 227		**RR**	P	AR	NC	52227 57227	Sir Alf Ramsey
150 228		**RR**	P	SR	HA	52228 57228	
150 229		**RR**	P	AR	NC	52229 57229	George Borrow
150 230		**RR**	P	WW	CF	52230 57230	
150 231		**RR**	P	AR	NC	52231 57231	King Edmund
150 232		**RR**	P	WW	CF	52232 57232	
150 233		**RR**	P	WW	CF	52233 57233	
150 234		**RR**	P	WW	CF	52234 57234	
150 235		**RR**	P	AR	NC	52235 57235	Cardinal Wolsey
150 236		**RR**	P	WW	CF	52236 57236	
150 237		**RR**	P	AR	NC	52237 57237	Hereward the Wake
150 238		**RR**	P	WW	CF	52238 57238	
150 239		**RR**	P	WW	CF	52239 57239	
150 240		**RR**	P	WW	CF	52240 57240	
150 241		**RR**	P	WW	CF	52241 57241	
150 242		**RR**	P	WW	CF	52242 57242	
150 243		**RR**	P	WW	CF	52243 57243	
150 244		**RR**	P	WW	CF	52244 57244	
150 245		**RR**	P	SR	HA	52245 57245	
150 246		**RR**	P	WW	CF	52246 57246	
150 247		**RR**	P	WW	CF	52247 57247	
150 248		**RR**	P	WW	CF	52248 57248	
150 249		**RR**	P	WW	CF	52249 57249	
150 250		**RR**	P	SR	HA	52250 57250	
150 251		**RR**	P	WW	CF	52251 57251	
150 252		**RR**	P	SR	HA	52252 57252	

150 253		**RR**	P	WW	CF	52253 57253	
150 254		**RR**	P	WW	CF	52254 57254	
150 255		**RR**	P	AR	NC	52255 57255	Henry Blogg
150 256		**RR**	P	SR	HA	52256 57256	
150 257		**RR**	P	AR	NC	52257 57257	Queen Boadicea
150 258		**RR**	P	SR	HA	52258 57258	
150 259		**RR**	P	SR	HA	52259 57259	
150 260		**RR**	P	SR	HA	52260 57260	
150 261		**RR**	P	WW	CF	52261 57261	
150 262		**RR**	P	SR	HA	52262 57262	
150 263		**RR**	P	WW	CF	52263 57263	
150 264		**RR**	P	SR	HA	52264 57264	
150 265	g	**RR**	P	CA	CF	52265 57265	
150 266	g	**RR**	P	CA	CF	52266 57266	
150 267	g	**RR**	P	CA	CF	52267 57267	
150 268	g	**RR**	P	CA	CF	52268 57268	
150 269	g	**RR**	P	CA	CF	52269 57269	
150 270	g	**RR**	P	CA	CF	52270 57270	
150 271	g	**RR**	P	CA	CF	52271 57271	
150 272	g	**RR**	P	CA	CF	52272 57272	
150 273	g	**RR**	P	CA	CF	52273 57273	
150 274		**RR**	P	NW	NH	52274 57274	
150 275	g	**RR**	P	CA	CF	52275 57275	
150 276	g	**RR**	P	CA	CF	52276 57276	
150 277	g	**RR**	P	CA	CF	52277 57277	
150 278	g	**RR**	P	CA	CF	52278 57278	
150 279	g	**RR**	P	CA	CF	52279 57279	
150 280	g	**RR**	P	CA	CF	52280 57280	
150 281	g	**RR**	P	CA	CF	52281 57281	
150 282	g	**RR**	P	CA	CF	52282 57282	
150 283		**RR**	P	SR	HA	52283 57283	
150 284		**RR**	P	SR	HA	52284 57284	
150 285		**RR**	P	SR	HA	52285 57285	EDINBURGH – BATHGATE 1986 – 1996

CLASS 153   LEYLAND BUS SUPER SPRINTER

DMSL. Converted by Hunslet-Barclay, Kilmarnock from Class 155 two-car units.

Engines: One Cummins NT855R5 of 213 kW (285 hp) per car.
Transmission: Hydraulic. Voith T211r with Gmeinder final drive.
Bogies: One P3-10 and one BT38.
Gangways: Throughout.
Doors: Sliding plug.
Accommodation: 2 + 2 facing/unidirectional with wheelchair space.
Dimensions: 23.21 x 2.70 m.
Maximum Speed: 75 mph.

52301 – 52335. DMSL. Dia. DX203. Lot No. 31026 1987 – 8. Converted under Lot No. 31115 1991 – 2. –/72 1TD + 3 tip-up seats. 41.2 t.
57301 – 57335. DMSL. Dia. DX203. Lot No. 31027 1987 – 8. Converted under Lot No. 31115 1991 – 2. –/72 1TD + 3 tip-up seats. 41.2 t.

Notes:

Cars numbered in the 573XX series have been renumbered by adding 50 to the number so that the last two digits correspond with the set number.
Certain Central Trains units have been fitted with new-style seating.

153 301	**RR**	A	NE	HT	52301	
153 302	**RR**	A	WW	CF	52302	
153 303	**RR**	A	WW	CF	52303	
153 304	**RR**	A	NE	HT	52304	
153 305	**RR**	A	WW	CF	52305	
153 306	**RR**	P	AR	NC	52306	Edith Cavell
153 307	**RR**	A	NE	HT	52307	
153 308	**RR**	A	WW	CF	52308	
153 309	**RR**	P	AR	NC	52309	Gerard Fiennes
153 310	**RR**	P	NW	NH	52310	
153 311	**RR**	P	AR	NC	52311	John Constable
153 312	**RR**	A	WW	CF	52312	
153 313	**RR**	P	NW	NH	52313	
153 314	**RR**	P	AR	NC	52314	Delia Smith
153 315	**RR**	A	NE	HT	52315	
153 316	**RR**	P	NW	NH	52316	
153 317	**RR**	A	NE	HT	52317	
153 318	**RR**	A	WW	CF	52318	
153 319	**RR**	A	NE	HT	52319	
153 320	**RR**	P	CT	TS	52320	
153 321	**RR**	P	CT	TS	52321	
153 322	**RR**	P	AR	NC	52322	Benjamin Britten
153 323	**RR**	P	CT	TS	52323	
153 324	**RR**	P	NW	NH	52324	
153 325	**RR**	P	CT	TS	52325	
153 326	**RR**	P	AR	NC	52326	Ted Ellis
153 327	**RR**	A	WW	CF	52327	
153 328	**RR**	A	NE	HT	52328	
153 329	**RR**	P	CT	TS	52329	
153 330	**RR**	P	NW	NH	52330	
153 331	**RR**	A	NE	HT	52331	
153 332	**RR**	P	NW	NH	52332	
153 333	**RR**	P	CT	TS	52333	
153 334	**RR**	P	CT	TS	52334	
153 335	**RR**	P	AR	NC	52335	
153 351	**RR**	A	NE	HT	57351	
153 352	**RR**	A	NE	HT	57352	
153 353	**RR**	A	WW	CF	57353	
153 354	**RR**	P	CT	TS	57354	
153 355	**RR**	A	WW	CF	57355	
153 356	**RR**	P	CT	TS	57356	
153 357	**RR**	A	NE	HT	57357	
153 358	**RR**	P	NW	NH	57358	
153 359	**RR**	P	NW	NH	57359	
153 360	**RR**	P	NW	NH	57360	
153 361	**RR**	P	NW	NH	57361	

153 362	RR	A	WW	CF	57362
153 363	RR	P	NW	NH	57363
153 364	RR	P	CT	TS	57364
153 365	RR	P	CT	TS	57365
153 366	RR	P	CT	TS	57366
153 367	RR	P	NW	NH	57367
153 368	RR	A	WW	CF	57368
153 369	RR	P	CT	TS	57369
153 370	RR	A	WW	CF	57370
153 371	RR	P	CT	TS	57371
153 372	RR	A	WW	CF	57372
153 373	RR	A	WW	CF	57373
153 374	RR	A	WW	CF	57374
153 375	RR	P	CT	TS	57375
153 376	RR	P	CT	TS	57376
153 377	RR	A	WW	CF	57377
153 378	RR	A	NE	HT	57378
153 379	RR	P	CT	TS	57379
153 380	RR	A	WW	CF	57380
153 381	RR	P	CT	TS	57381
153 382	RR	A	WW	CF	57382
153 383	RR	P	CT	TS	57383
153 384	RR	P	CT	TS	57384
153 385	RR	P	CT	TS	57385

CLASS 155   LEYLAND BUS SUPER SPRINTER

DMSL – DMS.

Engines: One Cummins NT855R5 of 213 kW (285 hp) per car.
Transmission: Hydraulic. Voith T211r with Gmeinder final drive.
Bogies: One P3-10 and one BT38.
Gangways: Throughout.
Doors: Sliding plug.
Accommodation: 2 + 2 facing/unidirectional with wheelchair space in DMSL.
Dimensions: 23.21 x 2.70 m.
Maximum Speed: 75 mph.

DMSL. Dia. DP248. Lot No. 31057 1988. –/80 1TD. 39.0 t.
DMS. Dia. DP249. Lot No. 31058 1988. –/80 and parcels area. 38.7 t.

Note: These units are owned by West Yorkshire PTE, although managed by Porterbrook Leasing Company.

155 341	Y	P	NE	NL	52341 57341
155 342	Y	P	NE	NL	52342 57342
155 343	Y	P	NE	NL	52343 57343
155 344	Y	P	NE	NL	52344 57344
155 345	Y	P	NE	NL	52345 57345
155 346	Y	P	NE	NL	52346 57346
155 347	Y	P	NE	NL	52347 57347

CLASS 156   METRO-CAMMELL SUPER SPRINTER

DMSL – DMS.

Engines: One Cummins NT855R5 of 210 kW (285 hp) per car.
Transmission: Hydraulic. Voith T211r with Gmeinder final drive.
Bogies: One P3-10 and one BT38.
Gangways: Throughout.
Doors: Sliding.
Accommodation: 2 + 2 facing/unidirectional with wheelchair space in DMSL.
Dimensions: 23.03 x 2.73 m.
Maximum Speed: 75 mph.

DMSL. Dia. DP244. Lot No. 31028 1988 – 9. – /74 (– /70 ★ §) 1TD. 36.1 t.
DMS. Dia. DP245. Lot No. 31029 1987 – 9. 35.5 t. – /76 (72 ★) + parcels area.

Notes: 156 500 – 514 are owned by Strathclyde PTE, although managed by
Angel Trains Contracts. Units reliveried in "RE" or RN livery have been fitted
with new-style seats.

156 401		**RE**	P	CT	TS	52401 57401
156 402		**RE**	P	CT	TS	52402 57402
156 403		**RE**	P	CT	TS	52403 57403
156 404		**RE**	P	CT	TS	52404 57404
156 405		**RE**	P	CT	TS	52405 57405
156 406		**RE**	P	CT	TS	52406 57406
156 407		**RE**	P	CT	TS	52407 57407
156 408		**P**	P	CT	TS	52408 57408
156 409		**P**	P	CT	TS	52409 57409
156 410		**P**	P	CT	TS	52410 57410
156 411		**RE**	P	CT	TS	52411 57411
156 412		**P**	P	CT	TS	52412 57412
156 413		**P**	P	CT	TS	52413 57413
156 414		**P**	P	CT	TS	52414 57414
156 415		**RE**	P	CT	TS	52415 57415
156 416		**RE**	P	CT	TS	52416 57416
156 417		**RE**	P	CT	TS	52417 57417
156 418		**RE**	P	CT	TS	52418 57418
156 419		**RE**	P	CT	TS	52419 57419
156 420		**RN**	P	NW	NH	52420 57420
156 421		**RN**	P	NW	NH	52421 57421
156 422		**P**	P	CT	TS	52422 57422
156 423	§	**RN**	P	NW	NH	52423 57423
156 424	§	**RN**	P	NW	NH	52424 57424
156 425		**P**	P	NW	NH	52425 57425
156 426	§	**RN**	P	NW	NH	52426 57426
156 427	§	**RN**	P	NW	NH	52427 57427
156 428	§	**RN**	P	NW	NH	52428 57428
156 429	§	**RN**	P	NW	NH	52429 57429
156 430		**P**	A	SR	CK	52430 57430
156 431	r★	**P**	A	SR	CK	52431 57431
156 432	r★	**P**	A	SR	CK	52432 57432

156 433	**CC**	A	SR	CK	52433	57433	The Kilmarnock Edition
156 434	r★ **P**	A	SR	CK	52434	57434	
156 435	r★ **P**	A	SR	CK	52435	57435	
156 436	r★ **P**	A	SR	CK	52436	57436	
156 437	**P**	A	SR	CK	52437	57437	
156 438	**P**	A	NE	NL	52438	57438	
156 439	**P**	A	SR	CK	52439	57439	
156 440	§ **RN**	P	NW	NH	52440	57440	
156 441	§ **RN**	P	NW	NH	52441	57441	
156 442	**P**	A	SR	CK	52442	57442	
156 443	**P**	A	NE	HT	52443	57443	
156 444	**P**	A	NE	HT	52444	57444	
156 445	r★ **P**	A	SR	CK	52445	57445	
156 446	r★ **P**	A	SR	IS	52446	57446	
156 447	r★ **P**	A	SR	CK	52447	57447	
156 448	**P**	A	NE	HT	52448	57448	
156 449	r★ **P**	A	SR	CK	52449	57449	
156 450	r★ **P**	A	SR	CK	52450	57450	
156 451	**P**	A	NE	HT	52451	57451	
156 452	**RN**	P	NW	NH	52452	57452	
156 453	r★ **P**	A	SR	CK	52453	57453	
156 454	**P**	A	NE	HT	52454	57454	
156 455	**RN**	P	NW	NH	52455	57455	
156 456	r★ **P**	A	SR	CK	52456	57456	
156 457	r★ **P**	A	SR	IS	52457	57457	
156 458	r★ **P**	A	SR	IS	52458	57458	
156 459	**RN**	P	NW	NH	52459	57459	
156 460	**RN**	P	NW	NH	52460	57460	
156 461	**P**	P	NW	NH	52461	57461	
156 462	r★ **P**	A	SR	CK	52462	57462	
156 463	**P**	A	NE	HT	52463	57463	
156 464	**RN**	P	NW	NH	52464	57464	
156 465	r★ **P**	A	SR	CK	52465	57465	Bonnie Prince Charlie
156 466	**RN**	P	NW	NH	52466	57466	
156 467	r★ **P**	A	SR	CK	52467	57467	
156 468	**P**	A	NE	NL	52468	57468	
156 469	**P**	A	NE	HT	52469	57469	
156 470	**P**	A	NE	NL	52470	57470	
156 471	**P**	A	NE	NL	52471	57471	
156 472	**P**	A	NE	NL	52472	57472	
156 473	**P**	A	NE	NL	52473	57473	
156 474	r★ **P**	A	SR	IS	52474	57474	
156 475	**P**	A	NE	NL	52475	57475	
156 476	**P**	A	SR	CK	52476	57476	
156 477	r★ **P**	A	SR	IS	52477	57477	HIGHLAND FESTIVAL
156 478	r★ **P**	A	SR	IS	52478	57478	
156 479	**P**	A	NE	NL	52479	57479	
156 480	**P**	A	NE	NL	52480	57480	
156 481	**P**	A	NE	NL	52481	57481	
156 482	**P**	A	NE	NL	52482	57482	

156 483		P	A	NE	NL	52483 57483
156 484		P	A	NE	NL	52484 57484
156 485	r★	P	A	SR	CK	52485 57485
156 486		P	A	NE	NL	52486 57486
156 487		P	A	NE	NL	52487 57487
156 488		P	A	NE	NL	52488 57488
156 489		P	A	NE	NL	52489 57489
156 490		P	A	NE	NL	52490 57490
156 491		P	A	NE	NL	52491 57491
156 492	r★	P	A	SR	CK	52492 57492
156 493	r★	P	A	SR	CK	52493 57493
156 494	r★	P	A	SR	CK	52494 57494
156 495	r★	P	A	SR	CK	52495 57495
156 496	r★	P	A	SR	CK	52496 57496
156 497		P	A	NE	NL	52497 57497
156 498		P	A	NE	NL	52498 57498
156 499	r★	P	A	SR	IS	52499 57499
156 500	r★	P	A	SR	CK	52500 57500
156 501		S	A	SR	CK	52501 57501
156 502		S	A	SR	CK	52502 57502
156 503		S	A	SR	CK	52503 57503
156 504		S	A	SR	CK	52504 57504
156 505	r★	S	A	SR	CK	52505 57505
156 506		S	A	SR	CK	52506 57506
156 507		S	A	SR	CK	52507 57507
156 508		S	A	SR	CK	52508 57508
156 509		S	A	SR	CK	52509 57509
156 510		S	A	SR	CK	52510 57510
156 511		S	A	SR	CK	52511 57511
156 512		S	A	SR	CK	52512 57512
156 513		S	A	SR	CK	52513 57513
156 514		S	A	SR	CK	52514 57514

CLASS 158/0   BREL EXPRESS

DMSL (B) – DMSL (A) or DMCL – DMSL*§ or DMSL (B) – MSL – DMSL (A).

Engines: One Cummins NTA855R of 260 kW (350 hp) or 300 kW (400 hp)§
(One Perkins 2006-TWH of 260 kW (350 hp)★) per car.
Transmission: Hydraulic. Voith T211r with Gmeinder final drive.
Bogies: One BREL P4 and one BREL T4 per car.
Gangways: Throughout.
Doors: Sliding plug.
Accommodation: 2 + 2 facing/unidirectional (first & standard classes).
Dimensions: 23.21 x 2.70 m.
Maximum Speed: 90 mph.

DMSL (B).. Dia. DP252. Lot No. 31051 Derby 1990 – 2. –/68 + wheelchair
space 1TD. Public telephone and trolley space. 38.5 t.
DMCL.. Dia. DP252. Lot No. 31051 Derby 1989 – 90. 15/51*, 9/51§ +
wheelchair space 1TD. Public telephone and trolley space. 38.5 t.
MSL. Dia. DR207. Lot No. 31050 Derby 1991. 38 t. –/70 2T.

DMSL (A). Dia. DP251. Lot No. 31052 Derby 1990 – 92. –/70 1T and parcels area. 37.8 t.

158 701	*	RE	P	SR	HA	52701	57701 The Scottish Claymores
158 702	*	RE	P	SR	HA	52702	57702
158 703	*	RE	P	SR	HA	52703	57703
158 704	*	RE	P	SR	HA	52704	57704
158 705	*	RE	P	SR	HA	52705	57705
158 706	*	RE	P	SR	HA	52706	57706
158 707	*	RE .	P	SR	HA	52707	57707
158 708	*	RE	P	SR	HA	52708	57708
158 709	*	RE	P	SR	HA	52709	57709
158 710	*	RE	P	SR	HA	52710	57710
158 711	*	RE	P	SR	HA	52711	57711
158 712	*	RE	P	SR	HA	52712	57712
158 713	*	RE	P	SR	HA	52713	57713
158 714	*	RE	P	SR	HA	52714	57714
158 715	*	RE	P	SR	HA	52715	57715 Haymarket
158 716	*	RE	P	SR	HA	52716	57716
158 717	*	RE	P	SR	HA	52717	57717
158 718	*	RE	P	SR	HA	52718	57718
158 719	*	RE	P	SR	HA	52719	57719
158 720	*	RE	P	SR	HA	52720	57720
158 721	*	RE.	P	SR	HA	52721	57721
158 722	*	RE	P	SR	HA	52722	57722
158 723	*	RE	P	SR	HA	52723	57723
158 724	*	RE	P	SR	HA	52724	57724
158 725	*	RE	P	SR	HA	52725	57725
158 726	*	RE	P	SR	HA	52726	57726
158 727	*	RE	P	SR	HA	52727	57727
158 728	*	RE	P	SR	HA	52728	57728
158 729	*	RE	P	SR	HA	52729	57729
158 730	*	RE	P	SR	HA	52730	57730
158 731	*	RE	P	SR	HA	52731	57731
158 732	*	RE	P	SR	HA	52732	57732
158 733	*	RE	P	SR	HA	52733	57733
158 734	*	RE	P	SR	HA	52734	57734
158 735	*	RE	P	SR	HA	52735	57735
158 736	*	RE	P	SR	HA	52736	57736
158 737	*	RE	P	SR	HA	52737	57737
158 738	*	RE	P	SR	HA	52738	57738
158 739	*	RE	P	SR	HA	52739	57739
158 740	*	RE	P	SR	HA	52740	57740
158 741	*	RE	P	SR	HA	52741	57741
158 742	*	RE	P	SR	HA	52742	57742
158 743	*	RE	P	SR	HA	52743	57743
158 744	*	RE	P	SR	HA	52744	57744
158 745	*	RE	P	SR	HA	52745	57745
158 746	*	RE	P	SR	HA	52746	57746
158 747	§	RE	P	XC	NH	52747	57747
158 748	§	RE	P	XC	NH	52748	57748

158 749	§	**RE**	P	XC	NH	52749	57749
158 750	§	**RE**	P	XC	NH	52750	57750
158 751	§	**RE**	P	XC	NH	52751	57751
158 752		**RE**	P	NW	NH	52752	57752
158 753		**RE**	P	NW	NH	52753	57753
158 754		**RE**	P	NW	NH	52754	57754
158 755		**RE**	P	NW	NH	52755	57755
158 756		**RE**	P	NW	NH	52756	57756
158 757		**RE**	P	NW	NH	52757	57757
158 758		**RE**	P	NW	NH	52758	57758
158 759		**RE**	P	NW	NH	52759	57759
158 760		**RE**	P	NE	NL	52760	57760
158 761		**RE**	P	NE	NL	52761	57761
158 762		**RE**	P	NE	NL	52762	57762
158 763		**RE**	P	NE	NL	52763	57763
158 764		**RE**	P	NE	NL	52764	57764
158 765		**RE**	P	NE	NL	52765	57765
158 766		**RE**	P	NE	NL	52766	57766
158 767		**RE**	P	NE	NL	52767	57767
158 768		**RE**	P	NE	NL	52768	57768
158 769		**RE**	P	NE	NL	52769	57769
158 770		**RE**	P	NE	NL	52770	57770
158 771		**RE**	P	NE	HT	52771	57771
158 772		**RE**	P	NE	NL	52772	57772
158 773		**RE**	P	NE	NL	52773	57773
158 774		**RE**	P	NE	HT	52774	57774
158 775		**RE**	P	NE	HT	52775	57775
158 776		**RE**	P	NE	HT	52776	57776
158 777		**RE**	P	NE	HT	52777	57777
158 778		**RE**	P	NE	HT	52778	57778
158 779		**RE**	P	NE	HT	52779	57779
158 780	r	**RE**	A	CT	NC	52780	57780
158 781	r	**RE**	P	NE	HT	52781	57781
158 782	r	**RE**	A	CT	NC	52782	57782
158 783	r	**RE**	A	CT	NC	52783	57783
158 784	r	**RE**	A	CT	NC	52784	57784
158 785	r	**RE**	A	CT	NC	52785	57785
158 786	r	**RE**	A	CT	NC	52786	57786
158 787	r	**RE**	A	CT	NC	52787	57787
158 788	r	**RE**	A	CT	NC	52788	57788
158 789	r	**RE**	A	CT	NC	52789	57789
158 790	r	**RE**	A	CT	NC	52790	57790
158 791	r	**RE**	A	CT	NC	52791	57791
158 792	r	**RE**	A	CT	NC	52792	57792
158 793	r	**RE**	A	CT	NC	52793	57793
158 794	r	**RE**	A	CT	NC	52794	57794
158 795	r	**RE**	A	CT	NC	52795	57795
158 796	r	**RE**	A	CT	NC	52796	57796
158 797	r	**RE**	A	CT	NC	52797	57797
158 798		**RE**	P	NE	HT	52798	58715	57798
158 799		**RE**	P	NE	HT	52799	58716	57799

158 800		**RE**	P	NE	HT	52800	58717	57800
158 801		**RE**	P	NE	HT	52801	58701	57801
158 802		**RE**	P	NE	HT	52802	58702	57802
158 803		**RE**	P	NE	HT	52803	58703	57803
158 804		**RE**	P	NE	HT	52804	58704	57804
158 805		**RE**	P	NE	HT	52805	58705	57805
158 806		**RE**	P	NE	HT	52806	58706	57806
158 807		**RE**	P	NE	HT	52807	58707	57807
158 808		**RE**	P	NE	HT	52808	58708	57808
158 809		**RE**	P	NE	HT	52809	58709	57809
158 810		**RE**	P	NE	HT	52810	58710	57810
158 811		**RE**	P	NE	HT	52811	58711	57811
158 812		**RE**	P	NE	HT	52812	58712	57812
158 813		**RE**	P	NE	HT	52813	58713	57813
158 814		**RE**	P	NE	HT	52814	58714	57814
158 815	★	**RE**	A	WW	CF	52815		57815
158 816	★	**RE**	A	WW	CF	52816		57816
158 817	★	**RE**	A	WW	CF	52817		57817
158 818	★	**RE**	A	WW	CF	52818		57818
158 819	★	**RE**	A	WW	CF	52819		57819
158 820	★	**RE**	A	WW	CF	52820		57820
158 821	★	**RE**	A	WW	CF	52821		57821
158 822	★	**RE**	A	WW	CF	52822		57822
158 823	★	**RE**	A	WW	CF	52823		57823
158 824	★	**RE**	A	WW	CF	52824		57824
158 825	★	**RE**	A	WW	CF	52825		57825
158 826	★	**RE**	A	WW	CF	52826		57826
158 827	★	**RE**	A	WW	CF	52827		57827
158 828	★	**RE**	A	WW	CF	52828		57828
158 829	★	**RE**	A	WW	CF	52829		57829
158 830	★	**RE**	A	WW	CF	52830		57830
158 831	★	**RE**	A	WW	CF	52831		57831
158 832	★	**RE**	A	WW	CF	52832		57832
158 833	★	**RE**	A	WW	CF	52833		57833
158 834	★	**RE**	A	WW	CF	52834		57834
158 835	★	**RE**	A	WW	CF	52835		57835
158 836	★	**RE**	A	WW	CF	52836		57836
158 837	★	**RE**	A	WW	CF	52837		57837
158 838	★	**RE**	A	WW	CF	52838		57838
158 839	★	**RE**	A	WW	CF	52839		57839
158 840	★	**RE**	A	WW	CF	52840		57840
158 841	★	**RE**	A	WW	CF	52841		57841
158 842	★r	**RE**	A	WW	CF	52842		57842
158 843	★r	**RE**	A	WW	CF	52843		57843
158 844	★r	**RE**	A	CT	NC	52844		57844
158 845	★r	**RE**	A	CT	NC	52845		57845
158 846	★r	**RE**	A	CT	NC	52846		57846
158 847	★r	**RE**	A	CT	NC	52847		57847
158 848	★r	**RE**	A	CT	NC	52848		57848
158 849	★r	**RE**	A	CT	NC	52849		57849
158 850	★r	**RE**	A	CT	NC	52850		57850

158 851	★r **RE**	A	CT	NC	52851	57851
158 852	★r **RE**	A	CT	NC	52852	57852
158 853	★r **RE**	A	CT	NC	52853	57853
158 854	★r **RE**	A	CT	NC	52854	57854
158 855	★r **RE**	A	CT	NC	52855	57855
158 856	★r **RE**	A	CT	NC	52856	57856
158 857	★r **RE**	A	CT	NC	52857	57857
158 858	★r **RE**	A	CT	NC	52858	57858
158 859	★r **RE**	A	CT	NC	52859	57859
158 860	★r **RE**	A	CT	NC	52860	57860
158 861	★r **RE**	A	CT	NC	52861	57861
158 862	★r **RE**	A	CT	NC	52862	57862
158 863	§ **RE**	A	WW	CF	52863	57863
158 864	§ **RE**	A	WW	CF	52864	57864
158 865	§ **RE**	A	WW	CF	52865	57865
158 866	§ **RE**	A	WW	CF	52866	57866
158 867	§ **RE**	A	WW	CF	52867	57867
158 868	§ **RE**	A	WW	CF	52868	57868
158 869	§ **RE**	A	WW	CF	52869	57869
158 870	§ **RE**	A	WW	CF	52870	57870
158 871	§ **RE**	A	WW	CF	52871	57871
158 872	§ **RE**	A	WW	CF	52872	57872

CLASS 158/9   BREL EXPRESS

DMSL – DMS. Units leased by West Yorkshire PTE. Details as for Class 158/0 except for seating layout and toilets.

DMSL.. Dia. DP252. Lot No. 31051 Derby 1990 – 2. – /70 + wheelchair space 1TD. Public telephone and trolley space. 38.1 t.
DMS. Dia. DP251. Lot No. 31052 Derby 1990 – 92. – /72 and parcels area. 37.8 t.

Note: Although these units are leased by West Yorkshire PTE, they are managed by Porterbrook Leasing Company.

158 901	Y	P	NE	NL	52901	57901
158 902	Y	P	NE	NL	52902	57902
158 903	Y	P	NE	NL	52903	57903
158 904	Y	P	NE	NL	52904	57904
158 905	Y	P	NE	NL	52905	57905
158 906	Y	P	NE	NL	52906	57906
158 907	Y	P	NE	NL	52907	57907
158 908	Y	P	NE	NL	52908	57908
158 909	Y	P	NE	NL	52909	57909
158 910	Y	P	NE	NL	52910	57910

CLASS 159   BREL EXPRESS

DMCL – MSL – DMSL. Built as Class 158 by BREL. Converted before entering passenger service to Class 159 by Rosyth Dockyard.

Engines: One Cummins NTA855R of 300 kW (400 hp) per car.

Transmission: Hydraulic. Voith T211r with Gmeinder final drive.
Bogies: One BREL P4 and one BREL T4 per car.
Gangways: Throughout.
Doors: Sliding plug.
Accommodation: 2 + 2 facing/unidirectional (standard class), 2 + 1 facing (first class).
Dimensions: 23.21 x 2.82 m.
Maximum Speed: 90 mph.

DMCL.. Dia. DP322. Lot No. 31051 Derby 1992. 24/28 1TD. 38.5 t.
MSL. Dia. DR209. Lot No. 31050 Derby 1992. 38 t. –/72 2T.
DMSL. Dia. DP260. Lot No. 31052 Derby 1992. –/72 1T and parcels area. 37.8 t.

159 001	NW P	SW	SA	52873	58718	57873	CITY OF EXETER
159 002	NW P	SW	SA	52874	58719	57874	CITY OF SALISBURY
159 003	NW P	SW	SA	52875	58720	57875	TEMPLECOMBE
159 004	NW P	SW	SA	52876	58721	57876	BASINGSTOKE AND DEANE
159 005	NW P	SW	SA	52877	58722	57877	
159 006	NW P	SW	SA	52878	58723	57878	
159 007	NW P	SW	SA	52879	58724	57879	
159 008	NW P	SW	SA	52880	58725	57880	
159 009	NW P	SW	SA	52881	58726	57881	
159 010	NW P	SW	SA	52882	58727	57882	
159 011	NW P	SW	SA	52883	58728	57883	
159 012	NW P	SW	SA	52884	58729	57884	
159 013	NW P	SW	SA	52885	58730	57885	
159 014	NW P	SW	SA	52886	58731	57886	
159 015	NW P	SW	SA	52887	58732	57887	
159 016	NW P	SW	SA	52888	58733	57888	
159 017	NW P	SW	SA	52889	58734	57889	
159 018	NW P	SW	SA	52890	58735	57890	
159 019	NW P	SW	SA	52891	58736	57891	
159 020	NW P	SW	SA	52892	58737	57892	
159 021	NW P	SW	SA	52893	58738	57893	
159 022	NW P	SW	SA	52894	58739	57894	

CLASS 165/0   BREL NETWORK TURBO

DMCL – DMS or DMCL – MS – DMS. Built for Chiltern Line services.

Engines: One Perkins 2006-TWH of 260 kW (350 hp) per car.
Transmission: Hydraulic. Voith T211r with Gmeinder final drive.
Bogies: One BREL P3 and one BREL T3 per car.
Gangways: Within unit only.
Doors: Sliding plug.
Accommodation: 2 + 3 facing/unidirectional (standard class), 2 + 2 facing (first class).
Dimensions: 23.50 x 2.85 m.
Maximum Speed: 75 mph.

58801 – 58822. 58873 – 58878. DMCL. Dia. DP319. Lot No. 31087 York.

1990. 16/72 1T. 37.0 t.
58823 – 58833. DMCL. Dia. DP320. Lot No. 31089 York 1991 – 1992. 24/60
1T. 37.0 t.
MS. Dia. DR208. Lot No. 31090 York 1991 – 1992. 106S. 37.0 t.
DMS. Dia. DP253. Lot No. 31088 York 1991 – 1992. 98S. 37.0 t.

165 001	**NW**	A	TT	RG	58801	58834
165 002	**NW**	A	TT	RG	58802	58835
165 003	**NW**	A	TT	RG	58803	58836
165 004	**NW**	A	TT	RG	58804	58837
165 005	**NW**	A	TT	RG	58805	58838
165 006	**NW**	A	CH	AL	58806	58839
165 007	**NW**	A	CH	AL	58807	58840
165 008	**NW**	A	CH	AL	58808	58841
165 009	**NW**	A	CH	AL	58809	58842
165 010	**NW**	A	CH	AL	58810	58843
165 011	**NW**	A	CH	AL	58811	58844
165 012	**NW**	A	CH	AL	58812	58845
165 013	**NW**	A	CH	AL	58813	58846
165 014	**NW**	A	CH	AL	58814	58847
165 015	**NW**	A	CH	AL	58815	58848
165 016	**NW**	A	CH	AL	58816	58849
165 017	**NW**	A	CH	AL	58817	58850
165 018	**NW**	A	CH	AL	58818	58851
165 019	**NW**	A	CH	AL	58819	58852
165 020	**NW**	A	CH	AL	58820	58853
165 021	**NW**	A	CH	AL	58821	58854
165 022	**NW**	A	CH	AL	58822	58855
165 023	**NW**	A	CH	AL	58873	58867
165 024	**NW**	A	CH	AL	58874	58868
165 025	**NW**	A	CH	AL	58875	58869
165 026	**NW**	A	CH	AL	58876	58870
165 027	**NW**	A	CH	AL	58877	58871
165 028	**NW**	A	CH	AL	58878	58872
165 029	**NW**	A	CH	AL	58823 55404	58856
165 030	**NW**	A	CH	AL	58824 55405	58857
165 031	**NW**	A	CH	AL	58825 55406	58858
165 032	**NW**	A	CH	AL	58826 55407	58859
165 033	**NW**	A	CH	AL	58827 55408	58860
165 034	**NW**	A	CH	AL	58828 55409	58861
165 035	**NW**	A	CH	AL	58829 55410	58862
165 036	**NW**	A	CH	AL	58830 55411	58863
165 037	**NW**	A	CH	AL	58831 55412	58864
165 038	**NW**	A	CH	AL	58832 55413	58865
165 039	**NW**	A	CH	AL	58833 55414	58866

CLASS 165/1   BREL NETWORK TURBO

DMCL – DMS or DMCL – MS – DMS. Built for Thames Trains services.

Engines: One Perkins 2006-TWH of 260 kW (350 hp) per car.
Bogies: One BREL P3 and one BREL T3 per car.

Transmission: Hydraulic. Voith T211r with Gmeinder final drive.
Gangways: Within unit only.
Doors: Sliding plug.
Accommodation: 2 + 3 facing/unidirectional (standard class), 2 + 2 facing (first class).
Dimensions: 23.50 x 2.85 m.
Maximum Speed: 90 mph.

58953 – 58969. DMCL. Dia. DP320. Lot No. 31098 York 1992. 24/60 1T. 37.0 t.
58879 – 58898. DMCL. Dia. DP319. Lot No. 31096 York 1992. 16/72 1T. 37.0 t.
MS. Dia. DR208. Lot No. 31099 York 1992. –/106. 37.0 t.
DMS. Dia. DP253. Lot No. 31097 York 1992. –/98. 37.0 t.

165 101	NW	A	TT	RG	58916	55415	58953
165 102	NW	A	TT	RG	58917	55416	58954
165 103	NW	A	TT	RG	58918	55417	58955
165 104	NW	A	TT	RG	58919	55418	58956
165 105	NW	A	TT	RG	58920	55419	58957
165 106	NW	A	TT	RG	58921	55420	58958
165 107	NW	A	TT	RG	58922	55421	58959
165 108	NW	A	TT	RG	58923	55422	58960
165 109	NW	A	TT	RG	58924	55423	58961
165 110	NW	A	TT	RG	58925	55424	58962
165 111	NW	A	TT	RG	58926	55425	58963
165 112	NW	A	TT	RG	58927	55426	58964
165 113	NW	A	TT	RG	58928	55427	58965
165 114	NW	A	TT	RG	58929	55428	58966
165 115	NW	A	TT	RG	58930	55429	58967
165 116	NW	A	TT	RG	58931	55430	58968
165 117	NW	A	TT	RG	58932	55431	58969
165 118	NW	A	TT	RG	58879		58933
165 119	NW	A	TT	RG	58880		58934
165 120	NW	A	TT	RG	58881		58935
165 121	NW	A	TT	RG	58882		58936
165 122	NW	A	TT	RG	58883		58937
165 123	NW	A	TT	RG	58884		58938
165 124	NW	A	TT	RG	58885		58939
165 125	NW	A	TT	RG	58886		58940
165 126	NW	A	TT	RG	58887		58941
165 127	NW	A	TT	RG	58888		58942
165 128	NW	A	TT	RG	58889		58943
165 129	NW	A	TT	RG	58890		58944
165 130	NW	A	TT	RG	58891		58945
165 131	NW	A	TT	RG	58892		58946
165 132	NW	A	TT	RG	58893		58947
165 133	NW	A	TT	RG	58894		58948
165 134	NW	A	TT	RG	58895		58949
165 135	NW	A	TT	RG	58896		58950
165 136	NW	A	TT	RG	58897		58951
165 137	NW	A	TT	RG	58898		58952

CLASS 166   ABB NETWORK EXPRESS TURBO

DMCL (A) – MS – DMCL (B). Built for Paddington – Oxford/ Newbury services.
Air conditioned.

Engines: One Perkins 2006-TWH of 260 kW (350 hp) per car.
Bogies: One BREL P3 and one BREL T3 per car.
Transmission: Hydraulic. Voith T211r with Gmeinder final drive.
Gangways: Within unit only.
Doors: Sliding plug.
Accommodation: 2 + 3 facing/unidirectional (standard class) with 20 standard
class seats in 2 + 2 format in DMCL(B), 2 + 2 facing (first class).
Dimensions: 22.91 x 2.81 m (DMCL), 22.72 x 2.81 m (MS).
Maximum Speed: 90 mph.

DMCL (A). Dia. DP321. Lot No. 31116 York 1992 – 3. 16/75 1T. 40.62 t.
MS. Dia. DR209. Lot No. 31117 York 1992 – 3. –/96. 38.04 t.
DMCL (B). Dia. DP321. Lot No. 31116 York 1992 – 3. 16/72 1T. 40.64 t.

166 201	**NW**	A	TT	RG	58101 58601 58122
166 202	**NW**	A	TT	RG	58102 58602 58123
166 203	**NW**	A	TT	RG	58103 58603 58124
166 204	**NW**	A	TT	RG	58104 58604 58125
166 205	**NW**	A	TT	RG	58105 58605 58126
166 206	**NW**	A	TT	RG	58106 58606 58127
166 207	**NW**	A	TT	RG	58107 58607 58128
166 208	**NW**	A	TT	RG	58108 58608 58129
166 209	**NW**	A	TT	RG	58109 58609 58130
166 210	**NW**	A	TT	RG	58110 58610 58131
166 211	**NW**	A	TT	RG	58111 58611 58132
166 212	**NW**	A	TT	RG	58112 58612 58133
166 213	**NW**	A	TT	RG	58113 58613 58134
166 214	**NW**	A	TT	RG	58114 58614 58135
166 215	**NW**	A	TT	RG	58115 58615 58136
166 216	**NW**	A	TT	RG	58116 58616 58137
166 217	**NW**	A	TT	RG	58117 58617 58138
166 218	**NW**	A	TT	RG	58118 58618 58139
166 219	**NW**	A	TT	RG	58119 58619 58140
166 220	**NW**	A	TT	RG	58120 58620 58141
166 221	**NW**	A	TT	RG	58121 58621 58142

3.3. DIESEL ELECTRIC MULTIPLE UNITS

All diesel-electric multiple unit power cars have above-floor-mounted engines and all vehicles are equipped with buckeye couplings and were built at Eastleigh with frames laid at Ashford.

Note: Vehicles shown as depot 'SE' are kept at St. Leonards Railway Engineering Ltd.

CLASS 201/202   PRESERVED 'HASTINGS' UNIT

DMBSO – 3TSOL – DMBSO.
Preserved unit made up from 2 Class 201 short-frame cars and 2 Class 202 long-frame cars. The 'Hastings' units were made with narrow body-profiles for use on the section between Tonbridge and Battle which had tunnels of restricted loading gauge. These tunnels were converted to single track operation in the 1980s thus allowing standard loading gauge stock to be used. The set also contains a Class 411 EMU trailer (not Hastings line gauge).

Engine: English Electric 4SRKT engines of 370 kW (500 hp).
Transmission: Two EE 507 traction motors on the inner bogie.
Gangways: Within unit only.
Dimensions: 17.68 x 2.50 m (60000/60501), 19.66 x 2.50 m. (60118/60529). 19.75 x 2.82 m (70262).
Maximum Speed: 75 mph.

60000. DMBSO. Dia DB203. Lot No. 30329 1957. – /22. 54 t.
60118. DMBSO. Dia DB203. Lot No. 30395 1957. – /30. 55 t. Renumbered from 60018.
60501. TSOL. Dia DB204. Lot No. 30331 1957. – /52 2T. 29 t.
60529. TSOL. Dia DH203. Lot No. 30397 1957. – /60 2T. 30 t.
70262. TSOL (ex Class 411/5 EMU). Dia. EH282. Lot No. 30455 1958 – 9. – /64 2T. 33.78 t.

O – Owner is Hastings Diesels Ltd.

201 001   **SG**   O   SS   SE   60000 60501 70262 60529 60118

60000 is named 'HASTINGS'.

CLASS 205/0   3H

DMBSO – TSOL – DTCsoL or DMBSO – DTCsoL.

Engine: English Electric 4SRKT engines of 450 kW (600 hp).
Transmission: Two EE 507 traction motors on the inner bogie.
Gangways: Non-gangwayed.
Dimensions: 20.28 x 2.82 m.
Maximum Speed: 75 mph.

60108 – 117/154. DMBSO. Dia DB203. Lot No. 30332 1957. – /52. 56 t.
60122 – 124. DMBSO. Dia DB203. Lot No. 30540 1958 – 59. – /52. 56 t.
60145 – 151. DMBSO. Dia DB204. Lot No. 30671 1960 – 62. – /42. 56 t.

60650 – 670. TSO. Dia DH203. Lot No. 30542 1958 – 59. –/104. 30 t.
60673 – 678. TSO. Dia DH203. Lot No. 30672 1960 – 62. –/104. 30 t.
60800 – 811. DTCsoL. Dia DE302. Lot No. 30333 1956 – 57. 19/50 2T. 32 t.
60822 – 824. DTCsoL. Dia DE302. Lot No. 30541 1958 – 59. 19/50 2T. 32 t.
60827 – 832. DTCsoL. Dia DE303. Lot No. 30673 1960 – 62. 13/62 2T. 32 t.

§ One compartment of DTCsoL converted to luggage compartment. 13/50 2T. Dia. DE301.

Notes:

60154 was renumbered from 60100.
205 023 is awaiting a decision on repair.

205 001	§	N	P	SC	SU	60154	60650	60800
205 009		N	P	SC	SU	60108	60658	60808
205 012		N	P	SC	SU	60111	60661	60811
205 018		N	P	SC	SU	60117	60674	60828
205 023		N	P		ZG	60122		60822
205 024	§	N	P	SC	SU	60123	60669	60823
205 025	§	N	P	SC	SU	60124	60670	60824
205 028		N	P	SC	SU	60146	60673	60827
205 032		N	P	SC	SU	60150	60677	60831
205 033		N	P	SC	SU	60151	60678	60832
Spare		N	P		SE	60664		
Spare		N	P		SE	60665		
Spare		N	P		SE	60668		

CLASS 205/1   3H

DMBSO – TSOL – DTSOL. Refurbished 1980. Fluorescent lighting. PA.

Engine: English Electric 4SRKT engines of 450 kW (600 hp).
Transmission: Two EE 507 traction motors on the inner bogie.
Gangways: Within unit only.
Dimensions: 20.28 x 2.82 m.
Maximum Speed: 75 mph.

DMBSO. Dia DB203. Lot No. 30332 1957. –/39. 57 t.
TSOL (ex Class 411/5 EMU). Dia. EH282. Converted from loco-hauled TSO 4059
Lot No. 30149 Ashford/Swindon 1955 – 7. –/64 2T. 33.78 t.
DTSOL. Dia DE204. Lot No. 30333 1957. –/76 2T. 32 t.

205 205		N	P	SC	SU	60110	71634	60810

CLASS 207/0   2D

DMBSO – DTSO (formerly DMBSO – TCsoL – DTSO).
These units were built for the Oxted line and therefore referred to as 'Oxted' units. They were made with a narrower body-profile which also allowed them to be used through the restricted loading-gauge Somerhill Tunnel between Tonbridge and Grove Junction (Tunbridge Wells). This tunnel was converted to single track operation in the 1980s thus allowing standard loading gauge stock to be used.

Engine: English Electric 4SRKT engines of 450 kW (600 hp).
Transmission: Two EE 507 traction motors on the inner bogie.
Gangways: Non-gangwayed.
Dimensions: 20.34 x 2.74 m. (DMBSO), 20.32 x 2.74 m. (DTSO), 20.34 x 2.74 m. (TCsoL).
Maximum Speed: 75 mph.

DMBSO. Dia DB205. Lot No. 30625 1962. –/42. 56 t.
TCsoL. Dia DH301. Lot No. 30626 1962. 24/42 1T. 31 t.
DTSO. Dia DE201. Lot No. 30627 1962. –/76. 32 t.

207 017	N	P	SC	SU	60142		60916
Spare	N	P		SE	60135		
Spare	N	P		ZG	60138		
Spare	N	P		SE		60616	

CLASS 207/1   3D

DMBSO – TSOL – DTSO.
Gangwayed sets with a Class 411 EMU trailer in the centre.

Engine: English Electric 4SRKT engines of 450 kW (600 hp).
Transmission: Two EE 507 traction motors on the inner bogie.
Gangways: Fitted with gangways within unit.
Dimensions: 20.34 x 2.74 m. (DMBSO), 20.32 x 2.74 m. (DTS).
Maximum Speed: 75 mph.

DMBSO. Dia DB205. Lot No. 30625 1962. –/40. 56 t.
70286. TSOL (ex Class 411/5 EMU). Dia. EH282. Lot No. 30455 1958 – 9. –/64 2T. 33.78 t.
70547/9. TSOL (ex Class 411/5 EMU). Dia. EH282. Lot No. 30620 1960 – 61 –/64 2T. 33.78 t.
DTSO. Dia DE201. Lot No. 30627 1962. –/75. 32 t.

207 201	N	P	SC	SU	60129	70286	60903	Ashford Fayre
207 202	N	P	SC	SU	60130	70549	60904	Brighton Royal Pavilion
207 203	N	P	SC	SU	60127	70547	60901	

3.4. SERVICE DMUs

This section contains service vehicles, i.e. vehicles not used for the carrying of passengers which are numbered or renumbered in the special service stock number series or in the internal user series. The last capital stock number carried is shown in parentheses.

LABORATORY COACH   DERBY LIGHTWEIGHT

Laboratory Coach 19. Converted from a Derby Lightweight single unit.

Engines: Two BUT of 112 kW (150 hp).
Transmission: Mechanical. Cardan shaft and freewheel to a four-speed epicylic gearbox with a further cardan shaft to the final drive, each engine driving the inner axle of one bogie.
Gangways: Non gangwayed single car with cab at each end.
Dimensions: 17.53 x 2.82 m.

DMBS. Lot No. 30380 Derby 1957.

	G	R	RS	ZA	975010	(79900)

CLASS 101   METRO-CAMMELL

DMBS – DMCL or DMBS – DMBS or DTCL. For details see page 8. Converted 1990 (i,l), 1993 (s).

51427. DMBS. Dia. DQ202. Lot No. 30500 1959. 32.5 t.
53193. DMCL. Dia. DP317. Lot No. 30256 1957. 32.5 t.
53200 – 53208. DMBS. Dia. DQ202. Lot No. 30259 1957. 32.5 t.
53222 – 53231. DMBS. Dia. DQ202. Lot No. 30261 1957. 32.5 t.
53291. DMBS. Dia. DQ202. Lot No. 30270 1957. 32.5 t.
53308. DMBS. Dia. DQ202. Lot No. 30275 1959. 32.5 t.
53321 – 53338. DMCL. Dia. DP317. Lot No. 30276 1958. 32.5 t.
54342. DTCL. Dia. DS302. Lot No. 30468 1959. 25.5 t.

Non-standard livery: Grey.

i – Internal user (stores van).
l – Lab Coach 19. Iris 2.

–	l	**0**	Z	TE	ZA	977693 (53222)	977694 (53338)
960 991		**N**	Q	SA	LO	977895 (53308)	977896 (53331)
960 992			Q	SA	LO	977897 (53203)	977898 (53193)
960 993			Q	SA	LO	977899 (51427)	977900 (53321)
960 994			Q	SA	LO	977901 (53200)	977902 (53231)
960 995			Q	SA	LO	977903 (53208)	977904 (53291)
–	i		M	ST	NL	042222 (54342)	

CLASS 114   DERBY HEAVYWEIGHT

Converted 1992. Used as a route learning unit.

Engines: Two Leyland TL11 of 152 kW (205 hp) per power car.
Transmission: Mechanical. Cardan shaft and freewheel to a four-speed epicyclic gearbox with a further cardan shaft to the final drive, each engine driving the inner axle of one bogie.
Gangways: Midland scissors type. Within unit only.
Doors: Slam.
Bogies: DD9 (motor) and DT9c (trailer).
Dimensions: 20.45 x 2.82 m.

55929. DMPMV. Lot No. 30209 Derby 1958. 29.0 t.
54904. DTPMV. Lot No. 30210 Derby 1958. 29.2 t.

Non-standard livery: Grey, red and yellow.

–	0	W	EW	TS	977775	(55929)	977776	(54904)

CLASS 121/122   PRESSED STEEL/GLOUCESTER

Sandite cars. For DMBS details see page 11.

55019. Class 122 DMBS. Dia. DX202. Lot No. 30419 Gloucester 1958. 36.5 t.
55020 – 55028. Class 121 DMBS. Dia. DX201. Lot No. 30518 Pressed Steel 1960. 38.0 t.

960 002	N	Q	SA	RG	977722	(55020)
960 010	N	Q	SA	AL	977858	(55024)
960 011	N	Q	SA	LO	977859	(55025)
960 012	N	Q	SA	RG	977873	(55022)
960 013	N	Q	SA	NC	977866	(55030)
960 014	N	Q	SA	RG	977860	(55028)
960 015	B	Q	SA	BY	975042	(55019)
960 021	N	Q	SA	BY	977723	(55021)

CLASS 205   SANDITE

DMBSO – TSO – DMBSO.
Converted 1993. For details see pages 43/44.

951 069		Q	SA SU	977939	(60145)	977870	(60660) 977940	(60149)

ULTRASONIC TEST TRAIN UNIT

Converted 1986 from Class 101 DMBS's plus a Class 432 EMU DMSO. For details of Class 101 see page 8.

51433. DMBS. Lot No. 30500 Metro-Cammell 1959. 32.5 t.
62483. DMSO. Lot No. 30862 York 1974. 19.66 x 2.82 m. 52.5 t.
53167. DMBS. Lot No. 30254 Metro-Cammell 1957. 32.5 t.

Non-standard livery: Grey.

—   **0** T TE ZA 977391 (51433) 999602 (62483) 977392 (53167)

WICKHAM SELF PROPELLED LABORATORY

Built new 1958. (4-wheeled).

Non-standard livery: BR Research blue and red.

—   **0** Z TE ZA 999507

TRACK RECORDING UNIT

Built new 1987. Class 150 derivative.

Non-standard livery: Blue and white with a red stripe below windows.

—   **0**   T TE   ZA   999600   999601

3.5. DMUs AWAITING DISPOSAL

The following withdrawn DMUs are awaiting disposal with the last known storage location shown.

Ex-Capital Stock

51340	ZH		55402	ZA
54350	Crewe Brook Sidings		55403	ZA
54367	Mossend Yard		55709	NH
55202	ZA		59228	Crewe Brook Sidings
55203	ZA		59518	OM
55302	ZA		60200	ZG
55303	ZA		60201	ZG

Ex-Service Stock

975023	(55001)	LO	977699	(60153)	ZG
975025	(60755)	WD	977753	(51321)	TS
977191	(56106)	CP	977813	(52060)	TO
977466	(54286)	LA	977814	(53926)	TO
977486	(54285)	TS	977825	(53881)	TS
977554	(54182)	Buxton LIP	977829	(53093)	TS
977696	(60522)	EH	977853	(53627)	ZC
977697	(60523)	ZG	977854	(51567)	ZC
977698	(60152)	ZG			

INTRODUCTION

Electric Multiple Unit operation on BR has increased enormously since the end of the steam era, with most electrification schemes being carried out at 25 kV a.c. using overhead conductor wires. The notable exceptions to this are the lines of the former Southern Railway, where the existing 660-750 V d.c. third rail system has been extended, with the voltage increased to 850 V in certain areas. The other exception is the Merseyrail network, which has also been extended using the third rail system.

NUMBERING

BR design electric multiple unit vehicles are numbered in the series 61000-78999. Isle of Wight vehicles are numbered in a separate series. In this book, stock is generally listed in order of the unit or set number. The unit or set number is stated first, followed by any notes applicable to the particular set. These are followed by codes for livery, owner, operation and depot respectively. Finally the numbers of the individual cars in the set are given, in order. Please note that reformations can and do occur. For off-loan vehicles, the last storage location is given when known.

DESIGN CONSIDERATIONS

Unless stated otherwise, all multiple unit vehicles are of BR design, or designed by contractors for BR and have buckeye couplings and tread brakes. Seating is 3 + 2 in standard class open vehicles, 2 + 2 in first class open vehicles, 8 to a corridor standard class compartment and 6 to a corridor first class compartment. In express stock, open standards have 2 + 2 seating and open firsts have 2 + 1 seating.

VEHICLE CODES

The codes used by the BR Operating Department to describe the various different types of electric multiple unit vehicles and quoted in the class headings are as follows:

M	Motor
DM	Driving Motor
BDM	Battery Driving Motor
T	Trailer
DT	Driving Trailer
BDT	Battery Driving Trailer
B	Brake, i.e. vehicle with luggage space and guards compartment.
F	First
S	Standard
C	Composite
RB	Buffet Car
RSM	Buffet Standard (Modular)
PMV	Parcels and Mails Van

▲ Caledonian blue liveried Class 101 No. 101 692 arrives at Whifflet with a Cumbernauld bound ScotRail service on 4th June 1996.
Colin J. Marsden

▼ Class 121 'bubble cars' L131 in Network SouthEast livery and L123 in BR green livery, pause at Ridgmont, Bedfordshire with the 13.00 Bletchley–Bedford North London Railways service on 10th October 1996.
Kevin Conkey

Network SouthEast liveried Class 117 No. 117 701 leaves Clapham Junction on 14th September 1996 with the 10.08 North London Railways service for Willesden Junction. This service is now worked by Class 313 EMUs.

Kevin Conkey

Class 141 No. 141 101 passes Outwood on 4th November 1995 whilst working the 13.14 Sheffield–Leeds Regional Railways North East service. This unit carries West Yorkshire PTE livery.

Dave McAlone

The 09.19 Whitehaven–Carlisle North West Regional Railways service approaches Wigton, Cumbria on 24th June 1996. The train is formed of Greater Manchester PTE liveried class 142 No. 142 008.

Kevin Conkey

Regional Railways liveried Class 143 No. 143 612 passes Bridgend East Junction with the 16.03 Cwmbran–Swansea Regional Railways South Wales and West service on 28th September 1996. This service is now operated by Prism Rail.

Nic Joynson

Class 144 No. 144 006 leaves Keighley on 4th November 1995 with the 10.31 Regional Railways North East service from Skipton to Bradford Forster Square. Trains on this route are now operated by EMUs.

Dave McAlone

Centro liveried Class 150/1 No. 150 013 passes GWR semaphore signals at Malvern Wells on 3rd May 1996. The train is the 09.27 Dorridge-Hereford Central Trains service.

Stephen Widdowson

Class 150/2 No. 150 224 leaves Bolton with a Buxton-bound North West Regional Railways service. The date is 25th July 1996.
Hugh Ballantyne

▲ Class 153 No. 153 324 draws away from Dalston, Cumbria with the 06.55 Barrow in Furness-Carlisle North West Regional Railways service on 8th June 1996. *Kevin Conkey*

▼ Class 156 No. 156 404 waits at Skegness on 8th May 1996, shortly before forming the 12.14 Central Trains service to Crewe. The unit carries Regional Railways Express livery as used on Class 158s. *Colin J. Marsden*

One of the West Yorkshire PTE Class 155s No. 155 342 passes Mills Hill, near Blackburn with a Leeds to Blackpool North West Regional Railways service during August 1996.   *Vincent Eastwood*

▲ Class 156 No. 156 433 'The Kilmarnock Edition' has recently been repainted into carmine and cream livery. The unit is pictured here awaiting departure from Glasgow Central with the 16.42 ScotRail service to East Kilbride on 24th September 1996.   *Brian Morrison*

▼ A four-car Class 158 formation, formed of unit Nos. 158 746 and 158 705, pauses at Montrose whilst working the 15.25 Aberdeen-Edinburgh/Glasgow Queen Street ScotRail service on 16th May 1996.
Colin J. Marsden

Network SouthEast liveried Class 159 No. 159 013 leads another unit of the same class along the sea wall at Dawlish on 18th August 1996 forming the 08.27 South West Trains service from Basingstoke to Paignton. This company is now owned by Stagecoach Rail.
Colin J. Marsden

'Turbo' units of Classes 165 and 166, Nos. 166 220 and 165 111 are caught side by side at Iver on 17th July 1996. The units are working Oxford–London Paddington and Reading–London Paddington trains respectively. These services are operated by Thames Trains.

Rodney Lissenden

▲ Class 205/0 No. 205 032 froms the 15.00 Uckfield–Oxted near Edenbridge on 30th May 1996. *Brian Denton*

▼ Class 207/2 No. 207 203 departs from Rye with the 09.24 Hastings–Ashford on 11th May 1996. The centre car of this unit was originally part of a Class 411/5 EMU. *David Brown*

▲ A Eurotunnel HGV shuttle is worked around the Cheriton loop by Euroshuttle locomotives 9008 and 9017 on 12th June 1996.
Chris Wilson

▼ Blackpool Transport's new livery is exemplified by this photograph of 1937-built Brush Railcoach No. 631 taken on 4th November 1995. Many of this class of vehicles are in advertising livery.
Peter Fox

▲ Manchester Metrolink Car No. 1026 arrives at Altrincham on 24th July 1995. *Hugh Ballantyne*

▼ South Yorkshire Supertram No. 05 with a Middlewood–Meadowhall working on 25th October 1996 at City Hall sporting the new logo. *Peter Fox*

H	handbrake fitted
LV	Luggage Van
K	Side corridor with lavatory
L	Open or semi-open Vehicle with lavatory
O	Open vehicle
so	Semi-open vehicle

The letters (A) and (B) may be added to the above codes to differentiate between two cars of the same operating type which have differences between them. The letter (T) denotes space for a catering trolley. Note that a consistent system is used, rather than the official operator codes which are sometimes inconsistent.

Notes:

(1) Compartment Stock (non-corridor) has no suffix.

(2) Semi-open composites generally have the first class accommodation in compartments and the standard class in open saloons.

(3) Unless stated otherwise, it is assumed that motor vehicles are fitted with pantographs. If the pantograph is on a trailer, then the trailer has the prefix 'P', e.g. PTSO - Pantograph trailer open standard.

A composite is a vehicle containing both First and Standard class accommodation.

A brake vehicle is a vehicle containing seperate specific accommodation for the guard (as opposed to the use of spare driving cabs on more recently-built units).

DIAGRAMS AND DESIGN CODES

For each type of vehicle, the official design code consists of a seven character code of two letters, four numbers and another letter, e.g. EC2040B. The first five characters of this are the diagram code and are given in the class heading or sub heading. These are explained as follows:

1st Letter

This is always 'E' for an electric multiple unit vehicle.

2nd Letter

as follows for various vehicle types:

A	Driving motor passenger vehicles.
B	Driving motor passenger vehicles with a brake compartment.
C	Non-Driving motor passenger vehicles.
D	Non-Driving trailer passenger vehicles with a brake compartment.
E	Driving Trailer passenger vehicles.
F	Battery Driving Trailer passenger vehicles.
G	Driving Trailer passenger vehicles with a brake compartment.
H	Trailer passenger vehicles.
I	Battery Driving Motor passenger vehicles.
J	Trailer passenger vehicles with a brake compartment.
N	Trailer passenger vehicles with a buffet compartment.
O	Battery Driving Trailer passenger vehicles with a brake compartment.
P	Trailer passenger vehicles with a handbrake.

X   Driving Motor Luggage Vans.

1st Figure

1   First class accommodation.
2   Standard class accommodation (incl. declassified seats).
3   Composite accommodation.
5   No passenger accommodation.

General information on on accommodation etc. will be found in the section on diesel multiple units.

LAYOUT

The layout in this section is as follows:

(1) Unit number.

(2) Notes (if any).
(3) Livery code.
(4) Owner code
(5) Operation code..
(5) Depot code.
(6) Individual car numbers.

Thus an example of the layout is as follows:

No.	Liv.	Owner	Operation	Depot	Car 1	Car 2	Car3	Car4
317 398	N	A	WN	HE	77027	62687	71604	77075

For off-loan vehicles, the last storage location is given when known.

4.1. 25kV a.c. OVERHEAD EMUs

Note: All units are 25 kV overhead only except where stated otherwise.

CLASS 302

BDTCOL – MBSO – TSOL – DTSO. All remaining units refurbished with new seats, fluorescent lighting and pa.
Gangways: Within unit.
Traction Motors: Four EE536A 143.5 kW.
Dimensions: 19.50 x 2.82 m (outer cars), 19.36 x 2.82 m (inner cars).
Maximum Speed: 75 mph.

75085 – 75205. BDTCOL. Lot No. 30436. York/Doncaster 1958 – 59. Dia. EF303. 24/52 1T. 39.5 t. B5 bogies.
75311 – 75358. BDTCOL. Lot No. 30440. York/Doncaster 1959. Dia. EF303. 24/52 1T. 39.5 t. B5 bogies.
61060 – 61091. MBSO. Lot No. 30434. York 1958 – 59. Dia. ED216. –/76. 55.3 t. Gresley Bogies.
61122 – 61226. MBSO. Lot No. 30438. York 1960. Dia. ED216. –/76. 55.3 t. Gresley Bogies.
70060 – 70091. TSOL. Lot No. 30437. York/Doncaster 1958 – 59. Dia. EH223. –/86 1T. 34.4 t. B4 bogies.
70122 – 70226. TSOL. Lot No. 30441. York 1959 – 61. Dia. EH223. –/86 1T. 34.4 t. B4 bogies.
75033 – 75079. DTSO. Lot No. 30435. York 1958 – 59. Dia. EE219. –/88. 33.4 t. B4 or B5 bogies.
75236 – 75283. DTSO. Lot No. 30439. York 1959 – 60. Dia. EE219. –/88. 33.4 t. B4 or B5 bogies.

302 201	N	E	LS	EM	75085	61060	70060	75033
302 202	N	E	LS	EM	75086	61061	70061	75034
302 203	N	E		Pig's Bay	75311	61122	70122	75236
302 204	N	E	LS	EM	75088	61063	70063	75036
302 205	N	E	LS	EM	75089	61064	70064	75037
302 206	N	E	LS	EM	75356	61065	70224	75281
302 207	N	E	LS	EM	75358	61226	70226	75283
302 210	N	E	LS	EM	75094	61069	70069	75042
302 211	N	E		EM	75095	61070	70070	75043
302 212	N	E		Pig's Bay	75096	61071	70071	75044
302 213	N	E	LS	EM	75097	61072	70072	75060
302 215	N	E	LS	EM	75099	61074	70074	75062
302 216	N	E	LS	EM	75100	61075	70075	75063
302 217	N	E	LS	EM	75190	61076	70076	75064
302 218	N	E	LS	EM	75191	61077	70077	75065
302 219	N	E	LS	EM	75192	61078	70078	75066
302 220	N	E	LS	EM	75193	61079	70079	75067
302 221	N	E	LS	EM	75194	61080	70080	75068
302 222	N	E		Pig's Bay	75195	61081	70081	75069
302 223	N	E	LS	EM	75341	61209	70209	75266

302 224	N	E	LS	EM	75197 61083 70083 75071
302 225	N	E	LS	EM	75198 61084 70084 75072
302 226	N	E	LS	EM	75199 61085 70085 75073
302 227	N	E	LS	EM	75325 61193 70193 75250
302 228	N	E	LS	EM	75201 61087 70087 75075
302 229	N	E		EM	75202 61088 70088 75076
302 230	N	E	LS	EM	75205 61091 70091 75079

CLASS 303

DTSO – MBSO – BDTSO. Sliding doors.
Bogies: Gresley.
Gangways: Gangwayed within units only (non-gangwayed *).
Traction Motors: Four MV 155 kW.
Dimensions: 19.50 x 2.82 m (outer cars), 19.36 x 2.82 m (inner cars).
Maximum Speed: 75 mph.

Class 303/0. Unrefurbished set*.

DTSO. Dia. EE206. –/83. 34.4 t.
MBSO. Dia. ED201. –/70. 56.4 t.
BDTSO. Dia. EF202. –/83. 38.4 t.

Non-standard Livery: Original Glasgow 'blue train' livery.

Note: 75752 carries "75758" and 75808 carries "75814"

Class 303/1. Refurbished with 2 + 2 seating and hopper-type window vents.

DTSO. Dia. EE241. –/56. 34.4 t.
MBSO. Dia. ED220. –/48. 56.4 t.
BDTSO. Dia. EF217. –/56. 38.4 t.

75566 – 75599. DTSO. Lot No. 30579 Pressed Steel 1959 – 60.
75747 – 75801. DTSO. Lot No. 30629 Pressed Steel 1960 – 61.
61481 – 61514. MBSO. Lot No. 30580 Pressed Steel 1959 – 60.
61813 – 61867. MBSO. Lot No. 30630 Pressed Steel 1960 – 61.
75601 – 75635. BDTSO. Lot No. 30581 Pressed Steel 1959 – 60.
75803 – 75857. BDTSO. Lot No. 30631 Pressed Steel 1960 – 61.

303 001	S	A	SR	GW	75566 61481 75601
303 003	S	A	SR	GW	75568 61483 75603
303 004	S	A	SR	GW	75569 61484 75604
303 006	S	A	SR	GW	75571 61486 75606
303 008	S	A	SR	GW	75573 61488 75608
303 009	S	A	SR	GW	75574 61489 75609
303 010	S	A	SR	GW	75575 61490 75610
303 011	S	A	SR	GW	75576 61491 75611
303 012	S	A	SR	GW	75577 61492 75612
303 013	S	A	SR	GW	75578 61493 75613
303 014	S	A	SR	GW	75579 61494 75614
303 016	S	A	SR	GW	75750 61496 75616
303 019	S	A	SR	GW	75584 61499 75619
303 020	S	A	SR	GW	75585 61500 75620
303 021	S	A	SR	GW	75586 61501 75621

303 023	S	A	SR	GW	75588	61503	75623
303 024	S	A	SR	GW	75589	61504	75624
303 025	S	A	SR	GW	75590	61505	75625
303 027	S	A	SR	GW	75592	61507	75627
303 028	S	A	SR	GW	75600	61508	75635
303 032	S	A	SR	GW	75597	61512	75632
303 033	S	A	SR	GW	75595	61860	75817
303 034	S	A	SR	GW	75599	61514	75634
303 037	S	A	SR	GW	75781	61813	75803
303 040	S	A	SR	GW	75581	61816	75806
303 043	S	A	SR	GW	75572	61819	75809
303 045	S	A	SR	GW	75755	61821	75811
303 046	S	A		ZH	75756	61822	75812
303 047	S	A	SR	GW	75757	61823	75813
303 048	* 0	A	SR	GW (S)	75752	61824	75808
303 054	S	A	SR	GW	75764	61830	75820
303 055	S	A	SR	GW	75765	61831	75821
303 056	S	A	SR	GW	75766	61832	75822
303 058	S	A	SR	GW	75768	61834	75824
303 061	S	A	SR	GW	75771	61837	75827
303 065	S	A	SR	GW	75775	61841	75831
303 070	S	A	SR	GW	75780	61846	75836
303 077	S	A	SR	GW	75787	61853	75843
303 079	S	A	SR	GW	75789	61855	75845
303 080	S	A	SR	GW	75790	61856	75846
303 083	S	A	SR	GW	75793	61859	75849
303 085	S	A	SR	GW	75795	61861	75851
303 087	S	A	SR	GW	75797	61863	75853
303 088	S	A	SR	GW	75798	61864	75854
303 089	S	A	SR	GW	75799	61865	75855
303 090	S	A	SR	GW	75800	61866	75856
303 091	S	A	SR	GW	75801	61867	75857
Spare	S	A			75747		

CLASS 305/2

BDTCOL – MBSO – TSOL – DTSO or BDTCOL – MBSO – DTSO. All refurbished with fluorescent lighting, new seats and PA.
Bogies: Gresley.
Gangways: Originally non-gangwayed, but now gangwayed within unit.
Traction Motors: Four GEC WT380 of 153 kW.
Dimensions: 19.53 x 2.82 m (outer cars), 19.36 x 2.82 m (inner cars).
Maximum Speed: 75 mph.

BDTCOL. Dia. EF304. Lot No. 30566 York/Doncaster 1960. 24/52 1T. 36.5 t.
MBSO. Dia. ED216. Lot No. 30567 York/Doncaster 1960. – /76. 56.5 t.
TSOL. Dia. EH223. Lot No. 30568 York/Doncaster 1960. – /86 1T. 31.5 t.
DTSO. Dia. EE220. Lot No. 30569 York/Doncaster 1960. – /88. 32.7 t.

305 501	RR	A	SR	GW	75424	61410	70356	75443
305 502	RR	A	SR	GW	75425	61421	70357	75444
305 503	GM	A	NW	LG	75426	61412		75445

305 506	**GM**	A	NW	LG	75429	61415		75448
305 507	**RR**	A	NW	LG	75430	61416		75449
305 508	**RR**	A	SR	GW	75431	61417	70363	75450
305 510	**GM**	A	NW	LG	75433	61419		75452
305 511	**GM**	A	NW	LG	75434	61420		75453
305 515	**GM**	A	NW	LG	75438	61424		75457
305 516	**GM**	A	NW	LG	75439	61425		75458
305 517	**RR**	A	SR	GW	75440	61426	70372	75459
305 518	**RR**	A		LG	75441	61427		75460
305 519	**RR**	A	SR	GW	75442	61428	70374	75461
Spare	**RR**	A		LG		61418		

CLASS 308

BDTCOL (declassified) – MBSO – DTSO. Refurbished with new seats, fluorescent lighting and PA. Originally 4-car units, but all TSOL now withdrawn.
Bogies: Gresley.
Gangways: Originally non-gangwayed, but now gangwayed within unit.
Traction Motors: Four EE 536A of 143.5 kW.
Dimensions: 19.36 x 2.82 m (outer cars), 19.35 x 2.82 m (inner cars).
Maximum Speed: 75 mph.

75879 – 75886. BDTCOL. Dia. EF304. Lot No. 30652 York 1961. 24/52 1T. 36.3 t.
75897 – 75919. BDTCOL. Dia. EF304. Lot No. 30656 York 1961. 24/52 1T. 36.3 t.
61884 – 61891. MBSO. Dia. ED216. Lot No. 30653 York 1961. -/76. 55.0 t.
61893 – 61915. MBSO. Dia. ED216. Lot No. 30657 York 1961. -/76. 55.0 t.
75888 – 75895. DTSO. Dia. EE220. Lot No. 30655 York 1961. – /88. 33 t.
75930 – 75952. DTSO. Dia. EE220. Lot No. 30659 York 1961. – /88. 33 t.

308 134	Y	A	NE	NL	75879	61884	75888
308 136	Y	A	NE	NL	75881	61886	75890
308 137	Y	A	NE	NL	75882	61887	75891
308 138	Y	A	NE	NL	75883	61888	75892
308 141	Y	A	NE	NL	75886	61891	75895
308 143	Y	A	NE	NL	75897	61893	75930
308 144	Y	A	NE	NL	75880	61894	75931
308 145	Y	A	NE	NL	75899	61895	75932
308 147	Y	A	NE	NL	75901	61897	75934
308 152	Y	A	NE	NL	75913	61902	75939
308 153	Y	A	NE	NL	75907	61903	75940
308 154	Y	A	NE	NL	75908	61904	75941
308 155	Y	A	NE	NL	75909	61905	75942
308 157	Y	A	NE	NL	75915	61907	75944
308 158	Y	A	NE	NL	75912	61908	75945
308 159	Y	A	NE	NL	75906	61909	75946
308 161	Y	A	NE	NL	75911	61911	75948
308 162	Y	A	NE	NL	75916	61912	75949
308 163	Y	A	NE	NL	75917	61913	75950
308 164	Y	A	NE	NL	75918	61914	75951
308 165	Y	A	NE	NL	75919	61915	75952

CLASS 309/1   ESSEX EXPRESS STOCK

DMBSO(T) – TSOL – TCsoL – BDTSOL. Built 1962 – 3 as 2 car units. Made up to four cars by the conversion of loco-hauled stock in 1973. All now refurbished with fluorescent lighting, hopper ventilators, new seating, PA.
Bogies: Commonwealth.
Gangways: Throughout.
Traction Motors: Four GEC of 210 kW.
Dimensions: 19.76 x 2.82 m (outer cars), 19.67 x 2.82 m (inner cars).
Maximum Speed: 100 mph.

DMBSO(T). Dia. EB206. Lot No. 30684 York 1962 – 63. – /44. 60 t.
TSOL. Dia. EH227. Lot No. 30871 Wolverton 1973 – 74. – /64 2T. 35 t.
TCsoL. Dia. EH309. Lot No. 30872 Wolverton 1973 – 74. 24/28 1T. 36 t.
BDTSOL. Dia. EF213. Lot No. 30683 York 1960 – 62. – /60 1T. 40 t.

309 605	N	A		Long Marston	61944	71108	71113	75988
309 606	N	A		Long Marston	61945	71109	71112	75989
309 607	N	A		BP	61946	71107	71111	75990

Former numbers of converted hauled stock:

71107 (26203)	71109 (26196)	71112 (16249)	71113 (16244)
71108 (26189)	71111 (16246)		

CLASS 309/2   ESSEX EXPRESS STOCK

BDTCsoL – MBSOL(T) – TSO – DTSOL. Built 1962 – 3. Units 309 613 – 309 618 formerly contained griddle cars, but these were withdrawn and their place has been taken by the conversion of loco-hauled TSOs on refurbishment. All refurbished with fluorescent lighting, hopper ventilators, new seating, PA.
Bogies: Commonwealth.
Gangways: Throughout.
Traction Motors: Four GEC of 210 kW.
Dimensions: 19.76 x 2.82 m (outer cars), 19.67 x 2.82 m (inner cars).
Maximum Speed: 100 mph.

75639 – 44. BDTCsoL. Dia. EF301. Lot No. 30679 York 1962. 18/32 2T. 40 t.
75965 – 67. BDTCsoL. Dia. EF213. Lot No. 30675 York 1962. 18/32 2T. 40 t.
61927 – 31. MBSOL(T). Dia. ED209. Lot No. 30676 York 1962. – /44 2T. 58 t.
61934 – 39. MBSOL(T). Dia. ED209. Lot No. 30680 York 1962. – /44 2T. 58 t.
70256 – 59. TSO. Dia. EH229. Lot No. 30677 York 1962. – /68 35 t.
71756 – 61. TSO. Dia. EH228. Lot No. 31001 Wolverton 1984 – 87. – /68. 35 t.
75972 – 75. DTSOL. Dia. EF213. Lot No. 30678 York 1962. – /56 2T 37 t.
75978 – 83. DTSOL. Dia. EF213. Lot No. 30682 York 1962 – 1963. – /56 2T. 37 t.

Non-standard liveries: 309 624 is in Manchester Airport Air Express livery (blue and white). 309 616/8/26 are in Network SouthEast livery with the red stripe replaced by a blue one.

309 613	p	RN	A	NW	LG		75639	61934	71756	75978

309 616	p	0	A	NW	LG	75642 61937 71759 75981
309 617	p	RN	A	NW	LG	75643 61938 71760 75982
309 618	p	0	A		BP	75966 61939 71761 75983
309 623		RN	A	NW	LG	75641 61927 71758 75980
309 624		0	A	NW	LG	75965 61928 70256 75972
309 626		0	A		BP	75967 61930 70258 75974
309 627		RN	A	NW	LG	75644 61931 70259 75975

Former numbers of converted hauled stock:

71756 (5068)	71759 (5062)	71760 (5056)	71761 (5066)
71758 (5058)			

CLASS 310

Disc brakes. All facelifted. with new panels and PA.
Bogies: B4.
Gangways: Within unit.
Traction Motors: Four EE546 of 201.5 kW.
Dimensions: 19.86 x 2.82 m (outer cars), 19.93 x 2.82 m (inner cars).
Maximum Speed: 75 mph.
Non-standard Livery: As 'P' but with grey and cream stripes.

BDTSOL. Dia. EF211. Lot No. 30745 Derby 1965 – 67. – /80 2T. 37.3 t.
76228. BDTSOL. Formerly a DTCOL to Lot 30748. Dia. EF210. Accomodation – /68 2T.
76998. BDTSOL. Rebuilt from TSO 70756 to Lot 30747. Dia. EF214. Accommodation – /75 2T.
MBSO. Dia. ED219. Lot No. 30746 Derby 1965 – 67. – /68. 57.2 t.
TSO. Dia. EH232. Lot No. 30747 Derby 1965 – 67. – /98. 31.7 t.
DTCOL (310/0). Dia. EE306. Lot No. 30748 Derby 1965 – 67. 25/43 2T. 34.4 t.
DTSOL (310/1). Dia. EE237. Lot No. 30748 Derby 1965 – 67. – /75 2T. 34.4 t.

Class 310/0. BDTSOL – MBSO – TSO – DTCOL.

310 046	N	E	LS	EM	76130 62071 70731 76180
310 047	N	E	LS	EM	76131 62072 70732 76181
310 049	N	E	LS	EM	76133 62074 70734 76183
310 050	N	E	LS	EM	76134 62075 70735 76184
310 051	N	E	LS	EM	76135 62076 70736 76185
310 052	N	E	LS	EM	76136 62077 70737 76186
310 057	N	E	LS	EM	76141 62082 70742 76191
310 058	N	E	LS	EM	76142 62083 70743 76192
310 059	N	E	LS	EM	76143 62084 70744 76205
310 060	N	E	LS	EM	76144 62085 70745 76194
310 064	N	E	LS	EM	76148 62089 70749 76198
310 066	N	E	LS	EM	76228 62091 70751 76200
310 067	N	E	LS	EM	76151 62092 70752 76201
310 068	N	E	LS	EM	76152 62093 70753 76202
310 069	N	E	LS	EM	76153 62094 70754 76203
310 070	N	E	LS	EM	76154 62095 70755 76204
310 074	N	E	LS	EM	76145 62099 70759 76208
310 075	N	E	LS	EM	76159 62100 70760 76209

310 077	N	E	LS	EM	76161	62102	70762	76211
310 079	N	E	LS	EM	76163	62104	70764	76222
310 080	N	E	LS	EM	76164	62105	70765	76214
310 081	N	E	LS	EM	76165	62106	70766	76215
310 082	N	E	LS	EM	76166	62107	70767	76216
310 083	N	E	LS	EM	76167	62108	70768	76217
310 084	N	E	LS	EM	76168	62109	70769	76218
310 085	N	E	LS	EM	76169	62110	70770	76219
310 086	N	E	LS	EM	76170	62111	70771	76220
310 087	N	E	LS	EM	76171	62112	70772	76221
310 088	N	E	LS	EM	76172	62113	70773	76213
310 089	N	E	LS	EM	76173	62114	70774	76223
310 091	N	E	LS	EM	76175	62116	70776	76225
310 092	N	E	LS	EM	76176	62117	70777	76226
310 093	N	E	LS	EM	76177	62118	70778	76190
310 094	N	E	LS	EM	76998	62119	70780	76193
310 095	N	E	LS	EM	76179	62120	70779	76229
Spare	N	E		EM	76149		70750	
Spare	N	E		ZD				76199

Name: Set 310 058 is named 'Chafford Hundred'.

Class 310/1. BDTSOL – MBSO – DTSOL (DTCOL (declassified)*).

310 101	RR	E	CT	BY	76157	62098	76207
310 102	RR	E	CT	BY	76139	62080	76189
310 103	RR	E	CT	BY	76160	62101	76210
310 104	RR	E	CT	BY	76162	62103	76212
310 105	RR	E	CT	BY	76174	62115	76224
310 106	RR	E	CT	BY	76156	62097	76206
310 107	RR	E	CT	BY	76146	62087	76196
310 108	RR	E	CT	BY	76132	62073	76182
310 109	O	E	CT	BY	76137	62078	76187
310 110	RR	E	CT	BY	76138	62079	76188
310 111	O	E	CT	BY	76147	62088	76197
310 112 *	RR	E	CT	BY	76140	62086	76227
310 113 *	RR	E	CT	BY	76158	62090	76195

Spare TSO.

70733	E	BY		70746	E	Kineton		70758	E	TS
70738	E	TS		70747	E	Kineton		70761	E	ZD
70739	E	Kineton		70748	E	BY		70763	E	Kineton
70740	E	TS		70757	E	Kineton		70775	E	ZN

CLASS 312

BDTSOL – MBSO – TSO – DTCOL. Disc brakes PA.
Bogies: B4.
Gangways: Within unit.
Traction Motors: Four EE546 of 201.5 kW.
Dimensions: 19.86 x 2.82 m (outer cars), 19.93 x 2.82 m (inner cars).
Maximum Speed: 90 mph.

Class 312/0. Standard design.

76994 – 97 BDTSOL. Dia. EF213. Lot No. 30891 York 1976. – /84 1T. 34.9 t.
62657 – 60 MBSO. Dia. ED214. Lot No. 30892 York 1976. – /68. 56 t.
71277 – 80 TSO. Dia. EH209. Lot No. 30893 York 1976. – /98. 30.5 t.
78045 – 48 DTCOL. Dia. EE305. Lot No. 30894 York 1976. 25/47 2T.
76949 – 74 BDTSOL. Dia. EF213. Lot No. 30863 York 1977 – 78. – /84 1T. 34.9 t.
62484 – 509 MBSO. Dia. ED212. Lot No. 30864 York 1977 – 78. – /68. 56 t.
71168 – 93 TSO. Dia. EH209. Lot No. 30865 York 1977 – 78. – /98. 30.5 t.
78000 – 25 DTCOL. Dia. EE305. Lot No. 30866 York 1977 – 78. 25/47 2T.

312 701	N	A	GE	IL	76949	62484	71168	78000
312 702	N	A	GE	IL	76950	62485	71169	78001
312 703	N	A	GE	IL	76951	62486	71170	78002
312 704	N	A	GE	IL	76952	62487	71171	78003
312 705	N	A	GE	IL	76953	62488	71172	78004
312 706	N	A	GE	IL	76954	62489	71173	78005
312 707	N	A	GE	IL	76955	62490	71174	78006
312 708	N	A	GE	IL	76956	62491	71175	78007
312 709	N	A	GE	IL	76957	62492	71176	78008
312 710	N	A	GE	IL	76958	62493	71177	78009
312 711	N	A	GE	IL	76959	62494	71178	78010
312 712	N	A	GE	IL	76960	62495	71179	78011
312 713	N	A	GE	IL	76961	62496	71180	78012
312 714	N	A	GE	IL	76962	62497	71181	78013
312 715	N	A	GE	IL	76963	62498	71182	78014
312 716	N	A	GE	IL	76964	62499	71183	78015
312 717	N	A	GE	IL	76965	62500	71184	78016
312 718	N	A	GE	IL	76966	62501	71185	78017
312 719	N	A	GE	IL	76967	62502	71186	78018
312 720	N	A	GE	IL	76968	62503	71187	78019
312 721	N	A	GE	IL	76969	62504	71188	78020
312 722	N	A	GE	IL	76970	62505	71189	78021
312 723	N	A	GE	IL	76971	62506	71190	78022
312 724	N	A	GE	IL	76972	62507	71191	78023
312 725	RR	A	CT	LG	76973	62509	71193	78025
312 726	RR	A	CT	LG	76974	62508	71192	78024
312 727	RR	A	CT	LG	76994	62657	71277	78045
312 728	RR	A	CT	LG	76995	62658	71278	78046
312 729	N	A	LS	EM	76996	62659	71279	78047
312 730	N	A	LS	EM	76997	62660	71280	78048

Class 312/1. Could also operate on 6.25 kV a.c. overhead.

BDTSOL. Dia. EF213. Lot No. 30867 York 1975 – 76. – /84 2T. 34.9 t.
MBSO. Dia. ED213. Lot No. 30868 York 1975 – 76. – /68. 56 t.
TSO. Dia. EH209. Lot No. 30869 York 1975 – 76. – /98. 30.5 t.
DTCOL. Dia. EE305. Lot No. 30870 York 1975 – 76. 25/47 2T.

312 781	N	A	LS	EM	76975	62510	71194	78026
312 782	N	A	LS	EM	76976	62511	71195	78027
312 783	N	A	LS	EM	76977	62512	71196	78028

312 784	N	A	LS	EM	76978 62513 71197 78029
312 785	N	A	LS	EM	76979 62514 71198 78030
312 786	N	A	LS	EM	76980 62515 71199 78031
312 787	N	A	LS	EM	76981 62516 71200 78032
312 788	N	A	LS	EM	76982 62517 71201 78033
312 789	N	A	LS	EM	76983 62518 71202 78034
312 790	N	A	LS	EM	76984 62519 71203 78035
312 791	N	A	LS	EM	76985 62520 71204 78036
312 792	N	A	LS	EM	76986 62521 71205 78037
312 793	N	A	LS	EM	76987 62522 71206 78038
312 794	N	A	LS	EM	76988 62523 71207 78039
312 795	N	A	LS	EM	76989 62524 71208 78040
312 796	N	A	LS	EM	76990 62525 71209 78041
312 797	N	A	LS	EM	76991 62526 71210 78042
312 798	N	A	LS	EM	76992 62527 71211 78043
312 799	N	A	LS	EM	76993 62528 71212 78044

CLASS 313

DMSO – PTSO – BDMSO. Tightlock couplers. Sliding doors. Disc and rheostatic brakes. PA. Cab to shore radio.
System: 25 kV a.c. overhead/750 V d.c. third rail.
Bogies: BX1.
Gangways: Within unit. End doors.
Traction Motors: Four GEC G310AZ of 82.125 kW.
Dimensions: 19.80 x 2.82 m (outer cars), 19.92 x 2.82 m (inner cars).
Maximum Speed: 75 mph.

DMSO. Dia. EA204. Lot No. 30879 York 1976 – 77. – /74. 36.4 t.
PTSO. Dia. EH210. Lot No. 30880 York 1976 – 77. – /84. 30.5 t.
BDMSO. Dia. EI201. Lot No. 30885 York 1976 – 77. – /74. 37.6 t.

* – Extra shoegear for Euston – Watford and Richmond – North Woolwich line services. Class 313/1.

313 001	*	N	E	NL	BY	62529 71213 62593
313 002	*	N	E	NL	BY	62530 71214 62594
313 003	*	N	E	NL	BY	62531 71215 62595
313 004	*	N	E	NL	BY	62532 71216 62596
313 005	*	N	E	NL	BY	62533 71217 62597
313 006	*	N	E	NL	BY	62534 71218 62598
313 007	*	N	E	NL	BY	62535 71219 62599
313 008	*	N	E	NL	BY	62536 71220 62600
313 009	*	N	E	NL	BY	62537 71221 62601
313 010	*	N	E	NL	BY	62538 71222 62602
313 011	*	N	E	NL	BY	62539 71223 62603
313 012	*	N	E	NL	BY	62540 71224 62604
313 013	*	N	E	NL	BY	62541 71225 62605
313 014	*	N	E	NL	BY	62542 71226 62606
313 015	*	N	E	NL	BY	62543 71227 62607

313 016	*	N	E	NL	BY	62544	71228	62608
313 017	*	N	E	NL	BY	62545	71229	62609
313 018	*	N	E	WN	HE	62546	71230	62610
313 019	*	N	E	NL	BY	62547	71231	62611
313 020	*	N	E	NL	BY	62548	71232	62612
313 021	*	N	E	NL	BY	62549	71233	62613
313 022	*	N	E	NL	BY	62550	71234	62614
313 023	*	N	E	NL	BY	62551	71235	62615
313 024		N	E	WN	HE	62552	71236	62616
313 025		N	E	WN	HE	62553	71237	62617
313 026		N	E	WN	HE	62554	71238	62618
313 027		N	E	WN	HE	62555	71239	62619
313 028		N	E	WN	HE	62556	71240	62620
313 029		N	E	WN	HE	62557	71241	62621
313 030		N	E	WN	HE	62558	71242	62622
313 031		N	E	WN	HE	62559	71243	62623
313 032		N	E	WN	HE	62560	71244	62624
313 033		N	E	WN	HE	62561	71245	62625
313 034		N	E	NL	BY	62562	71246	62626
313 035		N	E	WN	HE	62563	71247	62627
313 036		N	E	WN	HE	62564	71248	62628
313 037		N	E	WN	HE	62565	71249	62629
313 038		N	E	WN	HE	62566	71250	62630
313 039		N	E	WN	HE	62567	71251	62631
313 040		N	E	WN	HE	62568	71252	62632
313 041		N	E	WN	HE	62569	71253	62633
313 042		N	E	WN	HE	62570	71254	62634
313 043		N	E	WN	HE	62571	71255	62635
313 044		N	E	WN	HE	62572	71256	62636
313 045		N	E	WN	HE	62573	71257	62637
313 046		N	E	WN	HE	62574	71258	62638
313 047		N	E	WN	HE	62575	71259	62639
313 048		N	E	WN	HE	62576	71260	62640
313 049		N	E	WN	HE	62577	71261	62641
313 050		N	E	WN	HE	62578	71262	62649
313 051		N	E	WN	HE	62579	71263	62643
313 052		N	E	WN	HE	62580	71264	62644
313 053		N	E	WN	HE	62581	71265	62645
313 054		N	E	WN	HE	62582	71266	62646
313 055		N	E	WN	HE	62583	71267	62647
313 056		N	E	WN	HE	62584	71268	62648
313 057		N	E	WN	HE	62585	71269	62642
313 058		N	E	WN	HE	62586	71270	62650
313 059		N	E	WN	HE	62587	71271	62651
313 060		N	E	WN	HE	62588	71272	62652
313 061		N	E	WN	HE	62589	71273	62653
313 062		N	E	WN	HE	62590	71274	62654
313 063		N	E	WN	HE	62591	71275	62655
313 064		N	E	WN	HE	62592	71276	62656

Name: PTSO 71232 of 313 020 is named 'PARLIAMENT HILL'.

CLASS 314

DMSO – PTSO – DMSO. Thyristor control. Tightlock couplers. Sliding doors. Disc and rheostatic brakes. PA. Cab to shore radio.
Bogies: BX1.
Gangways: Within unit. End doors.
Traction Motors: Four GEC G310AZ (Brush TM61-53*) of 82.125 kW.
Dimensions: 19.80 x 2.82 m (outer cars), 19.92 x 2.82 m (inner cars).
Maximum Speed: 75 mph.

64583 – 64614. DMSO. Dia. EA206. Lot No. 30912 York 1979. –/68. 34.5 t.
64588^{II}. DMSO. Dia. EA207. Lot No. 30908 York 1978 – 80. –/74. 35.63 t.
Converted from Class 507 No. 64426. The original 64588 has been scrapped.
This vehicle has an experimental seating layout.
PTSO. Dia. EH211. Lot No. 30913 York 1979. –/76. 33.0 t.

314 201	*	S	A	SR	GW	64583 71450 64584
314 202	*	S	A	SR	GW	64585 71451 64586
314 203	*	S	A	SR	GW	64587 71452 64588^{II}
314 204	*	S	A	SR	GW	64589 71453 64590
314 205	*	S	A	SR	GW	64591 71454 64592
314 206	*	S	A	SR	GW	64593 71455 64594
314 207		S	A	SR	GW	64595 71456 64596
314 208		S	A	SR	GW	64597 71457 64598
314 209		S	A	SR	GW	64599 71458 64600
314 210		S	A	SR	GW	64601 71459 64602
314 211		S	A	SR	GW	64603 71460 64604
314 212		S	A	SR	GW	64605 71461 64606
314 213		S	A	SR	GW	64607 71462 64608
314 214		S	A	SR	GW	64609 71463 64610
314 215		S	A	SR	GW	64611 71464 64612
314 216		S	A	SR	GW	64613 71465 64614

Name: PTSO No. 71452 of set 314 203 is named 'European Union'.

CLASS 315

DMSO – TSO – PTSO – DMSO. Thyristor control. Tightlock couplers. Sliding doors. Disc and rheostatic brakes. PA.
Bogies: BX1.
Gangways: Within unit. End doors.
Traction Motors: Four Brush TM61-53 (GEC G310AZ*) of 82.125 kW.
Dimensions: 19.80 x 2.82 m (outer cars), 19.92 x 2.82 m (inner cars).
Maximum Speed: 75 mph.

64461 – 64582. DMSO. Dia. EA207. Lot No. 30902 York 1980 – 81. –/74. 35 t.
71281 – 71341. TSO. Dia. EH216. Lot No. 30904 York 1980 – 81. –/86. 25.5 t.
71389 – 71449. PTSO. Dia. EH217. Lot No. 30903 York 1980 – 81. –/84. 32 t.

315 801		N	E	GE	IL	64461	71281	71389	64462
315 802		N	E	GE	IL	64463	71282	71390	64464
315 803		N	E	GE	IL	64465	71283	71391	64466
315 804		N	E	GE	IL	64467	71284	71392	64468
315 805		N	E	GE	IL	64469	71285	71393	64470
315 806		N	E	GE	IL	64471	71286	71394	64472
315 807		N	E	GE	IL	64473	71287	71395	64474
315 808		N	E	GE	IL	64475	71288	71396	64476
315 809		N	E	GE	IL	64477	71289	71397	64478
315 810		N	E	GE	IL	64479	71290	71398	64480
315 811		N	E	GE	IL	64481	71291	71399	64482
315 812		N	E	GE	IL	64483	71292	71400	64484
315 813		N	E	GE	IL	64485	71293	71401	64486
315 814		N	E	GE	IL	64487	71294	71402	64488
315 815		N	E	GE	IL	64489	71295	71403	64490
315 816		N	E	GE	IL	64491	71296	71404	64492
315 817		N	E	GE	IL	64493	71297	71405	64494
315 818		N	E	GE	IL	64495	71298	71406	64496
315 819		N	E	GE	IL	64497	71299	71407	64498
315 820		N	E	GE	IL	64499	71300	71408	64500
315 821		N	E	GE	IL	64501	71301	71409	64502
315 822		N	E	GE	IL	64503	71302	71410	64504
315 823		N	E	GE	IL	64505	71303	71411	64506
315 824		N	E	GE	IL	64507	71304	71412	64508
315 825		N	E	GE	IL	64509	71305	71413	64510
315 826		N	E	GE	IL	64511	71306	71414	64512
315 827		N	E	GE	IL	64513	71307	71415	64514
315 828		N	E	GE	IL	64515	71308	71416	64516
315 829		N	E	GE	IL	64517	71309	71417	64518
315 830		N	E	GE	IL	64519	71310	71418	64520
315 831		N	E	GE	IL	64521	71311	71419	64522
315 832		N	E	GE	IL	64523	71312	71420	64524
315 833		N	E	GE	IL	64525	71313	71421	64526
315 834		N	E	GE	IL	64527	71314	71422	64528
315 835		N	E	GE	IL	64529	71315	71423	64530
315 836		N	E	GE	IL	64531	71316	71424	64532
315 837		N	E	GE	IL	64533	71317	71425	64534
315 838		N	E	GE	IL	64535	71318	71426	64536
315 839		N	E	GE	IL	64537	71319	71427	64538
315 840		N	E	GE	IL	64539	71320	71428	64540
315 841		N	E	GE	IL	64541	71321	71429	64542
315 842	*	N	E	GE	IL	64543	71322	71430	64544
315 843	*	N	E	GE	IL	64545	71323	71431	64546
315 844	*	N	E	GE	IL	64547	71324	71432	64548
315 845	*	N	E	GE	IL	64549	71325	71433	64550
315 846	*	N	E	WN	HE	64551	71326	71434	64552
315 847	*	N	E	WN	HE	64553	71327	71435	64554
315 848	*	N	E	WN	HE	64555	71328	71436	64556
315 849	*	N	E	WN	HE	64557	71329	71437	64558
315 850	*	N	E	WN	HE	64559	71330	71438	64560
315 851	*	N	E	WN	HE	64561	71331	71439	64562

315 852	*	N	E	WN	HE	64563 71332 71440 64564
315 853	*	N	E	WN	HE	64565 71333 71441 64566
315 854	*	N	E	WN	HE	64567 71334 71442 64568
315 855	*	N	E	WN	HE	64569 71335 71443 64570
315 856	*	N	E	WN	HE	64571 71336 71444 64572
315 857	*	N	E	WN	HE	64573 71337 71445 64574
315 858	*	N	E	WN	HE	64575 71338 71446 64576
315 859	*	N	E	WN	HE	64577 71339 71447 64578
315 860	*	N	E	WN	HE	64579 71340 71448 64580
315 861	*	N	E	WN	HE	64581 71341 71449 64582

CLASS 317

DTSO(A) – MSO – TCOL – DTSO(B). Thyristor control. Tightlock couplers.
Sliding doors. Disc brakes. PA.
Bogies: BP20 (MSO), BT13 (others).
Gangways: Throughout.
Traction Motors: Four GEC G315BZ of 247.5 kW.
Dimensions: 19.83 x 2.82 m (outer cars), 19.92 x 2.82 m (inner cars).
Maximum Speed: 100 mph.

Class 317/1. Pressure ventilated.

DTSO(A) Dia. EE216. Lot No. 30955 York 1981–82. –/74. 29.44 t.
MSO. Dia. EC202. Lot No. 30958 York 1981–82. –/79. 49.76 t.
TCOL. Dia. EH307. Lot No. 30957 Derby 1981–82. 22/46 2T. 28.80 t. Controlled emission toilets (but decommisioned).
DTSO(B) Dia. EE235 (EE232★). Lot No. 30956 York 1981–82. –/70. (–/71★). 29.28 t.

317 301	N	A	LS	EM	77024 62661 71577 77048
317 302	N	A	LS	EM	77001 62662 71578 77049
317 303	N	A	WN	HE	77002 62663 71579 77050
317 304	N	A	WN	HE	77003 62664 71580 77051
317 305	N	A	WN	HE	77004 62665 71581 77052
317 306	N	A	WN	HE	77005 62666 71582 77053
317 307	N	A	WN	HE	77006 62667 71583 77054
317 308	N	A	WN	HE	77007 62668 71584 77055
317 309	N	A	WN	HE	77008 62669 71585 77056
317 310	N	A	WN	HE	77009 62670 71586 77057
317 311	N	A	WN	HE	77010 62697 71587 77058
317 312	N	A	WN	HE	77011 62672 71588 77059
317 313	N	A	WN	HE	77012 62673 71589 77060
317 314	N	A	WN	HE	77013 62674 71590 77061
317 315	N	A	WN	HE	77014 62675 71591 77062
317 316	N	A	WN	HE	77015 62676 71592 77063
317 317	N	A	WN	HE	77016 62677 71593 77064
317 318	N	A	WN	HE	77017 62678 71594 77065
317 319	N	A	WN	HE	77018 62679 71595 77066
317 320	N	A	WN	HE	77019 62680 71596 77067
317 321	N	A	WN	HE	77020 62681 71597 77068
317 329	N	A	WN	HE	77028 62689 71605 77076

317 330		**N**	A	WN	HE	77029	62690	71606	77077
317 331		**N**	A	WN	HE	77030	62691	71607	77078
317 332		**N**	A	WN	HE	77031	62692	71608	77079
317 333		**N**	A	WN	HE	77032	62693	71609	77080
317 334		**N**	A	WN	HE	77033	62694	71610	77081
317 335		**N**	A	WN	HE	77034	62695	71611	77082
317 336		**N**	A	WN	HE	77035	62696	71612	77083
317 337	★	**N**	A	WN	HE	77036	62697	71613	77084
317 338	★	**N**	A	WN	HE	77037	62698	71614	77085
317 339	★	**N**	A	WN	HE	77038	62699	71615	77086
317 340	★	**N**	A	WN	HE	77039	62700	71616	77087
317 341	★	**N**	A	WN	HE	77040	62701	71617	77088
317 342	★	**N**	A	WN	HE	77041	62702	71618	77089
317 343	★	**N**	A	WN	HE	77042	62703	71619	77090
317 344	★	**N**	A	WN	HE	77043	62704	71620	77091
317 345	★	**N**	A	WN	HE	77044	62705	71621	77092
317 346	★	**N**	A	WN	HE	77045	62706	71622	77093
317 347	★	**N**	A	WN	HE	77046	62707	71623	77094
317 348	★	**N**	A	WN	HE	77047	62708	71624	77095

Class 317/2. Convection heating.

77200 – 19. DTSO(A). Dia. EE224. Lot No. 30994 York 1985 – 86. – /74. 29.31 t.
77280 – 83. DTSO(A). Dia. EE224. Lot No. 31007 York 1987. – /74. 29.31 t.
62846 – 65. MSO. Dia. EC205. Lot No. 30996 York 1985 – 86. – /79. 50.08 t.
62886 – 89. MSO. Dia. EC205. Lot No. 31009 York 1987. – /79. 50.08 t.
71734 – 53. TCOL. Dia. EH308. Lot No. 30997 York 1985 – 86. 22/46 2T. 28.28 t.
71762 – 65. TCOL. Dia. EH308. Lot No. 31010 York 1987. 22/46 2T. 28.28 t.
77220 – 39. DTSO(B). Dia. EE225. Lot No. 30995 York 1985 – 86. 29.28 t. – /71.
77284 – 87. DTSO(B). Dia. EE225. Lot No. 31008 York 1987. 29.28 t. – /71.

317 349	**N**	A	WN	HE	77200	62846	71734	77220
317 350	**N**	A	WN	HE	77201	62847	71735	77221
317 351	**N**	A	WN	HE	77202	62848	71736	77222
317 352	**N**	A	WN	HE	77203	62849	71739	77223
317 353	**N**	A	WN	HE	77204	62850	71738	77224
317 354	**N**	A	WN	HE	77205	62851	71737	77225
317 355	**N**	A	WN	HE	77206	62852	71740	77226
317 356	**N**	A	WN	HE	77207	62853	71742	77227
317 357	**N**	A	WN	HE	77208	62854	71741	77228
317 358	**N**	A	WN	HE	77209	62855	71743	77229
317 359	**N**	A	WN	HE	77210	62856	71744	77230
317 360	**N**	A	WN	HE	77211	62857	71745	77231
317 361	**N**	A	WN	HE	77212	62858	71746	77232
317 362	**N**	A	WN	HE	77213	62859	71747	77233
317 363	**N**	A	WN	HE	77214	62860	71748	77234
317 364	**N**	A	WN	HE	77215	62861	71749	77235
317 365	**N**	A	WN	HE	77216	62862	71750	77236
317 366	**N**	A	WN	HE	77217	62863	71752	77237

317 367	N	A	WN	HE	77218 62864 71751 77238
317 368	N	A	WN	HE	77219 62865 71753 77239
317 369	N	A	WN	HE	77280 62886 71762 77284
317 370	N	A	WN	HE	77281 62887 71763 77285
317 371	N	A	WN	HE	77282 62888 71764 77286
317 372	N	A	WN	HE	77283 62889 71765 77287

Class 317/0. As Class 317/1, but TCOL has first class seating declassified.

317 392	N	A	WN	HE	77021 62682 71598 77069
317 393	N	A	WN	HE	77022 62683 71599 77070
317 394	N	A	WN	HE	77023 62684 71600 77071
317 395	N	A	WN	HE	77000 62685 71601 77072
317 396	N	A	WN	HE	77025 62686 71602 77073
317 397	N	A	WN	HE	77026 62687 71603 77074
317 398	N	A	WN	HE	77027 62688 71604 77075

Names:

TCOL No. 71746 of set 317 361 is named 'Kings Lynn Festival'.
TCOL No. 71752 of set 317 366 is named 'Letchworth Garden City'.
TCOL No. 71764 of set 317 371 is named 'STEVENAGE new town 50 years
1946 – 1996'.
TCOL No. 71765 of set 317 372 is named 'Welwyn Garden City'.

CLASS 318

DTSOL – MSO – DTSO. Thyristor control. Tightlock couplers. Sliding doors. Disc
brakes. PA. Cab to shore radio.
Bogies: BP20 (MSO), BT13 (others).
Gangways: Throughout.
Traction Motors: Four Brush TM 2141 of 268 kW.
Dimensions: 19.83 x 2.82 m (outer cars), 19.92 x 2.82 m (inner cars).
Maximum Speed: 90 mph.

77240 – 59. DTSOL. Dia. EE227. Lot No. 30999 York 1985 – 86. –/66 1T.
30.01 t.
77288. DTSOL. Dia. EE227. Lot No. 31020 York 1986 – 87. –/66 1T. 30.01 t.
62866 – 85. MSO. Dia. EC207. Lot No. 30998 York 1985 – 86. –/79. 50.90 t.
62890. MSO. Dia. EC207. Lot No. 31019 York 1987. –/79. 50.90 t.
77260 – 79. DTSO. Dia. EE228. Lot No. 31000 York 1985 – 86. –/71. 26.60 t.
77289. DTSO. Dia. EE228. Lot No. 31021 York 1987. –/71. 26.60 t.

318 250	S	E	SR	GW	77260 62866 77240
318 251	S	E	SR	GW	77261 62867 77241
318 252	S	E	SR	GW	77262 62868 77242
318 253	S	E	SR	GW	77263 62869 77243
318 254	S	E	SR	GW	77264 62870 77244
318 255	S	E	SR	GW	77265 62871 77245
318 256	S	E	SR	GW	77266 62872 77246
318 257	S	E	SR	GW	77267 62873 77247
318 258	S	E	SR	GW	77268 62874 77248
318 259	S	E	SR	GW	77269 62875 77249
318 260	S	E	SR	GW	77270 62876 77250

318 261	S	E	SR	GW	77271 62877 77251
318 262	S	E	SR	GW	77272 62878 77252
318 263	S	E	SR	GW	77273 62879 77253
318 264	S	E	SR	GW	77274 62880 77254
318 265	S	E	SR	GW	77275 62881 77255
318 266	S	E	SR	GW	77276 62882 77256
318 267	S	E	SR	GW	77277 62883 77257
318 268	S	E	SR	GW	77278 62884 77258
318 269	S	E	SR	GW	77279 62885 77259
318 270	S	E	SR	GW	77289 62890 77288

Names:
DTSOL No. 77256 of set 318 266 is named 'STRATHCLYDER'.

CLASS 319

Thyristor control. Tightlock couplers. Sliding doors. Disc brakes. PA. Cab to shore radio.
System: 25 kV a.c. overhead/750 V d.c. third rail.
Bogies: P7-4 (MSO), T3-7 (others).
Gangways: Within unit. End doors.
Traction Motors: Four GEC G315BZ of 268 kW.
Dimensions: 19.83 x 2.82 m (outer cars), 19.92 x 2.82 m (inner cars).
Maximum Speed: 100 mph.

Class 319/0. DTSO – MSO – TSOL – DTSO.

77291 – 381. DTSO. Dia. EE233. Lot No. 31022 (odd nos.) York 1987 – 8. – /82. 30 t.
77431 – 457. DTSO. Dia. EE233. Lot No. 31038 (odd nos.) York 1988. – /82. 30 t.
62891 – 936. MSO. Dia. EC209. Lot No. 31023 York 1987 – 8. – /82. 51 t.
62961 – 974. MSO. Dia. EC209. Lot No. 31039 York 1988. – /82. 51 t.
71772 – 817. TSOL. Dia. EH234. Lot No. 31024 York 1987 – 8. – /77 2T. 34 t.
71866 – 879. TSOL. Dia. EH234. Lot No. 31040 York 1988. – /77 2T. 34 t.
77290 – 380. DTSO. Dia. EE234. Lot No. 31025 (even nos.) York 1987 – 8. – /78. 30 t.
77430 – 456. DTSO. Dia. EE234. Lot No. 31041 (even nos.) York 1988. – /78. 30 t.

319 001	N	P	SC	SU	77291 62891 71772 77290
319 002	N	P	SC	SU	77293 62892 71773 77292
319 003	N	P	SC	SU	77295 62893 71774 77294
319 004	N	P	SC	SU	77297 62894 71775 77296
319 005	N	P	SC	SU	77299 62895 71776 77298
319 006	N	P	SC	SU	77301 62896 71777 77300
319 007	N	P	SC	SU	77303 62897 71778 77302
319 008	N	P	SC	SU	77305 62898 71779 77304
319 009	N	P	SC	SU	77307 62899 71780 77306
319 010	N	P	SC	SU	77309 62900 71781 77308
319 011	N	P	SC	SU	77311 62901 71782 77310
319 012	N	P	SC	SU	77313 62902 71783 77312

319 013	N	P	SC	SU	77315	62903	71784	77314
319 021	N	P	TL	SU	77331	62911	71792	77330
319 022	TL	P	TL	SU	77333	62912	71793	77332
319 023	N	P	TL	SU	77335	62913	71794	77334
319 024	N	P	TL	SU	77337	62914	71795	77336
319 025	N	P	TL	SU	77339	62915	71796	77338
319 026	N	P	TL	SU	77341	62916	71797	77340
319 027	N	P	TL	SU	77343	62917	71798	77342
319 028	N	P	TL	SU	77345	62918	71799	77344
319 029	N	P	TL	SU	77347	62919	71800	77346
319 030	TL	P	TL	SU	77349	62920	71801	77348
319 031	TL	P	TL	SU	77351	62921	71802	77350
319 032	TL	P	TL	SU	77353	62922	71803	77352
319 033	TL	P	TL	SU	77355	62923	71804	77354
319 034	TL	P	TL	SU	77357	62924	71805	77356
319 035	TL	P	TL	SU	77359	62925	71806	77358
319 036	TL	P	TL	SU	77361	62926	71807	77360
319 037	TL	P	TL	SU	77363	62927	71808	77362
319 038	TL	P	TL	SU	77365	62928	71809	77364
319 039	TL	P	TL	SU	77367	62929	71810	77366
319 040	TL	P	TL	SU	77369	62930	71811	77368
319 041	TL	P	TL	SU	77371	62931	71812	77370
319 042	TL	P	TL	SU	77373	62932	71813	77372
319 043	TL	P	TL	SU	77375	62933	71814	77374
319 044	TL	P	TL	SU	77377	62934	71815	77376
319 045	TL	P	TL	SU	77379	62935	71816	77378
319 046	TL	P	TL	SU	77381	62936	71817	77380
319 047	TL	P	TL	SU	77431	62961	71866	77430
319 048	TL	P	TL	SU	77433	62962	71867	77432
319 049	TL	P	TL	SU	77435	62963	71868	77434
319 050	TL	P	TL	SU	77437	62964	71869	77436
319 051	TL	P	TL	SU	77439	62965	71870	77438
319 052	TL	P	TL	SU	77441	62966	71871	77440
319 053	TL	P	TL	SU	77443	62967	71872	77442
319 054	TL	P	TL	SU	77445	62968	71873	77444
319 055	TL	P	TL	SU	77447	62969	71874	77446
319 056	TL	P	TL	SU	77449	62970	71875	77448
319 057	TL	P	TL	SU	77451	62971	71876	77450
319 058	TL	P	TL	SU	77453	62972	71877	77452
319 059	TL	P	TL	SU	77455	62973	71878	77454
319 060	TL	P	TL	SU	77457	62974	71879	77456

Names:

TSOL 71776 of set 319 005 is named 'Partnership For Progress'.
TSOL 71779 of set 319 008 is named 'Cheriton'.
TSOL 71780 of set 319 009 is named 'Coquelles'.
TSOL 71801 of set 319 030 is named 'Harlington Festival'.
TSOL 71874 of set 319 055 is named 'Brixton Challenge'.

Class 319/1. DTCO – MSO – TSOL – DTSO.

DTCO. Dia. EE310. Lot No. 31063 York 1990. 16/54. 29 t.

MSO. Dia. EC214. Lot No. 31064 York 1990. −/79. 50.6 t.
TSOL. Dia. EH238. Lot No. 31065 York 1990. −/74 2T. 31 t.
DTSO. Dia. EE240. Lot No. 31066 York 1990. −/78. 29.7 t.

319 161	**NW**	P	TL	SU	77459 63043 71929 77458
319 162	**NW**	P	TL	SU	77461 63044 71930 77460
319 163	**NW**	P	TL	SU	77463 63045 71931 77462
319 164	**NW**	P	TL	SU	77465 63046 71932 77464
319 165	**NW**	P	TL	SU	77467 63047 71933 77466
319 166	**NW**	P	TL	SU	77469 63048 71934 77468
319 167	**NW**	P	TL	SU	77471 63049 71935 77470
319 168	**NW**	P	TL	SU	77473 63050 71936 77472
319 169	**NW**	P	TL	SU	77475 63051 71937 77474
319 170	**NW**	P	TL	SU	77477 63052 71938 77476
319 171	**NW**	P	TL	SU	77479 63053 71939 77478
319 172	**NW**	P	TL	SU	77481 63054 71940 77480
319 173	**NW**	P	TL	SU	77483 63055 71941 77482
319 174	**NW**	P	TL	SU	77485 63056 71942 77484
319 175	**NW**	P	TL	SU	77487 63057 71943 77486
319 176	**NW**	P	TL	SU	77489 63058 71944 77488
319 177	**NW**	P	TL	SU	77491 63059 71945 77490
319 178	**NW**	P	TL	SU	77493 63060 71946 77492
319 179	**NW**	P	TL	SU	77495 63061 71947 77494
319 180	**NW**	P	TL	SU	77497 63062 71948 77496
319 181	**NW**	P	TL	SU	77973 63093 71979 77974
319 182	**NW**	P	TL	SU	77975 63094 71980 77976
319 183	**NW**	P	TL	SU	77977 63095 71981 77978
319 184	**NW**	P	TL	SU	77979 63096 71982 77980
319 185	**NW**	P	TL	SU	77981 63097 71983 77982
319 186	**NW**	P	TL	SU	77983 63098 71984 77984

Class 319/2. Units converted from Class 319/0 for Connex Express services from London to Brighton. DTSO – MSO – TSOL – DTCO.

DTSO. Dia. EE244. −/64. 30.2 t.
MSO. Dia. EN262. −/60 (including 12 seats in a 'snug' under the pantograph area. External sliding doors sealed adjacent to this area. 51 t.
TSOL. Dia. EH212. −/52 1T 1TD. 34 t.
DTCO. Dia. EE374. 18/36. 30 t.

For lot Nos. see Class 3190.

319 214	(319 014)	**CX**	P	SC	SU	77317 62904 71785 77316
319 215	(319 015)	**CX**	P	SC	SU	77319 62905 71786 77318
319 216	(319 016)	**CX**	P	SC	SU	77321 62906 71787 77320
319 217	(319 017)	**CX**	P	SC	SU	77323 62907 71788 77322
319 218	(319 018)	**CX**	P	SC	SU	77325 62908 71789 77324
319 219	(319 019)	**CX**	P	SC	SU	77327 62909 71790 77326
319 220	(319 020)	**CX**	P	SC	SU	77329 62910 71791 77328

Names:

71786 of 319 215 is named 'London'
71788 of 319 217 is named 'Brighton'
71789 of 319 218 is named 'Croydon'

CLASS 320

DTSO(A) – MSO – DTSO(B). Thyristor control. Tightlock couplers. Sliding doors.
Disc brakes. PA.
Bogies: P7-4 (MSO), T3-7 (others).
Gangways: Within unit.
Traction Motors: Brush TM2141B of 268 kW.
Dimensions: 19.83 x 2.82 m (outer cars), 19.92 x 2.82 m (inner car).
Maximum Speed: 75 mph.

DTSO (A). Dia. EE238. Lot No. 31060 York 1990. –/77. 30.7 t.
MSO. Dia. EC212. Lot No. 31062 York 1990. –/77. 52.1 t.
DTSO (B). Dia. EE239. Lot No. 31061 York 1990. –/76 31.7 t.

320 301	S	E	SR	GW	77899	63021 77921
320 302	S	E	SR	GW	77900	63022 77922
320 303	S	E	SR	GW	77901	63023 77923
320 304	S	E	SR	GW	77902	63024 77924
320 305	S	E	SR	GW	77903	63025 77925
320 306	S	E	SR	GW	77904	63026 77926
320 307	S	E	SR	GW	77905	63027 77927
320 308	S	E	SR	GW	77906	63028 77928
320 309	S	E	SR	GW	77907	63029 77929
320 310	S	E	SR	GW	77908	63030 77930
320 311	S	E	SR	GW	77909	63031 77931
320 312	S	E	SR	GW	77910	63032 77932
320 313	S	E	SR	GW	77911	63033 77933
320 314	S	E	SR	GW	77912	63034 77934
320 315	S	E	SR	GW	77913	63035 77935
320 316	S	E	SR	GW	77914	63036 77936
320 317	S	E	SR	GW	77915	63037 77937
320 318	S	E	SR	GW	77916	63038 77938
320 319	S	E	SR	GW	77917	63039 77939
320 320	S	E	SR	GW	77918	63040 77940
320 321	S	E	SR	GW	77919	63041 77941
320 322	S	E	SR	GW	77920	63042 77942

Names:

MSO 63025 of set 320 305 is named GLASGOW SCHOOL OF ART.
MSO 63042 of set 320 322 is named FESTIVE GLASGOW ORCHID.

CLASS 321

DTCO (DTSO on Class 321/9) – MSO – TSOL – DTSO. Thyristor control.
Tightlock couplers. Sliding doors. Disc brakes. PA.
Bogies: P7-4 (MSO), T3-7 (others).
Gangways: Within unit.
Traction Motors: Brush TM2141C of 268 kW.
Dimensions: 19.83 x 2.82 m (outer cars), 19.92 x 2.82 m (inner cars).
Maximum Speed: 100 mph.

Non-Standard Livery: NS (Netherlands Railways) Intercity livery (yellow and deep blue).

Note: Lot numbers and diagrams were officially changed on 09/02/90.

Class 321/3. Units built for Liverpool Street workings.

DTCO. Dia. EE308. Lot No. 31053 York 1988 – 90. 12/56. 29.3 t.
MSO. Dia. EC210. Lot No. 31054 York 1988 – 90. –/79. 51.5 t.
TSOL. Dia. EH235. Lot No. 31055 York 1988 – 90. –/74 2T. 28 t.
DTSO. Dia. EE236. Lot No. 31056 York 1988 – 90. –/78. 29.1 t.

321 301	NW	E	GE	IL	78049	62975	71880	77853
321 302	NW	E	GE	IL	78050	62976	71881	77854
321 303	NW	E	GE	IL	78051	62977	71882	77855
321 304	NW	E	GE	IL	78052	62978	71883	77856
321 305	NW	E	GE	IL	78053	62979	71884	77857
321 306	NW	E	GE	IL	78054	62980	71885	77858
321 307	NW	E	GE	IL	78055	62981	71886	77859
321 308	NW	E	GE	IL	78056	62982	71887	77860
321 309	NW	E	GE	IL	78057	62983	71888	77861
321 310	NW	E	GE	IL	78058	62984	71889	77862
321 311	NW	E	GE	IL	78059	62985	71890	77863
321 312	NW	E	GE	IL	78060	62986	71891	77864
321 313	NW	E	GE	IL	78061	62987	71892	77865
321 314	NW	E	GE	IL	78062	62988	71893	77866
321 315	NW	E	GE	IL	78063	62989	71894	77867
321 316	NW	E	GE	IL	78064	62990	71895	77868
321 317	NW	E	GE	IL	78065	62991	71896	77869
321 318	NW	E	GE	IL	78066	62992	71897	77870
321 319	NW	E	GE	IL	78067	62993	71898	77871
321 320	NW	E	GE	IL	78068	62994	71899	77872
321 321	NW	E	GE	IL	78069	62995	71900	77873
321 322	NW	E	GE	IL	78070	62996	71901	77874
321 323	NW	E	GE	IL	78071	62997	71902	77875
321 324	NW	E	GE	IL	78072	62998	71903	77876
321 325	NW	E	GE	IL	78073	62999	71904	77877
321 326	NW	E	GE	IL	78074	63000	71905	77878
321 327	NW	E	GE	IL	78075	63001	71906	77879
321 328	NW	E	GE	IL	78076	63002	71907	77880
321 329	NW	E	GE	IL	78077	63003	71908	77881
321 330	NW	E	GE	IL	78078	63004	71909	77882
321 331	NW	E	GE	IL	78079	63005	71910	77883
321 332	NW	E	GE	IL	78080	63006	71911	77884
321 333	NW	E	GE	IL	78081	63007	71912	77885
321 334	0	E	GE	IL	78082	63008	71913	77886
321 335	NW	E	GE	IL	78083	63009	71914	77887
321 336	NW	E	GE	IL	78084	63010	71915	77888
321 337	NW	E	GE	IL	78085	63011	71916	77889
321 338	NW	E	GE	IL	78086	63012	71917	77890
321 339	NW	E	GE	IL	78087	63013	71918	77891
321 340	NW	E	GE	IL	78088	63014	71919	77892
321 341	NW	E	GE	IL	78089	63015	71920	77893

321 342	NW	E	GE	IL	78090	63016	71921	77894
321 343	NW	E	GE	IL	78091	63017	71922	77895
321 344	NW	E	GE	IL	78092	63018	71923	77896
321 345	NW	E	GE	IL	78093	63019	71924	77897
321 346	NW	E	GE	IL	78094	63020	71925	77898
321 347	NW	E	GE	IL	78131	63105	71991	78280
321 348	NW	E	GE	IL	78132	63106	71992	78281
321 349	NW	E	GE	IL	78133	63107	71993	78282
321 350	NW	E	GE	IL	78134	63108	71994	78283
321 351	NW	E	GE	IL	78135	63109	71995	78284
321 352	NW	E	GE	IL	78136	63110	71996	78285
321 353	NW	E	GE	IL	78137	63111	71997	78286
321 354	NW	E	GE	IL	78138	63112	71998	78287
321 355	NW	E	GE	IL	78139	63113	71999	78288
321 356	NW	E	GE	IL	78140	63114	72000	78289
321 357	NW	E	GE	IL	78141	63115	72001	78290
321 358	NW	E	GE	IL	78142	63116	72002	78291
321 359	NW	E	GE	IL	78143	63117	72003	78292
321 360	NW	E	GE	IL	78144	63118	72004	78293
321 361	NW	E	GE	IL	78145	63119	72005	78294
321 362	NW	E	GE	IL	78146	63120	72006	78295
321 363	NW	E	GE	IL	78147	63121	72007	78296
321 364	NW	E	GE	IL	78148	63122	72008	78297
321 365	NW	E	GE	IL	78149	63123	72009	78298
321 366	NW	E	GE	IL	78150	63124	72010	78299

Names:

TSOL No. 71891 of set 321 312 is named 'Southend-on-Sea'.
TSOL No. 71913 of set 321 334 is named 'Amsterdam'.
TSOL No. 71915 of set 321 336 is named 'Geoffrey Freeman Allen'.
TSOL No. 71995 of set 321 351 is named 'GURKHA'.

Class 321/4. Units built for WCML workings.

DTCO. Dia. EE309. Lot No. 31067 York 1989 – 90. 28/40. 29.3 t.
MSO. Dia. EC210. Lot No. 31068 York 1989 – 90. –/79. 51.5 t.
TSOL. Dia. EH235. Lot No. 31069 York 1989 – 90. –/74 2T. 28 t.
DTSO. Dia. EE236. Lot No. 31070 York 1989 – 90. –/78. 29.1 t.

Note: The DTCOs of sets allocated to IL have 12 First Class seats declassified.

321 401	NW	E	NL	BY	78095	63063	71949	77943
321 402	NW	E	NL	BY	78096	63064	71950	77944
321 403	NW	E	NL	BY	78097	63065	71951	77945
321 404	NW	E	NL	BY	78098	63066	71952	77946
321 405	NW	E	NL	BY	78099	63067	71953	77947
321 406	NW	E	NL	BY	78100	63068	71954	77948
321 407	NW	E	NL	BY	78101	63069	71955	77949
321 408	NW	E	NL	BY	78102	63070	71956	77950
321 409	NW	E	NL	BY	78103	63071	71957	77951
321 410	NW	E	NL	BY	78104	63072	71958	77952
321 411	NW	E	NL	BY	78105	63073	71959	77953
321 412	NW	E	NL	BY	78106	63074	71960	77954

321 413	NW	E	NL	BY	78107 63075 71961 77955
321 414	NW	E	NL	BY	78108 63076 71962 77956
321 415	NW	E	NL	BY	78109 63077 71963 77957
321 416	NW	E	NL	BY	78110 63078 71964 77958
321 417	NW	E	NL	BY	78111 63079 71965 77959
321 418	NW	E		BY	78112 63080 71966 77960
321 419	NW	E	NL	BY	78113 63081 71967 77961
321 420	NW	E		BY	78114 63082 71968 77962
321 421	NW	E	NL	BY	78115 63083 71969 77963
321 422	NW	E	NL	BY	78116 63084 71970 77964
321 423	NW	E	NL	BY	78117 63085 71971 77965
321 424	NW	E	NL	BY	78118 63086 71972 77966
321 425	NW	E	NL	BY	78119 63087 71973 77967
321 426	NW	E	NL	BY	78120 63088 71974 77968
321 427	NW	E	NL	BY	78121 63089 71975 77969
321 428	NW	E	NL	BY	78122 63090 71976 77970
321 429	NW	E	NL	BY	78123 63091 71977 77971
321 430	NW	E	NL	BY	78124 63092 71978 77972
321 431	NW	E	NL	BY	78151 63125 72011 78300
321 432	NW	E	NL	BY	78152 63126 72012 78301
321 433	NW	E	NL	BY	78153 63127 72013 78302
321 434	NW	E	NL	BY	78154 63128 72014 78303
321 435	NW	E	NL	BY	78155 63129 72015 78304
321 436	NW	E	NL	BY	78156 63130 72016 78305
321 437	NW	E	NL	BY	78157 63131 72017 78306
321 438	NW	E	GE	IL	78158 63132 72018 78307
321 439	NW	E	GE	IL	78159 63133 72019 78308
321 440	NW	E	GE	IL	78160 63134 72020 78309
321 441	NW	E	GE	IL	78161 63135 72021 78310
321 442	NW	E	GE	IL	78162 63136 72022 78311
321 443	NW	E	GE	IL	78125 63099 71985 78274
321 444	NW	E	GE	IL	78126 63100 71986 78275
321 445	NW	E	GE	IL	78127 63101 71987 78276
321 446	NW	E	GE	IL	78128 63102 71988 78277
321 447	NW	E	GE	IL	78129 63103 71989 78278
321 448	NW	E	NL	BY	78130 63104 71990 78279

Name: TSOL No. 71955 of set 321 407 is named 'HERTFORDSHIRE WRVS'.

Class 321/9. Units owned by West Yorkshire PTE although managed by Porterbrook Train Leasing. DTSO(A) – MSO – TSOL – DTSO(B).

DTSO (A). Dia. EE277. Lot No. 31108 York 1991. –/77. 29.3 t.
MSO. Dia. EC216. Lot No. 31109 York 1991. –/79. 51.5 t.
TSOL. Dia. EH240. Lot No. 31110 York 1991. –/74 2T. 28 t.
DTSO (B). Dia. EE277. Lot No. 31111 York 1991. –/77. 29.1 t.

321 901	Y	P	NE	NL	77990 63153 72128 77993
321 902	Y	P	NE	NL	77991 63154 72129 77994
321 903	Y	P	NE	NL	77992 63155 72130 77995

CLASS 322   STANSTED EXPRESS STOCK

DTCO – MSO – TSOL – DTSO. Units dedicated for use on Stansted Airport services. Thyristor control. Tightlock couplers. Sliding doors. Disc brakes. PA.
Bogies: P7-4 (MSO), T3-7 (others).
Gangways: Within unit.
Traction Motors: Brush TM2141C of 268 kW.
Dimensions: 19.83 x 2.82 m (outer cars), 19.92 x 2.82 m (inner cars).
Maximum Speed: 100 mph.
Non-Standard Livery: 322 481/2/4/5 are light grey with broad green band and narrow white and dark grey bands. White at cantrail level and on outer ends of end cars with 'Stansted Express' lettering. 322 483 is in Stansted skytrain livery (grey with a yellow stripe).

DTCO. Dia. EE313. Lot No. 31094 York 1990. 35/22. 30.43 t.
MSO. Dia. EC215. Lot No. 31092 York 1990. –/70. 52.27 t.
TSOL. Dia. EH239. Lot No. 31093 York 1990. –/60 2T. 29.51 t.
DTSO. Dia. EE242. Lot No. 31091 York 1990. –/65. 29.77 t.

322 481	0	E	WN	HE	78163	63137	72023	77985
322 482	0	E	WN	HE	78164	63138	72024	77986
322 483	0	E	WN	HE	78165	63139	72025	77987
322 484	0	E	WN	HE	78166	63140	72026	77988
322 485	0	E	WN	HE	78167	63141	72027	77989

CLASS 323

DMSO(A) – TSOL – DMSO(B). Aluminium alloy bodies. Thyristor control. Tightlock couplers. Sliding doors. Disc brakes. PA.
Bogies: RFS BP62 (power cars) and BT52 (trailer car).
Gangways: Within unit.
Traction Motors: Four Holec DMKT 52/24 of 146 kW per car.
Dimensions: 23.37 x 2.80 m (outer cars), 23.44 x 2.80 m (inner cars).
Maximum Speed: 75 mph.

DMSO (A). Dia. EA272. Lot No. 31112 Hunslet 1992 – 3. –/98 (–/82*). 41.0 t.
TSOL. Dia. EH296. Lot No. 31113 Hunslet 1992 – 3. –/88 1T (–/80 1T*). 39.4 t.
DMSO (B). Dia. EA272. Lot No. 31114 Hunslet 1992 – 3. –/98 (–/82*). 23.37 t.

323 201	CE	P	CT	BY	64001	72201	65001
323 202	CE	P	CT	BY	64002	72202	65002
323 203	CE	P	CT	BY	64003	72203	65005
323 204	CE	P	CT	BY	64004	72204	65004
323 205	CE	P	CT	BY	64005	72205	65003
323 206	CE	P	CT	BY	64006	72206	65006
323 207	CE	P	CT	BY	64007	72207	65007
323 208	CE	P	CT	BY	64008	72208	65008

323 209		CE	P	CT	BY	64009 72209 65009
323 210		CE	P	CT	BY	64010 72210 65010
323 211		CE	P	CT	BY	64011 72211 65011
323 212		CE	P	CT	BY	64012 72212 65012
323 213		CE	P	CT	BY	64013 72213 65013
323 214		CE	P	CT	BY	64014 72214 65014
323 215		CE	P	CT	BY	64015 72215 65015
323 216		CE	P	CT	BY	64016 72216 65016
323 217		CE	P	CT	BY	64017 72217 65017
323 218		CE	P	CT	BY	64018 72218 65018
323 219		CE	P	CT	BY	64019 72219 65019
323 220		CE	P	CT	BY	64020 72220 65020
323 221		CE	P	CT	BY	64021 72221 65021
323 222		CE	P	CT	BY	64022 72222 65022
323 223	*	GM	P	NW	LG	64023 72223 65023
323 224	*	GM	P	NW	LG	64024 72224 65024
323 225	*	GM	P	NW	LG	64025 72225 65025
323 226		GM	P	NW	LG	64026 72226 65026
323 227		GM	P	NW	LG	64027 72227 65027
323 228		GM	P	NW	LG	64028 72228 65028
323 229		GM	P	NW	LG	64029 72229 65029
323 230		GM	P	NW	LG	64030 72230 65030
323 231		GM	P	NW	LG	64031 72231 65031
323 232		GM	P	NW	LG	64032 72232 65032
323 233		GM	P	NW	LG	64033 72233 65033
323 234		GM	P	NW	LG	64034 72234 65034
323 235		GM	P	NW	LG	64035 72235 65035
323 236		GM	P	NW	LG	64036 72236 65036
323 237		GM	P	NW	LG	64037 72237 65037
323 238		GM	P	NW	LG	64038 72238 65038
323 239		GM	P	NW	LG	64039 72239 65039
323 240		CE	P	CT	BY	64040 72340 65040
323 241		CE	P	CT	BY	64041 72341 65041
323 242		CE	P	CT	BY	64042 72342 65042
323 243		CE	P	CT	BY	64043 72343 65043

CLASS 325

DTPMV(A) – MPMV – TPMV – DTPMV(B). New units owned by Royal Mail but operated on their behalf by EWS. Based on Class 319. Roller shutter doors and compatibility with diesel locomotive haulage. Cab to shore radio.

System: 25 kV a.c. overhead/750 V d.c. third rail.
Bogies: P7-4 (MSO), T3-7 (others).
Gangways: Non-gangwayed.
Traction Motors: Four GEC G315BZ of 247.5 kW.
Dimensions: 19.83 x 2.82 m (outer cars), 19.92 x 2.82 m (inner cars).
Maximum Speed: 100 mph.

68300-68330 (Even Nos.). DTPMV(A). Dia. EE501. Lot No. 31144 ABB Derby 1995.
MPMV. Dia. EC501. Lot No. 31145 ABB Derby 1995.
TPMV. Dia. EH501. Lot No. 31146 ABB Derby 1995.
68301-68331 (Odd Nos.). DTPMV(B). Dia. EE501. Lot No. 31144 ABB Derby 1995.

325 001	RM	W	EW	SU	68300	68340	68360	68301
325 002	RM	W	EW	SU	68302	68341	68361	68303
325 003	RM	W	EW	SU	68304	68342	68362	68305
325 004	RM	W	EW	GW	68306	68343	68363	68307
325 005	RM	W	EW	GW	68308	68344	68364	68309
325 006	RM	W	EW	GW	68310	68345	68365	68311
325 007	RM	W	EW	SU	68312	68346	68366	68313
325 008	RM	W	EW	GW	68314	68347	68367	68315
325 009	RM	W	EW	SU	68316	68348	68368	68317
325 010	RM	W	EW	SU	68318	68349	68369	68319
325 011	RM	W	EW	SU	68320	68350	68370	68321
325 012	RM	W	EW	SU	68322	68351	68371	68323
325 013	RM	W	EW	SU	68324	68352	68372	68325
325 014	RM	W	EW	GW	68326	68353	68373	68327
325 015	RM	W	EW	SU	68328	68354	68374	68329
325 016	RM	W	EW	GW	68330	68355	68375	68331

Name: 325 008 is named 'Peter Howarth C.B.E.'

CLASS 332   HEATHROW EXPRESS

DMSO(A)-TSOL-TSOL-DMSO(B). New units under construction for Heathrow Express service. Air conditioning. GTO Thyristor control. Tightlock couplers. Sliding doors. Disc brakes. PA. Full details not yet available.
Bogies: CAF.
Gangways: Within unit.
Traction Motors: 4 CAF 175 kW three-phase asynchronous motors in each mortor car.
Dimensions: 23.00 m x . m.
Maximum Speed: 100 mph.

DMSO(A). Dia. EA . CAF 1997. . . t.
TSO. Dia. EH . CAF 1997. . . t.
PTSOL. Dia. EH . CAF 1997. . . t.
DMSO(B). Dia. EA . CAF 1997. . t.

332 001	HE	B	HE	64044	72400	72414	64045
332 002	HE	B	HE	64046	72401	72415	64047
332 003	HE	B	HE	64048	72402	72416	64049
332 004	HE	B	HE	64050	72403	72417	64051
332 005	HE	B	HE	64052	72404	72418	64053
332 006	HE	B	HE	64054	72405	72419	64055
332 007	HE	B	HE	64056	72406	72420	64057
332 008	HE	B	HE	64058	72407	72421	64059
332 009	HE	B	HE	64060	72408	72422	64061
332 010	HE	B	HE	64062	72409	72423	64063

332 011	HE	B	HE	64064 72410 72424 64065
332 012	HE	B	HE	64066 72411 72425 64067
332 013	HE	B	HE	64068 72412 72426 64069
332 014	HE	B	HE	64070 72413 72427 64071

CLASS 365   NETWORKER EXPRESS

DMCO-TSOL-PTSOL-DMSO(B). New units with aluminium bodies. GTO thyristor control. Tightlock couplers. Sliding doors. Disc rheostatic and regenerative braking. PA.
System: 25 kV a.c. overhead/750 V d.c. third rail.
Bogies: P7 (power cars), T3 (trailers).
Gangways: Within unit.
Traction Motors: Four Brush three-phase induction motors.
Dimensions: 20.89 x 2.81 m (outer cars), 20.06 x 2.81 m (inner cars).
Maximum Speed: 100 mph.

DMCO. Dia. EA301. Lot No. 31133 ABB York 1994-5. 12/56. 46.7 t.
TSOL. Dia. EH298. Lot No. 31134 ABB York 1994-5. -/59 + 5 tip-up 1TD. 32.9 t.
PTSOL. Dia. EH298. Lot No. 31135 ABB York 1994-5. -/68 1T. 34.6 t.

365 501	NW	E	SE	RE	65894 72241 72240 65935
365 502	NW	E	SE	RE	65895 72243 72242 65936
365 503	NW	E	SE	RE	65896 72245 72244 65937
365 504	NW	E	SE	RE	65897 72247 72246 65938
365 505	CN	E	SE	RE	65898 72249 72248 65939
365 506	NW	E	SE	RE	65899 72251 72250 65940
365 507	NW	E	SE	RE	65900 72253 72252 65941
365 508	NW	E	SE	RE	65901 72255 72254 65942
365 509	NW	E	SE	RE	65902 72257 72256 65943
365 510	NW	E	SE	RE	65903 72259 72258 65944
365 511	NW	E	SE	RE	65904 72261 72260 65945
365 512	NW	E	SE	RE	65905 72263 72262 65946
365 513	NW	E	SE	RE	65906 72265 72264 65947
365 514	NW	E	SE	RE	65907 72267 72266 65948
365 515	NW	E	SE	RE	65908 72269 72268 65949
365 516	NW	E	SE	RE	65909 72271 72270 65950
365 517	NW	E	WN	HE	65910 72273 72272 65951
365 518	NW	E	WN	HE	65911 72275 72274 65952
365 519	NW	E	WN	HE	65912 72277 72276 65953
365 520	NW	E	WN	HE	65913 72279 72278 65954
365 521	NW	E	WN	HE	65914 72281 72280 65955
365 522	NW	E	WN	HE	65915 72283 72282 65956
365 523	NW	E	WN	HE	65916 72285 72284 65957
365 524	NW	E	WN	HE	65917 72287 72286 65958
365 525	NW	E	WN	HE	65918 72289 72288 65959
365 526	NW	E	WN	HE	65919 72291 72290 65960
365 527	NW	E	WN	HE	65920 72293 72292 65961
365 528	NW	E	WN	HE	65921 72295 72294 65962
365 529	NW	E	WN	HE	65922 72297 72296 65963
365 530	NW	E	WN	HE	65923 72299 72298 65964

365 531	NW	E	WN	HE	65924	72301	72300	65965
365 532	NW	E	WN	HE	65925	72303	72302	65966
365 533	NW	E	WN	HE	65926	72305	72304	65967
365 534	NW	E	WN	HE	65927	72307	72306	65968
365 535	NW	E	WN	HE	65928	72309	72308	65969
365 536	NW	E	WN	HE	65929	72311	72310	65970
365 537	NW	E	WN	HE	65930	72313	72312	65971
365 538	NW	E	WN	HE	65931	72315	72314	65972
365 539	NW	E	WN	HE	65932	72317	72316	65973
365 540	NW	E	WN	HE	65933	72319	72318	65974
365 541	NW	E	WN	HE	65934	72321	72320	65975

4.2. FORMER SOUTHERN REGION d.c. EMUs

These classes are all allocated to the former Southern Region and operate on the third rail system at 750 – 850 V d.c. Except where stated otherwise, all multiple units can run in multiple with one another. Buffet cars have electric cooking. In addition to the class number, the old SR designations e.g. 4 Cig are quoted. Outer couplings are buckeyes on units built befored 1982 with bar couplings within units. Newer units have tightlock outer couplings.

CLASS 438   4 TC

DTSO – TFK – TBSK – DTSO. Converted from loco-hauled stock. Unpowered units which worked push & pull with class 431/2 tractor units and class 33/1 and 73 locos. Express stock.

Electrical Equipment: 1966-type.
Bogies: B5 (SR) bogies.
Gangways: Throughout.
Dimensions: 19.66 x 2.82 m.
Maximum Speed: 90 mph.

DTSO. Dia. EE266. Lot No. 30764 York 1966 – 67. – /64. 32 t.
TFK. Dia. EH160. Lot No. 30766 York 1966 – 67. 42/ – 2T. 33.5 t.
TBSK. Dia. EJ260. Lot No. 30765 York 1966 – 67. 32S 1T. 35.5 t.

Renumbered from 8010/8017. Formerly class 491.

Units off loan

Two units remain and regained their original numbers for use on charter and special services. They are at present stored.

410	**B**	P		ZG	76288	70859	70812	76287
417	**B**	P		Kineton	76302	70860*	70826	76301
Spare	**N**	P		ZG	76327			

Former numbers of vehicles converted from hauled stock:

70812 (34987)	70860 (13019)	76288 (4391)	76302 (4382)
70826 (34980)	76287 (4379)	76301 (4375)	76327 (4018)
70859 (13040)			* At ZG

CLASS 421/5   'GREYHOUND' 4 Cig (PHASE 2)

DTCsoL (A) – MBSO – TSO – DTCsoL (B). Express stock. All facelifted with new trim, fluorescent lighting in saloons, PA.

Note: The following details apply to all Class 421 (phase 2) sets.

Diagram Numbers: EE369, ED264, EH287, EE369.
Electrical Equipment: 1963-type.
Bogies: Two Mk. 6 motor bogies (MBSO). B5 (SR) bogies (trailer cars).
Gangways: Throughout.
Traction Motors: Four EE507 of 185 kW.

Dimensions: 19.75 x 2.82 m.
Maximum Speed: 90 mph.

76561 – 76567. DTCsoL(A). Lot No. 30802 York 1970. 18/36 2T. 35.5 t.
76581 – 76610. DTCsoL(A). Lot No. 30806 York 1970. 18/36 2T. 35.5 t.
76717 – 76787. DTCsoL(A). Lot No. 30814 York 1970 – 72. 18/36 2T. 35.5 t.
76859. DTCsoL(A). Lot No. 30827 York 1972. 18/36 2T. 35.5 t.
62277 – 62283. MBSO. Lot No. 30804 York 1970. –/56. 49t.
62287 – 62316. MBSO. Lot No. 30808 York 1970. –/56. 49t.
62355 – 62425. MBSO. Lot No. 30816 York 1970. –/56. 49t.
62430. MBSO. Lot No. 30829 York 1972. –/56. 49t.
70967 – 70996. TSO. Lot No. 30809 York 1970 – 71. –/72. 31.5t.
71035 – 71105. TSO. Lot No. 30817 York 1970. –/72. 31.5t.
71106. TSO. Lot No. 30830 York 1972. –/72. 31.5t.
71926 – 71928. TSO. Lot No. 30805 York 1970. –/72. 31.5t.
76571 – 76577. DTCsoL(B). Lot No. 30803 York 1970. 24/28 2T. 35 t.
76611 – 76640. DTCsoL(B). Lot No. 30807 York 1970. 24/28 2T. 35 t.
76788 – 76858. DTCsoL(B). Lot No. 30815 York 1970 – 72. 24/28 2T. 35 t.
76859. DTCsoL(B). Lot No. 30828 York 1972. 18/36 2T. 35 t.

These sets are known as 'Greyhound' units and are fitted with an additional
stage of field weakening to improve the maximum attainable speed. This term
is traditional on the lines of the former London & South Western Railway, as
it was formerly applied to their Class T9 4 – 4 – 0 steam locomotives.

1301	N	E	SW	FR	76595	62301	70981	76625
1302	N	E	SW	FR	76584	62290	70970	76614
1303	N	E	SW	FR	76581	62287	70967	76611
1304	N	E	SW	FR	76583	62289	70969	76613
1305	N	E	SW	FR	76717	62355	71035	76788
1306	N	E	SW	FR	76723	62361	71041	76794
1307	N	E	SW	FR	76586	62292	70972	76616
1308	N	E	SW	FR	76627	62298	70978	76622
1309	N	E	SW	FR	76594	62300	70980	76624
1310	N	E	SW	FR	76567	62283	71926	76577
1311	N	E	SW	FR	76561	62277	71927	76571
1312	N	E	SW	FR	76562	62278	71928	76572
1313	N	E	SW	FR	76596	62302	70982	76626
1314	N	E	SW	FR	76588	62292	70974	76618
1315	N	E	SW	FR	76608	62314	70994	76638
1316	N	E	SW	FR	76585	62291	70971	76615
1317	N	E	SW	FR	76597	62303	70983	76592
1318	N	E	SW	FR	76590	62296	70976	76620
1319	N	E	SW	FR	76591	62297	70977	76621
1320	N	E	SW	FR	76593	62299	70979	76623
1321	N	E	SW	FR	76589	62295	70975	76619
1322	N	E	SW	FR	76587	62293	70973	76617

Former numbers of converted buffet cars:

71926 (69315) |71927 (69330) |71928 (69331) |

Note: No new Lot Nos were issued for the above conversions.

CLASS 411/5   4 Cep

DMSO (A) – TBCK – TSOL – DMSO (B). Kent Coast Express Stock. Refurbished and renumbered from the 71/72xx series. Fitted with hopper ventilators, Inter-City 70 seats, fluorescent lighting and PA.

Electrical Equipment: 1957-type.
Bogies: One Mk. 4 (Mk 3B§) motor bogie (DMSO). Commonwealth trailer bogies.
Gangways: Throughout.
Traction Motors: Two EE507 of 185 kW.
Dimensions: 19.75 x 2.82 m.
Maximum Speed: 90 mph.
Non-standard Livery: Blue with a white stripe.

★ – 70345 is a TBFK with one compartment declassified. It is from the original refurbished unit (1500), has a different interior colour scheme and does not have hopper ventilators.

DMSO (A). Dia. EA263. –/64. 44.15 t.
TBCK. Dia. EJ361. 24/6 2T. 36.17 t.
TSOL. Dia. EH282. –/64 2T. 33.78 t.
DMSO (B). Dia. EA264. –/64. 43.54 t.

Lot numbers are as follows, all cars being built at Ashford/Eastleigh:

61229 – 61240. 30449 1958.	**70241.** 30640 1961.
61306 – 61409. 30454 1958 – 59.	**70261 – 70302.** 30455 1958 – 59.
61694 – 61811. 30619 1960 – 61.	**70304 – 70355.** 30456 1958 – 59.
61868 – 61869. 30638 1960 – 61.	**70503 – 70551.** 30620 1960 – 61.
61948 – 61959. 30708 1963.	**70552 – 70610.** 30621 1960 – 61.
70043 – 70044. 30639 1961.	**70653 – 70657.** 30709 1963.
70229 – 70234. 30450 1958.	**70660 – 70664.** 30710 1963.
70235 – 70239. 30451 1958.	

1507	N	P		BM	61363	70332	70289	61362
1509	N	P	SE	RE	61335	70318	70275	61334
1510	N	P	SE	RE	61365	70333	70290	61364
1511	N	P	SE	RE	61367	70334	70291	61366
1512	N	P		BM	61321	70311	70268	61320
1517	N	P	SE	RE	61317	70309	70266	61316
1518	N	P	SC	BI	61333	70317	70274	61332
1519	N	P		BM	61403	70352	70516	61402
1520	N	P	SE	RE	61343	70327	70284	61380
1527	N	P	SE	RE	61237	70239	70233	61238
1530	N	P	SE	RE	61331	70316	70273	61330
1531	N	P		BM	61233	70237	70231	61234
1532	N	P		BM	61391	70346	71626	61390
1533	N	P	SE	RE	61393	70347	71627	61385
1534	N	P		BM	61405	70353	71628	61404
1535	N	P		BM	61397	70349	71629	61396
1536	N	P	SE	RE	61399	70350	71631	61398
1537	N	P		BM	61229	70235	70229	61230
1538	N	P		BM	61307	70304	70261	61306

1539		N	P	SE	RE	61401	70351	71632	61400
1541		N	P	SE	RE	61409	70355	71633	61408
1543		N	P	SE	RE	61323	70312	70297	61322
1544		N	P		BM	61315	70308	70265	61349
1545		N	P		RE	61359	70330	70287	61358
1547	★	N	P		BM	61329	70345	70272	61328
1548		N	P		BM	61375	70338	70295	61374
1549		N	P	SE	RE	61339	70320	70277	61338
1550		N	P	SE	RE	61313	70307	70264	61312
1551		N	P	SE	RE	61325	70313	70270	61324
1553		N	P	SE	RE	61728	70306	70263	61350
1554		N	P	SE	RE	61369	70335	70292	61368
1555		N	P	SE	RE	61311	70326	70283	61310
1556		N	P	SE	RE	61371	70336	70293	61370
1557		N	P	SE	RE	61337	70331	70288	61360
1559		N	P	SE	RE	61377	70339	70296	61376
1560		N	P	SE	RE	61387	70344	70301	61386
1561		N	P	SE	RE	61231	70604	70230	61232
1562		N	P	SE	RE	61407	70236	70241	61406
1563	§	N	P	SE	RE	61740	70575	70526	61741
1564	§	N	P	SE	RE	61788	70599	70550	61789
1565	§	N	P	SE	RE	61762	70586	71711	61763
1566	§	N	P	SE	RE	61722	70566	70517	61723
1568	§	0	P	SW	FR	61766	70588	70539	61767
1570	§	N	P	SE	RE	61738	70574	70525	61739
1571	§	N	P	SE	RE	61806	70608	71636	61807
1572	§	N	P	SE	RE	61734	70572	70523	61735
1573	§	N	P		BM	61726	70568	70519	61727
1574	§	N	P	SE	RE	61792	70601	71635	61793
1575	§	N	P	SE	RE	61768	70583	70540	61769
1576	§	N	P	SE	RE	61770	70590	70541	61771
1577	§	N	P	SE	RE	61718	70564	70515	61719
1578	§	N	P	SC	BI	61700	70555	70506	61701
1580	§	N	P	SE	RE	61756	70589	70534	61757
1581	§	N	P		BM	61784	70597	70548	61785
1582	§	N	P	SE	RE	61748	70603	71630	61797
1584	§	N	P	SE	RE	61752	70581	70532	61753
1585	§	N	P	SE	RE	61710	70560	70511	61711
1586	§	N	P	SE	RE	61714	70562	70513	61715
1587	§	N	P		BM	61764	70587	71625	61765
1588	§	N	P	SE	RE	61720	70044	70520	61721
1589	§	N	P	SW	FR	61742	70576	70527	61743
1590	§	N	P	SE	RE	61696	70553	70504	61697
1591	§	N	P	SE	RE	61790	70600	70551	61791
1592	§	N	P	SE	RE	61778	70594	70545	61779
1593	§	N	P	SE	RE	61730	70570	70521	61731
1594	§	N	P	SE	RE	61754	70582	70533	61755
1595	§	N	P	SE	RE	61704	70557	70508	61705
1597	§	N	P	SE	RE	61708	70559	70510	61709
1599	§	N	P	SE	RE	61706	70558	70509	61707
1602	§	N	P	SE	RE	61958	70565	70279	61959

1606	§	N	P		AF	61694 70552 70503 61695
1607	§	N	P	SE	RE	61698 70554 70505 61699
1609	§	N	P	SE	RE	61744 70577 70528 61745
1610	§	N	P	SE	RE	61750 70580 70531 61751
1611	§	N	P	SE	RE	61758 70584 70537 61759
1612	§	N	P		BM	61794 70602 70535 61795
1613	§	N	P	SE	RE	61760 70585 70536 61761
1614	§	N	P	SE	RE	61702 70556 70507 61703
1615	§	N	P	SE	RE	61956 70657 70664 61957
1616	§	N	P	SE	RE	61950 70654 70543 61951
1617	§	N	P	SE	RE	61800 70605 70661 61801
1618	§	N	P	SE	RE	61868 70043 70663 61869
1619	§	N	P	SE	RE	61952 70655 70662 61953
1620	§	N	P		EH	61948 70653 70660 61949
Spare		N	P		ZG	70578

Units fitted with B5(SR) trailer bogies.

1695	( )					
1696	( )					
1697	(1552)		N	P	SC	BI	61373 70337 70294 61372
1698	(1540)		N	P	SC	BI	61355 70343 70300 61384
1699	(1605)	§	N	P	SC	BI	61712 70561 70512 61713

Former numbers of converted hauled stock:

71625 (4381)	71628 (3844)	71631 (4436)	71635 (3990)
71626 (3916)	71629 (3992)	71632 (4063)	71636 (4065)
71627 (3921)	71630 (3988)	71633 (4072)	71711 (3994)

Note: No new lot numbers were issued for the above conversions.

CLASS 421/3   4 Cig (PHASE 1)

DTCsoL(A) – MBSO – TSO – DTCsoL(B). Express stock. Fitted with electric parking brake. Facelifted with new trim, fluorescent lighting in saloons, PA.

Electrical Equipment: 1963-type.
Bogies: Two Mk. 4 motor bogies (MBSO). B5 (SR) bogies (trailer cars).
Gangways: Throughout.
Traction Motors: Four EE507 of 185 kW.
Dimensions: 19.75 x 2.82 m.
Maximum Speed: 90 mph.

DTCsoL(A). Dia. EE364. Lot No. 30741 York 1964 – 65. 18/36 2T. 35.5 t.
MBSO. Dia. ED260. Lot No. 30742 York 1964 – 65. – /56. 49 t.
70695 – 70730. TSO. Dia. EH275. Lot No. 30734 York 1964 – 65. – /72. 31.5 t.
71044 – 71097. TSO. Dia. EH275. Lot No. 30817 York 1970. – /72. 31.5 t.
71766 – 71770. TSO. Dia. EH275. Lot No. 30784 York 1964 – 65. – /72. 31.5 t.
DTCsoL(B). Dia. EE363. Lot No. 30740 York 1964 – 65. 24/28 2T.

* Units reformed from Class 422 to enable all Class 422 power cars to have Mk. 6 motor bogies. Phase 1 units with phase 2 TSOs.

1701		N	A	SC	BI	76087	62028	70706	76033
1702		N	A	SC	BI	76101	62042	70720	76047
1703		N	A	SC	BI	76097	62038	70716	76043
1704		N	A		AF	76092	62033	70711	76038
1705		N	A	SC	BI	76076	62017	70695	76022
1706		N	A	SC	BI	76094	62035	70713	76040
1707		N	A	SC	BI	76084	62025	70703	76030
1708		N	A	SC	BI	76110	62051	70729	76056
1709		N	A	SC	BI	76103	62044	70722	76049
1710		N	A	SC	BI	76078	62019	70697	76024
1711		N	A	SC	BI	76114	62055	71766	76060
1712		N	A	SC	BI	76079	62020	70698	76025
1713		N	A	SC	BI	76128	62069	71767	76074
1714		N	A	SC	BI	76077	62018	70696	76023
1717		N	A	SC	BI	76083	62024	70702	76029
1719		N	A	SC	BI	76116	62057	70719	76062
1720		N	A	SC	BI	76098	62039	71769	76044
1721		N	A	SC	BI	76090	62031	70709	76036
1722		N	A	SC	BI	76106	62047	70725	76052
1724		N	A	SC	BI	76120	62061	71770	76066
1725		N	A	SC	BI	76088	62029	70707	76034
1726		N	A	SC	BI	76109	62050	70728	76055
1727		N	A	SC	BI	76111	62052	70730	76057
1731		N	A	SC	BI	76095	62036	70714	76041
1733	*	N	A	SC	BI	76122	62063	71047	76068
1734	*	N	A	SC	BI	76063	62054	71044	76059
1735	*	N	A	SC	BI	76117	62058	71050	76051
1736	*	N	A	SC	BI	76124	62065	71052	76070
1737	*	N	A	SC	BI	76121	62062	71058	76067
1738	*	N	A	SC	BI	76129	62064	71046	76069
1739	*	N	A	SC	BI	76123	62070	71066	76075
1740	*	N	A		ZG	76126	62067	71097	76072
1741		N	A		ZG	76089	62030	70708	76035
1742		N	A	SC	BI	76086	62027	70705	76032
1743	*	N	A		ZG	76118	62059	71065	76064
1744	*	N	A		ZG	76127	62068	71064	76073
1745		N	A	SC	BI	76085	62026	70704	76031
1746		N	A	SC	BI	76091	62032	70710	76037
1747		N	A	SC	BI	76026	62034	70712	76093
1748	*	N	A	SC	BI	76115	62056	71067	76061
1750		N	A	SC	BI	76080	62021	70699	76039
1751		N	A	SC	BI	76125	62066	71051	76071
1752		N	A	SC	BI	76119	62060	70717	76065
1753		N	A	SC	BI	76102	62043	70721	76048
Spare	*	N	A		ZF		62053	71068	76058

Former numbers of converted buffet cars:

71766 (69303) | 71768 (69317) | 71769 (69305) | 71770 (69308)
71767 (69314) |

Note: No new Lot Numbers were issued for the above conversions.

CLASS 421/4   4 Cig (PHASE 2)

DTCsoL – MBSO – TSO – DTCsoL. Express stock. Facelifted with new trim,
fluorescent lighting in saloons, PA. For details see Class 421/5.

1801	N	P	SC	BI	76777	62415	71095	76848
1802	N	P	SC	BI	76754	62392	71072	76825
1803	N	A	SC	BI	76780	62418	71098	76851
1804	N	A	SC	BI	76778	62416	71096	76849
1805	N	A	SC	BI	76782	62420	71100	76853
1806	N	E	SE	RE	76783	62421	71101	76854
1807	N	E	SE	RE	76784	62422	71102	76855
1808	N	E	SE	RE	76785	62423	71103	76856
1809	N	E	SE	RE	76786	62424	71104	76857
1810	N	E	SE	RE	76787	62425	71105	76858
1811	N	E	SE	RE	76781	62419	71099	76852
1812	N	E	SE	RE	76757	62395	71075	76828
1813	N	E	SE	RE	76859	62430	71106	76860
1831	N	A	SC	BI	76598	62304	70984	76628
1832	N	A	SC	BI	76719	62357	71037	76790
1833	N	A	SC	BI	76582	62288	70968	76612
1834	N	A	SC	BI	76566	62282	70988	76576
1835	N	A	SC	BI	76601	62307	70987	76631
1837	N	A	SC	BI	76722	62360	71040	76793
1839	N	E	SE	RE	76607	62313	70993	76637
1840	N	E	SE	RE	76724	62362	71042	76795
1841	N	E	SE	RE	76603	62309	70989	76633
1842	N	E	SE	RE	76725	62363	71043	76796
1843	N	E	SE	RE	76731	62369	71049	76802
1845	N	A	SC	BI	76599	62305	70985	76629
1846	N	A	SC	BI	76737	62375	71055	76808
1847	N	A	SC	BI	76600	62306	70986	76630
1848	N	A	SC	BI	76605	62311	70991	76635
1850	N	A	SC	BI	76718	62356	71036	76789
1851	N	A	SC	BI	76721	62359	71039	76792
1853	N	A	SC	BI	76606	62312	70992	76636
1854	N	A	SC	BI	76738	62376	71056	76809
1855	N	A	SC	BI	76720	62358	71038	76791
1856	N	A	SC	BI	76739	62377	71057	76810
1857	N	A	SC	BI	76610	62316	70996	76640
1858	N	A	SC	BI	76604	62310	70990	76634
1859	N	A	SC	BI	76727	62365	71045	76798
1860	N	A	SC	BI	76752	62390	71070	76823
1861	N	A	SC	BI	76735	62373	71053	76806
1862	CW	A	SC	BI	76736	62374	71054	76807
1863	N	A	SC	BI	76742	62380	71060	76813
1864	N	A	SC	BI	76741	62379	71059	76812
1865	N	A	SC	BI	76745	62383	71063	76639
1866	N	A	SC	BI	76743	62381	71061	76814
1867	N	A	SC	BI	76744	62382	71062	76815

1868	N	A	SC	BI	76751	62389	71069	76822
1869	N	A	SC	BI	76753	62391	71071	76804
1870	N	E	SE	RE	76108	62409	71089	76842
1871	N	E	SE	RE	76756	62394	71074	76827
1872	N	E	SE	RE	76771	62396	71076	76829
1873	N	E	SE	RE	76759	62397	71077	76830
1874	N	A	SC	BI	76755	62393	71073	76826
1876	N	E	SE	RE	76761	62399	71079	76832
1877	N	E	SE	RE	76763	62401	71081	76834
1878	N	E	SE	RE	76768	62406	71086	76839
1879	N	E	SE	RE	76760	62398	71078	76831
1880	N	E	SW	FR	76770	62408	71088	76841
1881	N	E	SW	FR	76762	62400	71080	76833
1882	N	E	SW	FR	76765	62403	71083	76836
1883	N	E	SW	FR	76764	62402	71082	76835
1884	N	E	SW	FR	76767	62405	71085	76838
1885	N	E	SW	FR	76769	62407	71087	76840
1886	N	E	SW	FR	76772	62410	71090	76843
1887	N	E	SW	FR	76766	62404	71084	76837
1888	N	E	SW	FR	76773	62411	71091	76844
1889	N	E	SW	FR	76774	62412	71092	76845
1890	N	E	SW	FR	76775	62413	71093	76846
1891	N	E	SW	FR	76776	62414	71094	76847
Spare		A		ZG			70995	

CLASS 421/9   4 Cig (PHASE 1)

DTCsoL(A) – MBSO – TSO – DTCsoL(B). Express stock. Fitted with electric parking brake. Facelifted with new trim, fluorescent lighting in saloons, PA. For details see Class 421/3. These units are fitted with ex-Class 432 Mark 6 motor bogies.

1901	N	P	SC	BI	76082	62023	70701	76028
1902	N	P	SC	BI	76100	62041	71768	76046
1903	CW	A	SC	BI	76081	62022	70700	62027
1904	N	A	SC	BI	76107	62048	70726	76053
1905	N	A	SC	BI	76099	62040	70718	76045
1906	N	A	SC	BI	76105	62046	70724	76113
1907	N	A	SC	BI	76104	62045	70723	76050
1908	N	A	SC	BI	76096	62037	70715	76042

CLASS 422/2   4 Big (PHASE 2)

DTCsoL (A) – MBSO – TSRB – DTCsoL (B). Express stock.

Diagram Numbers: EE369, ED264, EN260, EE369.
Electrical Equipment: 1963-type.
Bogies: Two Mk. 6 motor bogies (MBSO). B5 (SR) bogies (trailer cars).
Gangways: Throughout.
Traction Motors: Four EE507 of 185 kW.
Dimensions: 19.75 x 2.82 m.
Maximum Speed: 90 mph.

76563 – 76570. DTCsoL(A). Lot No. 30802 York 1970. 18/36 2T. 35.5 t.
76602. DTCsoL(A). Lot No. 30806 York 1970. 18/36 2T. 35.5 t.
62279 – 62286. MBSO. Lot No. 30804 York 1970. – /56. 49t.
62308. MBSO. Lot No. 30808 York 1970. – /56. 49t.
69332 – 69339. TSRB. Lot No. 30805 York 1970. – /40. 35 t.
76573 – 76580. DTCsoL(B). Lot No. 30803 York 1970. 24/28 2T. 35 t.
76632. DTCsoL(B). Lot No. 30807 York 1970. 24/28 2T. 35 t.

2203	N	P	SC	BI	76563	62279	69332 76573
2204	N	P	SC	BI	76564	62280	69336 76574
2205	N	P	SC	BI	76565	62281	69339 76575
2206	N	P	SC	BI	76602	62308	69338 76632
2208	N	P	SC	BI	76568	62284	69334 76578
2209	N	P	SC	BI	76569	62285	69335 76579
2210	N	P	SC	BI	76570	62286	69337 76580

CLASS 422/3   Facelifted 4 Big (PHASE 2/1)

DTCsoL (A) – MBSO – TSRB – DTCsoL (B). Express stock. Units reformed from
Class 421 to ensure that all Class 422 power cars have Mk. 6 motor bogies.
Phase 2 units with phase 1 TSRBs. For other details see Class 421/5.

Diagram Numbers: EE369, ED264, EN260, EE369.
Electrical Equipment: 1963-type.
Bogies: Two Mk. 6 motor bogies (MBSO). B5 (SR) bogies (trailer cars).
Gangways: Throughout.
Traction Motors: Four EE507 of 185 kW.
Dimensions: 19.75 x 2.82 m.
Maximum Speed: 90 mph.

69301 – 69318. TSRB. Lot No. 30744 York 1966. 40S. 35 t.

2251	N	P	SC	BI	76726	62364	69302 76797
2252	N	P	SC	BI	76728	62366	69312 76799
2253	N	P	SC	BI	76734	62372	69313 76805
2254	**■**	**P**	**SC**	**BI**	**76732**	**62370**	**69306 76803**
2255	**■**	**P**	**SC**	**BI**	**76740**	**62378**	**69310 76811**
2256	N	P	SC	BI	76747	62385	69307 76818
2257	N	P	SC	BI	76800	62367	69311 76729
2258	N	P	SC	BI	76746	62384	69316 76817
2259	**■**	**P**	**SC**	**BI**	**76748**	**62386**	**69318 76819**
2260	N	P	SC	BI	76749	62387	69304 76820
2261	N	P	SC	BI	76750	62388	69301 76821
2262	**■**	**P**	**SC**	**BI**	**76779**	**62417**	**69333 76850**

CLASS 412   REFURBISHED 4 Bep

DMSO (A) – TBCK – TRB – DMSO (B). Kent Coast Express Stock. Refurbished
and renumbered from the 70xx series. Fitted with hopper ventilators, Inter-City
70 seats, fluorescent lighting and PA.

Electrical Equipment: 1957-type.
Bogies: Mk 6 motor bogies and B5(SR) trailer bogies.
Gangways: Throughout.
Traction Motors: Four EE507 of 185 kW.
Dimensions: 19.75 x 2.82 m.
Maximum Speed: 90 mph.

DMSO (A). Dia. EA263. – /64. 44.15 t.
TBCK. Dia. EJ361. 24/6 2T. 36.17 t.
TRSB. Dia. EN261. – /24 1T + 9 longitudinal buffet chairs. 35.5 t.
DMSO (B). Dia. EA264. – /64. 43.54 t.
Lot numbers are as follows, all cars being built at Ashford/Eastleigh:

61736 – 61809. 30619 1960 – 61.	**70354.** 30456 1959.
61954 – 61955. 30708 1963.	**70573 – 70609.** 30621 1960 – 61.
69341 – 69347. 30622 1961.	**70656.** 30709 1963.

2301	N	P	SW	FR	61804	70607	69341 61805
2302	N	P	SW	FR	61774	70592	69342 61809
2303	N	P	SW	FR	61954	70656	69347 61955
2304	N	P	SW	FR	61736	70573	69344 61737
2305	N	P	SW	FR	61798	70354	69345 61799
2306	N	P	SW	FR	61808	70609	69346 61775
2307	N	P	SW	FR	61802	70606	69343 61803

Former numbers of converted buffet cars:

69341 (69014)	69343 (69018)	69345 (69013)	69347 (69015)
69342 (69019)	69344 (69012)	69346 (69016)	

Note: No new lot numbers were issued for the above conversions.

CLASS 442   WESSEX EXPRESS STOCK

DTFsoL – TSOL(A) – MBRSM – TSOL(B) – DTSOL. Express stock built for
Waterloo – Bournemouth – Weymouth service. Now also used on certain Portsmouth Harbour services. Air conditioned (heat pump system). Power-operated
sliding plug doors. PA. Can be hauled and heated by any BR ETH fitted
locomotive. Multiple working with class 33/1 and 73 locomotives.

Electrical Equipment: 1986-type.
Bogies: Mk 6 motor bogies (MBRSM). T4 trailer bogies.
Gangways: Throughout.
Traction Motors: Four EE546 of 300 kW recovered from class 432.
Dimensions: 23.00 x 2.74 m (inner cars), 23.15 x 2.74 m (outer cars).
Maximum Speed: 100 mph.

DTFsoL. Dia. EE160. Lot No. 31030 Derby 1988 – 89. 50/ – 1T. (36 in six compartments and 14 2 + 2 in one saloon). Public Telephone. 39.06 t.
TSOL (A). Dia. EH288. Lot No. 31032 Derby 1988 – 89. – /80 2T. 35.26 t.
MBRSM. Dia. ED265. Lot No. 31034 Derby 1988 – 89. – /14. 54.10 t.
TSOL (B). Dia. EH289. Lot No. 31033 Derby 1988 – 89. – /76 2T + wheelchair space. + 2 tip-up seats. 35.36 t.
DTSOL. Dia. EE273. Lot No. 31031 Derby 1988 – 89. – /78 1T. 39.06 t.

2401	NW	E	SW	BM	77382	71818	62937	71842	77406
2402	SC	E	SW	BM	77383	71819	62938	71843	77407
2403	NW	E	SW	BM	77384	71820	62941	71844	77408
2404	NW	E	SW	BM	77385	71821	62939	71845	77409
2405	NW	E	SW	BM	77386	71822	62944	71846	77410
2406	NW	E	SW	BM	77389	71823	62942	71847	77411
2407	NW	E	SW	BM	77388	71824	62943	71848	77412
2408	NW	E	SW	BM	77387	71825	62945	71849	77413
2409	NW	E	SW	BM	77390	71826	62946	71850	77414
2410	NW	E	SW	BM	77391	71827	62948	71851	77415
2411	NW	E	SW	BM	77392	71828	62940	71858	77422
2412	NW	E	SW	BM	77393	71829	62947	71853	77417
2413	NW	E	SW	BM	77394	71830	62949	71854	77418
2414	NW	E	SW	BM	77395	71831	62950	71855	77419
2415	NW	E	SW	BM	77396	71832	62951	71856	77420
2416	NW	E	SW	BM	77397	71833	62952	71857	77421
2417	NW	E	SW	BM	77398	71834	62953	71852	77416
2418	NW	E	SW	BM	77399	71835	62954	71859	77423
2419	NW	E	SW	BM	77400	71836	62955	71860	77424
2420	NW	E	SW	BM	77401	71837	62956	71861	77425
2421	NW	E	SW	BM	77402	71838	62957	71862	77426
2422	NW	E	SW	BM	77403	71839	62958	71863	77427
2423	NW	E	SW	BM	77404	71840	62959	71864	77428
2424	NW	E	SW	BM	77405	71841	62960	71865	77429

Names:

62937 BEAULIEU	62946 BOURNEMOUTH ORCHESTRAS
62938 COUNTY OF HAMPSHIRE	62948 MERIDIAN TONIGHT
62939 BOROUGH OF WOKING	62951 MARY ROSE
62941 THE NEW FOREST	62954 WESSEX CANCER TRUST
62942 VICTORY	62955 BBC SOUTH TODAY
62943 THOMAS HARDY	62956 CITY OF SOUTHAMPTON
62944 CITY OF PORTSMOUTH	62958 OPERATION OVERLORD
62945 COUNTY OF DORSET	62959 COUNTY OF SURREY

CLASS 423/0   4 Vep

DTCsoL – MBSO – TSO – DTCsoL. Outer suburban stock. Facelifted with fluorescent lighting, PA.

Electrical Equipment: 1963-type.
Bogies: Two Mk. 4 motor bogies (MBSO). B5 (SR) bogies (trailer cars).
Gangways: Throughout.
Traction Motors: Four EE507 of 185 kW.

Dimensions: 19.75 x 2.82 m.
Maximum Speed: 90 mph.

62121 – 40. MBSO. Dia. ED266. Lot No. 30760 Derby 1967. – /76. 49 t.
62182 – 216. MBSO. Dia. ED266. Lot No. 30773 York 1967 – 68. – /76. 49 t.
62217 – 66. MBSO. Dia. ED266. Lot No. 30794 York 1968 – 69. – /76. 49 t.
62267 – 76. MBSO. Dia. ED266. Lot No. 30800 York 1970. – /76. 49 t.
62317 – 54. MBSO. Dia. ED266. Lot No. 30813 York 1970 – 73. – /76. 49 t.
62435 – 75. MBSO. Dia. ED266. Lot No. 30851 York 1973 – 74. – /76. 49 t.
70781 – 800. TSO. Dia. EH291. Lot No. 30759 Derby 1967. – /98. 31.5 t.
70872 – 906. TSO. Dia. EH291. Lot No. 30772 York 1967 – 68. – /98. 31.5 t.
70907 – 56. TSO. Dia. EH291. Lot No. 30793 York 1968 – 69. – /98. 31.5 t.
70957 – 66. TSO. Dia. EH291. Lot No. 30801 York 1970. – /98. 31.5 t.
70997 – 71034. TSO. Dia. EH291. Lot No. 30812 York 1970 – 73. – /98. 31.5 t.
71115 – 55. TSO. Dia. EH291. Lot No. 30852 York 1973 – 74. – /98. 31.5 t.
76230 – 69. DTCsoL. Dia. EE373. Lot No. 30758 York 1967. 18/46 1T. 35 t.
76275. DTSO (Class 438). Dia. EE266. Lot No. 30764 York 1966. – /64. 32 t. (Converted from hauled TSO 3929).
76333 – 402. DTCsoL. Dia. EE373. Lot No. 30771 York 1967 – 68. 18/46 1T. 35 t.
76441 – 540. DTCsoL. Dia. EE373. Lot No. 30792 York 1968 – 69. 18/46 1T. 35 t.
76541 – 60. DTCsoL. Dia. EE373. Lot No. 30799 York 1970. 18/46 1T. 35 t.
76641 – 716. DTCsoL. Dia. EE373. Lot No. 30811 York 1970 – 73. 18/46 1T. 35 t.
76861 – 942. DTCsoL. Dia. EE373. Lot No. 30853 York 1973 – 74. 18/46 1T. 35 t.

Note: Porterbrook units allocated to Connex South Eastern have been renumbered in the 3800 series to differentiate them from the Angel Trains units operating on the same services.

3401	(3001)	**N**	E	SW	WD	76230 62276 70781 76231
3402	(3002)	**N**	E	SW	WD	76233 62123 70782 76232
3403	(3003)	**N**	E	SW	WD	76234 62254 70783 76235
3404	(3441)	**N**	E	SW	WD	76378 62261 70894 76236
3405	(3005)	**N**	E	SW	WD	76239 62271 70785 76238
3406	(3006)	**N**	E	SW	WD	76241 62130 70786 76240
3407	(3007)	**N**	E	SW	WD	76243 62348 70787 76242
3408	(3008)	**N**	E	SW	WD	76244 62435 70788 76245
3409	(3009)	**N**	E	SW	WD	76246 62239 70789 76247
3410	(3010)	**N**	E	SW	WD	76369 62442 70790 76249
3411	(3011)	**N**	E	SW	WD	76251 62342 70791 76250
3412	(3012)	**N**	A	SE	RE	76252 62340 70792 76253
3413	(3013)	**N**	E	SW	WD	76255 62441 70793 76254
3414	(3014)	**N**	E	SW	WD	76257 62446 70794 76248
3415	(3015)	**N**	E	SW	WD	76258 62462 70795 76259
3416	(3016)	**N**	A	SE	RE	76261 62451 70796 76260
3417	(3017)	**N**	E	SW	WD	76262 62236 70797 76263
3418	(3018)	**N**	E	SW	WD	76265 62133 70875 76264
3419	(3019)	**N**	E	SW	WD	76267 62354 70799 76266

3420	(3020)	N	E	SW	WD	76269	62349	70800	76268
3421	(3168)	N	A	SE	RE	76889	62449	71129	76890
3422	(3040)	N	A	SE	RE	76372	62201	70891	76371
3423	(3061)	N	A	SE	RE	76452	62222	70912	76451
3424	(3031)	N	A	SE	RE	76354	62185	70882	76353
3425	(3023)	N	E	SW	WD	76338	62192	70874	76358
3426	(3047)	N	E	SW	WD	76386	62208	70898	76385
3427	(3041)	N	E	SW	WD	76374	62184	70892	76373
3428	(3062)	N	E	SW	WD	76454	62223	70913	76453
3429	(3021)	N	E	SW	WD	76334	62202	70872	76333
3430	(3028)	N	E	SW	WD	76348	62189	70879	76347
3431	(3064)	N	E	SW	WD	76458	62182	70915	76457
3432	(3054)	N	E	SW	WD	76400	62225	70905	76399
3433	(3057)	N	E	SW	WD	76444	62215	70908	76443
3434	(3066)	N	E	SW	WD	76462	62218	70917	76461
3435	(3025)	N	P	SC	BI	76342	62228	70876	76341
3436	(3029)	N	P	SC	BI	76350	62190	70880	76349
3437	(3027)	N	P	SC	BI	76346	62186	70878	76345
3438	(3100)	N	P	SC	BI	76530	62262	70951	76529
3439	(3055)	N	P	SC	BI	76402	62227	70906	76401
3442	(3081)	N	P	SC	BI	76492	62216	70932	76491
3445	(3060)	N	A	SE	RE	76450	62242	70911	76449
3446	(3101)	N	A	SE	RE	76532	62243	70952	76531
3447	(3044)	N	A	SE	RE	76380	62199	70895	76379
3448	(3042)	N	A	SE	RE	76376	62221	70886	76375
3449	(3022)	N	A	SE	RE	76336	62205	70873	76335
3450	(3060)	N	A	SE	RE	76460	62203	70916	76459
3451	(3079)	N	A	SE	RE	76488	62240	70930	76487
3452		N	A	SE	RE	76340	62183	71021	76690
3453	(3045)	N	A	SE	RE	76382	62226	70896	76381
3454		N	A	SE	RE	76390	62200	70798	76389
3455	(3048)	N	E	SW	WD	76388	62206	70899	76387
3456	(3063)	N	E	SW	WD	76456	62210	70914	76455
3457	(3050)	N	E	SW	WD	76392	62197	70901	76391
3458	(3051)	N	E	SW	WD	76394	62209	70902	76393
3459	(3052)	N	E	SW	WD	76396	62224	70903	76395
3462	(3103)	N	P	SC	BI	76536	62213	70954	76535
3463	(3053)	N	P	SC	BI	76398	62266	70904	76397
3464	(3056)	N	P	SC	BI	76442	62265	70907	76441
3466	(3067)	N	E	SW	WD	76464	62214	70918	76463
3467	(3058)	N	E	SW	WD	76446	62217	70909	76445
3468	(3059)	N	E	SW	WD	76448	62267	70910	76447
3469	(3108)	N	E	SW	WD	76546	62219	70959	76545
3470	(3083)	N	E	SW	WD	76496	62220	70934	76495
3471	(3084)	N	A	SE	RE	76498	62269	70935	76497
3472	(3085)	N	A	SE	RE	76500	62244	70936	76499
3473	(3086)	N	A	SE	RE	76502	62245	70937	76339
3474	(3087)	N	A	SE	RE	76504	62246	70938	76503
3475	(3111)	N	A	SE	RE	76552	62270	70962	76551
3476	(3109)	N	P	SC	BI	76548	62247	70960	76547
3478	(3122)	N	P	SC	BI	76653	62125	71003	76654

3479	(3123)	**N**	E	SW	WD	76655	62272	71004	76656
3480	(3072)	**N**	E	SW	WD	76474	62323	70923	76473
3481	(3119)	**N**	E	SW	WD	76648	62324	70900	76647
3482	(3124)	**N**	E	SW	WD	76657	62320	71005	76658
3483	(3126)	**N**	E	SW	WD	76661	62233	71007	76662
3484	(3073)	**N**	E	SW	WD	76476	62325	70924	76475
3485	(3089)	**N**	E	SW	WD	76508	62327	70940	76507
3486	(3074)	**N**	E	SW	WD	76478	62234	70925	76477
3487	(3090)	**N**	A	SE	RE	76645	62250	70941	76509
3488	(3127)	**N**	E	SW	WD	76663	62235	71008	76664
3489	(3128)	**N**	E	SW	WD	76665	62251	71009	76666
3490	(3143)	**N**	E	SW	WD	76695	62328	71024	76696
3491	(3076)	**N**	A	SE	RE	76337	62436	70927	76481
3492	(3129)	**N**	A	SE	RE	76667	62344	71010	76668
3493	(3130)	**N**	A	SE	RE	76669	62237	71011	76670
3494	(3133)	**N**	A	SE	RE	76675	62330	71014	76676
3495	(3145)	**N**	A	SE	RE	76699	62331	71026	76700
3496	(3132)	**N**	A	SE	RE	76673	62334	71013	76674
3497	(3131)	**N**	A	SE	RE	76671	62346	71012	76672
3498	(3146)	**N**	A	SE	RE	76701	62333	71027	76702
3499	(3174)	**N**	A	SE	RE	76901	62347	71135	76902
3500	(3070)	**N**	A	SE	RE	76470	62455	70921	76469
3501	(3091)	**N**	P	SC	BI	76512	62332	70942	76511
3503	(3136)	**N**	P	SC	BI	76681	62231	71017	76682
3504	(3151)	**N**	P	SC	BI	76711	62351	71032	76712
3505	(3071)	**N**	P	SC	BI	76472	62352	70922	76471
3506	(3112)	**N**	P	SC	BI	76554	62217	70963	76553
3507	(3114)	**N**	P	SC	BI	76558	62232	70965	76557
3508	(3117)	**N**	E	SW	WD	76643	62273	70998	76644
3509	(3115)	**N**	E	SW	WD	76560	62275	70966	76559
3510	(3116)	**N**	E	SW	WD	76641	62318	70997	76642
3511	(3118)	**N**	A	SE	RE	76893	62135	70999	76646
3512	(3135)	**N**	P	SC	BI	76679	62337	71016	76680
3513	(3141)	**N**	P	SC	BI	76691	62336	71022	76692
3514	(3137)	**N**	P	SC	BI	76683	62136	71018	76684
3515	(3107)	**N**	P	SC	BI	76544	62319	70958	76543
3516	(3142)	**N**	E	SW	WD	76693	62268	71023	76694
3517	(3138)	**N**	P	SC	BI	76685	62338	71019	76686
3518	(3140)	**N**	P	SC	BI	76689	62343	70887	76363
3519	(3113)	**N**	E	SW	WD	76556	62274	70964	76555
3520	(3144)	**N**	E	SW	WD	76697	62131	71025	76698
3521	(3077)	**N**	A	SE	RE	76484	62345	70928	76483
3522	(3148)	**N**	P	SC	BI	76705	62341	71029	76706
3523	(3121)	**N**	E	SW	WD	76651	62139	71002	76652
3524	(3068)	**N**	E	SW	WD	76466	62322	70919	76370
3526	(3097)	**N**	P	SC	BI	76524	62255	70948	76523
3527	(3095)	**N**	P	SC	BI	76520	62326	70946	76519
3528	(3094)	**N**	P	SC	BI	76518	62258	70945	76517
3529	(3125)	**N**	E	SW	WD	76659	62257	71006	76660
3530	(3069)	**N**	E	SW	WD	76468	62256	70920	76467
3531	(3120)	**N**	E	SW	WD	76649	62222	71001	76650

3532	(3099)	N	P	SC	BI	76528	62321	70950	76527
3533	(3098)	N	P	SC	BI	76364	62260	70949	76525
3534	(3088)	N	P	SC	BI	76506	62259	70939	76505
3535	(3134)	N	P	SC	BI	76677	62335	71015	76678
3536	(3046)	N	E	SW	WD	76384	62207	70897	76383
3537	(3092)	N	P	SC	BI	76514	62249	70943	76513
3539	(3154)	N	E	SW	WD	76861	62122	71115	76862
3540	(3155)	N	E	SW	WD	76863	62128	71116	76864
3541	(3147)	N	P	SC	BI	76703	62238	71028	76704
3542	(3075)	N	E	SW	WD	76480	62127	70926	76479
3543	(3173)	N	A	SE	RE	76899	62137	71134	76900
3544	(3170)	N	A	SE	RE	76892	62454	71131	76894
3545	(3161)	N	A	SE	RE	76875	62121	71122	76876
3546	(3139)	N	P	SC	BI	76687	62339	71020	76688
3547	(3171)	N	A	SE	RE	76895	62126	71132	76896
3548	(3175)	N	A	SE	RE	76903	62452	71136	76904
3549	(3149)	N	P	SC	BI	76707	62132	71030	76708
3550	(3080)	N	P	SC	BI	76490	62350	70931	76489
3551	(3152)	N	P	SC	BI	76465	62456	71033	76714
3552	(3153)	N	E	SW	WD	76715	62353	71034	76716
3553	(3180)	N	A	SE	RE	76913	62241	71141	76914
3554	(3176)	N	A	SE	RE	76905	62461	71137	76906
3555	(3156)	N	E	SW	WD	76865	62140	71117	76866
3556	(3166)	N	A	SE	RE	76885	62457	71127	76886
3557	(3158)	N	E	SW	WD	76869	62437	71119	76870
3558	(3030)	N	E	SW	WD	76352	62447	70881	76351
3559	(3078)	N	E	SW	WD	76486	62439	70929	76485
3560	(3172)	N	A	SE	RE	76897	62191	71133	76898
3561	(3157)	N	E	SW	WD	76867	62453	71118	76868
3562	(3177)	N	A	SE	RE	76907	62129	71138	76908
3563	(3160)	N	E	SW	WD	76873	62438	71121	76874
3564	(3165)	N	A	SE	RE	76883	62458	71126	76884
3565	(3162)	N	A	SE	RE	76877	62134	71123	76878
3566	(3181)	N	A	SE	RE	76915	62443	71142	76916
3567	(3159)	N	E	SW	WD	76871	62138	71120	76872
3568	(3167)	N	A	SE	RE	76887	62440	71128	76888
3569	(3026)	N	E	SW	WD	76344	62448	70877	76343
3570	(3178)	N	A	SE	RE	76909	62187	71139	76910
3571	(3187)	N	A	SE	RE	76927	62463	71148	76928
3572	(3163)	N	A	SE	RE	76879	62468	71124	76880
3573	(3183)	N	A	SE	RE	76919	62444	71144	76920
3574	(3188)	N	A	SE	RE	76929	62464	71149	76930
3575	(3189)	N	A	SE	RE	76931	62469	71150	76932
3576	(3035)	N	E	SW	WD	76362	62196	70890	76361
3577	(3190)	N	A	SE	RE	76933	62459	71151	76934
3578	(3032)	N	E	SW	WD	76356	62193	70883	76355
3579	(3191)	N	A	SE	RE	76935	62471	71152	76936
3580	(3034)	N	E	SW	WD	76360	62195	70885	76359
3581	(3037)	N	E	SW	WD	76366	62198	70888	76365
3582	(3169)	N	A	SE	RE	76891	62472	71130	76275
3583	(3192)	N	A	SE	RE	76937	62450	71153	76938

3584	(3164)	N	A	SE	RE	76881 62473 71125 76882
3585	(3193)	N	A	SE	RE	76939* 62445 71154 76940
3586	(3184)	N	A	SE	RE	76921 62474 71145 76922
3587	(3186)	N	A	SE	RE	76925 62465 71147 76926
3588	(3185)	N	A	SE	RE	76923 62467 71146 76924
3589	(3179)	N	A	SE	RE	76911 62466 71140 76912
3590	(3194)	N	A	SE	RE	76941 62460 71155 76942
3591	(3182)	N	A	SE	RE	76917 62475 71143 76918
3801	(3525)	N	P	SE	RE	76522 62229 70947 76521
3802	(3440)	N	P	SE	RE	76534 62188 70953 76533
3803	(3443)	N	P	SE	RE.	76494 62263 70933 76493
3804	(3444)	N	P	SE	RE	76368 62204 70889 76367
3805	(3460)	N	P	SE	RE	76540 62211 70956 76539
3806	(3461)	N	P	SE	RE	76538 62212 70955 76537
3807	(3465)	N	P	SE	RE	76542 62264 70957 76541
3808	(3477)	N	P	SE	RE	76550 62248 70961 76549
3809	(3538)	N	P	SE	RE	76516 62253 70944 76515
3810	(3502)	N	P	SE	RE	76709 62252 71031 76710
Spare		N	P		ZG	62470
Spare			A		ZG	76510

CLASS 455/7

DTSO – MSO – TSO – DTSO. Sliding doors. Disc brakes. Fluorescent lighting.
PA. Second series with TSOs originally in Class 508. Pressure ventilation.

Bogies: BT13 (DTSO), BP27 (MSO), BX1 (TSO).
Gangways: Through gangwayed.
Traction Motors: Four EE507 of 185 kW.
Dimensions: 19.83 x 2.82 m. (outer cars), 19.92 x 2.82 m (inner cars).
Maximum Speed: 75 mph.

DTSO. Dia. EE218. Lot No. 30976 York 1984 – 85. – /74. 29.5 t.
MSO. Dia. EC203. Lot No. 30975 York 1984 – 85. – /84. 45 t.
TSO. Dia. EH219. Lot No. 30944 York 1977 – 80. – /86. 25.48 t.

Note: 5750 was renumberd from 5743 as a gimmick (BS 5750 is the quality
assurance standard).

5701	N	P	SW	WD	77727 62783 71545 77728
5702	N	P	SW	WD	77729 62784 71547 77730
5703	N	P	SW	WD	77731 62785 71540 77732
5704	N	P	SW	WD	77733 62786 71548 77734
5705	N	P	SW	WD	77735 62787 71565 77736
5706	N	P	SW	WD	77737 62788 71534 77738
5707	N	P	SW	WD	77739 62789 71536* 77740
5708	N	P	SW	WD	77741 62790 71560 77742
5709	N	P	SW	WD	77743 62791 71532 77744
5710	N	P	SW	WD	77745 62792 71566 77746
5711	N	P	SW	WD	77747 62793 71542 77748
5712	N	P	SW	WD	77749 62794 71546 77750
5713	N	P	SW	WD	77751 62795 71567 77752
5714	N	P	SW	WD	77753 62796 71539 77754

5715	**N**	P	SW	WD	77755 62797 71535 77756
5716	**N**	P	SW	WD	77757 62798 71564 77758
5717	**N**	P	SW	WD	77759 62799 71528 77760
5718	**N**	P	SW	WD	77761 62800 71557 77762
5719	**N**	P	SW	WD	77763 62801 71558 77764
5720	**N**	P	SW	WD	77765 62802 71568 77766
5721	**N**	P	SW	WD	77767 62803 71553 77768
5722	**N**	P	SW	WD	77769 62804 71533 77770
5723	**N**	P	SW	WD	77771 62805 71526 77772
5724	**N**	P	SW	WD	77773 62806 71561 77774
5725	**N**	P	SW	WD	77775 62807 71541 77776
5726	**N**	P	SW	WD	77777 62808 71556 77778
5727	**N**	P	SW	WD	77779 62809 71562 77780
5728	**N**	P	SW	WD	77781 62810 71527 77782
5729	**N**	P	SW	WD	77783 62811 71550 77784
5730	**N**	P	SW	WD	77785 62812 71551 77786
5731	**N**	P	SW	WD	77787 62813 71555 77788
5732	**N**	P	SW	WD	77789 62814 71552 77790
5733	**N**	P	SW	WD	77791 62815 71549 77792
5734	**N**	P	SW	WD	77793 62816 71531 77794
5735	**N**	P	SW	WD	77795 62817 71563 77796
5736	**N**	P	SW	WD	77797 62818 71554 77798
5737	**N**	P	SW	WD	77799 62819 71544 77800
5738	**N**	P	SW	WD	77801 62820 71529 77802
5739	**N**	P	SW	WD	77803 62821 71537 77804
5740	**N**	P	SW	WD	77805 62822 71530 77806
5741	**N**	P	SW	WD	77807 62823 71559 77808
5742	**N**	P	SW	WD	77809 62824 71543 77810
5750	**N**	P	SW	WD	77811 62825 71538 77812

Names:

5711   SPIRIT OF RUGBY
5735   The Royal Borough of Kingston
5750   Wimbledon Train Care

CLASS 455/8

DTSO – MSO – TSO – DTSO. Sliding doors. Disc brakes. Fluorescent lighting. PA. First series. Pressure ventilation.

Bogies: BP20 (MSO), BT13 (trailer cars).
Gangways: Through gangwayed.
Traction Motors: Four EE507 of 185 kW.
Dimensions: 19.83 x 2.82 m. (outer cars), 19.92 x 2.82 m (inner cars).
Maximum Speed: 75 mph.

DTSO. Dia. EE218. Lot No. 30972 York 1982 – 84. – /74. 29.5 t.
MSO. Dia. EC203. Lot No. 30973 York 1982 – 84. – /84. 45.6 t.
TSO. Dia. EH221. Lot No. 30974 York 1982 – 84. – /84. 27.1 t.

| 5801 | **N** | E | SC | SU | 77579 62709 71637 77580 |
| 5802 | **N** | E | SC | SU | 77581 62710 71664 77582 |

5803	**CX**	E	SC	SU	77583	62711	71639	77584
5804	**CX**	E	SC	SU	77585	62712	71640	77586
5805	**N**	E	SC	SU	77587	62713	71641	77588
5806	**N**	E	SC	SU	77589	62714	71642	77590
5807	**N**	E	SC	SU	77591	62715	71643	77592
5808	**N**	E	SC	SU	77593	62716	71644	77594
5809	**N**	E	SC	SU	77595	62717	71645	77596
5810	**N**	E	SC	SU	77597	62718	71646	77598
5811	**N**	E	SC	SU	77599	62719	71647	77600
5812	**N**	E	SC	SU	77601	62720	71648	77602
5813	**N**	E	SC	SU	77603	62721	71649	77604
5814	**N**	E	SC	SU	77605	62722	71650	77606
5815	**N**	E	SC	SU	77607	62723	71651	77608
5816	**N**	E	SC	SU	77609	62724	71652	77633
5817	**N**	E	SC	SU	77611	62725	71653	77612
5818	**N**	E	SC	SU	77613	62726	71654	77614
5819	**N**	E	SC	SU	77615	62727	71655	77616
5820	**N**	E	SC	SU	77617	62728	71656	77618
5821	**N**	E	SC	SU	77619	62729	71657	77620
5822	**N**	E	SC	SU	77621	62730	71658	77622
5823	**N**	E	SC	SU	77623	62731	71659	77624
5824	**N**	E	SC	SU	77637	62732	71660	77626
5825	**N**	E	SC	SU	77627	62733	71661	77628
5826	**N**	E	SC	SU	77629	62734	71662	77630
5827	**N**	E	SC	SU	77610	62735	71663	77632
5828	**N**	E	SC	SU	77634	62736	71638	77631
5829	**N**	E	SC	SU	77635	62737	71665	77636
5830	**N**	E	SC	SU	77625	62743	71666	77638
5831	**N**	E	SC	SU	77639	62739	71667	77640
5832	**N**	E	SC	SU	77641	62740	71668	77642
5833	**N**	E	SC	SU	77643	62741	71669	77644
5834	**N**	E	SC	SU	77645	62742	71670	77646
5835	**N**	E	SC	SU	77647	62738	71671	77648
5836	**N**	E	SC	SU	77649	62744	71672	77650
5837	**N**	E	SC	SU	77651	62745	71673	77652
5838	**N**	E	SC	SU	77653	62746	71674	77654
5839	**N**	E	SC	SU	77655	62747	71675	77656
5840	**N**	E	SC	SU	77657	62748	71676	77658
5841	**N**	E	SC	SU	77659	62749	71677	77660
5842	**N**	E	SC	SU	77661	62750	71678	77662
5843	**N**	E	SC	SU	77663	62751	71679	77664
5844	**N**	E	SC	SU	77665	62752	71680	77666
5845	**N**	E	SC	SU	77667	62753	71681	77668
5846	**N**	E	SC	SU	77669	62754	71682	77670
5847	**N**	P	SW	WD	77671	62755	71683	77672
5848	**N**	P	SW	WD	77673	62756	71684	77674
5849	**N**	P	SW	WD	77675	62757	71685	77676
5850	**N**	P	SW	WD	77677	62758	71686	77678
5851	**N**	P	SW	WD	77679	62759	71687	77680
5852	**N**	P	SW	WD	77681	62760	71688	77682
5853	**N**	P	SW	WD	77683	62761	71689	77684

5854	N	P	SW	WD	77685 62762 71690 77686
5855	N	P	SW	WD	77687 62763 71691 77688
5856	N	P	SW	WD	77689 62764 71692 77690
5857	N	P	SW	WD	77691 62765 71693 77692
5858	N	P	SW	WD	77693 62766 71694 77694
5859	N	P	SW	WD	77695 62767 71695 77696
5860	N	P	SW	WD	77697 62768 71696 77698
5861	N	P	SW	WD	77699 62769 71697 77700
5862	N	P	SW	WD	77701 62770 71698 77702
5863	N	P	SW	WD	77703 62771 71699 77704
5864	N	P	SW	WD	77705 62772 71700 77706
5865	N	P	SW	WD	77707 62773 71701 77708
5866	N	P	SW	WD	77709 62774 71702 77710
5867	N	P	SW	WD	77711 62775 71703 77712
5868	N	P	SW	WD	77713 62776 71704 77714
5869	N	P	SW	WD	77715 62777 71705 77716
5870	N	P	SW	WD	77717 62778 71706 77718
5871	N	P	SW	WD	77719 62779 71707 77720
5872	N	P	SW	WD	77721 62780 71708 77722
5873	N	P	SW	WD	77723 62781 71709 77724
5874	N	P	SW	WD	77725 62782 71710 77726

CLASS 455/9

DTSO – MSO – TSO – DTSO. Sliding doors. Disc brakes. Fluorescent lighting. PA. Third series. Convection heating.

Bogies: BP20 (MSO), BT13 (trailer cars).
Gangways: Through gangwayed.
Traction Motors: Four EE507 of 185 kW.
Dimensions: 19.83 x 2.82 m. (outer cars), 19.92 x 2.82 m (inner cars).
Maximum Speed: 75 mph.

DTSO. Dia. EE226. Lot No. 30991 York 1985. –/74. 29.5 t.
MSO. Dia. EC206. Lot No. 30992 York 1985. –/84. 45.6 t.
TSO. Dia. EH224. Lot No. 30993 York 1985. –/84. 27.1 t.
TSO n. Dia. EH224. Lot No. 30932 Derby 1981. –/84. 27.1 t.

* Chopper control.
§ Tread brakes.
c ''Crossrail'' interiors.
n Prototype vehicle converted from a Class 210 DMU.

5901		N	P	SW	WD	77813 62826 71714 77814
5902		N	P	SW	WD	77815 62827 71715 77816
5903		N	P	SW	WD	77817 62828 71716 77818
5904		N	P	SW	WD	77819 62829 71717 77820
5905	c	N	P	SW	WD	77821 62830 71731 77822
5906		N	P	SW	WD	77823 62831 71719 77824
5907		N	P	SW	WD	77825 62832 71720 77826
5908		N	P	SW	WD	77827 62833 71721 77828
5909		N	P	SW	WD	77829 62834 71722 77830
5910		N	P	SW	WD	77831 62835 71723 77832

5911		**N**	P	SW	WD	77833 62836 71724 77834
5912	*	**N**	P	SW	WD	77835 62837 71725 77836
5913	§	**N**	P	SW	WD	77837 62838 71726 77838
5914	§	**N**	P	SW	WD	77839 62839 71727 77840
5915	§	**N**	P	SW	WD	77841 62840 71728 77842
5916	*	**N**	P	SW	WD	77843 62841 71729 77844
5917	*	**N**	P	SW	WD	77845 62842 71730 77846
5918	*c	**N**	P	SW	WD	77847 62843 71732 77848
5919	*.	**N**	P	SW	WD	77849 62844 71718 77850
5920	*	**N**	P	SW	WD	77851 62845 71733 77852
Spsre	n	**N**	P	SW	WD	67400

CLASS 488   VICTORIA – GATWICK TRAILER SETS

TFOLH – TSOL (Class 488/3 only) – TSOLH. Converted 1983 – 84 from loco-hauled Mk. 2F FOs and TSOs for Victoria – Gatwick service. Express stock. Air conditioned. Fluorescent lighting. PA. Conversion consisted of a modified seating layout and the removal of one toilet to provide additional luggage space.

Bogies: B4.
Gangways: Throughout.
Dimensions: 20.12 x 2.82 m.
Maximum Speed: 90 mph.

72500 – 72509. TFOLH. Dia. EP101. Lot No. 30859 Derby 1973 – 74. 41/ – 1T. 35 t.
72602 – 14/6 – 8/20 – 44/46/7. TSOLH. Dia. EP201. Lot No. 30860 Derby 1973 – 74. – /48 1T. 35 t.
72615/19/45. TSOLH. Dia. EP201. Lot No. 30846 Derby 1973. – /48 1T. 35 t.
72701 – 72718. TSOL. Dia. EH285. Lot No. 30860 Derby 1973 – 74. – /48 1T. 35 t.

CLASS 488/2. Note: TFOLH fitted with public telephone.

8201	**GX**	P	GX	SL	72500 (3413)	72638 (6068)
8202	**GX**	P	GX	SL	72501 (3382)	72617 (6086)
8203	**GX**	P	GX	SL	72502 (3321)	72640 (6097)
8204	**GX**	P	GX	SL	72503 (3407)	72641 (6079)
8205	**GX**	P	GX	SL	72504 (3406)	72628 (6058)
8206	**GX**	P	GX	SL	72505 (3415)	72629 (6048)
8207	**GX**	P	GX	SL	72506 (3335)	72642 (6076)
8208	**GX**	P	GX	SL	72507 (3412)	72643 (6040)
8209	**GX**	P	GX	SL	72508 (3409)	72644 (6039)
8210	**GX**	P	GX	SL	72509 (3398)	72635 (6128)

CLASS 488/3. TSOLH – TSOL – TSOLH.

8302	**GX**	P	GX	SL	72602 (6130)	72701 (6088)	72604 (6087)
8303	**GX**	P	GX	SL	72603 (6093)	72702 (6099)	72608 (6077)
8304	**GX**	P	GX	SL	72606 (6084)	72703 (6075)	72611 (6083)
8305	**GX**	P	GX	SL	72605 (6082)	72704 (6132)	72609 (6080)
8306	**GX**	P	GX	SL	72607 (6020)	72705 (6032)	72610 (6074)
8307	**GX**	P	GX	SL	72612 (6156)	72706 (6143)	72613 (6126)
8308	**GX**	P	GX	SL	72614 (6090)	72707 (6127)	72615 (5938)

8309	**GX**	P	GX	SL	72616 (6007)	72708 (6095)	72639 (6070)
8310	**GX**	P	GX	SL	72618 (6044)	72709 (5982)	72619 (5909)
8311	**GX**	P	GX	SL	72620 (6140)	72710 (6003)	72621 (6108)
8312	**GX**	P	GX	SL	72622 (6004)	72711 (6109)	72623 (6118)
8313	**GX**	P	GX	SL	72624 (5972)	72712 (6091)	72625 (6085)
8314	**GX**	P	GX	SL	72626 (6017)	72713 (6023)	72627 (5974)
8315	**GX**	P	GX	SL	72636 (6071)	72714 (6092)	72645 (5942)
8316	**GX**	P	GX	SL	72630 (6094)	72715 (6019)	72631 (6096)
8317	**GX**	P	GX	SL	72632 (6072)	72716 (6114)	72633 (6129)
8318	**GX**	P	GX	SL	72634 (6089)	72717 (6069)	72637 (6098)
8319	**GX**	P	GX	SL	72646 (6078)	72718 (5979)	72647 (6081)

CLASS 489   VICTORIA – GATWICK GLV

Converted 1983 – 84 from class 414/3 (2 Hap) DMBSOs to work with class 488.

Bogies: Mk 4.
Gangways: Gangwayed at inner end only.
Traction Motors: Two EE507 of 185 kW.
Dimensions: 19.49 x 2.82 m.
Maximum Speed: 90 mph.

DMLV. Dia. EX561. Lot No. 30452 Ashford/Eastleigh 1959. 40.5 t.

9101	**GX**	P	GX	SL	68500 (61269)
9102	**GX**	P	GX	SL	68501 (61281)
9103	**GX**	P	GX	SL	68502 (61274)
9104	**GX**	P	GX	SL	68503 (61277)
9105	**GX**	P	GX	SL	68504 (61286)
9106	**GX**	P	GX	SL	68505 (61299)
9107	**GX**	P	GX	SL	68506 (61292)
9108	**GX**	P	GX	SL	68507 (61267)
9109	**GX**	P	GX	SL	68508 (61272)
9110	**GX**	P	GX	SL	68509 (61280)

CLASS 456

DMSO – DTSO. Sliding doors. Disc brakes. Fluorescent lighting. PA.

Bogies: P7 (motor) and T3 trailer.
Gangways: Within set.
Traction Motors: Two EE507 of 185 kW.
Dimensions: 19.83 x 2.82 m.
Maximum Speed: 75 mph.

DMSO. Dia. EA267. Lot No. 31073 York 1990 – 1. –/79. 41.1 t.
DTSO. Dia. EE276. Lot No. 31074 York 1990 – 1. –/51. 31.4 t.

456 001	**N**	P	SC	SU	64735	78250
456 002	**N**	P	SC	SU	64736	78251
456 003	**N**	P	SC	SU	64737	78252
456 004	**N**	P	SC	SU	64738	78253
456 005	**N**	P	SC	SU	64739	78254
456 006	**N**	P	SC	SU	64740	78255

456 007	N	P	SC	SU	64741	78256
456 008	N	P	SC	SU	64742	78257
456 009	N	P	SC	SU	64743	78258
456 010	N	P	SC	SU	64744	78259
456 011	N	P	SC	SU	64745	78260
456 012	N	P	SC	SU	64746	78261
456 013	N	P	SC	SU	64747	78262
456 014	N	P	SC	SU	64748	78263
456 015	N	P	SC	SU	64749	78264
456 016	N	P	SC	SU	64750	78265
456 017	N	P	SC	SU	64751	78266
456 018	N	P	SC	SU	64752	78267
456 019	N	P	SC	SU	64753	78268
456 020	N	P	SC	SU	64754	78269
456 021	N	P	SC	SU	64755	78270
456 022	N	P	SC	SU	64756	78271
456 023	N	P	SC	SU	64757	78272
456 024	CX	P	SC	SU	64758	78273

CLASS 465   NETWORKER

DMSO(A) – TSO – TSOL – DMSO(B). New units with Aluminium bodies. Sliding doors. Disc, rheostatic and regenerative brakes. PA.

Electrical Equipment: Networker.
Bogies: P3 (Power cars), T3 (trailers).
Gangways: Within set.
Traction Motors: Four Brush totally-enclosed squirrel-caged three-phase induction motors per car driven by four GTO inverters.
Dimensions: 20.89 x 2.81 m (outer cars), 20.06 x 2.81 m (inner cars).
Maximum Speed: 75 mph.

64759 – 64808. DMSO(A). Dia. EA268. Lot No. 31100 BREL York 1991 – 3. –/86. 38.9 t.
64809 – 64858. DMSO(B). Dia. EA268. Lot No. 31100 BREL York 1991 – 3. –/86. 39 t.
65700 – 65749. DMSO(A). Dia. EA269. Lot No. 31103 Metro-Cammell 1991 – 3. –/86. 38.8 t.
65750 – 65799. DMSO(B). Dia. EA269. Lot No. 31103 Metro-Cammell 1991 – 3. –/86. 38.9 t.
65800 – 65846. DMSO(A). Dia. EA268. Lot No. 31130 ABB York 1993 – 4. –/86.   t.
65847 – 65893. DMSO(A). Dia. EA268. Lot No. 31130 ABB York 1993 – 4. –/86.   t.
72028 – 72126 (even Nos.). TSO. Dia. EH293. Lot No. 31102 BREL York 1991 – 3. –/86. 29.5 t.
72029 – 72127 (odd Nos.). TSOL. Dia. EH292. Lot No. 31101 BREL York 1991 – 3. –/86. 28.6 t.
72719 – 72817 (odd Nos.). TSOL. Dia. EH294. Lot No. 31104 Metro-Cammell 1991 – 3. –/86. 30.2 t.
72720 – 72818 (even Nos.). TSO. Dia. EH295. Lot No. 31105 Metro-Cammell 1991 – 3. –/86. 29.1 t.

72900 – 72992 (even Nos.). TSO. Dia. EH293. Lot No. 31102 ABB York
1993 – 4. – /86.   t.
72901 – 72993 (odd Nos.). TSOL. Dia. EH292. Lot No. 31101 ABB York
1993 – 4. – /86.   t.

Class 465/0. Built by ABB.

465 001	**NW**	E	SE	SG	64759	72028	72029	64809
465 002	**NW**	E	SE	SG	64760	72030	72031	64810
465 003	**NW**	E	SE	SG	64761	72032	72033	64811
465 004	**NW**	E	SE	SG	64762	72034	72035	64812
465 005	**NW**	E	SE	SG	64763	72036	72037	64813
465 006	**NW**	E	SE	SG	64764	72038	72039	64814
465 007	**NW**	E	SE	SG	64765	72040	72041	64815
465 008	**NW**	E	SE	SG	64766	72042	72043	64816
465 009	**NW**	E	SE	SG	64767	72044	72045	64817
465 010	**NW**	E	SE	SG	64768	72046	72047	64818
465 011	**NW**	E	SE	SG	64769	72048	72049	64819
465 012	**NW**	E	SE	SG	64770	72050	72051	64820
465 013	**NW**	E	SE	SG	64771	72052	72053	64821
465 014	**NW**	E	SE	SG	64772	72054	72055	64822
465 015	**NW**	E	SE	SG	64773	72056	72057	64823
465 016	**NW**	E	SE	SG	64774	72058	72059	64824
465 017	**NW**	E	SE	SG	64775	72060	72061	64825
465 018	**NW**	E	SE	SG	64776	72062	72063	64826
465 019	**NW**	E	SE	SG	64777	72064	72065	64827
465 020	**NW**	E	SE	SG	64778	72066	72067	64828
465 021	**NW**	E	SE	SG	64779	72068	72069	64829
465 022	**NW**	E	SE	SG	64780	72070	72071	64830
465 023	**NW**	E	SE	SG	64781	72072	72073	64831
465 024	**NW**	E	SE	SG	64782	72074	72075	64832
465 025	**NW**	E	SE	SG	64783	72076	72077	64833
465 026	**NW**	E	SE	SG	64784	72078	72079	64834
465 027	**NW**	E	SE	SG	64785	72080	72081	64835
465 028	**NW**	E	SE	SG	64786	72082	72083	64836
465 029	**NW**	E	SE	SG	64787	72084	72085	64837
465 030	**NW**	E	SE	SG	64788	72086	72087	64838
465 031	**NW**	E	SE	SG	64789	72088	72089	64839
465 032	**NW**	E	SE	SG	64790	72090	72091	64840
465 033	**NW**	E	SE	SG	64791	72092	72093	64841
465 034	**NW**	E	SE	SG	64792	72094	72095	64842
465 035	**NW**	E	SE	SG	64793	72096	72097	64843
465 036	**NW**	E	SE	SG	64794	72098	72099	64844
465 037	**NW**	E	SE	SG	64795	72100	72101	64845
465 038	**NW**	E	SE	SG	64796	72102	72103	64846
465 039	**NW**	E	SE	SG	64797	72104	72105	64847
465 040	**NW**	E	SE	SG	64798	72106	72107	64848
465 041	**NW**	E	SE	SG	64799	72108	72109	64849
465 042	**NW**	E	SE	SG	64800	72110	72111	64850
465 043	**NW**	E	SE	SG	64801	72112	72113	64851
465 044	**NW**	E	SE	SG	64802	72114	72115	64852
465 045	**NW**	E	SE	SG	64803	72116	72117	64853

465 247	**NW**	E	SE	SG	65746	72811	72812	65796
465 248	**NW**	E	SE	SG	65747	72813	72814	65797
465 249	**NW**	E	SE	SG	65748	72815	72816	65798
465 250	**NW**	E	SE	SG	65749	72817	72818	65799

CLASS 466   NETWORKER

DMSO – DTSO. New units with Aluminium bodies. Sliding doors. Disc, rheostatic and regenerative brakes. PA.

Electrical Equipment: Networker.
Bogies: P3 (Power car), T3 (trailer).
Gangways: Within set.
Traction Motors: Four Brush totally-enclosed squirrel-caged three-phase induction motors per car driven by four GTO inverters.
Dimensions: 20.89 x 2.81 m.
Maximum Speed: 75 mph.

DMSO. Dia. EA271. Lot No. 31128 Metro-Cammell 1992 – 3. – /86. 39.2 t.
DTSO. Dia. EE279. Lot No. 31129 Metro-Cammell 1991 – 2. – /82. 33.2 t.

466 001	**NW**	E	SE	SG	64860	78312
466 002	**NW**	E	SE	SG	64861	78313
466 003	**NW**	E	SE	SG	64862	78314
466 004	**NW**	E	SE	SG	64863	78315
466 005	**NW**	E	SE	SG	64864	78316
466 006	**NW**	E	SE	SG	64865	78317
466 007	**NW**	E	SE	SG	64866	78318
466 008	**NW**	E	SE	SG	64867	78319
466 009	**NW**	E	SE	SG	64868	78320
466 010	**NW**	E	SE	SG	64869	78321
466 011	**NW**	E	SE	SG	64870	78322
466 012	**NW**	E	SE	SG	64871	78323
466 013	**NW**	E	SE	SG	64872	78324
466 014	**NW**	E	SE	SG	64873	78325
466 015	**NW**	E	SE	SG	64874	78326
466 016	**NW**	E	SE	SG	64875	78327
466 017	**NW**	E	SE	SG	64876	78328
466 018	**NW**	E	SE	SG	64877	78329
466 019	**NW**	E	SE	SG	64878	78330
466 020	**NW**	E	SE	SG	64879	78331
466 021	**NW**	E	SE	SG	64880	78332
466 022	**NW**	E	SE	SG	64881	78333
466 023	**NW**	E	SE	SG	64882	78334
466 024	**NW**	E	SE	SG	64883	78335
466 025	**NW**	E	SE	SG	64884	78336
466 026	**NW**	E	SE	SG	64885	78337
466 027	**NW**	E	SE	SG	64886	78338
466 028	**NW**	E	SE	SG	64887	78339
466 029	**NW**	E	SE	SG	64888	78340
466 030	**NW**	E	SE	SG	64889	78341
466 031	**NW**	E	SE	SG	64890	78342

466 032	**NW**	E	SE	SG	64891 78343
466 033	**NW**	E	SE	SG	64892 78344
466 034	**NW**	E	SE	SG	64893 78345
466 035	**NW**	E	SE	SG	64894 78346
466 036	**NW**	E	SE	SG	64895 78347
466 037	**NW**	E	SE	SG	64896 78348
466 038	**NW**	E	SE	SG	64897 78349
466 039	**NW**	E	SE	SG	64898 78350
466 040	**NW**	E	SE	SG	64899 78351
466 041	**NW**	E	SE	SG	64900 78352
466 042	**NW**	E	SE	SG	64901 78353
466 043	**NW**	E	SE	SG	64902 78354

CLASS 483   'NEW' ISLE OF WIGHT STOCK

DMSO(A) – DMSO(B). Tube stock. Built 1938 onwards for LTE. Converted 1989 – 90 for Isle of Wight Line. Sliding doors. End doors. dg. pa. Former London Underground numbers are shown in parentheses.

System: 660 V d.c. third rail.
Gangways: Non-gangwayed.
Traction Motors: Two of 130 kW.
Dimensions: 15.95 x 2.69 m.
Maximum Speed: 45 mph.

DMSO (A). Lot No. 31071. Dia. EA265. –/42. 27.5 t.
DMSO (B). Lot No. 31072. Dia. EA266. –/42. 27.5 t.

483 001	**NW**	E	IL	RY	121	(10184)	222 (11221)
483 002	**NW**	E	IL	RY	122	(10221)	225 (11142)
483 003	**NW**	E	IL	RY	123	(10116)	221 (11184)
483 004	**NW**	E	IL	RY	124	(10205)	224 (11205)
483 005	**NW**	E	IL	RY	125	(10142)	223 (11116)
483 006	**NW**	E	IL	RY	126	(10297)	226 (11297)
483 007	**NW**	E	IL	RY	127	(10291)	227 (11291)
483 008	**NW**	E	IL	RY	128	(10255)	228 (11255)
483 009	**NW**	E	IL	RY	129	(10289)	229 (11229)

4.3. MERSEYRAIL 750 V d.c. EMUs

CLASS 507

BDMSO – TSO – DMSO. Tightlock couplers. Sliding doors. Disc and rheostatic brakes. PA.

System: 750 V d.c. third rail.
Bogies: BX1.
Gangways: Gangwayed within unit. End doors.
Traction Motors: Four GEC G310AZ of 82.125 kW.
Dimensions: 19.80 x 2.82 m (outer cars), 19.92 x 2.82 m (inner cars).
Maximum Speed: 75 mph.

BDMSO. Dia. EI202. Lot No. 30906 York 1978 – 80. – /74 (– /68*). 37.06 t.
TSO. Dia. EH205. Lot No. 30907 York 1978 – 80. – /82 (– /86*). 25.60 t.
DMSO. Dia. EA201. Lot No. 30908 York 1978 – 80. – /74 (– /68*). 35.62 t.

507 001	**MT**	A	ME	HR	64367	71342	64405
507 002	**MT**	A	ME	HR	64368	71343	64406
507 003	**MT**	A	ME	HR	64369	71344	64407
507 004		A	ME	HR	64388	71345	64408
507 005	**MT**	A	ME	HR	64371	71346	64409
507 006	* **MT**	A	ME	HR	64372	71347	64410
507 007	**MT**	A	ME	HR	64373	71348	64411
507 008	**MT**	A	ME	HR	64374	71349	64412
507 009	**MT**	A	ME	HR	64375	71350	64413
507 010	**MT**	A	ME	HR	64376	71351	64414
507 011	**MT**	A	ME	HR	64377	71352	64415
507 012	**MT**	A	ME	HR	64378	71353	64416
507 013	**MT**	A	ME	HR	64379	71354	64417
507 014	**MT**	A	ME	HR	64380	71355	64418
507 015	**MT**	A	ME	HR	64381	71356	64419
507 016	**MT**	A	ME	HR	64382	71357	64420
507 017	* **MT**	A	ME	HR	64383	71358	64421
507 018	**MT**	A	ME	HR	64384	71359	64422
507 019	**MT**	A	ME	HR	64385	71360	64423
507 020	**MT**	A	ME	HR	64386	71361	64424
507 021	**MT**	A	ME	HR	64387	71362	64425
507 023	**MT**	A	ME	HR	64389	71364	64427
507 024	* **MT**	A	ME	HR	64390	71365	64428
507 025		A	ME	HR	64391	71366	64429
507 026	**MT**	A	ME	HR	64392	71367	64430
507 027	**MT**	A	ME	HR	64393	71368	64431
507 028	**MT**	A	ME	HR	64394	71369	64432
507 029	**MT**	A	ME	HR	64395	71370	64433
507 030	**MT**	A	ME	HR	64396	71371	64434
507 031	**MT**	A	ME	HR	64397	71372	64435
507 032	**MT**	A	ME	HR	64398	71373	64436
507 033		A	ME	HR	64399	71374	64437

CLASS 508

DMSO – TSO – BDMSO. Tightlock couplers. Sliding doors. Disc and rheostatic brakes. PA. Originally built as four car units and numbered 508 001 – 043. One trailer removed and used for class 455/7 on transfer from the SR.

System: 750 V d.c. third rail.
Bogies: BX1.
Gangways: Gangwayed within unit. End doors.
Traction Motors: Four GEC G310AZ of 82.125 kW.
Dimensions: 19.80 x 2.82 m (outer cars), 19.92 x 2.82 m (inner cars).
Maximum Speed: 75 mph.

64649 – 64691. DMSO. Dia. EA208. Lot No. 30979 York 1979 – 80. – /74.
36.15 t.
71483 – 71525. TSO. Dia. EH218. Lot No. 30980 York 1979 – 80. – /82.
26.72 t.
64692 – 64734. BDMSO. Dia. EI203. Lot No. 30981 York 1979 – 80. – /74.
36.61 t.

508 101		A		Kineton	64649	71483	64692
508 102	**MT**	A	ME	BD	64650	71484	64693
508 103	**MT**	A	ME	BD	64651	71485	64694
508 104	**MT**	A	ME	BD	64652	71486	64695
508 105		A		Kineton	64653	71487	64696
508 106		A		Kineton	64654	71488	64697
508 107		A		Kineton	64655	71489	64698
508 108		A	ME	BD	64656	71490	64699
508 109		A		Kineton	64657	71491	64700
508 110	**MT**	A	ME	BD	64658	71492	64701
508 111	**MT**	A	ME	BD	64659	71493	64702
508 112		A	ME	BD	64660	71494	64703
508 113		A		Kineton	64661	71495	64704
508 114	**MT**	A	ME	BD	64662	71496	64705
508 115	**MT**	A	ME	BD	64663	71497	64706
508 116		A		Kineton	64664	71498	64707
508 117	**MT**	A	ME	BD	64665	71499	64708
508 118	**MT**	A	ME	BD	64666	71500	64709
508 119		A		Kineton	64667	71501	64710
508 120	**MT**	A	ME	BD	64668	71502	64711
508 121		A		Kineton	64669	71503	64712
508 122	**MT**	A	ME	BD	64670	71504	64713
508 123	**MT**	A	ME	BD	64671	71505	64714
508 124	**MT**	A	ME	BD	64672	71506	64715
508 125		A	ME	BD	64673	71507	64716
508 126	**MT**	A	ME	BD	64674	71508	64717
508 127	**MT**	A	ME	BD	64675	71509	64718
508 128	**MT**	A	ME	BD	64676	71510	64719
508 129		A		Southport CS	64677	71511	64720
508 130	**MT**	A	ME	BD	64678	71512	64721
508 131	**MT**	A	ME	BD	64679	71513	64722

508 132		A		Southport CS	64680	71514	64723
508 133		A		Southport CS	64681	71515	64724
508 134		A	ME	BD	64682	71516	64725
508 135	**MT**	A	ME	BD	64683	71517	64726
508 136		A	ME	BD	64684	71518	64727
508 137		A	ME	BD	64685	71519	64728
508 138	**MT**	A	ME	BD	64686	71520	64729
508 139		A	ME	HR	64687	71521	64730
508 140	**MT**	A	ME	HR	64688	71522	64731
508 141	**MT**	A	ME	HR	64689	71523	64732
508 142		A	ME	HR	64690	71524	64733
508 143	**MT**	A	ME	HR	64691	71525	64734

4.4 . EUROSTAR SETS (CLASS 373)

Eurostar sets work services through the Channel Tunnel between London and Paris and Brussels. They are based on the French TGV design concept, and the individual cars are numbered like French TGVs.

Each train consists of two 9-coach sets back-to-back with a power car at the outer end. BR sets are allocated to North Pole (London), Belgian Railways (SNCB/NMBS) sets are allocated to Bruxelles Forest/Brussel Vorst and French Railways (SNCF) sets are allocated to Le Landy (Paris). Regional sets for operation north of London consisting of two 7-coach half-sets are not yet in service.

All sets are articulated with an extra motor bogie on the coach next to the power car. Coaches are numbered R1 – R9 (and in traffic R10 – R18 in the second set). Coaches R18 – R10 are identical to R1 – R9.

BR Sets:

3001	F15	U	ES	PI	3730010	3730011	3730012	3730013
3002	F15	U	ES	PI	3730020	3730021	3730022	3730023
3003	UK3	U	ES	PI	3730030	3730031	3730032	3730033
3004	UK3	U	ES	PI	3730040	3730041	3730042	3730043
3005	UK4	U	ES	PI	3730050	3730051	3730052	3730053
3006	UK4	U	ES	PI	3730060	3730061	3730062	3730063
3007	UK5	U	ES	PI	3730070	3730071	3730072	3730073
3008	UK5	U	ES	PI	3730080	3730081	3730082	3730083
3009	UK8	U	ES	PI	3730090	3730091	3730092	3730093
3010	UK8	U	ES	PI	3730100	3730101	3730102	3730103
3011	UK9	U	ES	PI	3730110	3730111	3730112	3730113
3012	UK9	U	ES	PI	3730120	3730121	3730122	3730123
3013	UK10	U	ES	PI	3730130	3730131	3730132	3730133
3014	UK10	U	ES	PI	3730140	3730141	3730142	3730143
3015	UK11	U	ES	PI	3730150	3730151	3730152	3730153
3016	UK11	U	ES	PI	3730160	3730161	3730162	3730163
3017	UK12	U	ES	PI	3730170	3730171	3730172	3730173
3018	UK12	U	ES	PI	3730180	3730181	3730182	3730183
3019	UK14	U	ES	PI	3730190	3730191	3730192	3730193
3020	UK14	U	ES	PI	3730200	3730201	3730202	3730203
3021	UK15	U	ES	PI	3730210	3730211	3730212	3730213
3022	UK15	U	ES	PI	3730220	3730221	3730222	3730223
3999		U	ES	PI	3739990 Spare power car.			

SNCB/NMBS Sets:

3101	UK1	B	ES	FF	3731010	3731011	3731012	3731013
3102	UK1	B	ES	FF	3731020	3731021	3731022	3731023
3103	UK2	B	ES	FF	3731030	3731031	3731032	3731033
3104	UK2	B	ES	FF	3731040	3731041	3731042	3731043
3105	UK6	B	ES	FF	3731050	3731051	3731052	3731053
3106	UK6	B	ES	FF	3731060	3731061	3731062	3731063
3107	UK7	B	ES	FF	3731070	3731071	3731072	3731073
3108	UK7	B	ES	FF	3731080	3731081	3731082	3731083

Systems: 25 kV a.c. overhead, 3000 V d.c. overhead and 750 V d.c. third rail.
* Also fitted for 1500 V d.c. operation.

Built: 1992 – 3 by GEC Alsthom at various works.
Wheel Arrangement: Bo – Bo + Bo – 2 – 2 – 2 – 2 – 2 – 2 – 2 – 2 – 2
Traction Motors: 6
Length: 22.15 + 21.845 + (7 x 18.70) + 21.845 m.
Max. Speed: 300 km/h (187.5 mph).
Livery: White with dark blue window band roof and yellow bodysides.

Car	Type	Seats	Lot No.	Car	Type	Seats	Lot No.
M	DM		31118	R5	TSOL	–/60 2T	31123
R1	MSOL	–/52 1T	31119	R6	Kitchen/bar		31124
R2	TSOL	–/60 1T	31120	R7	TFOL	39/– 1T	31125
R3	TSOL	–/60 2T	31121	R8	TFOL	39/– 1T	31126
R4	TSOL	–/60 1T	31122	R9	TBFOL	27/– 1T	31127

Note: The pairs of sets are also known by designations as follows: F/FN –
Assembled in France, UK/UN – Assembled in the UK.

```
3730014 3730015 3730016 3730017 3730018 3730019
3730024 3730025 3730026 3730027 3730028 3730029
3730034 3730035 3730036 3730037 3730038 3730039
3730044 3730045 3730046 3730047 3730048 3730049
3730054 3730055 3730056 3730057 3730058 3730059
3730064 3730065 3730066 3730067 3730068 3730069
3730074 3730075 3730076 3730077 3730078 3730079
3730084 3730085 3730086 3730087 3730088 3730089
3730094 3730095 3730096 3730097 3730098 3730099
3730104 3730105 3730106 3730107 3730108 3730109
3730114 3730115 3730116 3730117 3730118 3730119
3730124 3730125 3730126 3730127 3730128 3730129
3730134 3730135 3730136 3730137 3730138 3730139
3730144 3730145 3730146 3730147 3730148 3730149
3730154 3730155 3730156 3730157 3730158 3730159
3730164 3730165 3730166 3730167 3730168 3730169
3730174 3730175 3730176 3730177 3730178 3730179
3730184 3730185 3730186 3730187 3730188 3730189
3730194 3730195 3730196 3730197 3730198 3730199
3730204 3730205 3730206 3730207 3730208 3730209
3730214 3730215 3730216 3730217 3730218 3730219
3730224 3730225 3730226 3730227 3730228 3730229


3731014 3731015 3731016 3731017 3731018 3731019
3731024 3731025 3731026 3731027 3731028 3731029
3731034 3731035 3731036 3731037 3731038 3731039
3731044 3731045 3731046 3731047 3731048 3731049
3731054 3731055 3731056 3731057 3731058 3731059
3731064 3731065 3731066 3731067 3731068 3731069
3731074 3731075 3731076 3731077 3731078 3731079
3731084 3731085 3731086 3731087 3731088 3731089
```

SNCF Sets:

3201	F16	F	ES	LY	3732010 3732011 3732012 3732013
3202	F16	F	ES	LY	3732020 3732021 3732022 3732023
3203*	F1	F	ES	LY	3732030 3732031 3732032 3732033
3204*	F1	F	ES	LY	3732040 3732041 3732042 3732043
3205	F2	F	ES	LY	3732050 3732051 3732052 3732053
3206	F2	F	ES	LY	3732060 3732061 3732062 3732063
3207	F3	F	ES	LY	3732070 3732071 3732072 3732073
3208	F3	F	ES	LY	3732080 3732081 3732082 3732083
3209	F4	F	ES	LY	3732090 3732091 3732092 3732093
3210	F4	F	ES	LY	3732100 3732101 3732102 3732103
3211	F5	F	ES	LY	3732110 3732111 3732112 3732113
3212	F5	F	ES	LY	3732120 3732121 3732122 3732123
3213	F6	F	ES	LY	3732130 3732131 3732132 3732133
3214	F6	F	ES	LY	3732140 3732141 3732142 3732143
3215	F7	F	ES	LY	3732150 3732151 3732152 3732153
3216	F7	F	ES	LY	3732160 3732161 3732162 3732163
3217	F8	F	ES	LY	3732170 3732171 3732172 3732173
3218	F8	F	ES	LY	3732180 3732181 3732182 3732183
3219	F9	F	ES	LY	3732190 3732191 3732192 3732193
3220	F9	F	ES	LY	3732200 3732201 3732202 3732203
3221	F10	F	ES	LY	3732210 3732211 3732212 3732213
3222	F10	F	ES	LY	3732220 3732221 3732222 3732223
3223	F11	F	ES	LY	3732230 3732231 3732232 3732233
3224	F11	F	ES	LY	3732240 3732241 3732242 3732243
3225*	F12	F	ES	LY	3732250 3732251 3732252 3732253
3226*	F12	F	ES	LY	3732260 3732261 3732262 3732263
3227	F13	F	ES	LY	3732270 3732271 3732272 3732273
3228	F13	F	ES	LY	3732280 3732281 3732282 3732283
3229	F14	F	ES	LY	3732290 3732291 3732292 3732293
3230	F14	F	ES	LY	3732300 3732301 3732302 3732303
3231	UK13	F	ES	LY	3732310 3732311 3732312 3732313
3232	UK13	F	ES	LY	3732320 3732321 3732322 3732323

'Regional Eurostar' Sets for services from the North of England & Scotland:

These are 7 coach sets consisting of PC + R1/3/2/5/6/7/9 only.

3301	FN1	U	PI	3733010 3733011 3733013 3733012
3302	FN1	U	PI	3733020 3733021 3733023 3733022
3303	FN2	U	PI	3733030 3733031 3733033 3733032
3304	FN2	U	PI	3733040 3733041 3733043 3733042
3305	UN1	U	PI	3733050 3733051 3733053 3733052
3306	UN1	U	PI	3733060 3733061 3733063 3733062
3307	UN2	U	PI	3733070 3733071 3733073 3733072
3308	UN2	U	PI	3733080 3733081 3733083 3733082
3309	UN3	U	PI	3733090 3733091 3733093 3733102
3310	UN3	U	PI	3733100 3733101 3733103 3733102
3311	UN4	U	PI	3733110 3733111 3733113 3733112
3312	UN4	U	PI	3733120 3733121 3733123 3733122
3313	UN5	U	PI	3733130 3733131 3733133 3733132
3314	UN5	U	PI	3733140 3733141 3733143 3733142

```
3732014 3732015 3732016 3732017 3732018 3732019
3732024 3732025 3732026 3732027 3732028 3732029
3732034 3732035 3732036 3732037 3732038 3732039
3732044 3732045 3732046 3732047 3732048 3732049
3732054 3732055 3732056 3732057 3732058 3732059
3732064 3732065 3732066 3732067 3732068 3732069
3732074 3732075 3732076 3732077 3732078 3732079
3732084 3732085 3732086 3732087 3732088 3732089
3732094 3732095 3732096 3732097 3732098 3732099
3732104 3732105 3732106 3732107 3732108 3732109
3732114 3732115 3732116 3732117 3732118 3732119
3732124 3732125 3732126 3732127 3732128 3732129
3732134 3732135 3732136 3732137 3732138 3732139
3732144 3732145 3732146 3732147 3732148 3732149
3732154 3732155 3732156 3732157 3732158 3732159
3732164 3732165 3732166 3732167 3732168 3732169
3732174 3732175 3732176 3732177 3732178 3732179
3732184 3732185 3732186 3732187 3732188 3732189
3732194 3732195 3732196 3732197 3732198 3732199
3732204 3732205 3732206 3732207 3732208 3732209
3732214 3732215 3732216 3732217 3732218 3732219
3732224 3732225 3732226 3732227 3732228 3732229
3732234 3732235 3732236 3732237 3732238 3732239
3732244 3732245 3732246 3732247 3732248 3732249
3732254 3732255 3732256 3732257 3732258 3732259
3732264 3732265 3732266 3732267 3732268 3732269
3732274 3732275 3732276 3732277 3732278 3732279
3732284 3732285 3732286 3732287 3732288 3732289
3732294 3732295 3732296 3732297 3732298 3732299
3732304 3732305 3732306 3732307 3732308 3732309
3732314 3732315 3732316 3732317 3732318 3732319
3732324 3732325 3732326 3732327 3732328 3732329
```

```
3733015 3733016 3733017 3733019
3733025 3733026 3733027 3733029
3733035 3733036 3733037 3733039
3733045 3733046 3733047 3733049
3733055 3733056 3733057 3733059
3733065 3733066 3733067 3733069
3733075 3733076 3733077 3733079
3733085 3733086 3733087 3733089
3733095 3733096 3733097 3733099
3733105 3733106 3733107 3733109
3733115 3733116 3733117 3733119
3733125 3733126 3733127 3733129
3733135 3733136 3733137 3733139
3733145 3733146 3733147 3733149
```

▲ Networks SouthEast liveried Class 302s Nos. 302 204 & 302 202 approach Shadwell shortly after departure from London Fenchurch Street with the 11.00 LTS Rail service to Shoeburyness. The date is 2nd October 1996. *Kevin Conkey*

▼ Class 303 No. 303 033 arrives at Hillingdon East on 11th August 1995 with a Glasgow Central bound ScotRail train. The unit carries Strathclyde PTE livery. *Hugh Ballantyne*

▲ A few Class 305s are based in Scotland for the North Berwick line services. One them, No. 305 502, is pictured here at North Berwick with an Edinburgh bound ScotRail service on 13th April 1996. The unit carries Regional Railways livery. *Les Nixon*

▼ West Yorkshire PTE liveried Class 308 No. 308 163 at Guiseley with a Regional Railways North East service on 5th October 1995. *G.W. Morrison*

▲ Manchester Airport Air Express liveried Class 309 No. 309 624 passes a Class 90 at Slindon, Staffordshire whilst working the 17.16 Manchester Piccadilly–Birmingham New Street North West Regional Railways service. The date is 4th September 1996.
Hugh Ballantyne

▼ The 07.29 Wolverhampton–Stoke-on-Trent Central Trains local service approaches Norton Bridge on 17th July 1996. The train is formed of Provincial Midline liveried Class 310 No. 310 108. This livery will shortly be extinct. *Hugh Ballantyne*

▲ Class 312s Nos. 312 794 & 312 785 coast through Shadwell on 2nd October 1996 with the 10.40 London Fenchurch Street–Shoeburyness LTS Rail service. *Kevin Conkey*

▼ Class 313 pioneer, No. 313 001 approaches Kensal Rise on 21st September 1995 with the 10.14 Richmond–Stratford North London Railways service. *Kevin Conkey*

▲ Overhauled Class 314 No. 314 203 'European Union' is pictured displaying revised seating at Milngavie on 16th May 1996. This unit contains a DMSO rebuilt from a Class 507 unit.   *Colin J. Marsden*

▼ Class 315 No. 315 848 at Bethnal Green on 13th June 1996 with the 10.34 London Liverpool Street–Chingford West Anglia Great Northern Railway (WAGN) service.   *Kevin Conkey*

▲ Class 317/0 No. 317 396 passes through Bethnal Green with the 09.37 London Liverpool Street–Hertford East WAGN Railway service on 13th June 1996. *Kevin Conkey*

▼ Class 318 No. 318 260 passes over Clyde Bridge with a Largs bound Scotrail train on 11th August 1996. *Hugh Ballantyne*

▲ Thameslink liveried Class 319 No. 319 049 forms the 08.57 Brighton–Bedford Thameslink service at Coulsden on 20th July 1996.
Michael J. Collins

▼ The 15.04 London Euston–Milton Keynes North London Railways service passes Leighton Buzzard on 21st April 1995, formed of Class 321/4 No. 321 423.
Hugh Ballantyne

▲ Stansted Express liveried Class 322 No. 322 483 passes through Bethnal Green on 13th June 1996 with the 11.00 London Liverpool Street–Stansted WAGN Railway service.   *Kevin Conkey*

▼ A Wilmslow to Manchester Piccadilly North West Regional Railways service, formed of Greater Manchester PTE liveried Class 323 No. 323 223, enters Manchester Airport station on 20th May 1996.
                                                                          Brian Morrison

▲ Soon after being introduced on mail services, Royal Mail liveried Class 325 postal unit No. 325 006 passes Slindon, Staffordshire with the 16.20 London Euston–Crewe on 4th September 1996.
Hugh Ballantyne

▼ Class 365s operated by Connex South Eastern are having vinyl transfers applied to cover the old Network SouthEast stripes. The makeshift livery is pictured here on 365 505 as it stands at London Victoria. *Colin J. Marsden*

▲ Class 411/5 (4 Cep) No. 1568 is pictured near Port Creek Junction on the rear of the 08.50 Portsmouth–London Waterloo South West Trains service on 28th September 1996. The unit was on short term loan from Porterbrook Train Leasing and carries a blue and white livery. *Chris Wilson*

▼ Class 421/3 (4 Cig) No. 1731 passes St Denys with the 14.17 London Victoria–Bournemouth passes St Denys with 14.17 London Victoria-Bournemouth Connex South Central service on 17th August 1996. *Nic Joynson*

▲ Class 422/0 (8 Dig) No. 2001 and Class 423/0 (4 Vep) No. 3513 pass South Croydon on 3rd June 1996 with the 11.08 London Victoria–Brighton Connex South Central 'Capital Coast Express' service.
David Brown

▼ Class 412 (4 Bep) No. 2305 pulls the 11.20 London Waterloo–Portsmouth Harbour South West Trains service away from Clapham Junction on 14th September 1996. Class 411/5 No. 1619 is at the rear. *Kevin Conkey*

▲ The 13.41 Poole–London Waterloo passes Southampton behind Stagecoach liveried Class 442 No. 2402 on 10th May 1996. This service is operated by South West Trains. *Rodney Lissenden*

▼ The 16.35 Eastleigh–Southampton South West Trains service approaches its destination on 27th April 1996. Class 423/0 (4 Vep) No. 3426 is the unit in charge. *Nic Joynson*

▲ Class 455/9 No. 5847 at Surbiton on 15th July 1996.

Colin J. Marsden

▼ Gatwick Express liveried Class 489 GLV No. 9108 passes Coulsdon with a Gatwick Airport-London Victoria service on 20th July 1996. Class 73 No. 73210 is propelling at the rear. *Michael J. Collins*

▲ Connex liveried Class 456 No. 456 024 arrives at Wandsworth Road with a London Victoria to London Bridge Connex South Central service on 4th October 1996. *Hugh Ballantyne*

▼ Class 465 Networker No. 465 238 leaves Bat & Ball on 13th June 1996 with a Connex South Eastern Sevenoaks to London Blackfriars service. *Rodney Lissenden*

▲ Class 483 No. 483 007 waits at Ryde St Johns Road with the 17.04 Ryde Pier Head–Shanklin Island Line service on 31st July 1996. *Martyn Hilbert*

▼ Merseytravel liveried Class 507 No. 507 016 pauses at Hillside with a Southport to Hunts Cross Merseyrail service. The date is 9th July 1995. *Martyn Hilbert*

North of London Eurostar set 3310/09 pass Wandsworth Road with
a North Pole to Dollands Moor crew training run on 17th July 1996.

John A. Day

4.5. SERVICE EMUs

INDIVIDUAL VEHICLES

-	T	ZA	977335	(76277)	MTA Pool Generator coach for DB999550.
930	Q	DI	RE	977364	(10400)	
930 078	Q	SA	HE	977578	(77101)	Works with Class 313/317.
930 079	Q	SA	SU	977579	(77109)	Works with Class 319.

COMPLETE UNITS

Note: Most service units do not carry '93x' numbers.

Class 930/931. Ex-Southern Region 750 V d.c. units.

Other private owner: Connex.

930 003	**N**	Q	DI	SU	975594	(12658)	975595	(10904)
930 004		Q	DI	WD	975586	(10907)	975587	(10908)
930 005		Q	DI	WD	975588	(10981)	975589	(10982)
930 006		Q	DI	WD	975590	(10833)	975591	(10834)
930 007		Q	DI	RE	975592	(10933)	975593	(12659)
930 008	**N**	Q	DI	RE	975596	(10844)	975597	(10987)
930 009		Q	DI	BI	975598	(10989)	975599	(10990)
930 010		Q	DI	SU	975600	(10988)	975601	(10843)
930 011	**RT**	Q	DI	SU	975602	(10991)	975603	(10992)
930 012		Q	DI	SU	975604	(10939)	975605	(10940)
930 013	**RT**	Q	DI	RE	975896	(11387)	975897	(11388)
930 014		Q	DI	WD	977609	(65414)	977207	(61658)
930 016		Q	DI	FR	977533	(14273)	977534	(14384)
930 017		Q	DI	BM	977566	(65312)	977567	(65314)
930 030		Q	DI	FR	977004	(65336)	977805	(65357)
930 031		Q	DI	RE	977864	(65341)	977865	(65355)
930 032		Q	DI	RE	977874	(65302)	977875	(65304)
930 033		Q	DI	RE	977871	(65353)	977872	(65367)
930 034		Q	DI	WD	977924	(65382)	977925	(65379)
930 082	**CX**	O	CR	SU	977861	(61044)	977862	(70039)
					977863	(61038)	
931 001	**N**	Q	CR	SL	977857	(65346)	977856	(77531)
931 002	**N**	U	CR	RE	977917	(65331)	977918	(77516)

Class 936/0. Merseyrail 750 V d.c. Unit.

936 003	**MD**	Q	SA	BD	977349	(61183)	977350	(75183)

Class 936/1. 25 kV a.c. Units (ex Class 311).

936 103	Q	SA	GW	977844	(76414)	977845	(62174)
				977846	(76433)	
936 104	Q	SA	GW	977847	(76415)	977848	(62175)
				977849	(76434)	

Class 937. Miscellaneous 25 kV a.c. units.

937 908	Q	SA	IL	977741	(75469)	977742 (61436)
				977743	(75521)	
937 990	Q	SA	EM	977876	(75905)	977877 (61901)
				977878	(75938)	
937 991	Q	SA	IL	977926	(75900)	977927 (61896)
				977928	(75933)	
937 998	Q	SA	IL	977604	(75077)	977605 (61062)
				977606	(75070)	

Class 316. Test Unit. Works with 1620.

316 997	T	TE	EH	977708	(75118)	977709 (61018)
				977710	(75018)	

Service numbers not carried.

CLASS 931 (Formerly 419)   1957 type MLV

DMLV. Built 1959 – 61. Dual braked. These units are now officially in service stock, but they retain their capital stock side numbers.

Electrical Equipment: 1957-type.
Bogies: Mk 3B.
Gangways: Non-gangwayed.
Traction Motors: Two EE507 of 185 kW.
Dimensions: 19.64 x 2.82 m.
Maximum Speed: 90 mph.

68001. DMLV. Dia. EX560. Lot No. 30458 Ashford/Eastleigh. 1959. 45.5 t.
68003 – 10. DMLV. Dia. EX560. Lot No. 30623 Ashford./Eastleigh. 1960 – 61. 45.5 t.

931 090	(9010)	J	P	BM	68010
931 091	(9001)	N	P	BM	68001
931 092	(9002)	N	P	BM	68002
931 093	(9003)	B	P	BM	68003
931 094	(9004)	N	P	BM	68004
931 095	(9005)	N	P	BM	68005
931 097	(9007)	N	P	BM	68007
931 098	(9008)	N	P	BM	68008
931 099	(9009)	J	P	BM	68009

4.6. EMUs AWAITING DISPOSAL

The following withdrawn EMUs are awaiting disposal with the last known storage location shown.

Former Capital Stock Units

304 003	Crewe Brook Sidings	75047	61047	75647	
304 006	Stafford Salop Sidings	75050	61050	75650	
304 008	CP	75052	61052	75652	
304 013	Stafford Salop Sidings	75057	61057	75657	
304 021	Crewe Carriage Shed	75685	61633	75665	
304 024	Crewe Brook Sidings	75688	61636	75668	
304 027	Crewe Carriage Shed	75691	61639	75671	
304 029	Crewe Carriage Shed	75693	61641	75673	
304 030	Crewe Carriage Shed	75694	61642	75674	
305 403	LG	75506	61473	75558	
306 017	IL	65217	65417	65617	
308 142	NL	75929	61892	75896	
4308	Long Marston	61275	75395		
4311	Long Marston	61287	75407		
4732	Long Marston	12795	10239	12354	12796
5001	Long Marston	14001	15207	15101	14002
5176	Long Marston	14352	15396	15354	14351
6213	Long Marston	65327	77512		
6259	Long Marston	65373	77558		
6307	Long Marston	14573	16117		
6308	Long Marston	14564	16108		
6309	Long Marston	14562	16106		
6402	Long Marston	65362	77547		
7001	ZG	67300	67401	67301	

Former Service Stock Vehicles

975032	(75165)	SH	977506	(65323)	SH
977296	(65319)	SH	977598	(75080)	IL
977304	(65317)	WD	977599	(61073)	IL
977305	(65322)	WD	977600	(75061)	IL
977345	(61180)	BD	977639	(75548)	Southall ECD
977347	(61178)	BD	977640	(61463)	Southall ECD
977385	(61148)	SH	977641	(75214)	Southall ECD

Loose Cars

61224	IL	70003	OM	75026	OM
61433	LG	70008	OM	75030	OM
70612	Crewe Brook Sdgs	70010	OM	75003	Kineton
70621	Crewe Brook Sdgs	70011	OM	75015	Kineton
70622	Crewe Brook Sdgs	75002	OM	75019	Kineton
70631	Crewe Brook Sdgs	75020	OM	75023	Kineton
70640	Crewe Brook Sdgs	75025	OM	75773	Yoker

5. NON-PASSENGER-CARRYING COACHING STOCK

The notes shown for locomotive-hauled passenger stock generally apply also to non-passenger-carrying coaching stock (often abbreviated to NPCCS).

TOPS CODES

TOPS codes for NPCCS are made up as follows:

(1) Two letters denoting the type of the vehicle:

NA Propelling control vehicle.
NB High security gangwayed brake van (100 mph).
NC Gangwayed brake van modified for newspaper conveyance (100 mph).
ND Gangwayed brake van (90 mph).
NE Gangwayed brake van (100 mph).
NF Gangwayed brake van with guard's safety equipment removed.
NG Motorail loading wagon.
NH Gangwayed brake van (110 mph).
NJ General utility van (90 mph).
NK High Security general utility van (100 mph).
NL Newspaper van.
NN Courier vehicle.
NO General utility van (100 mph e.t.h. wired).
NP General utility van for Post Office use or Motorail van (110 mph).
NR BAA Container van (100 mph).
NS Post office sorting van.
NT Post office stowage van.
NU Brake post office stowage van.
NX Motorail van (100 mph).
NY Exhibition van.
NZ Driving brake van (also known as driving van trailer).

A third letter denoting the brake type:

A   Air braked
V   Vacuum braked
X   Dual braked

OPERATOR CODES

The normal operator codes are given in brackets after the TOPS codes. These are as follows:

BG   Gangwayed brake van.
BPOT   Brake post office stowage van.
DLV   Driving brake van (also known as driving van trailer – DVT).
GUV   General utility van.
POS   Post office sorting van.
POT   Post office stowage van.

AK51 (RK)   KITCHEN CAR

Dia. AK503. Mark 1. Gas cooking. Converted from RBR. Fluorescent lighting.
d. Commonwealth bogies. ETH 2X.

Note: Kitchen cars have traditionally been numbered in the NPCCS series, but
have passenger coach diagram numbers!

Lot No. 30628 Pressed Steel 1960 – 61. 39 t.

| 80041 | (1690) | I | M | SS | BN |

NN   COURIER VEHICLE

Dia. NN504. Converted 1986 – 7 from Mark 1 BSKs. One compartment retained for courier use. Roller shutter doors. ETH 2.
Non-Standard Liveries: 80211 is purple and 80220 is GWR plain brown.

80207. Lot No. 30721 Wolverton 1963. Commonwealth bogies. 37 t.
80211 – 7/235. Lot No. 30699 Wolverton 1962. Commonwealth bogies. 37 t.
80220. Lot No. 30573 Gloucester 1960. B4 bogies. 33 t.

80207	(35466)	x	PC	V	SS	SL
80211	(35296)	a	0	M	SS	BN
80212	(35307)	x	RM	W		OM
80213	(35316)	x	CH	R	SS	CO
80214	(35323)	x	RY	X		Ferme Park
80216	(35295)	x	RM	W		OM
80217	(35299)	x	M	O	LS	GT
80220	(35276)	x	0	O	LS	RO
80223	(35331)	x	RY	X		DY
80225	(35327)	x		O		SO

NP   POST OFFICE GUV

Dia. NP502. Converted 1991 – 93 from newspaper vans. Mark 1. Short frames
(57'). Originally converted from GUV. Fluorescent lighting, toilets and gangways
fitted. Load 14 t. ETH 3X. B5 bogies.

Lot No. 30922 Wolverton or Doncaster 1977 – 8. 31 t.

80250	(86838, 94008)	a	RM	W		BK
80251	(86467, 94017)	x	RM	W		OM
80252	(86718, 94022)	a	RM	W		OM
80253	(86170, 94018)	a	RM	W		OM
80254	(86082, 94012)	x	RM	W		OM
80255	(86098, 94019)	x	RM	W		OM
80256	(86408, 94013)	x	RM	W		OM
80257	(86221, 94023)	x	RM	W		OM
80258	(86651, 94002)	a	RM	W		OM
80259	(86845, 94005)	x	RM	W		OM

NS (POS)   POST OFFICE SORTING VAN

Used in travelling post office (TPO) trains. Mark 1. Various diagrams.

The following lots are v and have Mark 1 bogies except * − B5 bogies. x. (subtract 2 t from weight).

80300 − 80305. Lot No. 30486 Wolverton 1959. Dia. NS501. Originally built with nets for collecting mail bags in motion. Equipment now removed. ETH 3X. 36 t.
80306 − 80308. Lot No. 30487 Wolverton 1959. Dia. NS502. ETH 3. 36 t.
80309 − 80314. Lot No. 30661 Wolverton 1961. Dia. NS501. ETH 3. 37 t.
80315 − 80316. Lot No. 30662 Wolverton 1961. Dia. NS501. ETH 3X. 36 t.

80300	**RM** W		DY	80310	**RM** W		OM
80301	**RM** W		DY	80312	**RM** W		OM
80303 *	**RM** W		OM	80313	**RM** W		ZH
80305	**RM** W		OM	80314 *	**RM** W		OM
80306	**RM** W		OM	80315	**RM** W		OM
80308 *	**RM** W		OM	80316 *	**RM** W		OM
80309 *	**RM** W		OM				

The following lots are pressure ventilated and have B5 bogies.

80319 − 80327. Dia. NS504. Lot No. 30778 York 1968 − 9. ETH 4. 35 t.
80328 − 80338. Dia. NS505. Lot No. 30779 York 1968 − 9. ETH 4. 35 t.
80339 − 80355. Dia. NS506. Lot No. 30780 York 1968 − 9. ETH 4. 35 t.

80319 x	**RM** W	EW	EN	80338 x	**RM** W	EW	BK
80320 a	**RM** W	EW	NC	80339 a	**RM** W	EW	EN
80321 a	**RM** W	EW	BK	80340 a	**RM** W	EW	BK
80322 a	**RM** W	EW	EN	80341 a	**RM** W	EW	EN
80323 x	**RM** W		CF	80342 x	**RM** W	EW	BK
80324 a	**RM** W	EW	EN	80343 a	**RM** W	EW	BK
80325 a	**RM** W	EW	EN	80344 a	**RM** W	EW	NC
80326 a	**RM** W	EW	NC	80345 a	**RM** W	EW	BK
80327 a	**RM** W	EW	BK	80346 a	**RM** W	EW	EN
80328 x	**RM** W	EW	EN	80347 x	**RM** W	EW	EN
80329 a	**RM** W	EW	NC	80348 x	**RM** W	EW	BK
80330 a	**RM** W	EW	EN	80349 a	**RM** W	EW	EN
80331 a	**RM** W	EW	NC	80350 x	**RM** W	EW	BK
80332 a	**RM** W	EW	EN	80351 x	**RM** W	EW	PZ
80333 a	**RM** W	EW	EN	80352 x	**RM** W	EW	BK
80334 x	**RM** W	EW	BK	80353 x	**RM** W	EW	EN
80335 x	**RM** W	EW	EN	80354 a	**RM** W	EW	BK
80336 x	**RM** W	EW	BK	80355 a	**RM** W	EW	EN
80337 a	**RM** W	EW	BK				

Names:

80320	The Borders Mail
80327	George James

80356 – 80380. Lot No. 30839 York 1972 – 3. Dia. NS501. Pressure ventilated. Fluorescent lighting. B5 bogies. ETH 4X. 37 t.

80356	a	RM	W	EW	EN	80369	a	RM	W	EW	EN
80357	x	RM	W	EW	BK	80370	a	RM	W	EW	EN
80358	a	RM	W	EW	NC	80371	a	RM	W	EW	PZ
80359	a	RM	W	EW	BK	80372	a	RM	W	EW	EN
80360	a	RM	W	EW	NC	80373	a	RM	W	EW	EN
80361	a	RM	W	EW	EN	80374	a	RM	W	EW	EN
80362	x	RM	W	EW	EN	80375	a	RM	W	EW	BK
80363	a	RM	W	EW	BK	80376	a	RM	W	EW	BK
80364	x	RM	W	EW	EN	80377	a	RM	W	EW	EN
80365	a	RM	W	EW	EN	80378	a	RM	W	EW	EN
80366	a	RM	W	EW	EN	80379	a	RM	W	EW	EN
80367	a	RM	W	EW	BK	80380	a	RM	W	EW	PZ
80368	a	RM	W	EW	EN						

Names:

80360	Derek Carter	80380	Ernie Gosling
80367	M.G. Berry		

80381 – 80395. Lot No. 30900 Wolverton 1977. Dia NS531. Converted from SK. Pressure ventilated. Fluorescent lighting. B5 bogies. ETH 4X. 38 t.

80381	(25112)	a	RM	W	EW	EN	80389	(25103)	a	RM	W		ZG
80382	(25109)	a	RM	W	EW	EN	80390	(25047)	a	RM	W	EW	EN
80383	(25033)	a	RM	W	EW	BK	80392	(25082)	a	RM	W	EW	EN
80384	(25078)	a	RM	W	EW	NC	80393	(25118)	a	RM	W	EW	EN
80385	(25083)	a	RM	W	EW	EN	80394	(25156)	a	RM	W	EW	NC
80386	(25099)	a	RM	W	EW	EN	80395	(25056)	x	RM	W	EW	EN
80387	(25045)	x	RM	W	EW	EN							

NT (POT)   POST OFFICE STOWAGE VAN

Mark 1. Open vans used for stowage of mail bags in conjunction with POS. Various diagrams.

Lot No. 30488 Wolverton 1959. Dia. NT502. Originally built with nets for collecting mail bags in motion. Equipment now removed. B5 bogies. ETH 3. 35 t.

80400	a	RM	W	EW	BK	80402	x	RM	W	EW	BK
80401	a	RM	W	EW	EN						

The following eight vehicles were converted at York from BSK to lot 30143 (80403) and 30229 (80404 – 80414). No new lot number was issued. Dia. NT503. B5 bogies. 35 t. (*dia. NT501 BR2 bogies 38 t. ETH 3 (3X*).

80403	(34361)	a	RM	W	EW	NC	80411	(35003)	x *RM	W	EW	EN
80404	(35014)	a	RM	W	EW	NC	80412	(35002)	a *RM	W	EW	EN
80405	(35009)	x	RM	W	EW	EN	80413	(35004)	x *RM	W	EW	NC
80406	(35022)	a	RM	W	EW	EN	80414	(35005)	x *RM	W	EW	EN

Lot No. 30781 York 1968. Dia. NT505. Pressure ventilated. B5 bogies. ETH 4. 34 t.

```
80415 a RM W EW    EN        80421 a RM W EW    BK
80416 x RM W EW    EN        80422 a RM W EW    EN
80417 a RM W EW    EN        80423 a RM W EW    EN
80419 x RM W EW    BK        80424 x RM W EW    EN
80420 x RM W EW    BK
```

Lot No. 30840 York 1973. Dia. NT504. Pressure ventilated. fluorescent lighting.
B5 bogies. ETH 4X. 35 t.

```
80425 a RM W EW    BK        80428 a RM W EW    EN
80426 a RM W EW    EN        80429 a RM W EW    BK
80427 x RM W EW    EN        80430 a RM W EW    EN
```

Lot No. 30901 Wolverton 1977. converted from SK. Dia. NT521. Pressure ventilated. Fluorescent lighting. B5 bogies. ETH 4X. 35 t.

```
80431 (25104) x RM W EW    PZ    80436 (25077) x RM W EW    EN
80432 (25071) x RM W EW    BK    80437 (25068) a RM W EW    EN
80433 (25150) a RM W EW    BK    80438 (25139) x RM W EW    PZ
80434 (25119) a RM W EW    EN    80439 (25127) x RM W EW    EN
80435 (25117) a RM W EW    BK
```

NU (BPOT)   BRAKE POST OFFICE STOWAGE VAN

As NT but with brake. Mark 1.

Lot No. 30782 York 1968. Dia. NU502. Pressure ventilated. B5 bogies. ETH 4.
36 t.

```
80456 a RM W EW    EN        80458 x RM W EW    EN
80457 a RM W EW    EN
```

NZ (DLV)   DRIVING BRAKE VAN (110 mph)

Dia. NZ501. Mark 3B. Air conditioned. T4 bogies. a. dg. Cab to shore communication. ETH 5X.

Lot No. 31042 Derby 1988. 45.18 t.

```
82101  I  P  WC  PC        82117  I  P  WC  PC
82102  I  P  WC  OY        82118  I  P  WC  OY
82103  I  P  WC  OY        82119  I  P  WC  MA
82104  I  P  WC  PC        82120  I  P  WC  MA
82105  I  P  WC  MA        82121  I  P  WC  MA
82106  I  P  WC  OY        82122  I  P  WC  OY
82107  I  P  WC  PC        82123  I  P  WC  MA
82108  I  P  WC  MA        82124  I  P  WC  PC
82109  I  P  WC  MA        82125  I  P  WC  OY
82110  I  P  WC  PC        82126  I  P  WC  PC
82111  I  P  WC  PC        82127  I  P  WC  PC
82112  I  P  WC  MA        82128  I  P  WC  OY
82113  I  P  WC  OY        82129  I  P  WC  OY
82114  I  P  WC  PC        82130  I  P  WC  MA
82115  I  P  WC  PC        82131  I  P  WC  PC
82116  I  P  WC  MA        82132  I  P  WC  OY
```

82133	I	P	WC	OY		82143	I	P	WC	OY
82134	I	P	WC	PC		82144	I	P	WC	OY
82135	I	P	WC	PC		82145	I	P	WC	OY
82136	I	P	WC	MA		82146	I	P	WC	PC
82137	I	P	WC	PC		82147	I	P	WC	MA
82138	I	P	WC	PC		82148	I	P	WC	OY
82139	I	P	WC	MA		82149	I	P	WC	MA
82140	I	P	WC	PC		82150	I	P	WC	MA
82141	I	P	WC	MA		82151	I	P	WC	OY
82142	I	P	WC	PC		82152	I	P	WC	OY

Names::

82101	Wembley InterCity Depot
82115	Liverpool John Moores University
82120	Liverpool Chamber of Commerce
82132	West Midlands
82134	Sir Henry Doulton 1820 – 1897
82135	Spirit of Cumbria
82148	International Spring Fair

NZ (DLV)   DRIVING BRAKE VAN (140 mph)

Dia. NZ502. Mark 4. Air conditioned. Swiss-built (SIG) bogies. a. dg. Cab to shore communication. ETH 6X.

Lot No. 31043 Metro-Cammell 1988. 45.18 t.

82200	I	E	GN	BN		82216	I	E	GN	BN
82201	I	E	GN	BN		82217	I	E	GN	BN
82202	I	E	GN	BN		82218	I	E	GN	BN
82203	I	E	GN	BN		82219	I	E	GN	BN
82204	I	E	GN	BN		82220	I	E	GN	BN
82205	I	E	GN	BN		82221	GN	E	GN	BN
82206	I	E	GN	BN		82222	I	E	GN	BN
82207	GN	E	GN	BN		82223	I	E	GN	BN
82208	I	E	GN	BN		82224	I	E	GN	BN
82209	I	E	GN	BN		82225	I	E	GN	BN
82210	I	E	GN	BN		82226	GN	E	GN	BN
82211	I	E	GN	BN		82227	GN	E	GN	BN
82212	I	E	GN	BN		82228	GN	E	GN	BN
82213	I	E	GN	BN		82229	I	E	GN	BN
82214	I	E	GN	BN		82230	I	E	GN	BN
82215	I	E	GN	BN		82231	I	E	GN	BN

ND (BG)   GANGWAYED BRAKE VAN (90 mph)

Dia. ND501. These vans are built on short frames (57'). Load 10t. BR1 bogies. v. ETH 1. The full lot number list is listed here for reference purposes with renumbered vehicles.

b – (Dia. NB501). High security brake van. Converted at WB from ND 1985. Gangways removed. x. B4 bogies. Now used for movement of materials between EWS maintenance depots.

80525. Lot No. 30009 Derby 1952 – 3. 31 t.
80561. Lot No. 30039 Derby 1954. 31 t.
80620 – 80621. Lot No. 30046 York 1954. 31.5 t.
80700 – 80703. Lot No. 30136 Metro-Cammell 1955. 31.5 t.
80731 – 80791. Lot No. 30140 BRCW 1955 – 6. 31.5 t.
80805 – 80848. Lot No. 30144 Cravens 1955. 31.5 t.
80855 – 80962. Lot No. 30162 Pressed Steel 1956 – 7. 32 t.
80971 – 81014. Lot No. 30173 York 1956. 31.5 t.
81019 – 81051. Lot No. 30224 Cravens 1956. 31.5 t.
81055 – 81179. Lot No. 30228 Metro-Cammell 1957 – 8. 31.5 t.
81182 – 81200. Lot No. 30234 Cravens 1956 – 7. 31.5 t.
81205 – 81265. Lot No. 30163 Pressed Steel 1957. 31.5 t.
81266 – 81309. Lot No. 30323 Pressed Steel 1957. 32 t.
81313 – 81497. Lot No. 30400 Pressed Steel 1957 – 8. 32 t.
81498 – 81568. Lot No. 30484 Pressed Steel 1958. 32 t.
81588 – 81590. Lot No. 30715 Gloucester 1962. 31 t.
81598 – 81610. Lot No. 30716 Gloucester 1962. 31 t.

Note: All 84xxx vehicles were renumbered from the 81xxx series by adding 3000 to the original number.

84025	**M** D		Heysham	84387 b **B**	W EW BK
84197	W EW	BK		84477 b **B**	W EW BK
84382 b **RX**	W EW	BK			

84197 is kept at Shrewsbury Road Sidings, Sheffield for use when the station lifts are out of order.

NJ (GUV)   GENERAL UTILITY VAN

Mark 1. NJ501. Short frames. Load 14 t. Screw couplings. Dia. NJ501. All vehicles were built with BR Mark 2 bogies. ETH 0 or OX*. These vehicles had 7000 added to the original numbers to avoid confusion with Class 86. The full lot number list is listed here for reference purposes with renumbered vehicles. No unmodified vehicles remain in service.

86081 – 86499. Lot No. 30417 Pressed Steel 1958 – 9. 30 t.
86508 – 86518. Lot No. 30343 York 1957. 30 t.
86521 – 86651. Lot No. 30403 York/Glasgow 1958 – 60. 30 t.
86656 – 86834. Lot No. 30565 Pressed Steel 1959. 30 t.
86836 – 86980. Lot No. 30616 Pressed Steel 1959 – 60. 30 t.

NE/NH (BG) 100/110 mph GANGWAYED BRAKE VAN

As ND but rebogied with B4 bogies suitable for 100 mph – NE (110 mph with special maintenance – NH). ETH 1 (1X* and NHA). For lot numbers refer to original number series. Deduct 1.5t from weights. All NHA are a*pg.

92100 (81391)	a to **I**	X			Ferme Park
92111 (81432)	NHA **I**	E			Long Marston
92112 (81440)	x **RY**	W			BK
92114 (81443)	NHA **I**	E			Longtown
92116 (81450)	a to **O**	M	SS		BN

92121 (81457)	a*	**RX**	W		CF
92122 (81459)	x*to	**RY**	W		Carlisle Yard
92125 (81470)	a to l		A		OY
92146 (81498)	NHA I		E		Longtown
92155 (81525)	a*pg l		A	AT	LA
92159 (81534)	NHA I		E	SR	IS
92174 (81567)	NHA I		E	SR	IS
92175 (81568)	a pg l		E	GW	LA
92188 (81598)	a to		A	AT	LA
92193 (81604)	a pg l		W	EW	EN
92194 (81606)	a to l		E	GW	LA
92197 (81610)	a to l		A	AT	LA
92211 (81267)	a*	**R**	W		Carlisle Yard
92229 (80902)	a*	**R**	W		Carlisle Yard
92234 (81336, 84336)	a*	**RX**	W		DY
92238 (81563, 84563)	a	**RY**	W		DY
92243 (81489, 84489)	a*	**RY**	W		Carlisle Yard
92252 (80959)	x*	**RY**	W		Crewe South Yard
92258 (81346, 84346)	a	**RY**	W		Carlisle Yard
92259 (81313, 84313)	x	**RY**	W		Carlisle Yard
92261 (80988)	x*	**RY**	W		Carlisle Yard
92265 (80945)	x	**RY**	W		Carlisle Yard
92267 (81404, 84404)	x		W		Crewe South Yard
92271 (80962)	x*	**R**	W		OM

92193 is kept at Preston station.

NE (BG)   100 mph GANGWAYED BRAKE VAN

As ND but rebogied with Commonwealth bogies suitable for 100 mph. ETH 1 (1X*). For lot numbers refer to original number series. Add 1.5 t to weights to allow for the increased weight of the Commonwealth bogies.

92302 (81501, 84501)	a	**RX**	W	Carlisle Yard
92303 (81427, 84427)	a	**RX**	W	DY
92306 (81217, 84217)	a*	**RY**	W	Carlisle Yard
92307 (80805)	a*		W	Carlisle Yard
92309 (81043, 84043)	x*	**RX**	W	Carlisle Yard
92311 (81453, 84453)	x	**RY**	W	Crewe South Yard
92312 (81548, 84548)	a	**RX**	W	Carlisle Yard
92314 (80777)	x*	**RY**	W	Crewe South Yard
92316 (80980)	x*	**RY**	W	Carlisle Yard
92319 (81055, 84055)	a*	**RY**	W	Carlisle Yard
92321 (81566, 84566)	a	**RY**	W	BN
92323 (80832)	a*	**R**	W	Carlisle Yard
92324 (81087, 84087)	a	**RY**	W	Carlisle Yard
92325 (80791)	a	**RY**	W	Carlisle Yard
92328 (80999)	x*	**RY**	W	Carlisle Yard
92329 (81001, 84001)	a*	**RY**	W	Carlisle Yard
92330 (80995)	x*	**RY**	W	Carlisle Yard
92332 (80845)	a*	**RX**	W	Carlisle Yard
92333 (80982)	a*	**RY**	W	Carlisle Yard

92334 (80983)	x*	R	W		BK
92337 (81140, 84140)	a*	RX	W		Carlisle Yard
92340 (81059, 84059)	a*	RY	W		Carlisle Yard
92341 (81316, 84316)	x	RY	W		Carlisle Yard
92343 (81505, 84505)	x	R	W		Carlisle Yard
92344 (81154, 84154)	a*	RY	W		Carlisle Yard
92345 (81083, 84083)	x*	RY	W		Carlisle Yard
92346 (81091, 84091)	a	RY	W		Carlisle Yard
92347 (81326, 84326)	a	RX	W		DY
92348 (81075, 84075)	x*	RY	W		Carlisle Yard
92350 (81049, 84049)	a*	RY	W		DY
92351 (81174, 84174)	x	RX	Q	SD	PZ
92353 (81323, 84323)	a	R	W		Carlisle Yard
92355 (81517, 84517)	x	RX	W		DY
92356 (81535, 84535)	x		W		Carlisle Yard
92357 (81136, 84136)	a	RX	W		Carlisle Yard
92362 (81188, 84188)	x	RY	W		Carlisle Yard
92363 (81294, 84294)	x	RY	W		Crewe South Yard
92364 (81030, 84030)	x*	R	W		Carlisle Yard
92365 (81122, 84122)	a	RX	W		Carlisle Yard
92366 (81551, 84551)	a	RX	W		Carlisle Yard
92369 (80960)	x*		W	EW	BK
92370 (81324, 84324)	a	RX	W		Carlisle Yard
92377 (80928)	a*	RX	W		DY
92379 (80914)	a*	RX	W		Carlisle Yard
92380 (81247, 84247)	a*	R	W		Carlisle Yard
92381 (81476, 84476)	a	RX	W		Carlisle Yard
92382 (81561, 84561)	a	RX	W		DY
92384 (80893)	a	RY	W		Crewe South Yard
92385 (81261, 84261)	x*	RY	W		Carlisle Yard
92387 (81380, 84380)	x		W		BK
92389 (81026, 84026)	a*	RY	W		Carlisle Yard
92390 (80834)	a*		W		Carlisle Yard
92392 (80861)	a*	RY	W		Carlisle Yard
92395 (81274, 84274)	a		W		Carlisle Yard
92398 (80859)	x*	RY	W		Carlisle Yard
92399 (80781)	x*	RY	W		BK
92400 (81211, 84211)	a*		W		Crewe South Yard
92401 (81280, 84280)	x	RX	W		Carlisle Yard
92402 (81099, 84099)	a*	RY	W		Carlisle Yard
92403 (81273, 84273)	x	RY	W	EW	EN
92404 (81051, 84051)	x		W		Carlisle Yard
92406 (81475, 84475)	x	RY	Q	SD	PZ
92409 (81370, 84370)	x		W		OM
92410 (81469, 84469)	x		W		Crewe South Yard
92411 (81252, 84252)	x	RY	W	EW	PZ
92412 (81354, 84354)	a*	RY	W	EW	PZ
92413 (81472, 84472)	x	RY	W	EW	PZ
92414 (81458, 84458)	x		W		OM
92415 (81388, 84388)	a	RX	W		Carlisle Yard
92416 (81250, 84250)	a*	RY	W		Carlisle Yard

92417 (80885)	a*	**RX**	W		Carlisle Yard
92418 (81512, 84512)	a*	**RX**	W		Crewe South Yard

92369 is kept at Doncaster station for use when the lifts are out of order.
92403 is kept at Euston Downside CARMD for rubbish disposal.

NF (BG)   100/110 mph GANGWAYED BRAKE VAN

As NE but with emergency equipment removed. For details and lot numbers refer to original number series. 92503 – 92755 have B4 bogies whilst 92800 – 92897 have Commonwealth bogies

b – (Dia. NB501). High security brake van. Converted at WB from ND 1985. Gangways removed. Now used for movement of materials between EWS maintenance depots.

92503 (80864, 92903)	x	**RY**	W		Carlisle Yard
92505 (80876, 92905)	x	**I**	W		Carlisle Yard
92509 (80897, 92909)	a	**RX**	W		Carlisle Yard
92510 (80900, 92910)	x	**RX**	W		Carlisle Yard
92513 (80916, 92913)	x	**RX**	W		Carlisle Yard
92518 (80941, 92918)	x	**RX**	W		Crewe South Yard
92521 (80956, 92921)	x	**I**	W		OM
92530 (81461, 84461)	xb	**RX**	W	EW	BK
92542 (81207, 92942)	a	**RX**	W		Carlisle Yard
92547 (81216, 92947)	a	**RX**	W		Carlisle Yard
92550 (81220, 92950)	a	**RX**	W		Carlisle Yard
92555 (81225, 92955)	a	**RX**	W		Carlisle Yard
92558 (81228, 92958)	a	**RX**	W		Carlisle Yard
92562 (81232, 92962)	a	**RX**	W	EW	EN
92566 (81238, 92966)	a		W		BK
92568 (81244, 92968)	a	**RX**	W		Crewe South Yard
92576 (81257, 92976)	a	**RX**	W		Crewe South Yard
92577 (81258, 92977)	a		W		Carlisle Yard
92582 (81265, 92982)	a	**RY**	W	EW	EN
92607 (81410, 92107)	x	**RX**	W	EW	EN
92617 (81451, 92117)	x	**RY**	W		Carlisle Yard
92649 (81509, 92149)	x		W		Carlisle Yard
92650 (81514, 92150)	a to	**RY**	W		Carlisle Yard
92709 (80873, 92209)	x	**RX**	W		Carlisle Yard
92714 (81504, 92214)	a	**RX**	W		Carlisle Yard
92716 (81376, 92216)	x	**RY**	W		Carlisle Yard
92717 (80877, 92217)	x	**RY**	W		Carlisle Yard
92718 (81314, 92218)	x	**RY**	W		Carlisle Yard
92720 (80924, 92220)	x	**RY**	W		Carlisle Yard
92721 (80888, 92221)	x	**RY**	W		BK
92722 (80887, 92222)	x	**RX**	W		BK
92725 (80891, 92225)	a	**RX**	W		Carlisle Yard
92728 (80921, 92228)	x	**RX**	W		Crewe South Yard
92740 (80703, 92240)	x	**RY**	W		Crewe South Yard
92748 (80935, 92248)	a	**RX**	W	EW	EN
92750 (81235, 92250)	x	**RX**	W		Crewe South Yard

92753 (80936, 92253)	x	**RY**	W		Crewe South Yard
92755 (80871, 92255)	x	**RX**	W		Carlisle Yard
92800 (81200, 92300)	x	**RX**	Q	SD	PZ
92804 (81339, 92304)	x	**RX**	W		Carlisle Yard
92805 (81590, 92305)	x	**RX**	W		Carlisle Yard
92808 (80784, 92308)	x	**RX**	W		BK
92810 (81105, 92310)	a	**RX**	W		Carlisle Yard
92815 (80848, 92315)	a*	**RX**	W		Carlisle Yard
92817 (80836, 92317)	x	**RX**	W		Carlisle Yard
92820 (81166, 92320)	x		Q	SD	PZ
92822 (80771, 92322)	x	**RX**	W		Carlisle Yard
92827 (80842, 92327)	x	**RX**	W		Carlisle Yard
92831 (81365, 92331)	x	**RX**	W		Carlisle Yard
92842 (81397, 92342)	x	**RY**	W		Carlisle Yard
92852 (81182, 92352)	a*	**RX**	W		DY
92854 (81353, 92354)	x	**RX**	W		Carlisle Yard
92858 (84393, 92358)	x	**RX**	W		BK
92859 (81275, 92359)	a*	**RX**	W		DY
92860 (81431, 92360)	x	**RX**	W		BK
92861 (81463, 92361)	a	**R**	W		Carlisle Yard
92867 (81293, 92367)	x	**RX**	W		Carlisle Yard
92872 (81362, 92372)	x	**RY**	W		MA
92873 (81528, 92373)	a	**RX**	W		Carlisle Yard
92876 (81374, 92376)	a*	**RX**	W		Carlisle Yard
92883 (81429, 92383)	a*	**RX**	W		BK
92886 (80843, 92386)	x	**RX**	W		Carlisle Yard
92888 (80868, 92388)	a*	**RX**	W	EW	EN
92893 (80701, 92393)	x	**RX**	W		BK
92894 (81322, 92394)	x	**RX**	W		BK
92897 (80700, 92397)	x*	**RY**	W		Carlisle Yard

NE/NH (BG)   100/110 mph **GANGWAYED BRAKE VAN**

Renumbered from 920xx series by adding 900 to number to avoid conflict with Class 92 locos. Class continued from 92271.

92901 (80855, 92001)	NHA	**I**	E	SR	IS
92904 (80867, 92004)	a*pg	**G**	V	SS	SL
92907 (80880, 92007)	a*pg	**RX**	W		Carlisle Yard
92908 (80895, 92008)	NHA	**I**	E	SR	IS
92910 (80930, 92010)	a*pg	**I**	E		Long Marston
92916 (80930, 92016)	x*pg	**RY**	W		Carlisle Yard
92917 (80940, 92017)	a*to	**RX**	W		Carlisle Yard
92919 (80944, 92019)	a*pg	**I**	W		BK
92920 (80950, 92020)	x*pg	**I**	Q	SD	PZ
92922 (80958, 92022)	x*pg	**RX**	W		BK
92923 (80971, 92023)	a*pg	**I**	E		Longtown
92926 (81060, 92026)	NHA	**I**	E		Longtown
92927 (81061, 92027)	NHA	**I**	E		Longtown
92928 (81064, 92028)	NHA	**I**	E		Longtown
92929 (81077, 92029)	NHA	**I**	E		Long Marston

92931 (81102, 92031)	NHA	I	E	SR	IS
92932 (81117, 92032)	NHA	I	E	SR	IS
92933 (81123, 92033)	NHA	I	E		Long Marston
92934 (81142, 92034)	NHA	I	E		Longtown
92935 (81150, 92035)	a*pg	I	E	SR	IS
92936 (81158, 92036)	NHA	I	E	SR	IS
92937 (81165, 92037)	NHA	I	E	SR	IS
92938 (81173, 92038)	NHA	I	E	SR	IS
92939 (81175, 92039)	NHA	I	E		Long Marston
92940 (81186, 92040)	a pg	I	E	GW	LA
92946 (81214, 92046)	NHA	I	E	SR	IS
92948 (81218, 92048)	NHA	I	E	SR	IS
92957 (81227, 92057)	a to	I	X		Ferme Park
92961 (81231, 92061)	a	I	E		Longtown
92972 (81253, 92072)	a to	I	Q	SD	PZ
92986 (81282, 92086)	a to	I	E		CP
92988 (81284, 92088)	a to	I	E		Longtown
92989 (81303, 92089)	a to	I	A	AT	LA
92991 (81308, 92091)	a to	I	E		Longtown
92998 (81381, 92098)	NHA	I	E		Longtown

NL   NEWSPAPER VAN

Dia. NL501. Mark 1. Short frames (57'). Converted from NJ (GUV). Fluorescent lighting, toilets and gangways fitted. Load 14 t. ETH 3X. Not now used for News traffic. B5 bogies.

Lot No. 30922 Wolverton or Doncaster 1977 – 8. 31 t.

94003 (86281, 93999)	x	RX	W	OM
94004 (86156, 85504)	a	RY	W	OM
94006 (86202, 85506)	a	RX	W	OM
94007 (86572, 85507)	a	B	W	OM
94009 (86144, 85509)	a	RY	W	OM
94010 (86151, 85510)	x	RX	W	OM
94011 (86437, 85511)	a	RX	W	OM
94015 (86484, 85515)	x	B	W	BK
94016 (86317, 85516)	x	RY	W	OM
94020 (86220, 85520)	x	RY	W	OM
94021 (86204, 85521)	x	B	W	OM
94024 (86106, 85524)	a	B	W	OM
94025 (86377, 85525)	a	RY	W	OM
94026 (86703, 85526)	x	RY	W	OM
94027 (86732, 85527)	a	R	W	Ferme Park
94028 (86733, 85528)	x	RX	W	OM
94029 (86740, 85529)	x	RY	W	OM
94030 (86746, 85530)	x	B	W	OM
94031 (86747, 85531)	x	B	W	BK
94032 (86730, 85532)	a	RX	W	OM
94033 (86731, 85533)	x	RY	W	BK

NKA   HIGH SECURITY GENERAL UTILITY VAN

Dia. NK501. ay. ETH 0X. Commonwealth bogies. For lot Nos. see original number series. Add 2 t to weight. These vehicles are GUVs further modified with new floors, three roller shutter doors per side and the end doors removed.

94100 (86668, 95100)	RX	W	EW	EN
94101 (86142, 95101)	RX	W	EW	BK
94102 (86762, 95102)	RX	W	EW	BK
94103 (86956, 95103)	RX	W	EW	BK
94104 (86942, 95104)	RX	W	EW	BK
94106 (86353, 95106)	RX	W	EW	BK
94107 (86576, 95107)	RX	W	EW	EN
94108 (86600, 95108)	RX	W	EW	BK
94110 (86393, 95110)	RX	W	EW	EN
94111 (86578, 95111)	RX	W	EW	EN
94112 (86673, 95112)	RX	W	EW	EN
94113 (86235, 95113)	RX	W	EW	BK
94114 (86081, 95114)	RX	W	EW	BK
94116 (86426, 95116)	RX	W	EW	BK
94117 (86534, 95117)	RX	W	EW	BK
94118 (86675, 95118)	RX	W	EW	EN
94119 (86167, 95119)	RX	W	EW	EN
94121 (86518, 95121)	RX	W	EW	BK
94123 (86376, 95123)	RX	W	EW	BK
94126 (86692, 95126)	RX	W	EW	EN
94132 (86607, 95132)	RX	W	EW	BK
94133 (86604, 95133)	RX	W	EW	EN
94137 (86610, 95137)	RX	W	EW	EN
94138 (86212, 95138)	RX	W	EW	BK
94140 (86571, 95140)	RX	W	EW	BK
94146 (86648, 95146)	RX	W	EW	EN
94147 (86091, 95147)	RX	W	EW	BK
94148 (86416, 95148)	RX	W	EW	BK
94150 (86560, 95150)	RX	W	EW	BK
94153 (86798, 95153)	RX	W	EW	EN
94155 (86520, 95155)	RX	W	EW	EN
94157 (86523, 95157)	RX	W	EW	EN
94160 (86581, 95160)	RX	W	EW	BK
94164 (86104, 95164)	RX	W	EW	BK
94166 (86112, 95166)	RX	W	EW	BK
94168 (86914, 95168)	RX	W	EW	BK
94170 (86395, 95170)	RX	W	EW	BK
94172 (86429, 95172)	RX	W	EW	EN
94174 (86852, 95174)	RX	W	EW	BK
94175 (86521, 95175)	RX	W	EW	BK
94176 (86210, 95176)	RX	W	EW	EN
94177 (86411, 95177)	RX	W	EW	BK
94180 (86362, 95141)	RX	W	EW	BK
94182 (86710, 95182)	RX	W	EW	EN

94190	(86624, 95350)	**RX**	W	EW	EN
94191	(86596, 95351)	**RX**	W	EW	EN
94192	(86727, 95352)	**RX**	W	EW	EN
94193	(86514, 95353)	**RX**	W	EW	EN
94195	(86375, 95355)	**RX**	W	EW	EN
94196	(86478, 95356)	**RX**	W	EW	EN
94197	(86508, 95357)	**RX**	W	EW	BK
94198	(86195, 95358)	**RX**	W	EW	BK
94199	(86854, 95359)	**RX**	W	EW	EN
94200	(86207, 95360)	**RX**	W	EW	BK
94202	(86563, 95362)	**RX**	W	EW	BK
94203	(86345, 95363)	**RX**	W	EW	BK
94204	(86715, 95364)	**RX**	W	EW	BK
94205	(86857, 95365)	**RX**	W	EW	BK
94207	(86529, 95367)	**RX**	W	EW	EN
94208	(86656, 95368)	**RX**	W	EW	BK
94209	(86390, 95369)	**RX**	W	EW	BK
94211	(86713, 95371)	**RX**	W	EW	BK
94212	(86728, 95372)	**RX**	W	EW	EN
94213	(86258, 95373)	**RX**	W	EW	EN
94214	(86367, 95374)	**RX**	W	EW	BK
94215	(86862, 94077)	**RX**	W	EW	BK
94216	(86711, 93711)	**RX**	W	EW	BK
94217	(86131, 93131)	**RX**	W	EW	BK
94218	(86541, 93541)	**RX**	W	EW	BK
94221	(86905, 93905)	**RX**	W	EW	BK
94222	(86474, 93474)	**RX**	W	EW	BK
94223	(86660, 93660)	**RX**	W	EW	BK
94224	(86273, 93273)	**RX**	W	EW	BK
94225	(86849, 93849)	**RX**	W	EW	BK
94226	(86525, 93525)	**RX**	W	EW	EN
94227	(86585, 93585)	**RX**	W	EW	BK
94228	(86511, 93511)	**RX**	W	EW	BK
94229	(86720, 93720)	**RX**	W	EW	BK

NAA   PROPELLING CONTROL VEHICLE

Dia. NA508. (PCV) Mark 1. Class 307 driving trailers converted for use in propelling parcels trains out of termini. Fitted with roller shutter doors. Equipment fitted for communication between cab of PCV and locomotive.

Lot No. 30206 Ashford/Eastleigh 1954 – 6. Converted at RTC Derby 1993 (94300 – 1), Hunslet-Barclay, Kilmarnock 1994 – 6 (remainder).

94300	(75114)	**RX**	W	EW	BK	94308	(75125)	**RX**	W	EW	EN
94301	(75102)	**RX**	W	EW	BK	94309	(75130)	**RX**	W	EW	EN
94302	(75124)	**RX**	W	EW	BK	94310	(75119)	**RX**	W	EW	BK
94303	(75131)	**RX**	W	EW	NC	94311	(75105)	**RX**	W	EW	EN
94304	(75107)	**RX**	W	EW	EN	94312	(75126)	**RX**	W	EW	EN
94305	(75104)	**RX**	W	EW	BK	94313	(75129)	**RX**	W	EW	NC
94306	(75112)	**RX**	W	EW	EN	94314	(75109)	**RX**	W	EW	BK
94307	(75127)	**RX**	W	EW	BK	94315	(75132)	**RX**	W	EW	EN

94316 (75108)	**RX**	W	EW	EN	94333 (75016)	**RX**	W EW	BK
94317 (75117)	**RX**	W	EW	NC	94334 (75017)	**RX**	W EW	BK
94318 (75115)	**RX**	W	EW	BK	94335 (75032)	**RX**	W EW	BK
94319 (75128)	**RX**	W	EW	BK	94336 (75031)	**RX**	W EW	EN
94320 (75120)	**RX**	W	EW	EN	94337 (75029)	**RX**	W EW	EN
94321 (75122)	**RX**	W	EW	EN	94338 (75008)	**RX**	W EW	BK
94322 (75111)	**RX**	W	EW	EN	94339 (75024)	**RX**	W EW	BK
94323 (75110)	**RX**	W	EW	BK	94340 (75012)	**RX**	W EW	NC
94324 (75103)	**RX**	W	EW	EN	94341 (75007)	**RX**	W EW	EN
94325 (75113)	**RX**	W	EW	BK	94342 (75005)	**RX**	W EW	BK
94326 (75123)	**RX**	W	EW	BK	94343 (75027)	**RX**	W EW	EN
94327 (75116)	**RX**	W	EW	EN	94344 (75014)	**RX**	W EW	BK
94331 (75022)	**RX**	W	EW	EN	94345 (75004)	**RX**	W EW	BK
94332 (75011)	**RX**	W	EW	EN				

NBA   HIGH SECURITY BRAKE VAN

Dia. NB501. ETH 1X. B4 bogies. For lot Nos. refer to original number series.
These vehicles are NEs further modified with sealed gangways, new floors and
roller shutter doors.

94400 (81224, 92954)	**RX**	W	EW	EN
94401 (81277, 92224)	**RX**	W	EW	EN
94403 (81479, 92629)	**RX**	W	EW	BK
94404 (81486, 92135)	**RX**	W	EW	BK
94405 (80890, 92233)	**RX**	W	EW	EN
94406 (81226, 92956)	**RX**	W	EW	BK
94407 (81223, 92553)	**RX**	W	EW	BK
94408 (81264, 92981)	**RX**	W	EW	EN
94409 (81511, 92249)	**RX**	W	EW	BK
94410 (81205, 92941)	**RX**	W	EW	EN
94411 (81378, 92997)	**RX**	W	EW	EN
94412 (81210, 92945)	**RX**	W	EW	EN
94413 (80909, 92236)	**RX**	W	EW	PZ
94414 (81377, 92996)	**RX**	W	EW	PZ
94415 (81309, 92992)	**RX**	W	EW	BK
94416 (80929, 92746)	**RX**	W	EW	BK
94418 (81248, 92244)	**RX**	W	EW	BK
94419 (80858, 92902)	**RX**	W	EW	BK
94420 (81325, 92263)	**RX**	W	EW	EN
94421 (81230, 92960)	**RX**	W	EW	EN
94422 (81516, 92651)	**RX**	W	EW	BK
94423 (80923, 92914)	**RX**	W	EW	EN
94424 (81400, 92103)	**RX**	W	EW	BK
94425 (80937, 92212)	**RX**	W	EW	BK
94426 (81283, 92987)	**RX**	W	EW	EN
94427 (80894, 92754)	**RX**	W	EW	BK
94428 (81550, 92166)	**RX**	W	EW	BK
94429 (80870, 92232)	**RX**	W	EW	EN
94430 (80908, 94235)	**RX**	W	EW	BK
94431 (81401, 92604)	**RX**	W	EW	EN

94432 (81383, 92999)	**RX**	W	EW	BK
94433 (81495, 92643)	**RX**	W	EW	EN
94434 (81268, 92584)	**RX**	W	EW	BK
94435 (81485, 92134)	**RX**	W	EW	EN
94436 (81237, 92565)	**RX**	W	EW	BK
94437 (81403, 92208)	**RX**	W	EW	BK
94438 (81425, 92251)	**RX**	W	EW	EN
94439 (81480, 92130)	**RX**	W	EW	EN
94440 (81497, 92645)	**RX**	W	EW	BK
94441 (81492, 92140)	**RX**	W	EW	BK
94442 (80932, 92723)	**RX**	W	EW	BK
94443 (81473, 92127)	**RX**	W	EW	BK
94444 (81484, 92133)	**RX**	W	EW	BK
94445 (81444, 92615)	**RX**	W	EW	EN
94446 (80857, 92242)	**RX**	W	EW	EN
94447 (81515, 92266)	**RX**	W	EW	EN
94448 (81541, 92664)	**RX**	W	EW	BK
94449 (81536, 92747)	**RX**	W	EW	EN
94450 (80927, 92915)	**RX**	W	EW	BK
94451 (80955, 92257)	**RX**	W	EW	EN
94452 (81394, 92602)	**RX**	W	EW	BK
94453 (81170, 92239)	**RX**	W	EW	EN
94454 (81465, 92124)	**RX**	W	EW	BK
94455 (81239, 92264)	**RX**	W	EW	EN
94456 (80879, 92226)	**RX**	W	EW	BK
94457 (81454, 92119)	**RX**	W	EW	BK
94458 (81255, 92974)	**RX**	W	EW	EN
94459 (81490, 92138)	**RX**	W	EW	BK
94460 (81266, 92983)	**RX**	W	EW	EN
94461 (81487, 92136)	**RX**	W	EW	EN
94462 (81289, 92270)	**RX**	W	EW	EN
94463 (81375, 92995)	**RX**	W	EW	EN
94464 (81240, 92262)	**RX**	W	EW	EN
94465 (81481, 92131)	**RX**	W	EW	BK
94466 (81236, 92964)	**RX**	W	EW	EN
94467 (81245, 92969)	**RX**	W	EW	BK
94468 (81259, 92978)	**RX**	W	EW	BK
94469 (81260, 92979)	**RX**	W	EW	BK
94470 (81442, 92113)	**RX**	W	EW	BK
94471 (81518, 92152)	**RX**	W	EW	BK
94472 (81526, 92975)	**RX**	W	EW	EN
94473 (81262, 92272)	**RX**	W	EW	EN
94474 (81452, 92618)	**RX**	W	EW	EN
94475 (81208, 92943)	**RX**	W	EW	EN
94476 (81209, 92944)	**RX**	W	EW	BK
94477 (81494, 92642)	**RX**	W	EW	BK
94478 (81488, 92637)	**RX**	W	EW	EN
94479 (81482, 92132)	**RX**	W	EW	BK
94480 (81411, 92608)	**RX**	W	EW	EN
94481 (81493, 92641)	**RX**	W	EW	BK
94482 (81491, 92639)	**RX**	W	EW	EN

94483 (81500, 92647)	**RX**	W	EW	EN
94484 (81426, 92110)	**RX**	W	EW	BK
94485 (81496, 92644)	**RX**	W	EW	EN
94486 (81254, 92973)	**RX**	W	EW	EN
94487 (81413, 92609)	**RX**	W	EW	BK
94488 (81405, 92105)	**RX**	W	EW	BK
94489 (81423, 92230)	**RX**	W	EW	
94490 (81409, 92606)	**RX**	W	EW	BK

NOX (GUV)   GENERAL UTILITY VAN (100 MPH ETH WIRED)

Dia. NO513. ETH 0X. Commonwealth bogies except where shown otherwise.
For lot Nos. refer to original number series. Add 2 t to weight (Subtract 1 t for
B4).

95105 (86126, 93126)	a	**RX**	W	Carlisle Yard
95109 (86269, 93269)	x	**B**	W	Carlisle Yard
95120 (86468, 93468)	x	**RY**	W	Carlisle Yard
95124 (86836, 93836)	x	**R**	W	Carlisle Yard
95125 (86143, 93143)	x	**RY**	W	Carlisle Yard
95128 (86764, 93764)	x	**RY**	W	Crewe South Yard
95129 (86347, 93347)	x	**RY**	W	Crewe South Yard
95131 (86860, 93860)	a	**RX**	W	OM
95135 (86249, 93249)	x	**RY**	W	Carlisle Yard
95136 (86396, 93396)	x	**RX**	W	OM
95142 (86844, 93844)	x	**RX**	W	BK
95144 (86165, 93165)	x	**RY**	W	OM
95145 (86293, 93293)	x	**RX**	W	Carlisle Yard
95151 (86606, 93606)	x	**RX**	W	OM
95152 (86969, 93969)	x	**RY**	W	Carlisle Yard
95156 (86160, 93160)	x	**RX**	W	OM
95165 (86262, 93262)	x	**RX**	W	Carlisle Yard
95167 (86255, 93255)	a	**RX**	W	OM
95169 (86277, 93277)	a	**RX**	W	BK
95171 (86110, 93110)	x	**RX**	W	OM
95173 (86842, 94076)	x	**RX**	W	BK
95181 (86971, 95361)	x	**B**	W	BK
95190 (86643, 95393)	a B4	**RY**	W	OM
95191 (86278, 95391)	x B4	**B**	W	OM
95192 (86495, 95392)	x B4	**R**	W	BK
95194 (86192, 93192)	x B4	**RX**	W	OM
95195 (86539, 93539)	x B4	**RX**	W	OM
95196 (86775, 93775)	x B4	**RX**	W	OM
95197 (86590, 93590)	x B4	**RX**	W	OM
95198 (86134, 93134)	x B4	**RX**	W	OM
95199 (86141, 93141)	x B4	**RX**	W	OM

NCX   NEWSPAPER VAN (100 mph)

Dia. NC501. BGs modified to carry newspapers. x. ETH 3 (3X*). Commonwealth bogies. For lot Nos. refer to original number series. Add 2 t to weight. Not now used for news traffic.

95200 (81019, 84019)	*	RY	W		BK
95201 (80875)		RY	W		Carlisle Yard
95204 (80947)	*	RX	W		OM
95209 (81047, 84047)		RX	W		BK
95210 (80731)		RX	W		OM
95211 (80949)		RX	W		Carlisle Yard
95212 (81179, 84179)		B	Q	SD	PZ
95217 (81385, 84385)		B	W	EW	EN
95223 (80933)	*	RY	W		NC
95227 (81292, 95310)		RX	W		Carlisle Yard
95228 (81014, 95332)		RX	W		NC
95229 (81341, 95329)		RX	W		OM
95230 (80525, 95321)		RX	W		DY

95217 is kept at Euston Downside CARMD for rubbish disposal.

NOV   GENERAL UTILITY VAN (100 mph ETH WIRED)

Dia. NO513. vy. ETH 0X. Commonwealth bogies. For lot Nos. refer to original number series. Add 2 t to weight.

95366 (86251, 93251)	B	W	EW	BK

Kept at Gloucester station.

NRX   BAA CONTAINER VAN (100 mph)

Dia. NR503. Modified for carriage of British Airports Authority containers with roller shutter doors and roller floors and gangways removed. x. ETH 3 (3X*). Commonwealth bogies. For lot Nos. see original number series. Add 2 t to weight. Now used for movement of materials between EWS maintenance depots.

95400 (80621, 95203)	RX	W	EW	BK
95410 (80826, 95213)	RX	W	EW	BK

NOA   SUPER GENERAL UTILITY VAN

Dia. NO502. ay. ETH 0X. Commonwealth bogies. For lot Nos. see original number series. Add 2 t to weight. These vehicles are GUVs further modified with new floors, two roller shutter doors per side and the middle doors sealed and end doors removed.

95715 (86174, 95115)	R	W	EW	EN
95727 (86323, 95127)	R	W	EW	EN
95734 (86462, 95134)	RX	W	EW	EN

95739	(86172, 95139)	**R**	W	EW	EN
95743	(86485, 95143)	**RX**	W	EW	EN
95749	(86265, 95149)	**R**	W	EW	EN
95754	(86897, 95154)	**R**	W	EW	EN
95758	(86499, 95158)	**RX**	W	EW	EN
95759	(86084, 95159)	**RX**	W	EW	BK
95761	(86205, 95161)	**RX**	W	EW	EN
95762	(86122, 95162)	**RX**	W	EW	EN
95763	(86407, 95163)	**RX**	W	EW	EN

NX (GUV)   MOTORAIL VAN (100 mph)

Mark 1. Dia. NX501. For details and lot numbers see original number series.
ETH 0 (0X*). 100 mph.

96100	(86734, 93734)	a*B5I	E	Kineton
96101	(86741, 93741)	a*B5I	E	Kineton
96110	(86738, 93738)	a*C I	E	Kineton
96111	(86742, 93742)	a*C I	E	Kineton
96112	(86750, 93750)	a*C I	E	Longtown
96130	(86736, 93736)	a*C I	E	Kineton
96131	(86737, 93737)	a*C I	E	Kineton
96132	(86754, 93754)	a*C I	E	Longtown
96133	(86685, 93685)	a C I	E	Longtown
96134	(86691, 93691)	a C I	E	Longtown
96135	(86755, 93755)	a C I	E	Long Marston
96136	(86735, 93735)	a C I	E	Longtown
96137	(86748, 93748)	a C **B**	E	ZN
96138	(86749, 93749)	a C I	E	Longtown
96139	(86751, 93751)	a C I	E	Long Marston
96141	(86753, 93753)	a C **B**	E	Longtown
96150	(86097, 93097)	a*B5I	E	Kineton
96155	(86334, 93334)	a*B5I	E	Kineton
96156	(86337, 93337)	a*B5I	E	Kineton
96157	(86344, 93344)	a*B5I	E	Kineton
96162	(86647, 93647)	a*C I	E	Longtown
96163	(86646, 93646)	a*C I	E	Kineton
96164	(86880, 93880)	a*C I	E	Longtown
96165	(86784, 93784)	a*C I	E	Kineton
96166	(86834, 93834)	a*C I	E	Kineton
96167	(86756, 93756)	a*C I	E	Kineton
96168	(86978, 93978)	a*C I	E	Longtown
96169	(86937, 93937)	a*C I	E	Longtown
96170	(86159, 93159)	x*C I	E	Kineton
96171	(86326, 93326)	x*C I	E	Longtown
96172	(86363, 93363)	x*C I	E	Kineton
96173	(86440, 93440)	x*C I	E	Kineton
96174	(86453, 93453)	x*C I	E	Longtown
96175	(86628, 93628)	x*C I	E	Kineton
96176	(86641, 93641)	x*C I	E	Kineton
96177	(86980, 93980)	a*C I	E	Kineton

96178	(86782, 93782)	a*C I	E		Kineton
96179	(86910, 93910)	a*C I	E		Longtown
96181	(86875, 93875)	a*C I	E		Longtown
96182	(86944, 93944)	a*C I	E		Long Marston
96185	(86083, 93083)	x*C I	E		Longtown
96186	(86087, 93087)	x*C I	E		Longtown
96187	(86168, 93168)	x*C I	E		Longtown
96188	(86320, 93320)	x*C I	E		Kineton
96189	(86447, 93447)	x*C I	E		Longtown
96190	(86448, 93448)	x*C I	E		Longtown
96191	(86665, 93665)	x*C I	E		Kineton
96192	(86669, 93669)	x*C I	E		Kineton
96193	(86874, 93874)	x*C I	E		Longtown
96194	(86949, 93949)	x*C I	E		Longtown
96195	(86958, 93958)	x*C I	E		Longtown

NP (GUV)   MOTORAIL VAN (110 mph)

Mark 1. Dia. NP503. Vehicles modified with concertina end doors. For details
and lot numbers see original number series. B5 Bogies. a. ETH 0X*.

96210	(86355, 96159)	I	E	Longtown
96211	(86745, 96104)	I	E	Horsham
96212	(86443, 96161)	I	E	Longtown
96213	(86324, 96152)	I	E	Kineton
96214	(86331, 96154)	I	E	Horsham
96215	(86351, 96158)	I	E	Kineton
96216	(86385, 96160)	I	E	Kineton
96217	(86327, 96153)	I	E	Kineton
96218	(86286, 96151)	I	E	Longtown

NG   MOTORAIL LOADING WAGON

Dia. NG503. These vehicles have been renumbered from weltrol wagons and
are used for loading purposes.

Built Swindon 1960. wagon Lot No. 3102 (3192*).

96450	(B900920)		E	OL	Kineton
96451	(B900912)		E	OL	Kineton
96452	(B900917)		E	OL	Longtown
96453	(B900926)	*	E	OL	PC
96454	(B900938)	*	E	OL	ZH

NY   EXHIBITION VAN

Various interiors. Converted from various vehicle types. Electric heating from shore supply. In some cases new lot numbers were issued for conversions, but not always. Non-standard livery — varies according to job being undertaken.

Lot 30842 Swindon 1972 – 3. Dia. NY503. Converted from BSK to Lot No. 30156 Wolverton 1955.

| 99621 | (34697) x | BR1 | **0** | W | OM | Exhibition Coach. |
| 99625 | (34693) x | Mk4 | **0** | W | OM | Generator Van. |

Converted Salisbury 1981 from RB to Lot No. 30636 Pressed Steel 1962. Dia NY523/4 respectively.

| 99645 | (1765) v | C | **0** | W | Ferme Park | Club Car. |
| 99646 | (1766) v | C | **0** | W | Ferme Park | Club Car. |

Note: Mk4 denotes a Southern Region Mark 4 EMU trailer bogie.

Converted Railway Age, Crewe 1996 from TSO to Lot No. 30822 Derby 1971.

| 99662 | (5689) | | a B4 | **0** | M | SS | BN |

Converted Railway Age, Crewe 1996 from SO to Lot No. 30821 Derby 1971. Originally FO.

| 99663 | (3194, 6223) | a B4 | **0** | X | SS | BN |
| 99664 | (3189, 6231) | a B4 | **0** | M | SS | BN |

Converted Railway Age, Crewe 1996 from TSO to Lot No. 30837 Derby 1972.

| 99665 | (5755) | | a B4 | **0** | M | SS | BN |

Converted Railway Age, Crewe 1996 from FO to Lot No. 30843 Derby 1972 – 3.

| 99666 | (3250) | | a B4 \ | **0** | M | SS | BN |

5.2. NPCCS AWAITING DISPOSAL

This list contains the last known locations of non-passenger-carrying coaching
stock awaiting disposal. The definition of which vehicles are awaiting disposal
is somewhat vague, but generally speaking these are vehicles of types not now
in normal service or vehicles which have been damaged by fire, vandalism or
collision.

80735	Perth Holding Sidings
80977	LL
80865	Hornsey Sand Terminal
84361	Cambridge Station Yard
84364	Doncaster West Yard
84519	Crewe Coal Sidings
92067	Doncaster West Yard
92172	NC
92198	Doncaster West Yard
92199	Doncaster West Yard
92202	ZF
92371	ZC
92378	Cambridge Coldham Lane Sidings
93149	OY
93180	Derby South Dock Siding
93234	Hayes & Harlington
93259	LL
93446	Crewe South Yard
93457	Cricklewood Rubbish Terminal
93482	Bedford Civil Engineers Sidings
93542	Hayes & Harlington
93723	Bletchley T&RSMD
93930	Crewe South Yard
93952	Willesden Brent Sidings
93979	Willesden Brent Sidings
96250	Oxford Hinksey Yard
96256	Oxford Hinksey Yard
96260	Oxford Hinksey Yard
96265	Oxford Hinksey Yard
99648	Eastleigh Loco Holding Sidings

6. EUROTUNNEL STOCK

This book presents the complete rolling stock of Eurotunnel, the operator of the Channel Tunnel. Whilst through rail passengers travel in the 'Eurostar' sets sets detailed in the preceeding pages, motorised passengers travel in special car and lorry-carring vehicles.

Car passengers travel in special double deck car carrying vehicles. Coaches, campervans, caravans and light goods vehicles are accommodated in single deck carriers of similar design. Up to three motorbikes can be carried in each double deck loader. Cars with roof loads over 1.65 m must travel in the single deck stock. The double deck loaders have side sliding roof mechanism.

The system is drive-on – drive-off and car passengers are normally expected to remain in their vehicles, although it is possible to walk along the coach to a toilet or snack machine. The vehicles are well lit with information displays giving anticipated arrival times during the journey. All tourists are able to use a motorway service station style rest area before lining up for allocation. The platform to platform transit is about 35 minutes with 25 of that spent in the Tunnel.

For heavy goods vehicles (HGVs), drivers will not remain in their vehicles, but will travel in separate 'club' cars. An at seat meal service will be provided for the drivers.

The Tunnel itself consists of twin 50.5 km (31.4 mile) long large diameter tunnels up to 126 metres (413 ft.) below sea level. There is also a service tunnel between the two running tunnels. All 'Le Shuttle' workings have two locomotives.

Continuous Rating: 5760 kW (7725 hp) giving a tractive effort of 310 kN at 65 km/h.

Brake Force: 50 t.	**Length over Buffers:** 22.00 m.
Design Speed: 175 km/h (110 mph).	**Weight:** 132 t.
Max. Speed: 160 km/h (100 mph).	**RA:** Channel Tunnel only.
ETH Index:	**Wheel Diameter:** 1090 mm.
Train Brakes: Air.	**Electric Brake:** Regenerative.

Multiple Working: Time division multiplex system. RC232 data bus
Couplings: High level Scharfenberg plus UIC screw links.
Communication Equipment: Cab to shore radio and in-train system.
Cab Signalling: TVM 430.
Livery: Two-tone grey and white with green, blue bands.

9001	ET	LESLEY GARRETT
9002	ET	STUART BURROWS
9003	ET	BENJAMIN LUXON
9004	ET	
9005	ET	
9006	ET	
9007	ET	DAME JOAN SUTHERLAND
9008	ET	ELISABETH SODERSTROM
9009	ET	FRANCOIS POLLET
9010	ET	JEAN-PHILIPPE COURTIS
9011	ET	JOSE VAN DAM
9012	ET	LUCIANO PAVAROTTI
9013	ET	MARIA CALLAS
9014	ET	
9015	ET	
9016	ET	
9017	ET	JOSE CARRERAS
9018	ET	
9019	ET	
9020	ET	NICOLAI GHIAUROV
9021	ET	
9022	ET	DAME JANET BAKER
9023	ET	DAME ELISABETH LEGGE-SCHWARZKOPF
9024	ET	
9025	ET	
9026	ET	
9027	ET	BARBARA HENDRICKS
9028	ET	
9029	ET	
9031	ET	PLACIDO DOMINGO
9032	ET	
9033	ET	
9034	ET	
9035	ET	NICOLAI GEDDA
9036	ET	
9037	ET	GABRIEL BAQUIER
9038	ET	

'LE SHUTTLE' PASSENGER FLEET'

DOUBLE DECK CARRIER WAGON   DDCa

Builder: Bombardier (Canada)/ANF, Crespin, France.
Weight: 62 t.
Height: 5.575 m.
Length: 26.00 m.
Width: 4.1 m.
Couplings: Automatic Scharfenburg at one end, semi-automatic Scharfenburg at the other.

1001	1013	1025	1201	1213	1225
1002	1014	1026	1202	1214	1226
1003	1015	1027	1203	1215	1227
1004	1016	1028	1204	1216	1228
1005	1017	1029	1205	1217	1229
1006	1018	1030	1206	1218	1230
1007	1019	1031	1207	1219	1231
1008	1020	1032	1208	1220	1232
1009	1021	1033	1209	1221	1233
1010	1022	1034	1210	1222	1234
1011	1023	1035	1211	1223	1235
1012	1024	1036	1212	1224	1236

DOUBLE DECK CARRIER WAGON   DDCs

These vehicles have a toilet and stairs.

Builder: Bombardier (Canada)/ANF, Crespin, France.
Weight: 62 t.
Height: 5.575 m.
Length: 26.000 m.
Width: 4.1 m.
Couplings: Semi-automatic Scharfenburg at both ends.

1401	1407	1413	1419	1425	1431
1402	1408	1414	1420	1426	1432
1403	1409	1415	1421	1427	1433
1404	1410	1416	1422	1428	1434
1405	1411	1417	1423	1429	1435
1406	1412	1418	1424	1430	1436

DOUBLE DECK LOADER WAGON   DDL

Builder: Bombardier, Canada.
Weight: 64 t.
Height: 5.575 m.
Length: 27.25 m.
Width: 4.1 m.

Couplings: Low level Scharfenburg electro-pneumatic auto couplers.

1801	1805	1808	1811	1814	1817
1802	1806	1809	1812	1815	1818
1803	1807	1810	1813	1816	1819
1804					

Formations:

Formations are as follows:

Set 1 is 1801 + 1001 – 1401 – 1201 + 1002 – 1402 – 1202 + 1003 – 1403 – 1203 + 1004 – 1404 – 1204 + 1802 with other sets being in sequence.

SINGLE DECK CARRIER WAGON   SDCa

Builder: Bombardier BN, Brugge, Belgium.
Weight: 62.5 t.   **Length:** 26.00 m.
Height: 5.575 m.   **Width:** 4.1 m.
Couplings: Low level Scharfenburg electro-pneumatic auto coupler at one end and semi-auto Scharfenburg at other

3001	3013	3025	3201	3213	3225
3002	3014	3026	3202	3214	3226
3003	3015	3027	3203	3215	3227
3004	3016	3028	3204	3216	3228
3005	3017	3029	3205	3217	3229
3006	3018	3030	3206	3218	3230
3007	3019	3031	3207	3219	3231
3008	3020	3032	3208	3220	3232
3009	3021	3033	3209	3221	3233
3010	3022	3034	3210	3222	3234
3011	3023	3035	3211	3223	3235
3012	3024	3036	3212	3224	3236

SINGLE DECK CARRIER WAGON   SDCs

With toilet

Builder: Bombardier BN, Bruges, Belgium.
Weight: 63 t.
Height: 5.575 m.
Length: 26.000 m.
Width: 4.1 m.
Couplings: Low level semi-automatic Scharfenburg electro-pneumatic at both ends.

3401	3407	3413	3419	3425	3431
3402	3408	3414	3420	3426	3432
3403	3409	3415	3421	3427	3433
3404	3410	3416	3422	3428	3434
3405	3411	3417	3423	3429	3435
3406	3412	3418	3424	3430	3436

SINGLE DECK LOADER WAGON   SDL

Builder: Fiat, Savigliano, Italy.
Weight: 61 t.
Height: 5.570 m.
Length: 26.000 m.
Width: 4.1 m.
Couplings: Low level Scharfenburg electro-pneumatic auto couplers.

3801	3804	3807	3810	3813	3816
3802	3805	3808	3811	3814	3817
3803	3806	3809	3812	3815	3818

Formations:

Formations are as follows:

Set 1 is 3801 + 3001 – 3401 – 3201 + 3002 – 3402 – 3202 + 3003 – 3403 – 3203 + 3004 – 3404 – 3204 + 3802 with other sets being in sequence.

'LE SHUTTLE' HGV FLEET

LIGHT HGV CARRIER WAGON   LHGVC

Length: 20.506 m.
Height: 5.595 m.
Width: 4.1 m.
Weight: 34 t.
Builders: OMECA, Reggio, Calabria, Italy (110), Ferrosud, Materia, Italy (70) and Imesi, Palermo, Italy (48).

5001	5115	5201	5219	5305	5323
5002	5116	5202	5220	5306	5324
5003	5117	5203	5221	5307	5325
5004	5118	5204	5222	5308	5326
5101	5119	5205	5223	5309	5327
5102	5120	5206	5224	5310	5328
5103	5121	5207	5225	5311	5329
5104	5122	5208	5226	5312	5330
5105	5123	5209	5227	5313	5331
5106	5124	5210	5228	5314	5332
5107	5125	5211	5229	5315	5401
5108	5126	5212	5230	5316	5402
5109	5127	5213	5231	5317	5403
5110	5128	5214	5232	5318	5404
5111	5129	5215	5301	5319	5405
5112	5130	5216	5302	5320	5406
5113	5131	5217	5303	5321	5407
5114	5132	5218	5304	5322	5408

5409	5429	5517	5605	5625	5713
5410	5430	5518	5606	5626	5714
5411	5431	5519	5607	5627	5715
5412	5432	5520	5608	5628	5716
5413	5501	5521	5609	5629	5717
5414	5502	5522	5610	5630	5718
5415	5503	5523	5611	5631	5719
5416	5504	5524	5612	5632	5720
5417	5505	5525	5613	5701	5721
5418	5506	5526	5614	5702	5722
5419	5507	5527	5615	5703	5723
5420	5508	5528	5616	5704	5724
5421	5509	5529	5617	5705	5725
5422	5510	5530	5618	5706	5726
5423	5511	5531	5619	5707	5727
5424	5512	5532	5620	5708	5728
5425	5513	5601	5621	5709	5729
5426	5514	5602	5622	5710	5730
5427	5515	5603	5623	5711	5731
5428	5516	5604	5624	5712	5732

LIGHT HGV LOADER WAGON   LHGVL

Length: 25.100 m.
Height: 3.490 m.
Width: 4.1 m.
Weight: 45 t.
Builder: Fiat, Savigliano, Italy.

5801	5807	5813	5819	5824	5829
5802	5808	5814	5820	5825	5830
5803	5809	5815	5821	5826	5831
5804	5810	5816	5822	5827	5832
5805	5811	5817	5823	5828	5833
5806	5812	5818			

LIGHT AMENITY COACH-CLUB CAR   LAMC

Length: 25.720 m.
Height: 3.950 m.
Width: 3 m.
Weight: 45 t.
Builders: OMECA, Calabria, Italy (8) and Breda, Sisloia, Italy (1).

5901	5903	5905	5907	5908	5909
5902	5904	5906			

PLATFORM 5 EUROPEAN HANDBOOKS

The Platform 5 European Railway Handbooks are the most comprehensive guides to the rolling stock of selected European railway administrations available. Each book lists all locomotives and railcars of the country concerned, giving details of number carried, livery and depot allocations (when allocated), together with a wealth of technical data for each class of vehicle. In addition the Benelux book contains details of hauled coaching stock vehicles. Each book is A5 size, thread sewn and includes at least 32 pages of colour photographs (Irish Railways 16 in colour). The following are currently available:

No. 1	Benelux Railways 3rd edition	£10.50
No. 2	German Railways 3rd edition	£12.50
No. 3	Austrian Railways 3rd edition	£10.50
No. 6	Italian Railways 1st edition	£13.50
No. 7	Irish Railways 1st edition	£9.95

The new editions of our European Handbooks, No. 4: French Railways 3rd edition and No. 5: Swiss Railways 2nd edition, will be published in 1997. See ''Today's Railways'' magazine for details of publication dates.

If you are interested in purchasing any of these titles you can order them direct using the Mail Order form at the back of this book.

7. CODES

7.1. LIVERY CODES

Locomotives

Locomotives are blue unless otherwise indicated. The colour of the lower half of the bodyside is stated first. Minor variations to these liveries are ignored.

BR Revised blue (large bodyside numbers and full height BR logo).
BS Blue with red solebar stripe.
C Civil Engineers (grey and yellow).
CS Central services (grey and red with Central Services logo and lettering).
CT Civil Engineers livery with Transrail markings.
D Departmental (plain grey with black cab doors).
E Eurostar (UK) - As **F** with blue roof and cast Channel Tunnel logo.
EW English Welsh & Scottish Railway Ltd. (maroon with large maroon EW&S lettering and number on broad gold band between cabs).
F New Railfreight Unspecified (two-tone grey with no sub-sector markings).
FA Trainload Construction - As **F** with construction markings (blue blocks on a yellow background).
FC Trainload Coal - As **F** with coal markings (black diamonds on a yellow background).
FD Old Railfreight Distribution - As **F** with Railfreight Distribution markings (red diamonds on a yellow background).
FE New Railfreight Distribution - Two-tone grey with blue roof and Railfreight Distribution lettering and markings (red diamonds on a yellow background).
FF Freightliner 1995 - As **F** with Freightliner lettering and markings (red diagonal stripes behind right hand cab door).
FL New Railfreight Livery with Loadhaul lettering.
FM New Railfreight Livery with Mainline logo and lettering.
FO Old Railfreight (grey sides, yellow cabsides and full height BR logo).
FP Trainload Petroleum - As **F** with Trainload Petroleum markings (blue waves on a yellow background).
FR As **FO** but with a red solebar stripe and a slightly smaller BR logo.
FS Trainload Metals - As **F** with metals markings (blue chevrons on a yellow background).
FT Transrail - As **F** with Transrail lettering and logo (large white 'T' on a blue circle with a red outline, underlined with two red stripes).
G BR or GWR green.
GN Great North Eastern Railway (dark blue with an orange bodyside stripe and gold or silver GNER lettering).
GW Great Western Trains (green and ivory with Great Western Trains logo and lettering).
GX Gatwick Express (white and dark grey with claret stripe and Gatwick Express lettering and motif).
I InterCity (white and dark grey with red stripe and swallow motif).
I0 Old InterCity (light grey and dark grey with red stripe, yellow lower cab sides and BR logo).
LH Loadhaul (black with orange cabsides and Loadhaul lettering).

LIVERY CODES

M   Mainline (as **IO** but without the yellow lower cabsides and BR logo).
MD   Merseyrail Departmental (dark grey and yellow with Merseyrail logo and lettering).
ML   Mainline Freight (blue with thin silver body stripe and Mainline logo and lettering).
MM   Midland Mainline (grey and green with three orange bodyside stripes and Midland Mainline logo and lettering).
N   Network SouthEast (grey/white/red/white/blue/white with Network SouthEast lettering).
O   Other livery (non-standard - refer to text).
PL   Porterbrook Leasing (purple at one end, white at the other with small logo and lettering behind the left-hand cab doors. The livery represents an enlarged portion of the Porterbrook logo with the colours reversed on the other side).
R   Parcels (post office red and dark grey).
RR   Regional Railways (grey/light blue/white/dark blue with Regional Railways lettering).
RX   Rail express systems (post office red with the Res blue & black logo).
SC   Stagecoach (grey/orange/red/white/blue/white).
T   Racal-BRT (two-tone grey with green markings).
U   Grey undercoat. Certain locos emerged in undercoat whilst EWS and Great Western Trains were deciding on a livery to adopt as standard.
VC   Virgin CrossCountry (red with black inner ends on power cars and Virgin CrossCountry logo and lettering).
W   Waterman Railways (black with cream & red lining).

Coaching Stock & Multiple Units

Loco-hauled coaching stock vehicles are in Intercity livery and DMUs, EMUs and NPCCS are in the old blue & grey livery unless otherwise indicated. The colour of the lower half of the bodyside is stated first.

A   Advertising Livery.
B   Plain Blue.
BG   Blue & Grey (loco-hauled coaches).
CC   BR Carmine & Cream ("Blood & Custard").
CE   Centro (WMPTE) (grey/light blue/white/green).
CH   BR/GWR Chocolate & Cream.
CN   Connex Class 365 (yellow white and blue).
CX   Connex (yellow and white with blue solebar stripe).
CW   Connex (yellow and white with blue solebar stripe).
E   European Passenger Services (two-tone grey).
G   Southern Region Green or BR DMU Green.
GM   New Greater Manchester PTE (dark grey/red/white/light grey)
GN   Great North Eastern Railway (dark blue with an orange bodyside stripe and gold GNER lettering).
GW   Great Western Trains (green and ivory with Great Western Trains logo and lettering).
GX   Gatwick Express (white and dark grey with claret stripe and Gatwick Express lettering and motif)
H   LNER Tourist Green and Cream ("Highland Heritage").
HE   Heathrow Express (silver and blue).
I   InterCity (light grey (white on DVTs)/red stripe/dark grey).

J	Jaffacake livery (grey/dark brown with orange stripe).
LH	Loadhaul (orange and black).
M	BR Maroon.
MM	Midland Mainline (grey and green with three orange bodyside stripes).
MS	Merseyrail Service (yellow/brown).
MT	Merseytravel (yellow/blue/white/yellow).
N	Network SouthEast (grey/white/red/white/blue/white).
NR	Network SouthEast livery with the red stripe repainted blue.
NW	Network SouthEast (white/red/white/blue/white).
O	Other livery (non-standard - refer to text).
P	Provincial services (grey/light blue/white/dark blue).
PL	Porterbrook Leasing (purple and grey).
PR	Provincial Services railbus variant (dark blue/white/light blue).
R	Plain Red.
RE	Regional Railways Express (buff/light grey/dark grey/light grey/buff, with dark blue, white and light blue stripes).
RM	Red with Yellow stripes above solebar with Royal Mail insignia or "Royal Mail Travelling Post Office" markings.
RN	As **RR** but with green stripe under windows.
RR	Regional Railways (grey/light blue/white/dark blue with three black and white stripes at end of each light blue band under cabs.
RX	Rail Express Systems (Red and grey with blue/black markings).
RY	Red with yellow stripes above solebar and BR logo.
S	Strathclyde PTE (orange and black).
T	Tyne & Wear PTE (yellow blue & white).
TL	Thameslink (grey with orange and blue logos).
VC	Virgin CrossCountry (red with black doors and Virgin CrossCountry logo and lettering).
W	Waterman Railways (maroon with cream stripes).
WV	Waterman Railways (West Coast Joint Stock lined purple lake).
Y	West Yorkshire PTE (red and cream).

7.2. LOCOMOTIVE POOL CODES

Central Services
CDJD Derby Etches Park Class 08 (Research)

Railfreight Distribution
DAAN Allerton Class 08
DADC Crewe Electric Class 92 (Dollands Moor-Wembley)
DAEC Crewe Electric Class 92 (Not in Traffic)
DAET Tinsley Class 47
DAMC Crewe Electric Class 87/1 & 90
DASY Tinsley Class 08 (Saltley)
DATI Tinsley Class 08
DAVC Crewe Electric Class 92 (100 mph Maximum)
DAWE Allerton Class 08 (Wembley/Dagenham/Southampton)
DAXT Tinsley Class 47 (Awaiting Repair)
DAYX Stored Locomotives

Freightliner (1995)
DFLC Crewe Electric Class 90/1
DFLM Crewe Diesel Class 47 (Multiple Working Fitted)
DFLR Crewe Diesel Class 47 (Resilience Pool)
DFLS Allerton/Crewe Diesel/Eastleigh/Stratford/Tinsley Class 08
DFLT Crewe Diesel Class 47
DFNC Crewe Electric Class 86/6
DHLT Crewe Diesel Class 47 (Holding Pool)

English Welsh & Scottish Railway (Formerly Mainline)
ENAN Toton/Stewarts Lane Class 60
ENBN Toton Class 58
ENRN Toton Class 47 (Restricted Use)
ENSN Toton Class 08 (Toton/Peterborough)
ENTN Toton Class 31/37 (Infrastructure)
ENXX Stored Locomotives
ENZX Locomotives For Withdrawal
EWDB Stewarts Lane/Stratford Class 33/37 (Infrastructure)
EWEB Stewarts Lane Class 73 (Infrastructure)
EWEH Eastleigh Class 08
EWHG Stewarts Lane Class 09
EWOC Old Oak Common Class 08/09
EWRB Stewarts Lane Class 37/73 (Restricted)
EWSF Stratford Class 08/09
EWSU Selhurst Class 08/09
EWSX Stratford Class 08 (Stored/Reserve)

English Welsh & Scottish Railway (Formerly Loadhaul)
FDAI Immingham Class 60
FDBI Immingham Class 56
FDCI Immingham Class 37
FDKI Immingham Class 47 (Control Contingency)
FDRI Immingham Class 37 (Restricted)

FDSD	Doncaster Class 08
FDSI	Immingham Class 08
FDSK	Knottingley Class 08/09
FDSX	Stored Shunters
FDYX	Stored Locomotives
FMSY	Thornaby Class 08/09

Eurostar (UK)

GPSN	Stewarts Lane Class 73 (North Pole)
GPSS	Old Oak Common Class 08 (North Pole)
GPSV	Old Oak Common Class 37/6 (North Pole)

Passenger Train Operating Companies

HASS	ScotRail - Inverness Class 08
HBSH	Great North Eastern Railway - Bounds Green/Craigentinny Class 08
HEBD	Merseyrail - Birkenhead North Class 73
HFSL	West Coast - Longsight Class 08
HFSN	West Coast - Willesden Class 08
HGSS	Central - Tyseley Class 08
HISE	Midland Mainline - Derby Etches Park Class 08
HISL	Midland Mainline - Neville Hill Class 08
HJSE	Great Western Trains - Landore Class 08
HJSL	Great Western Trains - Laira Class 08
HJXX	Great Western Trains - Old Oak Common/St Phillips Marsh Class 08
HLSV	Cardiff Railway Company - Cardiff Canton Class 08
HSSN	Anglia Railways - Norwich Crown Point Class 08
HWSU	Connex South Central - Selhurst Class 09
HYSB	South Western Trains (Stagecoach) - Bournemouth Class 73/1
IANA	Anglia Railways - Norwich Crown Point Class 86/2
ICCA	Virgin CrossCountry - Longsight Class 86/2
ICCP	Virgin CrossCountry - Laira Class 43
ICCS	Virgin CrossCountry - Edinburgh Craigentinny Class 43
IECA	Great North Eastern Railway - Bounds Green Class 91
IECP	Great North Eastern Railway - Craigentinny/Neville Hill Class 43
ILRA	Virgin CrossCountry - Crewe Diesel Class 47/8
ILRB	Virgin CrossCountry - Crewe Diesel Class 47/8 (Spot Hire)
IMLP	Midland Mainline - Neville Hill Class 43
IVGA	Gatwick Express - Stewarts Lane Class 73
IWCA	West Coast - Willesden Class 87/90
IWCP	West Coast - Longsight Class 43
IWLA	Great Western Trains - Laira Class 47
IWLX	Great Western Trains - Laira Class 47 (Reserve)
IWPA	West Coast - Willesden Class 86
IWRP	Great Western Trains - Laira/St Phillips Marsh Class 43

English Welsh & Scottish Railway (Formerly Transrail)

LBBS	Bescot Class 08/09
LBSB	Bescot Class 37 (Sandite Fitted)
LCWX	Strategic Reserve Locomotives
LCXX	Stored Locomotives
LCYX	Locomotives For Withdrawal
LGAM	Motherwell Class 56

LGBM	Motherwell Class 37
LGHM	Motherwell Class 37/4 (West Highland)
LGML	Motherwell Class 08/09
LNAK	Cardiff Canton Class 60 (South Wales)
LNBK	Cardiff Canton Class 56 (South Wales)
LNCF	Cardiff Canton Class 08/09
LNCK	Cardiff Canton Class 37 (South Wales)
LNLK	Cardiff Canton Class 37 (St Blazey)
LNSK	Cardiff Canton Class 37 (Sandite Fitted)
LNWK	Cardiff Canton Class 08 (Allied Steel & Wire)
LWCW	Crewe Diesel Class 37 (North West)
LWMC	Crewe Diesel Class 37/4 (North West Passenger)
LWNW	Crewe Diesel Class 31
LWRC	Crewe Diesel Class 47 (Restricted)
LWSP	Springs Branch Class 08

Heritage Locomotives

MBDL	Diesel Locomotives
MBEL	Electric Locomotives

Carriage & Traction Company

PWLO	Crewe Diesel Class 47

English Welsh & Scottish Railway (Formerly Rail express systems)

PXLB	Crewe Diesel Class 47 (Extended Range)
PXLC	Crewe Diesel Class 47
PXLD	Crewe Diesel Class 47 (Reserve/Stored)
PXLE	Crewe Electric Class 86
PXLK	Crewe Diesel Class 47/9
PXLP	Crewe Diesel Class 47 (VIP Fleet)
PXLS	Crewe Diesel/Heaton/Old Oak Common/Willesden Class 08
PXLT	Crewe Diesel/Toton Class 08
PXXA	Locomotives For Withdrawal

Western Track Renewals

RNRG	Reading Class 97/6

Eversholt Holdings

SAXL	Locomotives Off Lease

Porterbrook Leasing Company

SBXL	Locomotives Off Lease

Racal-BRT

TAKB	Bescot Class 20
TAKX	Stored Locomotives

Other Operators

XHSD	Direct Rail Services Class 20/3
XYPA	ARC Class 59/1
XYPD	Hunslet Barclay Class 20/9
XYPN	National Power Class 59/2
XYPO	Foster Yeoman Class 59/0

7.3. COACHING STOCK OWNER & OPERATION CODES

This book now uses a (generally) logical system of codes instead of the gobbledygook codes of the BR Rolling Stock Library (RSL). We have decided to do this since RSL information is not officially available to the general public and a system of coding which is fairly obvious to the reader is preferred. Owner codes consist of one letter, whereas operation codes consist of two letters. For passenger train operating companies these are generally based on those used by Railtrack in the Great Britain passenger timetable, but there are a few changes for clarity or to reflect changes since the timetable was printed.

OWNER CODES

A   Angel Trains Contracts Ltd.
B   SNCB/NMBS
C   West Coast Railway Company Ltd.
D   Railfilms Ltd.
E   Eversholt Holdings
F   SNCF
G   Great Scottish & Western Railway Co. Ltd. (operators of the 'Royal Scotsman' train)
J   Ridings Railtours Ltd.
L   London & North Western Railway Co.Ltd.
M   Rail Charter Services Ltd.
N   Flying Scotsman Railways Ltd.
O   Other owners - refer to list below
P   Porterbrook Leasing Company Ltd.
Q   Railtrack plc
R   Riviera Trains Ltd. (operators of the 'Riviera Limited' set). includes vehicles owned by Titanstar Ltd., Vulcan Trains Ltd. and RPR Ltd.)
S   Scottish Railway Preservation Society
T   Railtest Ltd.
U   Eurostar (UK) Ltd. (also includes vehicles owned by European Night Services Ltd.)
V   Venice Simplon Orient Express Ltd. (operators of the VSOE Pullman set and Ocean Liner Express set)
W   English Welsh & Scottish Railway Ltd.
X   The Carriage and Traction Co. Ltd.
Y   Resco Railways Ltd. (owners of the 'Queen of Scots' set)

Other Owners

17007   Merchant Navy Locomotive Preservation Society Ltd.
17021   Humberside Locomotive Preservation Group
17041   Duke of Gloucester Steam Locomotive Trust Ltd.
21098   A4 Locomotive Society Ltd.
35322   Britannia Locomotive Society
35333   6024 Preservation Society Ltd.
35449   75014 Locomotive Operators Group
35457   Ian Storey Engineering Ltd.
35468   National Railway Museum

80217   75014 Locomotive Operators Group
80220   Mid-Hants Railway Preservation Society

OPERATION CODES

The two letter operating codes give the use to which the vehicle is at present
put. For vehicles in regular use, this is the code for the train operating company.
For other vehicles the actual type of use is shown. If no operating code is shown
then the vehicle is not at present in use.

Train Operating Companies

AR	Anglia Railways
CA	Cardiff Railway Company
CH	Chiltern Trains
CT	Central Trains
ES	Eurostar (UK)
EW	English Welsh & Scottish Railway Company
GE	Great Eastern Railway
GN	Great North Eastern Railway
GW	Great Western Trains
GX	Gatwick Express
IL	Island Line (Isle of Wight)
LS	LTS Rail (London Tilbury & Southend)
ME	Merseyrail Electrics
ML	Midland Mainline
NE	Regional Railways North East
NL	North London Railways
NW	North West Regional Railways
SC	Connex South Central
SE	Connex South Eastern
SR	ScotRail
SW	South West Trains
TL	Thameslink Rail
TT	Thames Trains
WC	West Coast
WN	West Anglia Great Northern Railway
WW	South Wales & West Railway
XC	Virgin CrossCountry

Other Operation Codes

BV	Barrier vehicle
CR	Crew training
DI	Deicing or deicing and sandite spraying
RT	Royal train use
SA	Sandite spraying
SD	Sea defences
SS	Used normally only on special or charter passenger services
ST	Stores vehicle
SU	Locomotive support coach
TE	Test train

7.4. DEPOT & WORKS CODES

Note: This list includes various locations which are not necessarily official operating company maintenance depots.

Depot Codes

AF	Ashford Chart Leacon TMD
AL	Aylesbury TMD
AN	Allerton TMD (Liverpool)
AY	Ayr TMD
BD	Birkenhead North T&RSMD
BI	Brighton T&RSMD
BK	Bristol Barton Hill CWMD
BM	Bournemouth T&RSMD
BN	Bounds Green T&RSMD (London)
BO	Bo'Ness Station (West Lothian) (Bo'Ness & Kinneil Railway)
BP	Blackpool North CS
BQ	Bury (Greater Manchester) (East Lancashire Railway)
BS	Bescot TMD (Walsall)
BY	Bletchley TMD
CD	Crewe Diesel TMD
CE	Crewe International EMD
CF	Cardiff Canton T&RSMD
CJ	Clapham Yard CSD (London)
CK	Corkerhill SD (Glasgow)
CL	Carlisle Upperby CWMD
CM	Cranmore (Somerset) (Riviera Trains Ltd.)
CO	Cranmore (Somerset) (East Somerset Railway)
CP	Crewe Carriage Shed
CQ	Crewe (The Railway Age)
CS	Carnforth Steamtown (West Coast Railway Co. Ltd.)
DI	Didcot Railway Centre (Great Western Society)
DR	Doncaster TMD
DY	Derby Etches Park T&RSMD
EC	Craigentinny T&RSMD (Edinburgh)
EH	Eastleigh T&RSMD
EM	East Ham EMUD (London)
EN	Euston Downside CARMD (London)
ET	Coquelles (France) (Eurotunnel)
FB	Ferrybridge (National Power)
FF	Bruxelles Forest/Brussel Vorst (Belgium) (SNCB/NMBS)
FR	Fratton (Portsmouth)
GI	Gillingham EMUD
GT	Grosmont (North Yorkshire) (North Yorkshire Moors Railway)
GW	Glasgow Shields TMD
HA	Haymarket TMD (Edinburgh)
HE	Hornsey TMD (London)
HR	Hall Road EMUD (Merseyside)
HT	Heaton T&RSMD (Newcastle)
IL	Ilford T&RSMD (London)

IM	Immingham TMD (Lincolnshire)
IS	Inverness T&RSMD
KY	Knottingley TMD
LA	Laira T&RSMD (Plymouth)
LE	Landore T&RSMD (Swansea)
LG	Longsight TMD (E) (Manchester)
LL	Liverpool Edge Hill CARMD
LO	Longsight TMD (D) (Manchester)
LY	Le Landy (Paris) (SNCF)
MA	Manchester Longsight CARMD
MD	Merehead (Foster Yeoman)
ML	Motherwell TMD
NC	Norwich Crown Point T&RSMD
NH	Newton Heath T&RSMD (Manchester)
NL	Neville Hill T&RSMD (Leeds)
OC	Old Oak Common TMD (D) (London)
OM	Old Oak Common CARMD (London)
OO	Old Oak Common TMD (HST) (London)
OY	Oxley CARMD (Wolverhampton)
PC	Polmadie CARMD (Glasgow)
PI	North Pole International (London)
PM	St. Phillips Marsh T&RSMD (Bristol)
PZ	Penzance T&RSMD
RE	Ramsgate T&RSMD
RG	Reading T&RSMD
RO	Ropley (Mid Hants Railway)
RY	Ryde (Isle of Wight) T&RSMD
SA	Salisbury TMD
SD	Sellafield (Direct Rail Services)
SF	Stratford TMD (London)
SG	Slade Green T&RSMD
SH	Strawberry Hill EMUD (London)
SK	Swanwick Junction (Derbyshire) (Midland Railway Centre)
SL	Stewarts Lane T&RSMD (London)
SO	Southall (Greater London) (Southall Railway Centre)
SP	Springs Branch TMD (Wigan)
SU	Selhurst T&RSMD (London)
TE	Thornaby TMD
TI	Tinsley TMD (Sheffield)
TO	Toton TMD (Nottinghamshire)
TS	Tyseley TMD (Birmingham)
WB	Wembley InterCity CARMD (London)
WD	East Wimbledon EMUD (London)
WH	Whatley (ARC Limited)
WN	Willesden TMD (London)
YM	National Railway Museum (York)

Works Codes

ZA	Railway Technical Centre (Derby)
ZB	RFS (E) Ltd., Doncaster
ZC	ADtranz Crewe Works

ZD	ADtranz Derby Carriage Works
ZF	ADtranz Doncaster Works
ZG	Wessex Traincare Ltd., Eastleigh Works
ZH	Railcare Ltd., Springburn Works, Glasgow
ZI	ADtranz Ilford Works
ZK	Hunslet-Barclay Ltd., Kilmarnock Works
ZM	GEC-Aslthom Metro-Cammell Ltd., Washwood Heath, Birmingham
ZN	Railcare Ltd., Wolverton Works
ZP	Bombardier Prorail, Horbury, West Yorkshire
ZT	ADtranz Trafford Park Wheel Works, Manchester (unofficial code)

Depot Type Code

CARMD	Carriage Maintenance Depot
CS	Carriage Sidings
CSD	Carriage Servicing Depot
CWMD	Carriage and Wagon Maintenance Depot
EMUD	Electric Multiple Unit Depot
EMD	Electric Maintenance Depot
SD	Servicing Depot
TMD	Traction Maintenance Depot
TMD (D)	Traction Maintenance Depot (Diesel)
TMD (E)	Traction Maintenance Depot (Electric)
TMD (HST)	HST Maintenance Depot
T&RSMD	Traction and Rolling Stock Maintenance Depot
WRD	Wagon Repair Depot

7.5. GENERAL ABBREVIATIONS

BR	British Railways
EWS	English Welsh & Scottish Railway Company
GWR	Great Western Railway
LNER	London & North Eastern Railway
LMS	London Midland & Scottish Railway
SR	Southern Railway
NMBS	Nationale Maatschappij Belgische Spoorwegen *
SNCB	Société Nationale des Chemins de Fer Belges *
SNCF	Société Nationale des Chemins de Fer Francais §

DEMU	Diesel Electric Multiple Unit
DHMU	Diesel Hydraulic Multiple Unit
DMMU	Diesel Mechanical Multiple Unit
DMU	Diesel Multiple Unit (general term)
EMU	Electric Multiple Unit

a.c.	alternating current
d.c.	direct current
hp	horsepower
GTO	gate turn-off
km/h	kilometres per hour
kN	kilonewtons
kV	kilovolts
kW	kilowatts
lbf	pounds force
T	Toilets
TD	Toilets (suitable for disabled passengers)
m	metres
mm	millimetres
m.p.h.	miles per hour
rpm	revolutions per minute
t	tons
V	volts

(S)	Stored servicable.
(U)	Stored unservicable

* Belgian Railways in Dutch and French respectively
§ French Railways

7.6. BUILDERS

These are shown in class headings where the following abbreviations are used:

Alexander	Walter Alexander Ltd., Falkirk
ABB Derby	ABB Transportation Ltd., Derby Carriage Works
ABB York	ABB Transportation Ltd., York Works
ADtranz Derby	ADtranz Ltd., Derby Carriage Works
AEI	Associated Electrical InduStries Ltd.
Barclay	Andrew Barclay Ltd., Kilmamock
BRCW	The Birmingham Railway Carriage & Wagon Co. Ltd.
Brush	Brush Traction Ltd., Loughborough
BTH	The British Thomson Houston Co. Ltd.
Cravens	Cravens Ltd., Sheffield
CP	Crompton-Parkinson Ltd.
EE	The English Electric Company Ltd.
GEC	The General Electric Company Ltd. (Now GEC Alsthom).
Gloucester	The Gloucester Railway Carriage and Wagon Co. Ltd.
Hunslet	Hunslet Transportation Projects Ltd.
Leyland Bus	Leyland Bus Ltd., Workington
Metro	The Metropolitan Railway Carriage and Wagon Co. Ltd., Birmingham
Metro-Cammell	The Metropolitan Cammell Railway Carriage and Wagon Co. Ltd., Birmingham
Midland	The Midland Railway Carriage and Wagon Co. Ltd,. Oldbury, Worcs.
MV	The Metropolitan-Vickers Co. Ltd.
Pressed Steel	Pressed Steel Ltd., Swindon

This list generally excludes BR/BREL workshops which are denoted in the text by their town/city. Where a dual BR works builder is shown (e.g. Ashford/Eastleigh) the first named built the underframe and the last named built the body and assembled the vehicle. For second generation vehicles, the first name is that of the main contractor with the second name baing the underframe and final assembly sub-contractor.

PRESERVED LOCOMOTIVES OF BRITISH RAILWAYS 9th edition

Peter Hall & Peter Fox.

The complete guide to all remaining Ex-British Railways and Constituent Companies, steam, diesel & electric locomotives, and diesel & electric multiple units. For the first time this popular volume now includes locomotives & multiple units of London Underground Limited and its predecessors, plus expanded coverage of locomotives once owned by the British Military. Also includes a full list of preservation sites and industrial locations. A5 size. Thread Sewn. Illustrated in colour and black & white. **£7.95.**

PRESERVED COACHING STOCK OF BRITISH RAILWAYS

Part 1 - BR Design Stock. £7.95
Part 2 - Pre-Nationalisation Stock. £8.95

Peter Hall & Peter Fox.

The ideal companions to 'Preserved Locomotives of British Railways' are now available. Part One contains full details of all BR Design Coaching Stock together with Pullman cars from the same era. Background information and brief design details are included, plus all numbers carried and current locations for every vehicle. A complete BR hauled coaching stock lot number list is also provided. This is the first time such a listing has been published in the clear Platform 5 format which also includes a full index to preservation sites including OS grid references.

Part Two is now available. This volume lists all coaching stock vehicles designed between the 1923 grouping and nationalisation in 1948, which are known to be still in existence. Details of number, former number(s), current location and usage (where appropriate), are included for every vehicle, plus technical data for each class of vehicle. The informative narrative and explanatory notes from the authors make this book a must for all followers of Railway Preservation and coaching stock.

8. UK LIGHT RAIL SYSTEMS & METROS

8.1. BLACKPOOL & FLEETWOOD TRAMWAY

System: 660 V d.c. overhead.   **Depot:** Rigby Road.
Livery: Cream and green. (many in advertising livery).
Note: Numbers in brackets are pre-1968 numbers.

ONE-MAN CARS

Rebuilt 1972 – 76 from English Electric railcoaches built 1934 – 5. Radio fitted.
13 converted (1 – 13).
Seats: 48.
Traction Motors: Two EE305 of 40 kW.

Note: First numbers in brackets are post 1968 numbers prior to conversion.

5 (609, 221)(U)	11 (615, 268)

OPEN BOAT CARS

Built 1934 – 5 by English Electric. 12 built (225 – 236).
Seats: 56.
Traction Motors: Two EE327 of 30 kW.

600* (225)	604§ (230)	606b (235)
602★ (227)	605 (233)	607 (236)

* On loan to Heaton Park Tramway, Manchester.
★ Yellow and black livery.
§ Red and white livery.
b Blue & yellow livery.

REPLICA VANGUARD

Built 1987 on underframe of one man car No. 7.(619 – 282).
Seats: .
Traction Motors: Two EE327 of 30 kW.

619

BRUSH RAILCOACHES

Built 1937 by Brush. 20 built (284 – 303).
Seats: 48.
Traction Motors: Two EE305 of 40 kW. (EE327 of 30 kW*).

621 (284)	626 (289)	631 (294)	634 (297)
622* (285)	627 (290)	632 (295)	636 (299)
623 (286)	630 (293)	633 (296)	637 (300)
625 (288)			

CENTENARY CLASS

Built 1984 – 7. Body by East Lancs. Coachbuilders, Blackburn. One man operated. Radio fitted.
Seats: 52.
Traction Motors: Two EE305 of 40 kW.

* Rebuilt from GEC car 651.

641	643	645	647
642	644	646	648*

CORONATION CLASS

Built 1953 by Charles Roberts & Co. Resilient wheels. 25 built (304 – 328).
Seats: 56.
Traction motors: Four Crompton-Parkinson 92 of 34 kW.

660 (324)

PROGRESS TWIN CARS

Motor cars (671 – 677) rebuilt 1958 – 60 from English Electric railcoaches.
Seats: 53.
Traction Motors: Two EE305 of 40 kW.
Driving trailers (681 – 687) built 1960 by Metro-Cammell.
Seats: 53.

671 + 681 (281 + T1)	674 + 684 (284 + T4)	676 + 686 (286 + T6)
672 + 682 (282 + T2)	675 + 685 (285 + T5)	677 + 687 (287 + T7)
673 + 683 (283 + T1)		

SINGLE CARS

Rebuilt 1958 – 60 from English Electric railcoaches. Originally ran with trailers.
Seats: 48.
Traction Motors: Two EE305 of 40 kW.

678 (278)	679 (279)	680 (280)

"BALLOON" DOUBLE DECKERS

Built 1934 – 5 by English Electric. 700 – 712 were originally built with open tops, and 706 has now reverted to that condition and is named 'PRINCESS ALICE'.
Seats: 94.
Traction Motors: Two EE305 of 40 kW.

* Converted to ice cream tram seating 64 with an ice cream sales area in one of the lower saloons.
§ Red and white livery.

700 (237)	702 (239)	704 (241)
701§ (238)	703 (240)	706 (243)

707	(244)	713	(250)	720	(257)
708	(245)	715	(252)	721	(258)
709	(246)	716	(253)	722	(259)
710	(247)	717	(254)	723	(260)
711	(248)	718	(255)	724	(261)
712	(249)	719	(256)	726	(263)

ILLUMINATED CARS

732	(168)	Rocket	Seats: 47
733	(209)	Western Train loco. & tender	Seats: 35
734	(174)	Western Train coach	Seats: 60
735	(222)	Hovertram	Seats: 99
736	(170)	HMS Blackpool	Seats: 71

WORKS CARS

259	(748, 624)	PW gang towing car.
260	(751, 628, 291)	Crane car and rail carrier.
749	(S)	Tower wagon trailer.
750		Cable drum trailer.
752	(2, 1)	Rail grinder and snowplough.
754		New works car (unnumbered).

JUBILEE CLASS DOUBLE DECKERS

Rebuilt 1979/82 from Balloon cars. Standard bus ends, thyristor control and stairs at each end. 761 has one door per side whereas 762 has two. Radio fitted.
Seats: 100.
Traction Motors: Two EE305 of 40 kW.

761 (725, 262) |762 (714, 251)

PRESERVED CARS

| Blackpool & Fleetwood 40 | Box car. Bogie single decker built 1914 |
| Bolton 66 | Bogie double-decker built 1901 |

8.2. DOCKLANDS LIGHT RAILWAY

This is a light rail line running in London's East End from Bank, Tower Gateway and Stratford to Island Gardens and Beckton. It is being extended to Lewisham. Originally owned by London Transport, it is now owned by the London Docklands Development Corporation.

System: 750 V d.c. third rail (bottom contact).
Depots: Poplar, Beckton.

CLASS P89   B – 2 – B

Built 1990 by BREL Ltd. York Works. 28.80 x 2.65 m. Sliding doors. Chopper control. Scharfenberg Couplers.

Weight: 39 t.
Seats: 84.
Traction Motors: Two GEC of 185 kW.
Max. Speed: 80 km/h.
Electric Brake: Rheostatic.

12	15	18	20
13	16	19	21
14	17		

CLASS B90   B – 2 – B

Built 1991 – 2 by BN Construction, Bruges, Belgium. (now Bombardier BN). 28.80 x 2.65 m. Sliding doors. End doors for staff use. Chopper control. Scharfenberg Couplers. These units are to be converted for Seltrack signalling.

Weight: 36 t.
Seats: 66 + 4 tip-up.
Traction Motors: Two Brush of 140 kW.
Max. Speed: 80 km/h.
Electric Brake: Rheostatic.

22	28	34	40
23	29	35	41
24	30	36	42
25	31	37	43
26	32	38	44
27	33	39	

CLASS B92   B – 2 – B

Built 1992 – 5 by BN Construction, Bruges, Belgium. (now Bombardier BN).
28.80 x 2.65 m. Sliding doors. End doors for staff use. Chopper control.
Scharfenberg Couplers. Fitted with Seltrack signalling.

Weight: 36 t.
Seats: 66 + 4 tip-up.
Traction Motors: Two Brush of 140 kW.
Max. Speed: 80 km/h.
Electric Brake: Rheostatic.

45	57	69	81
46	58	70	82
47	59	71	83
48	60	72	84
49	61	73	85
50	62	74	86
51	63	75	87
52	64	76	88
53	65	77	89
54	66	78	90
55	67	79	91
56	68	80	

8.3. GREATER MANCHESTER METROLINK

This new light rail system runs from Bury to Altrincham through the streets of Manchester, with a spur to Piccadilly.

System: 750 V d.c. overhead.
Depot: Queens Road.

SIX-AXLE ARTICULATED CARS $\quad$ Bo – 2 – Bo

Built 1991 – 2 by Firema, Italy. Power operated sliding doors. Chopper control. Scharfenberg Couplers.

Weight: 45 t.
Seats: 84.
Dimensions: 29.00 x 2.65 m.
Traction Motors: Four GEC of 130 kW.
Braking: Rheostatic, regenerative, disc and emergency track brakes.

1001	CHILDREN'S HOSPITALS APPEAL 1
1002	
1003	
1004	THE ROBERT OWEN
1005	GREATER ALTRINCHAM ENTERPRISE
1006	
1007	
1008	MANCHESTER AIRPORT
1009	
1010	MANCHESTER CHAMPION
1011	
1012	KERRY
1013	THE FUSILIER
1014	THE CITY OF DRAMA
1015	SPARKY
1016	
1017	
1018	
1019	THE ERIC BLACK
1020	THE DAVID GRAHAM CBE
1021	THE GREATER MANCHESTER RADIO
1022	THE GRAHAM ASHWORTH
1023	
1024	THE JOHN GREENWOOD
1025	
1026	THE POWER

SPECIAL PURPOSE VEHICLE

Built 1991 by RFS Industries, Kilnhurst and Brown Root. Used for shunting and track maintenance. Includes a crane.

Unnumbered.

8.4. SOUTH YORKSHIRE SUPERTRAM

This light rail system has three lines, to Halfway in the south east of Sheffield with a spur from Gleadless Townend to Herdings, to Middlewood in the north west with a spur from Hillsborough to Malin Bridge and to Meadowhall Interchange in the north east adjacent to the large shopping complex. Because of the severe gradients in Sheffield (up to 1 in 10), all axles are powered on these vehicles. The company is effectively owned by South Yorkshire passenger Transport Executive, but is about to be privatised.

System: 750 V d.c. overhead.
Depot: Nunnery.

EIGHT-AXLE ARTICULATED UNITS   B – B – B – B

Built 1993 – 4 by Duewag, Düsseldorf, Germany.

Weight: 52 t.
Seats: 88.
Dimensions: 34.75 x 2.65 m.
Traction Motors: Four monomotors.
Braking: Rheostatic, regenerative, disc and emergency track brakes.

01	08	14	20
02	09	15	21
03	10	16	22
04	11	17	23
05	12	18	24
06	13	19	25
07			

FOUR WHEELED WORKS CAR   B

Built 1968 by Reichsbahn Ausbesserungswerke Schöneweide, Berlin, East Germany as single-ended passenger car with electrical equipment by LEW Henningsdorf. Converted 1980 to double-ended works car. Delivered to Sheffield on 7th November 1996.

Weight: .
Dimensions: .
Traction Motors: Two.

721 039-4   (5104, 217 303-7)

8.5. STRATHCLYDE PTE UNDERGROUND

This circular 4' gauge underground line in Glasgow is generally referred to as the ''Subway''.

System: 750 V d.c. third rail.
Depot: Broomloan.

SINGLE CARS   Bo – Bo

Built 1978 – 9 by Metro-Cammell. Power-operated sliding doors. 12.58 x 2.34 m.

Seats: 36.
Traction Motors: Two GEC G312AZ.

101	110	118	126
102	111	119	127
103	112	120	128
104	113	121	129
105	114	122	130
106	115	123	131
107	116	124	132
108	117	125	133
109			

INTERMEDIATE TRAILERS   2 – 2

Built 1992 by Metro-Cammell. Power-operated sliding doors. 12.58 x 2.34 m. No details available.

201	203	205	207
202	204	206	208

8.6. TYNE AND WEAR METRO

System: 1500 V d.c. overhead.
Depot: South Gosforth.

BATTERY/OVERHEAD ELECTRIC LOCOS

Built: 1989 – 80 by Hunslet, Leeds. BSI couplers.
Traction Motors: Hunslet-Greenbat T9-4P.
Weight: 26 t.

BL1   BL2   BL3

SIX-AXLE ARTICULATED UNITS   B – 2 – B

Built 1976, 1978 – 81 by Metro-Cammell. 27.80 x 2.65m. BSI couplers.
Weight: 39 t.
Seats: 84 (70 r – refurbished units, 76 p – Prototype refurbished unit).
Traction Motors: Two 187 kW monomotor bogies.

4001	4019	4037	4055 r R	4073
4002	4020 r R	4038	4056 A	4074
4003	4021 r R	4039 r A	4057	4075
4004 r G	4022	4040	4058	4076
4005 r R	4023	4041	4059	4077 r R
4006	4024	4042	4060	4078
4007 r R	4025	4043 r R	4061 r G	4079
4008 r B	4026 A	4044 r R	4062	4080 r R
4009	4027 r R	4045 r A	4063	4081
4010 r R	4028	4046	4064 r R	4082 r G
4011	4029	4047	4065 r R	4083
4012 . A	4030 r R	4048 r B	4066 B	4084
4013	4031	4049 r A	4067	4085 r B
4014	4032	4050	4068 r R	4086 r B
4015	4033 r B	4051 r R	4069	4087 p A
4016 r B	4034	4052	4070	4088 r R
4017 r R	4035	4053	4071	4089
4018	4036 r G	4054	4072	4090

Names:

4041   HARRY COWANS |4065   Catherine Cookson

Liveries:

A Advertising livery.
B Blue.
G Green.
R Red.
Standard livery is yellow and white.

BRITISH RAILWAYS LOCOMOTIVES & COACHING STOCK BACK ISSUES

Mislaid your early rolling stock guides?

Need to complete your record library?

No problem. Platform 5 Publishing's popular **LOCOMOTIVES & COACHING STOCK** books are still available for the years 1986-1996. The enthusiast's favourite rolling stock books reflect the great changes which have taken place on Britain's Railways over the past 11 years, making up an essential reference collection. Enhance YOUR collection today!

Locomotives & Coaching Stock 1986	£3.30
Locomotives & Coaching Stock 1987	£3.30
Locomotives & Coaching Stock 1988	£3.95
Locomotives & Coaching Stock 1989	£4.95
Locomotives & Coaching Stock 1990	£5.95
Locomotives & Coaching Stock 1991	£6.60
British Railways Locomotives & Coaching Stock 1992 ...	£7.00
British Railways Locomotives & Coaching Stock 1993 ...	£7.25
British Railways Locomotives & Coaching Stock 1994 ...	£7.50
British Railways Locomotives & Coaching Stock 1995 ...	£8.50
British Railways Locomotives & Coaching Stock 1996 ...	£8.95

Available from Platform 5 Publishing. To order, please see instructions on rear cover of this magazine.

PLATFORM 5 PUBLISHING LIMITED
MAIL ORDER

Modern British Railway Titles	Price
British Railways Locomotives & Coaching Stock 1997	9.95
BR Pocket Book No.1: Locomotives	2.50
BR Pocket Book No.2: Coaching Stock	2.50
BR Pocket Book No.3: DMUs & Light Rail Systems	2.50
BR Pocket Book No.4: Electric Multiple Units	2.50
Preserved Locomotives of British Railways 9th ed.	7.95
Preserved Coaching Stock Part 1: BR Design Stock	7.95
Preserved Coaching Stock Part 2: Pre-Nationalisation Stock	8.95
Valley Lines - The People's Railway	9.95
Diesel & Electric Loco Register 3rd edition	7.95
Underground Official Handbook (Capital)	7.95
Docklands Light Rail Official Handbook (Capital)	7.95
Air Braked Series Wagon Fleet (SCTP)	7.95
Departmental Coaching Stock 5th edition (SCTP)	6.95
On-Track Plant on British Railways 5th edition (SCTP)	7.95
Engineers Series Wagon Fleet 970000-999999 (SCTP)	6.95
British Rail Wagon Fleet - B-Prefix Series (SCTP)	6.95
British Rail Internal Users (SCTP)	7.95
Miles & Chains Volume 2 - London Midland (Milepost)	1.95
Miles & Chains Volume 3 - Scottish (Milepost)	1.95
Miles & Chains Volume 5 - Southern (Milepost)	1.95

Light Rail Transit & Trams	
Tram to Supertram (Sheffield Trams)	4.95
Light Rail Review 4	7.50
Light Rail Review 5	7.50
Light Rail Review 6	7.50
Light Rail Review 7	8.95
Manx Electric	8.95
Light Rail in Europe (Capital)	9.95
Tramway & Light Railway Atlas Germany 1996 (LRTA)	10.45
The Tramways of Portugal (LRTA)	9.05
Tramtracks & Trolleybooms (Chesterfield Trams) (Headstock)	6.95

Overseas Railways

High Speed in Japan 16.95
High Speed in Europe 9.95
European Handbook No. 1: Benelux Railways 3rd ed. 10.50
European Handbook No. 2: German Rlys Locos & MUs 3rd ed. 12.50
European Handbook No. 3: Austrian Railways 3rd ed. 10.50
European Handbook No. 4: French Railways 3rd ed. ★APRIL★ 13.50
European Handbook No. 5: Swiss Railways 2nd ed. ★JUNE★ 13.50
European Handbook No. 6: Italian Railways 1st ed. 13.50
European Handbook No. 7: Irish Railways 1st ed. 9.95
The Berlin S-Bahn (Capital) 7.50
The Berlin U-Bahn (Capital) 7.50
Locomotives & Railcars of Bord Na Mona (Midland) 4.99
Irish Railways In Colour: From Steam to Diesel 1955-1967 (Midland) . 16.99
Irish Railways In Colour: A Second Glance 1947-1970 (Midland) 19.99
Irish Narrow Gauge - Pictorial History Part 1 (Midland) 15.99
Irish Narrow Gauge - Pictorial History Part 2 (Midland) 15.99
Steam Locomotives of Czechoslovakia 16.95

European Railway Atlases (Ian Allan)

European Railway Atlas: France, Benelux 10.99

Rambling

Rambles by Rail 2 - Liskeard-Looe 1.95
Rambles by Rail 4 - The New Forest 1.95
Buxton Spa Line Rail Rambles 1.20

Historical Railway Titles

6203 'Princess Margaret Rose' 19.95
Steam Days on BR 1 - The Midland Line in Sheffield 4.95
Rails along the Sea Wall (Dawlish-Teignmouth Pictorial) 4.95
The Rolling Rivers 6.95
British Baltic Tanks 6.95
LNWR Branch Lines of West Leics & East Warwicks (Milepost) 7.95
Private Owner Wagons Volume 3 (Headstock) 9.95
Private Owner Wagons Volume 4 (Headstock) 9.95
Bradshaw's Guide 1850 (Kay) 7.95
London Tilbury & Southend Railway Part 1 (Kay) 9.95
Railway Carriages & Wagons (Kay) 8.95
Locomotive Management - Cleaning, Driving, Maintenance Part 1 (Kay) .. 8.95

Locomotive Management - Cleaning, Driving, Maintenance Part 2 (Kay) .. 8.95
Power Railway Signalling Part 1A (Kay) 12.50
Power Railway Signalling Part 1B (Kay) 9.95
Power Railway Signalling Part 2 (Kay) 15.95
Railway Signal Engineering - Mechanical (Kay) 12.50
The Twopenny Tube (Capital) 5.95

Postcards
Sheffield Supertram - crosses Sheffield Canal 0.30
Manchester Metrolink - in Aytoun Street 0.30

Maps and Track Diagrams
Railway Track Diagrams No. 1: Scotland & Isle of Man (Quail) 6.50
British Rail Track Diagrams No. 4: Midland - 1990 Reprint (Quail) ... 6.95
British Rail Track Diagrams No. 5: Southern (Quail) 6.95
Railway Track Diagrams No. 6: Ireland (Quail) 5.50
London Transport Railway Track Map (Quail) 1.75
Harzer Schmalspurbahnen Track Diagram (Quail) 0.60
Portugal Railway Map (Quail) 2.00
Greece Railway Map (Quail) 1.70
Poland Railway Map (Quail) 2.00
New York Railway Map (Quail) 1.70
Estonia Railway Map (Quail) 1.20
Czech Republic & Slovakia Railway Map (Quail) 1.70
Berlin Track Map (Quail) 2.20
Korea Railway Map (Quail) 2.00
Latvia & Lithuania Railway Map (Quail) 2.00
Track Diagram - South Yorkshire Supertram (HRT Rail Sales) 1.50
Track Diagram - Blackpool & Fleetwood (HRT Rail Sales) 1.00
Track Diagram - Tyne & Wear (HRT Rail Sales) 2.00

Bargain Books *
Today's Railways Review of the Year Volume 1 (was 11.95) 6.95
Today's Railways Review of the Year Volume 2 (was 11.95) 6.95
Today's Railways Review of the Year Volume 3 (was 13.95) 6.95
Today's Railways Review of the Year Volume 4 (was 14.95) 6.95
The Handbook of British Railways Steam Motive Power Depots
    Volume 2 - Central England, East Anglia & Wales (was 8.95) 3.95
    Volume 4 - Northern England & Scotland (was 9.95) 3.95
North West Rails in Colour (was 8.50) 3.95

The Battle for the Settle & Carlisle (was 6.95) 2.95
The Fifty 50s in Colour (was 5.95) 2.95
Steam Alive (Friends of the NRM) 2.95
* Postage on reduced price titles **must** be based on original book price.

Buses & Fire Engines

Bus Review 11 (Bus Enthusiast) 6.95
South East Bus Handbook (Capital) 12.50
The First RTs (Capital) 19.95
National Express Handbook (Capital) 7.95
Buses In Britain 2 (Capital) 19.95
London Trolleybus Routes (Capital) 18.95
Greater Manchester Buses (Capital) 19.95
London Buses Before the War (Capital) 19.95
Routemaster Volume Two 1970-1989 (Capital) 19.95
Routemaster Handbook (Capital) 10.95
The 1997 Stagecoach Bus Handbook (British Bus) 15.00
The 1997 Firstbus Bus Handbook (British Bus) 15.00
The South Midlands Bus Handbook (British Bus) 9.95
The East Midlands Bus Handbook (British Bus) 9.95
The South Wales Bus Handbook (British Bus) 9.95
The North & West Wales Bus Handbook (British Bus) 9.95
The North & West Midlands Bus Handbook (British Bus) 9.95
The Lancashire, Cumbria & Manchester Bus Handbook (British Bus) . 9.95
The Merseyside & Cheshire Bus Handbook (British Bus) 9.95
The Leyland Lynx Bus Handbook (British Bus) 8.95
The Model Bus Handbook (British Bus) 9.95
Fire Brigade Handbook 2nd edition (British Bus) 9.95

PVC Book Covers

A6 Pocket Book - in Blue, Red, Green or Grey 0.80
Locos & Coaching Stock - in Blue, Red, Green or Grey 1.00
A5 Book - in Blue, Red, Green or Grey 1.40

Loco & Coaching Stock Back Numbers

1986	3.30	1992	7.00
1987	3.30	1993	7.25
1988	3.95	1994	7.50
1989	4.95	1995	8.50
1990	5.95	1996	8.95
1991	6.60		

HOW TO ORDER

Fill in your name and address and complete the form on the next page. Please remember to calculate the post & packing applicable, then send this along with your remittance to:

Platform 5 Mail Order Department (LCS)
3 Wyvern House, Sark Road
SHEFFIELD, S2 4HG, ENGLAND

Tel: (+44) 0114 255 2625
Fax: (+44) 0114 255 2471.

Postage & Packing
Please add: 10% UK, 20% Europe or 30% Rest of World. (If P&P works out as less than 30p, then please add 30p, the minimum charge)

*Postage on reduced price titles must be based on original price.

NOTE. When ordering publications in conjunction with a **Today's Railways** subscription offer please add on post and packing **before** deducting the voucher. Vouchers may **not** be combined.

Ways To Pay
We accept payment by sterling cheque (drawn on a UK bank), money order, Eurocheque or British Postal Order - please make these payable to **'PLATFORM 5 PUBLISHING LTD'**

We also accept payment by Credit Card, - Visa/Access/Delta/Mastercard/Eurocard. Please state type of card, cardholder's name and address, card number and expiry date. **Minimum credit card order accepted - £3.00.**

For Order Form See Over

Quantity	Title	Price	Total
	SUB-TOTAL		
	Postage & Packing (see previous page for details)		
	TOTAL REMITTANCE		

Name: ....

Address: ....

....

.... Postcode: ....

Daytime Telephone No.: ....

Payment (Delete as appropriate)

I enclose my cheque/postal order for £ .... made payable to: 'PLATFORM 5 PUBLISHING LTD'.

Please debit my Access/Visa/Delta/Mastercard/Eurocard

Card No.: .... Expiry Date: ....

Signature: .... Date: ....